CORRECTIONS AND CHANGES

When *Barney's Book on the Olympic Peninsula* was written, I tried to make it as accurate and up-to-date as possible. As with all guide books though, errors creep in and the passage of time obsoletes some entries. Those errors which have surfaced so far appear to be minor, but nonetheless a nuisance, hence this list of corrections and clarifications.

If you spot any errors in the book, please make a note of them, and send it to me at Nosado Press, P.O. Box 634, Olympia, WA 98507-0634.

This listing will be updated as required, and the changes noted will be included in the appropriate description when the book goes into its next printing.

Barney Arender, December, 1990

MAPS - GENERAL CLARIFICATION
The maps in *Barney's Book on the Olympic Peninsula* are not meant to replace detailed maps drawn by someone with cartographic training. They are not drawn to scale, and may be distorted by manipulation with my computer. Their purpose is to provide a quick-reference supplement to the descriptive text to illustrate sequence and general relationships between the roads and trails included. See the Introduction for recommendations of detailed maps that should be taken on any trip to the remote areas of the Olympic Peninusla.

MAPS - SEASONAL RANGER STATIONS
Seasonal ranger stations are represented on the maps by the same symbol as that used for permanent ranger stations. The seasonal ranger stations are manned only in the summer months, and many have no permanent structure. Enquire at the information centers for the locations and dates of operation of the temporary ranger stations if you are planning a backcountry excursion.

INTRODUCTION
My comments about excessive detail in existing maps should not be construed as a criticism of their accuracy, or their adequacy for their intended purpose. My comments were meant to convey the difficulty that I have had in finding maps for quick-reference whilst driving or hiking.

My comments on the excellence of *Olympic Mountains Trail Guide* by Robert Wood have left some readers with the impression that it contains no errors. Unfortunately, this guide book, like all guide books contains errors and out-dated information. Hopefully any inaccuracies are minor.

Page 19
The restaurant at Westwater Inn is correctly spelled Ceazan's Restaurant.

Page 21
The 7-11 convenience store is now Black Lake Grocery and Deli. Saucey's Pizza is no longer there.

Rainier Bank has been renamed Security Pacific Bank.

Page 27
The appearance on this map of Olympic Hot Springs in large type implies that it is a major tourist area. It is in fact a backcountry area with no facilities and the springs can be fairly unsanitary, as they are not treated for purification.

Page 28
This map shows several trails which are not maintained. Some no longer exist, and should only be

attempted by experienced cross-country hikers. Routes that no longer exist are: 22 Crystal Ridge; 38 Tshletshy Creek; and 26 Aurora Divide.

The correct name of High Divide-Bailey Range Trail is High Divide Trail.

Trail 48 is correctly spelled O'Neil Pass Trail.

Page 30
Mason County Visitors Information Center has been opened on the right at Lynch Road, mile 353.5.

Page 63
Mount Washington is a class 4 climbing trail from the end of the maintained trail. There is an easier climbing route before you reach the maintained trail. (See route 1A in *Climber's Guide to the Olympic Mountains*, published by The Mountaineers.)

Page 65
There are only 60 sites at Staircase Campground. Although some sources show a maximum trailer length of 16 feet, there are a few sites that will accommodate 21 ft. trailers.

Page 66
The description of Staircase Rapids Trail implies that there is a bridge at Upper Skokomish Crossing. There is no bridge. Beyond the turnoff to Upper Skokomish Crossing the trail, though not maintained, continues to just past the Olympic National Forest boundary where it ends.

Page 67
Again, there is no bridge at Upper Skokomish Crossing.

Page 72
The caption for the photo on page 72 is incorrect. This peak is part of a ridge on Mt. Pershing.

Page 76
The "ranger station" mentioned at mile 5.6 of Hamma Hamma Road is actually a guard station which is used to house National Forest Service employees, and is not open to the public.

Page 82
Putvin Trail is actually a way trail and receives little or no maintenance.

Page 89 (Map), Page 90
"Heart" Lake is correctly spelled Hart Lake.

FSR 2610-010 and FSR 2610-011 from Highway 101 to the trailhead for Mount Jupiter Trail have been greatly improved.

Page 161
Although none of the maps in *Barney's Book on the Olympic Peninsula* are drawn to scale, this one has been distorted more than most by lengthening the North-South axis to enlarge the space available for labels. The result is that many trails appear to be much longer than they are.

The label for Klahhane Ridge is in the wrong place. It should appear under the segment of trail that runs in an easterly direction from the junction of Switchback Trail and Heather Park Trail. This segment of trail is a continuation of Lake Angeles Trail beyond Lake Angeles, but it is sometimes called Klahhane Ridge Trail.

An inconsistency in the format of the listing at mile 253.1 makes it appear that Deer Park Campground, Blue Mountain and the three trails listed are accessible from Highway 101. They are not on Highway 101. They are all located near the end of Deer Park Road, more than 16 miles of steep, narrow, twisty gravel road that is unsuitable for trailers or motor homes.

The street running north and south just east of Heart O' The Hills Parkway on the map does not exist.

Frugal's Take Away serves hamburgers, not fish.

On this map, the label "Dawn Lake" should read Lake Dawn.

The trail shown on the map near the label "Sunrise Ridge" is Hurricane Ridge Trail

The trail called ONP Visitor Center Nature Trail is correctly named Thomas T. Aldwell Nature Trail.

The descriptions of Heather Park Trail, Lake Angeles Trail and Switchback Trail are inaccurate due to my misunderstanding of exactly where these trails ended. Actually, they all end at the same place, in a three way junction at mile 6.3 of Heather Park Trail. There are signs for each trail at the junction. In the description I had Heather Park Trail continuing on to Hurricane Ridge Lodge. If you wish to go to Hurricane Ridge Lodge, continue on Switchback trail for 1.0 mile to its junction with Hurricane Ridge Trail, a 2.6 mile traverse to Hurricane Ridge Lodge. There is a path leading to the summit of Mount Angeles (6454 feet) 0.2 miles from the start of Hurricane Ridge Trail.

The descriptions of Lake Angeles Trail, Heather Park Trail and Switchback Trail are inaccurate due to my misunderstanding of exactly where they ended. Actually, they all end at the same place, in a three way junction at mile 6.5 of Lake Angeles Trail. There are signs for each trail at the junction.

The last two sentences of the second paragraph which start "You can turn left, and after one mile..." should be replaced with:
> You can turn left into Switchback Trail, and after one mile turn right into Hurricane Ridge Trail, a 2.6 mile traverse to Hurricane Ridge Lodge. There is a path leading to the summit of Mount Angeles (6454 feet) 0.2 miles from the start of Hurricane Ridge Trail. If you continue on Switchback Trail, past the Hurricane Ridge Trail turn off, for another 0.5 miles of steep descent, you will reach the trailhead of Switchback Trail at mile 15.8 of Hurricane Ridge Road.

The descriptions of Switchback Trail, Lake Angeles Trail and Heather Park Trail are inaccurate due to my misunderstanding of exactly where they ended. Actually, they all end at the same place, in a three way junction at mile 1.5 of Switchback Trail. There are signs for each trail at the junction.

The paragraph on Switchback Trail should be replaced with:
> Switchback Trail is 1.5 miles long and quite steep. According to one reader who has counted them, there are 27 switchbacks in the trail. From the parking lot you can see a little stream that cascades down from the rocky ridge above. Although the trail looks almost vertical, it is the shortest and fastest way to Mount Angeles. After 0.5 miles, you can turn left into Hurricane Ridge Trail, a 2.6 mile traverse to Hurricane Ridge Lodge. There is a path leading to the summit of Mount Angeles (6454 feet) 0.2 miles from the start of Hurricane Ridge Trail.

Continuing on Switchback Trail, you will ascend to the crest of Klahhane Ridge in 13 switchbacks over the remaining 1.0 mile to Switchback Trail's junction with Lake Angeles Trail and Heather Park Trail.

Page 181
Hurricane Hill Lookout Trail is paved for its entire length.

Page 183
The three lakes in the Grand Valley are mentioned under Grand Pass Trail as being stocked with trout. They are not stocked, and have not been stocked for many years.

Page 189
The museum's name is correctly spelled Makah Museum.

Page 192
State Highway 112 was re-opened after a wash-out cut it in the floods of early 1989. In the floods of November, 1990 the road was cut again by wash-outs, and remains closed from the community of Twin on the Twin Rivers to the community of Pysht near Pillar Point Recreation Area.Those people going to Clallam Bay, Sekiu, Ozette and Neah Bay should continue on Highway 101 to Burnt Mountain Road which goes north from Sappho at mile 203.9.

Page 207
Crystal Ridge Trail no longer exists. The route should only be attempted by experienced cross-country hikers.

Page 222
Crystal Ridge Trail no longer exists. The route should only be attempted by experienced cross-country hikers.

Boulder Creek Campground no longer has potable water or restrooms. It is managed as a backcountry area.

Page 224
Cat Creek Way Trail no longer exists. The route should only be attempted by experienced cross-country hikers.

Page 229
Aurora Divide Trail is a way trail, and is only minimally maintained.

The overlooks at Marymere Falls are not accessible by wheelchair. Wheelchairs (with assistance) can reach the river on this trail, but cannot cross the bridge over Barnes Creek.

Page 244
The correct name for the "High Divide-Bailey Range Trail" is High Divide Trail.

Page 268
The correct name for the "Tumwata Creek Trail" is Hoh-Bogachiel Trail.

Page 296
Tshletshy Creek Trail no longer exists as a trail, and should only be attempted by experienced cross-country hikers.

BARNEY'S BOOK

ON

THE OLYMPIC PENINSULA

A COMPENDIUM FOR MOTORISTS AND HIKERS
OF ALL MAJOR ROADS AND TRAILS

BY

BARNEY ARENDER

NOSADO PRESS
OLYMPIA, WASHINGTON

BARNEY'S BOOK ON THE OLYMPIC PENINSULA

A Compendium for Motorists and Hikers
of All Major Roads and Trails

By Barney Arender

Published by: Nosado Press
                    318 Security Building
                    203 East Fourth Street
                    Olympia, WA 98501 U.S.A.

Copyright © 1990 by L. B. Arender
First printing 1990

Cover photo: *Northeastern Slopes of the Olympic Mountains from Highway 101 West of Sequim.*

Publishers Cataloging in Publication Data

Arender, Louis B.
Barney's Book on The Olympic Peninsula: A Compendium for Motorists and Hikers of All Major Roads and Trails by Barney Arender—1st ed.

Includes Index
1.   Automobile Touring—Washington (State)—Olympic Peninsula—Guidebooks
2.   Hiking—Washington (State)—Olympic Peninsula—Guidebooks
3.   Backpacking—Washington (State)—Olympic Peninsula—Guidebooks
4.   Roads—Washington (State)—Olympic Peninsula—Guidebooks
5.   Trails—Washington (State)—Olympic Peninsula—Guidebooks
6.   Olympic Peninsula (Washington)—Description and Travel—Guidebooks
I.   Title

Library of Congress Catalog Card Number 90-91668
ISBN 1-878903-00-4 $17.95   Softcover

TABLE of CONTENTS

LIST of MAPS

Warning-Disclaimer

The intent of this book is to entertain and to provide a concise but comprehensive description of the roads and trails in the Olympic Peninsula. Simplified maps are included to help clarify these descriptions.

Hiking and driving in remote areas such as the Olympic Peninsula entail a certain amount of risk. For the careless, these activities are downright dangerous. One should always check with the forest service, the park service or the Department of Natural Resources for the latest information on such things as the weather, avalanche risks and the conditions of roads and trails. Detailed maps, trail guides and tide tables should also be obtained. Appropriate equipment and clothing should be taken to anticipate the rapid and severe changes in the weather that occur in the Olympics. Food supplies should be sufficient to last for a day or so beyond your planned return.

The author has made every effort to ensure that the information in this book is accurate and complete. **There may be mistakes**. These mistakes could be in the content or they could be typographical errors. Furthermore, there may have been changes since the research was done. It should also be noted that the maps in this book are not drawn to scale and they may have been distorted by their manipulation in the word processing and page layout systems.

In view of the above, this book should be used as a general guide, rather than as the final authority on roads and trails in the Olympic Peninsula.

The author and Nosado Press take no responsibility for, and shall have no liability to anyone for any loss or damage caused, or alleged to be caused, directly or indirectly, by the information in this book.

If you do not wish to be bound by this disclaimer, you may return this book to the publisher for a full refund.

INTRODUCTION

Over the years as I have driven and hiked in the wilderness areas the USA, Canada and Australia I have discovered two difficulties that are common to practically every excursion.

First, there is not enough detail available about the roads leading to trailheads and scenic attractions. Often the information that does exist is less than useful. Directions like "Turn left two miles before you get to where Joe Bloggs' barn burned down on Clear Spring Road in 1953" abound. Even if Mr. Bloggs' barn has not burned down, the authors of such directions assume that everyone is intimately familiar with the three roads that are between the main highway and Clear Spring Road, and that everyone knows that "Clear Spring Road" only appears on maps under its official designation - "County Road 30".

The second difficulty is too much detail on maps and in trail guides to allow you to quickly spot the next objective on your route. The maps include lines that represent roads, trails, rivers, contour lines and boundaries. All the lines are the same color and width. Then, to make sure that the lines are totally unintelligible, they are put on a dark, low-contrast background color.

OBJECTIVE

My objective in writing this book has been to address these two problems. I have tried to provide a description of the roads and trails in the Olympic Peninsula that is definitive enough to enable you to decide where you want to go, and to tell you exactly how to get there. I have also tried to limit the detail to information that is definitive enough to enable you to decide where you want to go, and to tell you exactly how to get there.

I have included information about attractions in the areas described, campgrounds, RV parks, restaurants, and other commercial establishment that are of interest to travellers in the peninsula. Detailed description of the many fascinating botanical and geological features of the peninsula has been deliberately excluded. I have also made simplified maps of areas of particular interest. I have taken this approach to enable the traveller to use this guide as he drives or hikes, to quickly find the next landmark on his route.

OTHER PUBLICATIONS

This book does not duplicate the work of others who have written excellent, detailed trail guides, and drawn superb maps. I recommend "Olympic Mountains Trail Guide" by Robert L. Wood (published by The Mountaineers, 306 2nd Ave. W., Seattle WA 98119) for comprehensive information about all the trails in both the national park and the national forest. I have found Wood's book invaluable in my own forays into Olympic National Park and Olympic National Forest. I owe Mr. Wood a debt of gratitude, as this book would have been much more difficult to compile in the absence of his trail guide. His book was arbiter when other sources disagreed on important details of the park service and forest service trails, and it provided a control to ensure that all major trails (and most minor trails) in the national park and national forest were included.

The forest service has prepared a map entitled "Olympic National Forest and Olympic National Park" which is essential for even the casual visitor to the peninsula. It includes the entire peninsula north of the southern boundary of Olympic National Forest. It is available at most ranger stations and information centers, or it can be purchased by mail from: Forest Supervisor, Olympic National Forest, P.O. Box 2288, Olympia, WA 98507, Phone (206) 753-9534. This map has all the new Forest Service Road numbers that came from the 1988 renumbering exercise that especially affected the Quilcene area.

For hiking, topographic maps are available from: Branch of Distribution, U.S. Geological Survey, Denver Federal Center, Denver CO 80225, or from the information centers. My personal preference for detailed hiking maps is the Custom Correct Maps which are available at the information centers or from: Little River Enterprises, 499 Little River Road, Port Angeles, WA 98362.

SEQUENCE AND FORMAT

The sequence and format of this book is structured to convey as much information as possible, with as little clutter as possible. Description of the peninsula roads and trails starts at mile 367.3, the end of US Highway 101, where it joins Interstate Highway 5 in Olympia in Chapter Three. The description follows the route of Highway 101 in a counter-clockwise loop through the peninsula to Aberdeen. There, where Highway 101 continues on south to Oregon, I have described US Highway 12 and Washington State Highway 8 to close the loop back to Olympia.

Note that the mile numbers on Highway 101 decrease as you proceed in a counter-clockwise direction. Where there are differences between my mileage figures and the mile numbers on the mileposts, I have adjusted my figures to the distances shown on the mileposts. By citing both the distance to I-5, and the mile number you should be able to get your bearings at any point at which you choose to join Highway 101. If you are travelling in a clockwise direction, you need only read the mileage listings from the bottom of the page to the top and substitute "Right" for "Left", and "Left" for "Right".

The format of the listings should also help you quickly find your way. Everything is listed in the sequence in which it is encountered on a counter-clockwise trip from Olympia. The road listings are divided into three columns. Landmarks and features which physically appear on the right side of the road appear on the right side of the page. Landmarks and features that physically appear on the left side of the road appear on the left side of the page. The narrow center column contains mileage figures, highlights of the information in the other two columns and information that pertains to both sides of the road, such as crossroads, or boundary information.

There is a four line heading at the beginning of each road described and at the top of each page of the description. It shows the road name on the first line, and reference points for two mileage figures shown in the center column. For example, the heading for Highway 101 first shows the mileage from Interstate Highway 5, where the description begins, then shows the official mile number as posted periodically along the roadside. A similar format has been adapted for all roads described. For roads which have no mileposts, the mile number is presumed to be 0.0 at the perimeter, (usually Highway 101) and it grows larger as you proceed toward the interior of the peninsula. In the example it is 135.6 miles to Highway 101's departure from Interstate Highway 5.

ROADS

The roads in the Olympic Peninsula range from superhighways to narrow, rough one-lane paths. All of them are reasonably safe so long as you drive slowly enough for the existing conditions and remain alert. You should also avoid the more primitive roads unless you have an appropriate, properly maintained vehicle. Good brakes are essential on all roads.

US AND STATE HIGHWAYS

US and State Highways are all paved roads with at least two-lanes. They seldom have grades steep enough to be noticeable. Two lane sections in the mountainous areas have slow vehicle turnouts. The use of the turnouts enables motorists to comply with the state law that requires slow vehicles to pull off the roadway when impeding five or more vehicles. These turnouts are sometimes used for overnight parking by people with RV,s. Although this practice is not illegal unless the turnout is posted with "no parking" signs, it is discouraged, as it detracts from the effectiveness of the turnouts in improving traffic flow. On the maps in this book, US Highways are represented by numbers within a shield, and state highways are represented by numbers within a circle or an ellipse.

FOREST SERVICE ROADS

Most Forest Service Roads are lower standard roads that are neither designed nor maintained for high speeds. Line of sight is also often obstructed by trees or sharp curves, and many of these roads are only one lane with turnouts. Remember, it always takes longer to stop on gravel and dirt surfaces than it does on paved surfaces. Grades that are too steep and roadways too narrow for underpowered or towing vehicles are not uncommon.

Those comments notwithstanding, don't be intimidated by the Forest Service Roads. All of the ones that are designed for automobile traffic (two digit and four digit road numbers) are safe for cars in good mechanical condition driven by alert drivers.

The National Forest Service provides these safety tips:

- Drive defensively.

- Keep to the right.

- Always expect to meet
logging trucks.

- Don't drive in the dust of other vehicles.

- Park well off the road.

- Don't block turnouts.

The signs on Forest Service Roads (abbreviated to FSR in this book) identify the nature of the road. Two types of road maintained for automobile traffic.

Primary, arterial roads are represented by two digit road numbers on a trapezoid-shaped sign with the words Forest Service at the bottom of the sign. Many of these roads are paved for at least part of their length.

Secondary roads are represented by four digit road numbers on a rectangular sign. They are often rougher, and they are not maintained as well as the primary roads.

The first two digits in the secondary road number usually indicate the primary road from which it originated. For example, FSR 2270 starts from FSR 22. The signs for both types of road use white numbers on a brown background and are usually clearly posted near their entrances and intersections.

Other roads in the national forest are represented by vertical signs with a three digit number, placed well away from their entrance, or by rectangular signs with a small four digit number at the top followed by a three digit number. (For example FSR 2610-010.) The four digit number is the road from which the primitive road originated. Primitive roads that originate from primary roads have two zeros added to the two digit road number. (For example FSR 2700-010)

In the maps in this book Forest Service Roads are represented by their number within a square for arterial roads, or within a rectangle for all other Forest Service Roads.

NATIONAL PARK ROADS
Most of the comments for Forest Service Roads also apply to Park Service Roads. The Park Service Roads, however, are named rather than numbered, and those going to popular attractions are, for the most part, paved.

DEPARTMENT OF NATURAL RESOURCES ROADS
Most Washington Department of Natural Resources roads were built for logging purposes. They probably compare in standard to the secondary and primitive Forest Service Roads. Those mentioned in this book are adequate for automobile traffic unless otherwise noted.

CAMPGROUNDS AND RV PARKS
I have included remarks on campgrounds and RV Parks for most of the Peninsula. Where I use the word "campground", I am referring to areas operated by the forest service, the park service or by a state or local government agency. Most of them have no hook-ups or showers and there are limitations on the vehicle size.

I have used the term "RV park" to refer to commercial RV parks. Most of them have hook-ups and showers and many of them have large pull-through sites. Other amenities such as laundries and recreation rooms are often available at RV Parks.

State Parks that have campgrounds have at least some sites with hook-ups and showers. Most of the showers are coin-operated pay showers.

CHAPTER 1

GETTING THERE

There are so many fascinating places along the way, that it often takes several attempts and tremendous will power to pass up the scenic attractions which will try to lay claim to your time before you reach the Olympic Peninsula. If you are easily led astray by the scenic wonders of the American West, skip this chapter, and make a vow not to leave the Interstate Highways until you reach Olympia.

For those who have very strong will power, or unlimited time, I will mention some of the attractions on each of the major routes. There are three main gateways to the Olympic Loop Highway.

Olympia   I-5 and CA-99 give you easy access to five National Parks and the grandeur of the Cascades before I-5 intersects with the end of US-101 (Mile 367.3) in Olympia. From this gateway you begin with the eastern leg of the Olympic Loop Highway starting with the trails and Wilderness Areas of the Olympic National Forest.

Port Angeles   After disembarking at the ferry terminal or the airport, and a mandatory visit to Hurricane Ridge, heading east on US-101 will start your adventure with the treats of the Strait of Juan de Fuca and the Hood Canal. US-101 to the west will start your journey with Lake Crescent and the hot springs of Elwha and Soleduck.

Aberdeen -
Hoquiam   US-101, after overwhelming you with the beauty of the coast in northern California, Oregon and southern Washington, becomes the western leg of The Olympic Loop Highway. This gateway will start your Olympic adventure with emphasis on the ocean beaches and rain forests of the Olympic National Park.

The major access routes to these gateways are shown on Map 1.1 below.

1

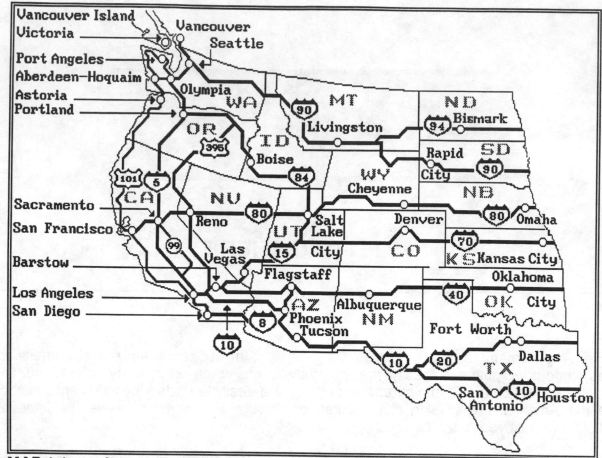

MAP 1-1 ACCESS ROUTES TO THE OLYMPIC PENINSULA

ACCESS FROM THE SOUTH

There are three major highways bringing people to southern California from the eastern states, and three major routes heading north for the Olympic Peninsula. Interstate Highways 8, 10 and 40 bring people from the southeastern states through Texas, New Mexico and Arizona to southern California. There, one can choose between a coastal (US-101/CA-1), central (I-5/CA-99) or desert (US-395) route to the Olympic Peninsula.

INTERSTATES 8, 10, AND 40

Interstate 8

I-8 ends in San Diego where one has the opportunity to visit Mexico before heading north on I-5. If you prefer a coastal route, take the CA-1 exit from I-5 just past San Clemente.

Interstate 10

I-10 ends in Los Angeles. There are exits for I-15, I-5 and US-101 before I-10 ends at CA-1, The Coast Road.

I-40 ends in Barstow, California. At its termination you are offered two options. You can take I-15 south to Los Angeles where you can join I-5, US-101 or CA-1. The other option is to continue west on CA-58 for 21 miles and join US-395.

US 101, INTERSTATE 5 AND US 395

Having sampled Universal Studios, Disneyland and some of southern California's many other temptations, you can now choose from three very different routes to complete your journey to the Olympic Peninsula.

US HIGHWAY 101

US-101 stretches from southern California to the Olympic Peninsula where it becomes the Olympic Loop Highway. Whilst you are in California, it often follows the coastline with its spectacular seascapes. US-101 occasionally goes inland. When it does, you are usually offered CA-1, The Coast Road, as an alternative to permit you to continue along the coastline.

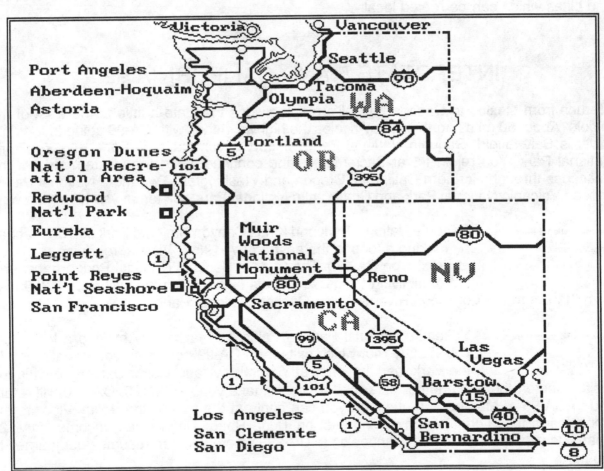

MAP 1-2   ACCESS FROM THE SOUTH, US-101 AND CA-1

Point Reyes

Shortly after you leave San Francisco via the Golden Gate Bridge on US-101, CA-1 goes to the east to take you back to the coast. CA-1 climbs high enough for you to get a good look at Marin County, then offers you Muir Woods National Monument, a cathedral-like grove of redwoods at the foot of Mount Tamalpais. A few miles further on is the Point Reyes National Seashore with long beaches, sand dunes and lagoons backed by tall cliffs and timber land. There are numerous hiking trails here, and whales, on their annual journey to Baja California, are often seen from the 100 year old Point Reyes Light. Sea lions bask on the rocks nearby.

Redwood National Park

You return to US-101 at Leggett. Allow time to admire Eureka's beautiful Victorian homes. Soon after you leave Eureka, you pass through Redwood National Park, a 106,000 acre forest of giant redwoods. Some of them are over 300 feet tall, and more than 400 years old. Along the seashore you often see hundreds of these gigantic trees littering the beach like match sticks where they have been strewn about by turbulent seas.

Oregon Dunes

As you continue north on US-101, the Oregon coast overwhelms you. Just about the time you become jaded and say to yourself that you will only take photos of incredible vistas, you come to Oregon Dunes National Recreation Area, a 50 mile long buffer zone in the continuing battle between the land and the sea. Even with your resolution, you notice that you have suddenly gone through another three rolls of film. In addition to the hiking trails, there are areas for dune buggies, and bikes which can be rented locally.

INTERSTATE 5 AND CALIFORNIA 99

I-5 runs from Mexico to Canada. In California, it divides the state a little to the west of the middle. About 80 miles north of Los Angeles the highway forks, with CA-99 going to the right towards Bakersfield, Sequoia National Park, Kings Canyon National Park, and Yosemite National Park. You rejoin I-5 at Sacramento, and continue along the western side of the Cascades through Northern California, Oregon and Washington. Two more National Parks, Lassen Volcanic National Park and Crater Lake National Park, will tempt you along the way.

Sequoia National Park
Kings Canyon

Sequoia National Park and Kings Canyon National Park can be reached by making a loop to the east on CA-198 at Visalia, returning to CA-99 at Fresno on CA-180. The trees in Sequoia National Park are the largest of all living things. America's highest Canyon wall rises 8,350 feet from the South Fork of Kings River in Kings Canyon National Park.

Yosemite National Park

Yosemite National Park can also be reached by making a loop from CA-99. CA-140, which exits from CA-99 near Merced, will take you to the Park road that ends at Yosemite Village Visitor Center. Leaving the Visitor Center, there is another park road which will take you to CA-120. CA-120 will return you to CA-99 at Manteca. In summer, you can contrast the visit to the Valley Floor to the pinnacles of the High Sierra by going east on Tioga Road. Tioga Road becomes CA-120 when it leaves the park, and continues on to US-395 where you can resume your journey to the north.

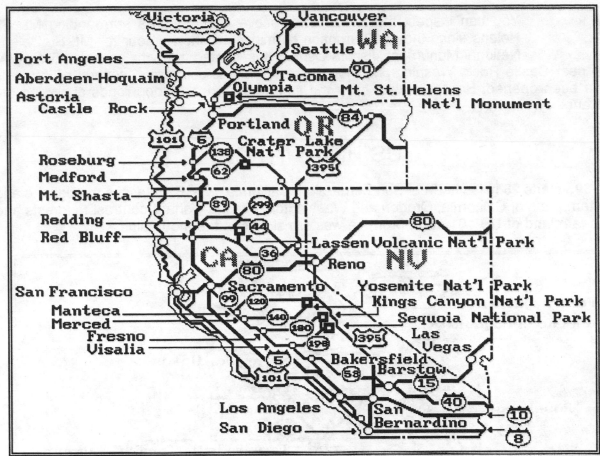

MAP 1-3 ACCESS FROM THE SOUTH, I-5 AND CA-99

Lassen Volcanic National Park

At the south end of the Cascades is Lassen Peak (10,457 ft.) which last erupted in 1914 and 1915. Lassen Peak is the focal point of Lassen Volcanic National Park, and the southern-most of a string of volcanos that reach north for 700 miles to British Columbia. The park is reached by making a loop from I-5 that starts by turning east on CA-36 at Red Bluff. Upon leaving the park, you can return to I-5 at Redding on CA-44. If the park has merely whetted your appetite for scenic beauty, CA-89 will return you to I-5 just south of the town of Mount Shasta. West on either CA-36 or CA-44 will take you to Susanville and US-395.

Crater Lake

Crater Lake National Park is the second of four National Parks that punctuate the Cascades as you head north. The lake is the deepest lake in the United States. It lies in a huge 20 square mile crater formed 6,840 years ago by the collapse of Mount Mazama during a massive eruption. To go there, make a loop, leaving I-5 at the OR-62 exit near Medford. OR-62 will take you to the west entrance of the park. The main park road will take you first to the Visitor Center, then around the western rim of the lake where you can either continue on to the north entrance to the park, or take the 35 mile Rim Drive around the rest of the lake. Leaving the park by the north entrance, you join OR-138 West to rejoin I-5 at Roseburg.

5

You can inspect the remarkable recovery of the area surrounding Mt. St. Helens since the 1980 eruption by making a short detour to Mt. St. Helens National Monument Visitors Center. It is located a few miles from I-5 on WA-504 near Castle Rock, Washington. Though the volcano is still active, several hiking trails have been opened. For those who have the time, there are two loop roads encircling the volcano.

US HIGHWAY 395

US-395 starts 28 miles north of San Bernardino, California on I-15. It passes through the arid eastern parts of California, Oregon and Washington, offering a sharp contrast to forests and lush farmland of US-101 and I-5 on the western slopes of the mountains.

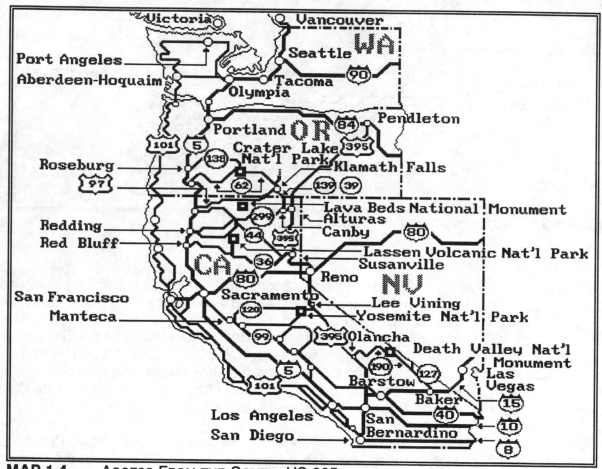

MAP 1-4   ACCESS FROM THE SOUTH, US-395

Death Valley   Death Valley National Monument is nearly two million acres of desert that includes the lowest point in the western hemisphere. It offers outstanding views for both hikers, and motorists. Many plants and animals are unique. There are even fish that are relics of the Pleistocene age. The best way to include Death Valley if you are coming from southern California, is to take I-15 north, past the US-395 exit, to Baker where you turn north on CA-127. To return to US-395 you take CA-190 to Olancha. Although this is a rather long diversion, it is well worth the effort if you have the time.

Yosemite Nat'l Park Although there is no convenient loop to Yosemite, CA-120 (starting just south of Lee Vining) will take you through the park to CA-99 at Manteca. CA-120 is known as Tioga Road within the boundaries of the Park. (See page 4.)

Lassen Volcanic National Park If you continue on through Susanville, 10 miles past the point where US-395 turns sharply to the east there is a fork in the road. CA-44 goes to the right and CA-36 goes left. Both roads take you to Lassen Volcanic National Park, and then to I-5 at Redding and Red Bluff respectively. (See page 5.)

Lava Beds National Monument Crater Lake Again, there is no convenient loop for returning you quickly to US-395 after visiting Lava Beds Nat'l Monument and Crater Lake National Park. There is however, an easy and scenic access to I-5 when you leave Crater Lake. There are over 200 caves in the 46,239 acre Lava Beds National Monument. Some of the caves have permanent ice in them; some are covered with ferns and mosses; and some of them even have Indian pictographs on their walls. To reach Lava Beds, you turn west on CA-299 at Alturas and follow it 18 miles to its junction with CA-139 at Canby where you turn right. When you leave Lava Beds, you rejoin CA-139, and continue north on it into Oregon, where it becomes OR-39. OR-39 takes you to Klamath Falls where you continue north on US-97. Twenty-two miles North of Klamath Falls, OR-62 branches to the left from US-97, taking you directly to Crater Lake. Leaving the park by the north entrance, take OR-138 west to join I-5 at Roseburg.

Columbia R. Gorge US-395 meets I-84 at Pendleton, Oregon. I-84 takes you through the beautiful Columbia River Gorge to Portland where you join I-5 to continue your trip to the Olympic Peninsula. Along the way are numerous State Parks and rest areas that contain interpretive information about the Lewis and Clark expedition, and the early days of Oregon Territory and the Oregon Trail.

ACCESS FROM THE EAST

Interstate Highways 70, 80, 90 and 94 concentrate the traffic from the central and Northern states and feed it into Interstate Highways 84 and 90 which serve the Pacific Northwest. Both I-84 and I-90 connect with I-5 to bring you to Olympia and the Olympic Loop Highway.

INTERSTATE HIGHWAY 70

Although there is short segment some 35 miles to the south, I-70 ends 30 miles short of I-15 at Salina, Utah. The final 30 miles to I-15 is on US-50. Salt Lake City is over a hundred miles north on I-15. If time permits, however, you should take a day to visit Bryce Canyon and Zion National Parks to the south.

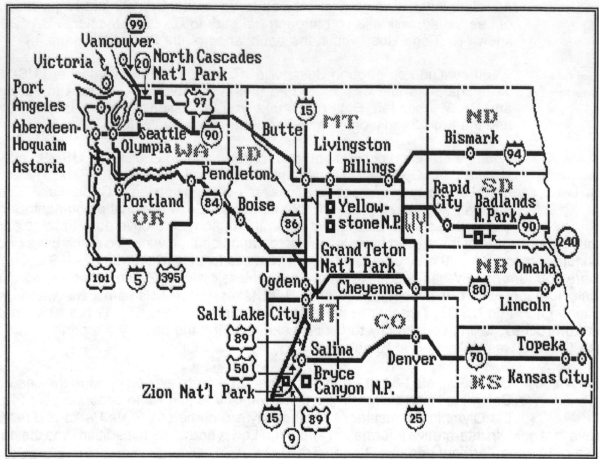

MAP 1-5   ACCESS FROM THE EAST

Bryce Canyon   Bryce Canyon has been delicately carved into the Pink Cliffs of The Grand Staircase over the last 50 or 60 million years. The Grand Staircase is the geological feature that starts with the Kaibab Plateau, which forms the north rim of the Grand Canyon, then rises through the Chocolate Cliffs, Vermillion Cliffs, White Cliffs and Grey Cliffs before it reaches the Pink Cliffs of Bryce Canyon. Where the Grand Canyon looks as though it has been scooped out of the Earth, each spire and arch of Bryce Canyon seems to have been individually carved, then painted with water colors. To get there, you go south on US-89 for 90 miles to UT-12 where you turn right and proceed another 14 miles to the park entrance.

Zion National Park   Zion National Park has several roads which have overcome the natural road blocks with tunnels and switchbacks that allow you to see a sizable amount of the park without even leaving your car. The Virgin River has incised Zion Canyon into the White Cliffs, and exposed the tallest cliffs in the Grand Staircase. UT-9 cuts across the south-eastern corner of Zion National Park. It leaves US-89 forty-four miles south of UT-12 (the access road to Bryce Canyon National Park), and, joins I-15 a few miles west of the park. Here you head north to resume your journey to the Olympic Peninsula.

8

INTERSTATE HIGHWAYS 80 AND 84

If you went to Bryce Canyon and Zion National Parks, you rejoin I-15 290 miles south of Salt Lake City. Just south of Ogden, I-15 merges with I-84. I-84 begins 31 miles to the east where it branches off from I-80 before I-80 heads south for Salt Lake City. I-84 passes through the arid West, offering vistas of mountains that seem to be only minutes away because of the clear air. Then it enters the grasslands of Idaho, and the historic and beautiful Columbia River Gorge. I-84 will bring you to I-5 at Portland, Oregon, where you head north to Olympia.

INTERSTATE HIGHWAY 90

I-94 rejoins I-90 at Billings Montana after having left it in Wisconsin to head north through central Minnesota and North Dakota. I-90 is the main access road for three of the most beautiful National Parks in America before it terminates at I-5 in Seattle, Washington.

Badlands Nat'l Park At mile 131 of I-90 you can exit to SD-240 to make a loop through the Badlands National Park. Here the land has eroded the prairies into fairyland shapes that expose delicate colors in each of the sedimentary layers laid down over millions of years. SD-240 will return to I-90 at Wall, South Dakota, home of the famous Wall Drug Store.

Yellowstone & Yellowstone National Park can be reached by leaving I-90 at mile 332 in
Grand Teton Livingston, Montana, and heading south on US 89. After you enter the park at
National Parks Gardiner, Montana, you come to Mammoth Hot Springs, and one of the five Visitor Centers. You then set out on the Grand Loop, a 145 mile long figure eight through the Park. There are several active thermal areas, and the spacious, rolling hills teem with wildlife. The Grand Canyon of the Yellowstone will provide an excellent contrast to the rolling hills with its roughly hewn grandeur. Heading south at the bottom of the figure eight will take you to the Grand Teton National Park. There, the sheer jagged peaks rise so suddenly from the plain called Jackson Hole that they seem to have been placed there as ornaments.

ACCESS FROM THE NORTH

I-5 brings people from northern Washington and Canada to the Olympic Peninsula and the Olympic Loop Highway. For those who want to get out of the fast lane before embarking on their Olympic adventure, a day or so in Victoria, at the tip of Vancouver Island will slow the pace.

INTERSTATE HIGHWAY 5

When Highway 99 from Vancouver enters Washington at Blaine it becomes I-5 and, on clear days, offers you glorious views of snow-capped Mt. Baker. The drive south is a scenic one, but increasingly as you approach Seattle, heavy traffic demands your attention on I-5.

North Cascades National Park As you head south on I-5, you parallel the Cascade Range. You can get a closer look, and enjoy a scenic drive by going east on WA-20 at Burlington. WA-20 goes through the park to US-97 at Okanogen. There are 360 miles of hiking trails in the park and nearby recreation areas. These tall steep mountains intercept the rain that drenches western Washington, turning eastern Washington into a desert.

VICTORIA FERRY

A very pleasant and relaxing way to reach the Olympic Peninsula is to take the ferry that leaves several times each day from Victoria, the capital of British Columbia. The passage across the Strait of Juan de Fuca to Port Angeles takes about an hour and a half and leaves you rested to begin your Olympic adventure immediately. Whilst you are in Victoria be sure to take in the British Columbia Provincial Museum.

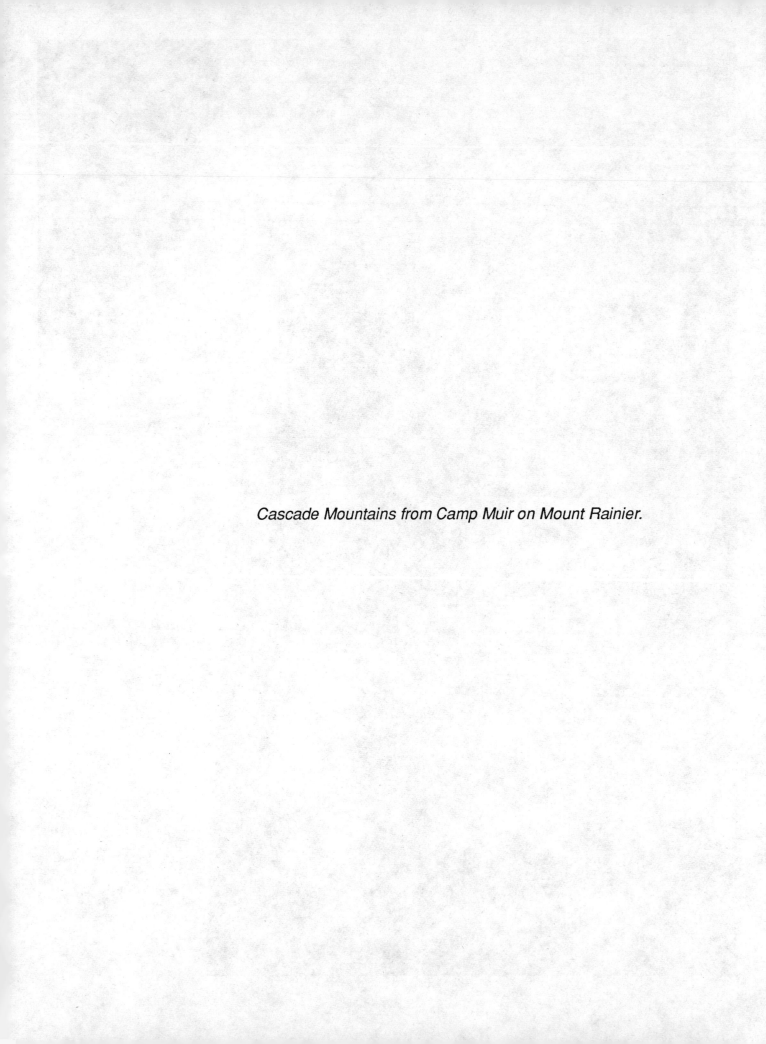

Cascade Mountains from Camp Muir on Mount Rainier.

CHAPTER 2

SEATTLE TACOMA MT RAINIER OLYMPIA

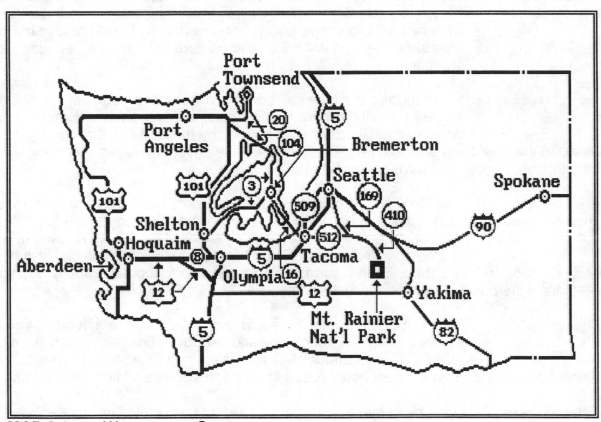

MAP 2-1   WASHINGTON STATE

Olympia is one of the gateways to the Olympic Peninsula and it, along with nearby Tacoma and Seattle offer many attractions for you to sample either before or after your Olympic adventure. Some of these attractions are highlighted below. Then, the adventure begins in earnest as we leave I-5 at exit number 104 to join US Highway 101 at its termination point, mile number 367.3.

13

SEATTLE

Seattle is a vacation objective in its own right, and it has been beefing up its convention facilities. Try not to let Seattle's many attractions erode the time you have reserved for the Olympic Peninsula.

SPACE NEEDLE   In Seattle the Space Needle will help you to get your bearings. The Olympics are to the west. The Cascades to the east. Either of the two revolving restaurants at the 500 foot level — The Emerald Suite for elegance, or The Space Needle Restaurant for more casual family dining — offers a very pleasant venue for a meal. On clear days the Olympic Mountains seem to sparkle. Elevator rides and passes to the Observation Deck are complimentary with meals. Reservations are recommended.

SEATTLE CENTER
PACIFIC SCIENCE CNTR   The Space Needle and the Pacific Science Center are both found in the 74 acre Seattle Center. The Pacific Science Center has six buildings crammed full of displays and hands-on exhibits. There are also brilliant laser shows and an IMAX Theater. Be sure to check the newspaper for schedules.

MONORAIL - FREE BUS   You can take the monorail downtown and have your own tour. Even with all the hills in downtown Seattle, walking tours are really great. When you get tired, you can just hop on the next bus that comes along. Busses in the downtown area are free. Be sure to ask the driver where the downtown Zone ends, though, or you may have to pay full fare.

PIKE PLACE
WATERFRONT - AQUARIUM   Head for Pike Place Market where vendors hawk their wares from farmers market stalls. Then go down to the waterfront for a full mile of seafood restaurants and interesting shops. The Seattle Aquarium, with its Underwater Dome and Touch Tank, is at Pier 59. You can also book coach tours on the waterfront. Even if you have no reservation, you can usually buy your tickets from the driver if there is space available.

PIONEER SQUARE   Pioneer Square is near the south end of the waterfront. It offers you 20 square blocks of historic stone and brick buildings that were built on the ashes of the disastrous 1889 fire. They have now been restored to their original beauty, and many of them now house gift shops, galleries and fine restaurants.

UNDERGROUND SEATTLE   Don't be content with what you see at street level in Pioneer Square. Take a tour of Underground Seattle which was created before the Denny Regrade, when Seattle's street level was one floor lower than it is today. For many years after the street level was raised, the establishments in the area continued to offer their customers entrances on both street level and on the underground sidewalk.

KLONDIKE GOLD RUSH NAT'L HISTORICAL PARK Two blocks from Pioneer Square is the Seattle unit of Klondike Gold Rush National Historical Park. It highlights Seattle's role as the major gateway to the 1897-98 Gold Rush. You visit this museum at your peril though. After I went there I had to see the 13,000 acre Skagway, Alaska unit of the park. That led to walking the 33 mile Chilkoot Trail from Dyea, Alaska near Skagway, to Bennett, British Columbia. The restored historical section of Skagway seemed to insist that I visit Dawson City, Yukon Territory to see the destination that drew thousands of would-be miners through horrendous hardships to the Klondike

SALT WATER STATE PARK The Salt Water State Park is located on Puget Sound below Kent Smith Canyon, two miles south of Des Moines on WA-509. It has 53 campsites (maximum length 60 feet), none have RV hook-ups. There are picnic tables, fireplaces, a dump station, flush toilets and pay showers. The park also has picnic and kitchen shelters, beach access, scuba diving, clamming (in season) and extensive hiking trails.

KINGDOME
MUSEUM OF FLIGHT
GOVERNMENT LOCKS Seattle has dozens of other fascinating attractions like the Kingdome, The Museum of Flight (located in Boeing's first real home) and the Government Locks between Lake Washington and Puget Sound. While you are at the Government Locks, see if you can figure out a way to keep the sea lions from eating all the salmon as they queue up for the fish ladder. (You are not allowed to hurt the sea lions in the process.)

TACOMA

The Tacoma area is a region of superlatives: the tallest mountain in the Cascade Range; the oldest incorporated town in Washington, with the state's oldest jail, protestant church, and library; and the world's largest wooden dome. These are but a few of Tacoma's many attractions.

MOUNT RAINIER Mount Rainier, the tallest mountain in the Cascades, is also the tallest mountain above its base in the lower 48 states. It looms over the city and appears to be in Tacoma's back yard rather than 70 miles away. (See Mt. Rainier National Park below.)

STEILACOOM Washington's oldest town, Steilacoom, southwest of Tacoma was incorporated in 1874, 15 years before Washington became a state. Steilacoom is also the location of the state's oldest jail, protestant church and library.

TACOMA DOME Tacoma Dome, can seat 30,000 people under the largest wooden dome in the world. It has a restaurant, and guided tours of the dome are available.

POINT DEFIANCE PARK Point Defiance Park is the home of the Zoo and Aquarium. History buffs will enjoy the unique logging relics at Camp Six Logging Museum and Fort Nisqually Historic Site overlooking the Tacoma Narrows Bridge. Fishermen can rent a boat, motor and tackle here to do a bit of fishing in the Puget Sound.

DASH POINT STATE PARK The Dash Point State Park is located five miles northeast of Tacoma on WA-509. There are 136 campsites (maximum length 35 feet) of which 28 have water and electricity. There are fireplaces, picnic tables, telephones, dump station, flush toilets and pay showers. Dash Point also has picnic shelters, beach access and fishing.

STATE HISTORY MUSEUM
BING CROSBY MUSEUM
PANTAGES THEATRE
Some of Tacoma's many other attractions are Washington State Historical Society Museum, the Bing Crosby Historical Society (Crosby was born in Tacoma), and the beautifully restored Pantages Center for the Performing Arts.

MOUNT RAINIER NATIONAL PARK

Mount Rainier National Park has 41 glaciers (including both the largest in area and the longest in the lower 48 states), 300 miles of trails, six campgrounds, two lodges, four visitors centers, a museum and roads that will take you up to an elevation of 6,500 feet.

CLIMBING MT. RAINIER For information about guides, climbing safety and instruction, or equipment rental, contact Rainier Mountaineering, Inc., Paradise, WA 98397, Phone (206) 569-2227. In winter: 201 St. Helens Avenue, Tacoma, WA 98402 (206) 627-6242. They also offer a supervised climb to the summit. It includes a one day snow and ice climbing school, then two days for the climb itself. The first day takes you to Camp Muir, a rock shelf at about 10,000 feet. The second day entails a 2 AM departure to ensure return before the mid-day sun begins to weaken the ice bridges. Its a somewhat difficult climb, so be sure you are in good condition before attempting it.

OLYMPIA

There are also many interesting attractions in the Olympia area before you embark on your Olympic adventure. In addition to its being the state capital, Olympia has several beautiful parks and historic sites.

TOURIST INFORMATION
HENDERSON HSE. MUSEUM
TUMWATER HIST. PARK
You can exit from I-5 at mile 103 for the Tourist Information Center. It is located in the Henderson House Museum in the Tumwater Historic The park teems with ducks and geese that like having their picture taken. There is also a trail that goes under the freeway, through some wetlands on a plank walk-way to an interpretive display about the creation of Capitol Lake.

OLYMPIA BREWERY TOUR Exit 103 will also take you to the Olympia Brewery, which has a beautiful collection of beer steins and conducts guided tours until 4:30 PM every day. In addition to showing you how the beer is made, they show you how to serve it. (Not too cold.)

TUMWATER FALLS PARK Across from the brewery is beautiful Tumwater Falls Park.

16

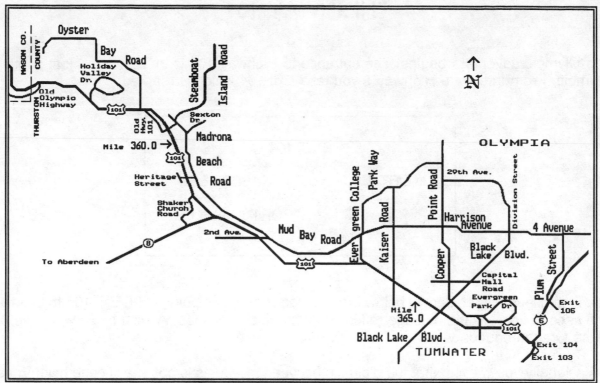

MAP 2-2   OLYMPIA - TUMWATER AREA

STATE CAPITOL   I-5 Exit 105 will take you to the State Capitol with its 287 foot dome. In the spring the cherry blossoms on the State Capitol grounds are glorious. Tours, guided and self-guided, can be organized. Be sure to include the Department of Natural Resources retail shop. It is two blocks north of the Capitol Campus on the left side of Capitol Way. There you will find a great selection of maps and photos of Washington's wilderness sites. Interestingly, the Capitol is the most frequently visited attraction in the state.

STATE CAPITOL MUSEUM   The State Capitol Museum and its exhibit of the eruption in May, 1980 that made Mount St. Helens 1,300 feet shorter, is located in the Clarence J. Lord Mansion, south of the Capitol campus. It is reached from I-5 Exit 105. There are also displays on Northwest native American culture and history here.

CITY CENTER   I-5 Exit 105 will also take you to Olympia's City Center via either the Capitol campus or the Post Office.

HIGHWAY 101

The Olympic adventure begins! The entrance to Highway 101 is in Tumwater, just south of Olympia. From Interstate Highway 5 you take Exit 104 which is marked:

```
+---------------------------------------------+
|                                             |
|                  EXIT 104                    |
|                                             |
|       NORTH              ABERDEEN            |
|                                             |
|        101              PORT ANGELES         |
|                                             |
+---------------------------------------------+
```

The first mileage figure shown below is the distance from this point — I-5 Exit 104 to US-101. The second figure is the mileage reflected in the official mileposts which begin with mile 0.0 at the Oregon boundary.

Occasionally you will find that the distance between mileposts is not exactly one mile. These discrepancies have usually occurred when improvements to the road have shortened it. Where differences exist, I have adjusted my figures to the official mileposts to enable you to quickly locate your position in this book. I have also used the center column to highlight attractions that are mentioned in the text so that you can home in on those things that are of particular interest to you.

Text on the left side of the page refers to attractions and other items of interest which are physically located on the left side of the road. The same is true for text on the right side of the page. It refers to attractions on the right. For Highway 101, "left" means left as you proceed away from mile 367.3 toward smaller mile numbers. Compass directions can be a little tricky on Highway 101, as it makes a complete loop in the Olympic Peninsula.

	HIGHWAY 101	
	MILES MILE	
	from NUMBER	
	I-5 ___	

DECATUR STREET SW	0.7 366.6	**COOPER POINT ROAD**
MOTTMAN ROAD	C-STORE	**EVERGREEN PARK DRIVE**
	PHONE	
To: S. Puget Sound Community	GAS	There is an AM/PM C-Store with
College		ARCO gas on your right, 0.1 miles
		from this exit. It is at the junction of
		Cooper Point Rd. and Evergreen
		Park Dr. Evergreen Park Dr. goes
		to the right in front of the AM/PM.

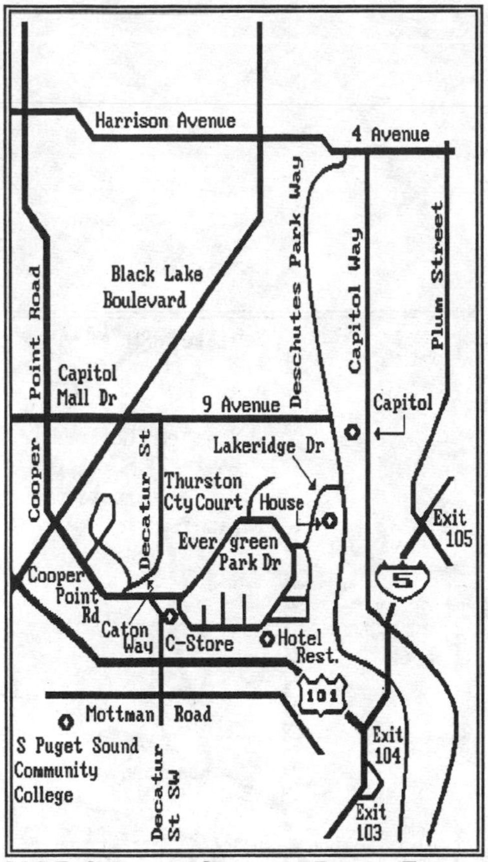

MAP 2-3   COOPER POINT ROAD-
DECATUR ST. EXIT

Map labels: Harrison Avenue, 4 Avenue, Black Lake Boulevard, Deschutes Park Way, Capitol Way, Plum Street, Black Lake Boulevard, Capitol Mall Dr, 9 Avenue, Capitol, Lakeridge Dr, Thurston Cty Court House, Cooper Point Road, Decatur St, Evergreen Park Dr, Exit 105, 5, Cooper Point Rd, Caton Way, C-Store, Hotel Rest., Mottman Road, 101, Exit 104, S Puget Sound Community College, Decatur St SW, Exit 103

THURSTON COUNTY
COURTHOUSE

Turn right into Evergreen Park Dr. for Thurston County Courthouse. After 0.6 miles, turn left into Lakeridge Drive, the second street on your left.

Lakeridge Drive continues past the courthouse to Deschutes Park Way and a view of the Capitol across the lake.

LODGING
RESTAURANT

After the two long blocks to Lakeridge drive, Evergreen Park Drive curves back toward Hwy. 101. Westwater Inn and Cezan's Restaurant are two short blocks further, on the left just as the road turns to the right to run parallel to Highway 101.

After the intersection with Evergreen Park Drive, Cooper Point Road continues, to intersect Black Lake Boulevard in 0.9 mile.

1.3   366.0

The right lane ends here, reducing the road from three north bound lanes to two.

BLACK LAKE BLVD.
WEST OLYMPIA

BLACK LAKE BOULEVARD

GAS
RESTAURANT
C-STORE

A left turn under Highway 101 will bring you to an Exxon Service Station immediately on the right. One tenth of a mile further south on Black Lake Boulevard are Kattleman's Steak and Omelette House, and a Shop Easy convenience store on your left.

PROPANE

C & D Propane is on your right as you continue south on Black Lake Boulevard, 1.1 miles from Highway 101. Their address is 2925 Black Lake Boulevard.

RV PARK

To reach Black Lake RV Park, follow Black Lake Blvd. south for two miles, turn left into Belmore Road. Go 0.3 miles, and turn right into Black Lake-Belmore Road. The RV park is on your right in 0.2 miles.

It has 56 campsites of which 46 have hook-ups. There are picnic tables, fireplaces, pay showers, flush toilets, recreation room, store and swimming area. It also has a boat launch and a dock. Rental boats are available. The address and phone are: 4325 Black Lake-Belmore Road SW, Olympia, WA 98502, Phone: (206) 357-6775.

RV PARK

Salmon Shores RV Resort is in Black Lake Blvd. on the left, 3.3 miles from Highway 101. It has 65 campsites, of which 45 have hook-ups. They also rent trailers. There are fireplaces, picnic tables flush toilets, free showers, recreation room, store, laundry, playground and a swimming area. It also has a boat launch and a dock. Rental boats are available. The address and phone number are: 5446 Black Lake Blvd., Olympia, WA 98502. Phone:(206) 357-8618.

RV PARK

Columbus Park is in Black Lake Blvd., on the left, 3.5 miles from Highway 101. It has 76 sites, with hook-ups. There are tables, fireplaces, flush toilets, pay showers, a store, recreation room, laundry, playground and a swimming area. It has a boat launch and dock. The address is: 5700 Black Lake Blvd., Olympia, WA 98502. Phone: (206) 786-9460.

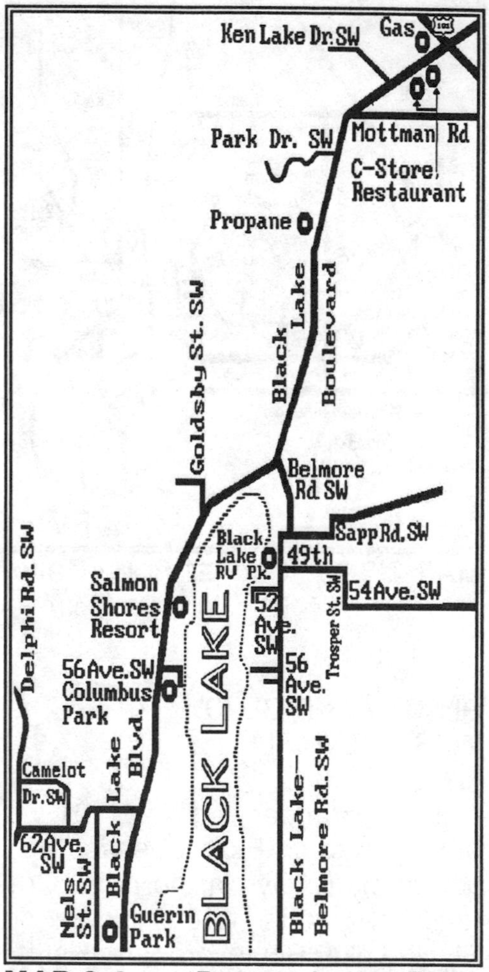

MAP 2-4   BLACK LAKE BLVD. SOUTH OF HIGHWAY 101

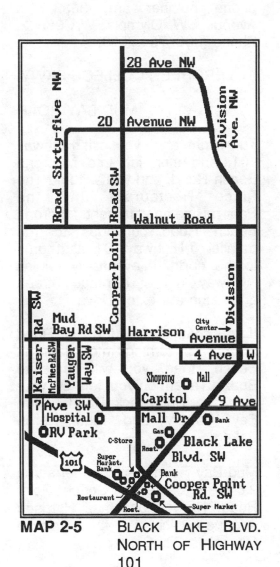

MAP 2-5 BLACK LAKE BLVD. NORTH OF HIGHWAY 101

RESTAURANT SUPERMARKET BANK	Denny's Restaurant, MEGA Foods, and Great American Bank are on your right in the first block of Black Lake Blvd. after you turn right from Hwy. 101.
BANK SUPERMARKET C-STORE, GAS FAST FOOD	Top 24 Hour Foods, a Seafirst Bank branch (inside the supermarket), a 7-11 C-Store (with gas) and Saucy's Pizza are on your left at this point.
HOSPITAL	To reach Black Hills Community Hospital, turn left at the first intersection, 0.2 miles from the Black Lake Blvd. (Cooper Point Rd.) and left again at Capital Mall Road, the second traffic light after you turn into Cooper Point Road.
RESTAURANT GAS BANK SHOPPING MALL	Continuing on Black Hills Blvd. to Capital Mall Rd., Coco's Family Restaurant and a Shell station are on the left. A Rainier Bank is on your right. Capital Mall is on the left.
CITY CENTER	Black Lake Boulevard becomes Division St. 0.4 miles from its Intersection with Capital Mall Road. Turn right at the next street, Harrison Ave., for Olympia's City Center.
2.3 365.0 MILEPOST	

KAISER ROAD

3.0 364.3 RV PARK	Coach Post Trailer Park is on your right just before the Kaiser Road intersection. A series of right turns will bring you to the entrance: right into Kaiser Road, right again at the first street, 7th Avenue, then right into the entrance.

HIGHWAY 101
MILES from I-5 | MILE NUMBER

Coach Post Trailer Park has 20 sites with hook-ups. There are picnic tables, flush toilets, pay showers and laundry. Guests also have access to golf, a stable and tennis courts. Their address and phone number are: 3633 7th Avenue SW, Olympia, WA 98502. Phone (206) 754 7580.

3.1 364.2

EVERGREEN COLLEGE PKWY.

2ND AVENUE SW

4.5 362.8

MUD BAY ROAD

RESTAURANT
PARK N RIDE

Turn right after you exit Highway 101, and then left into Madrona Beach Road, and you will find The Place Restaurant and the Park-n-Ride on your right. Madrona Beach Road continues to run parallel to Highway 101, as it turns to the north. It eventually rejoins Highway 101 at Heritage Street, and again at Sexton Drive.

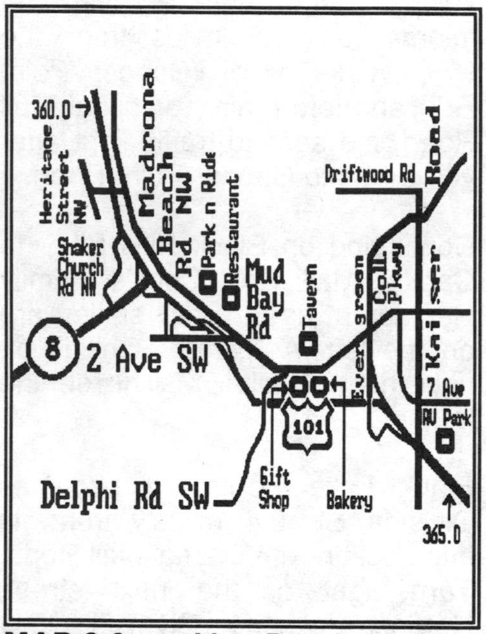

MAP 2-6 MUD BAY AREA

TAVERN
GIFT SHOP
BAKERY

If you continue on Mud Bay Road instead of turning into Madrona Beach Road, you will come to Buzz's Tavern on your left. On your right are Shipwreck Beads, Mud Bay Pottery and Blue Heron Bakery.

CITY CENTER

Mud Bay Road continues for some 2.6 miles to intersect Cooper Point Road. Here it becomes Harrison Avenue which will take you to Olympia's City Center.

WEST (8) OCEAN BEACHES ABERDEEN MONTESANO

State Highway 8 continues in the two left lanes.

5.7 361.6

NORTH (101) SHELTON PORT ANGELES BREMERTON HOOD CANAL

Highway 101 exits to a single lane on the right.

HERITAGE STREET

6.7   360.6

MADRONA BEACH ROAD

Madrona Beach Road runs along parallel to Hwy. 101 for several miles, from Mud Bay Road to Sexton Drive.

7.3   360.0

MILEPOST

OLD HIGHWAY 101

Old Highway 101 runs along parallel to Highway 101 until they intersect again at Oyster Bay Road.

7.5   359.8

GIFT SHOP
GAS
TAVERN

SEXTON DRIVE
STEAMBOAT ISLAND ROAD
HUNTER POINT

Ilene's Art and Gift Parlor is on your right as you enter Sexton Drive from the little access road. Turn left into Sexton Drive for Ken's Unocal 76 Station and Characters Corner Tavern.

SUPERMARKET
PHONE

Pat's Market is directly behind the service station and tavern. It is accessible from Steamboat Island Road.

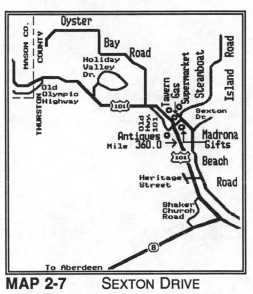

MAP 2-7   SEXTON DRIVE STEAMBOAT IS. ROAD

OLD HIGHWAY 101

Once Upon A Time Antiques is on your left where Old Highway 101 rejoins Highway 101 from the south.

8.3   359.0

ANTIQUES

OYSTER BAY ROAD

9.3   358.0

HOLIDAY VALLEY ROAD

The small gravel road to your right is a private driveway.

OLD OLYMPIC HIGHWAY

10.3 357.0

Old Olympic Highway goes to the left. It rejoins Highway 101 at mile 356.0.

The gravel road to the right is a private driveway.

MASON COUNTY - THURSTON COUNTY
      BOUNDARY

10.5 356.8

THURSTON COUNTY - MASON COUNTY
      BOUNDARY

Forest Service Road 2340 from Brown Creek Campground.

CHAPTER 3

SHELTON   SOUTH FORK SKOKOMISH

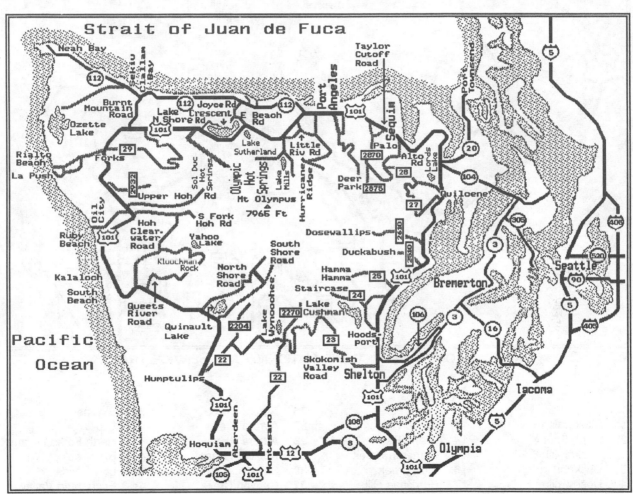

MAP 3-1   MAJOR ROADS IN THE OLYMPIC AND KITSAP PENINSULAS

As you can see on this map, Olympia is the last big city we will see until we return from the Olympic Peninsula. Most of one's needs can be satisfied in the towns like Shelton along Highway 101. If you need anything exotic or difficult to find however, you should probably

27

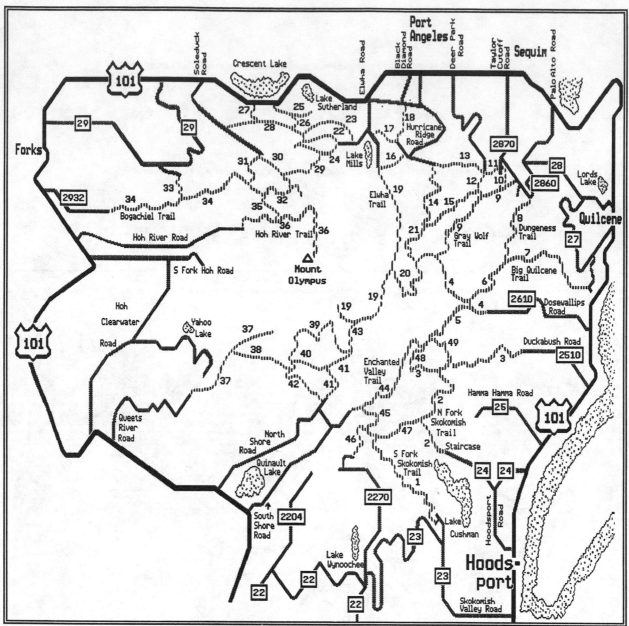

MAP 3-2 NATIONAL FOREST SERVICE AND NATIONAL PARK SERVICE TRAILS

1	South Fork Skokomish	12	Three Forks	26	Aurora Divide	39	Skyline
2	North Fork Skokomish	13	Grand Ridge	27	Aurora Creek	40	Elip
		14	Grand Pass	28	Aurora Ridge	41	North Fork Quinault
3	Duckabush	15	Cameron Creek	29	Appleton Pass	42	Big Creek
4	Dosewallips	16	Wolf Creek	30	Soleduck	43	Low Divide
5	West Fork Dosewallips	17	Hurricane Hill	31	Canyon Creek	44	Enchanted Valley
		18	Little River	32	High Divide-Bailey Range	45	Graves Creek
6	Constance Pass	19	Elwha	33	Rugged Ridge	46	Wynoochee
7	Big Quilcene	20	Hayden Pass	34	Bogachiel	47	Six Ridge
8	Dungeness	21	Lost Pass	35	Hoh Lake	48	O'Niel Pass
9	Gray Wolf	22	Crystal Ridge	36	Hoh River	49	La Crosse Pass
10	Slab Camp	23	Happy Lake Ridge	37	Queets River		
11	Deer Ridge	24	Boulder Lake	38	Tshletshy Creek		
		25	Barnes Creek				

stock up in Olympia. This is especially so for time-critical things like special prescription drugs. Although practically anything can be obtained in Port Angeles and some of the larger small towns, it may take a day or two to bring them in from Tacoma or Seattle.

After we leave Shelton we will get our first glimpse of the Olympic Mountains. Not long after that we will be in them, as we head for Brown Creek Campground and the trails that start from near the South Fork Skokomish River.

The map opposite shows the major trails that originate from roads that are accessible from Highway 101, and connect with other major trails in the interior of the peninsula. If you have access to two vehicles, leave one on the opposite side of the Peninsula from where you start. It is an exhilarating experience to enjoy the alpine scenery from the high passes as you cross to the other side.

If you have only one vehicle, do not despair. The return journey on Olympic trails is always vastly different from the outward hike.

Let's return now to Mile 356.8 of Highway 101, at the Thurston County - Mason County Boundary, and continue north towards Shelton.

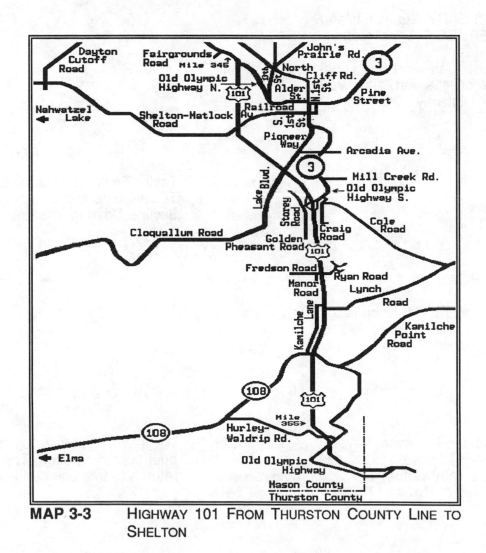

MAP 3-3   HIGHWAY 101 FROM THURSTON COUNTY LINE TO SHELTON

29

THURSTON COUNTY - MASON COUNTY BOUNDARY	10.5 356.8	MASON COUNTY - THURSTON COUNTY BOUNDARY

OLD OLYMPIC HIGHWAY

11.3 356.0

OLD OLYMPIC HIGHWAY   KAMILCHE
KAMILCHE POINT
OYSTER BAY

On the left, Old Olympic Highway goes south for one mile.

HURLEY - WALDRIP ROAD

12.1 355.2

HURLEY - WALDRIP ROAD

Left here takes you about two miles to State Highway 108.

Right here takes you half a mile to Old Pacific Highway.

12.3 355.0
MILEPOST

WEST McCLEARY Squaxin Island
(108) ABERDEEN Tribal Center

13.6 353.7

KAMILCHE

The Kamilche Cafe and the Tribal Center are on the left after you cross under Highway 101.

RESTAURANT

KAMILCHE LANE

14.8 352.5

LYNCH ROAD

RESTAURANT
PHONE C-STORE
GAS DIESEL
DRIVE-IN MOVIE

Taylor Towne Restaurant/Store
Texaco Gas and Diesel Fuel
Skyline Drive-in Theatre

FREDSON ROAD

15.9 351.4

RYAN ROAD

Betty's Candle and Gift Shop is 0.4 miles south on Manor Road, left as you enter Fredson Road.

GIFT SHOP

GOLDEN PHEASANT ROAD

17.1 350.2

NORTH   OLD OLYMPIC   SHELTON
(3)   HIGHWAY S.   BREMERTON

HOSPITAL
SUPERMARKET
C-STORE RV PARK
DIESEL PROPANE
LODGING TAVERN
GAS FAST FOOD
PARK-N-RIDE
RESTAURANT

To reach Golden Pheasant Tavern, turn left under Highway 101, pass the entrance ramps, turn left into Golden Pheasant Rd. and follow it for 0.9 mi.

We leave Highway 101 here for a brief visit to Shelton. The narrative returns to this point (Mile 350.2) on page 36.

30

SHELTON

Shelton is a very pleasant logging community mainly supported by Christmas tree farms and Simpson Timber. It has a population of 7,629, and is the County Seat of Mason County. Shelton is also Mason County's only incorporated town.

Shelton's commercial activity is distributed among three areas: Old Olympic Highway South (the approach we will use); the central business district; and Old Olympic Highway North. Traffic is usually light except when log trains creep across the road on the Simpson Timber Railroad. Parking is easy, even for large motor homes, and the fast food chains are well represented.

OLD OLYMPIC HIGHWAY LOOP

The point at which we leave Highway 101 is mile zero of State Highway 3 which continues on to Allyn, Belfair, Bremerton and the Kitsap Peninsula after it passes through Shelton. The mileage figures shown below are distances from Highway 101's junctions with Old Olympic Highway South, and Old Olympic Highway North.

MAP 3-4 SHELTON VIA OLD OLYMPIC HIGHWAY

SHELTON DISTANCE FROM HIGHWAY 101		
SOUTH	NORTH	
0.0	4.9	PARK-N-RIDE
		RV PARK

MILE ZERO OF STATE HIGHWAY ③

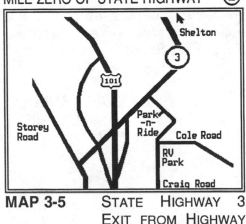

MAP 3-5 STATE HIGHWAY 3 EXIT FROM HIGHWAY 101

MILE ZERO OF STATE HIGHWAY ③
A Park-n-Ride is on your right just after you turn right.

Past the Park-n-Ride, the roadway bends to the right. Just before you get back even with Highway 101, the road goes to the left in front of We & U RV Park. You will need to be alert to find it, as it seems to be primarily a mobile home park and their sign is not readily apparent.

	0.9 4.0	Mill Creek Motel
	LODGING	

ARCADIA AVENUE	1.5 3.4	ARCADIA AVENUE
Chevron Service Station	GAS PROPANE	Log Cabin Tavern
	TAVERN	Marv's Hillcrest Texaco,

BELLEVUE AVENUE	1.6 3.3	DICKINSON AVENUE
Everybody's 25 Hour Supermarket	SUPERMARKET	Brad's Quick Stop and
	C-STORE GAS	Laundromat
	LAUNDROMAT	

CASCADE AVENUE	1.7 3.2	CASCADE AVENUE
	C-STORE	Nault's Grocery-Arco, Propane
	GAS PROPANE	

DEARBORN AVENUE	1.8 3.1	DEARBORN AVENUE
ELLINOR AVENUE		ELLINOR AVENUE
FAIRMOUNT AVENUE		FAIRMOUNT AVENUE

	1.9 3.0	Log Monument Lookout
	VIEWPOINT	

Kentucky Fried Chicken	2.2 2.7	Here, the street curves right at the bottom of a steep hill and becomes South First Street.
	FAST FOOD	

HARVARD AVENUE	2.3 2.6	HARVARD AVENUE
Donut Tree Restaurant	RESTAURANT	MILL STREET
Lucky Strike Restaurant	TAVERN	
Spare Room Lounge	BOWLING	

TURNER AVENUE KNEELAND PARK	2.4 2.5	
PARK STREET		

Simpson Timber Railroad **GOLDSBOROUGH CREEK**	2.5 2.4	Simpson Timber Railroad **GOLDSBOROUGH CREEK**

Paul Bunyan Express Lane-24 Hr.
 Foods, Gas, Diesel
Jackpot Self Service Gasoline

KNEELAND STREET
Smokey's Burgers

C-STORE
GAS DIESEL
RESTAURANT
TAVERN
FAST FOOD

Bob's Tavern

GROVE STREET
COTA STREET

2.6 2.3

GROVE STREET
COTA STREET

Price Setter Supermarket is to your left at Fifth and Cota.

SUPERMARKET
TAVERN
RESTAURANT

Sail Inn Tavern
Pine Tree Lounge and Restaurant

**RAILROAD   SHELTON CITY
AVENUE   CENTER**

2.7 2.2

**RAILROAD   NORTH   ALLYN
AVENUE   ③   BELFAIR
                          BREMERTON**

Shelton's City Center is to the left. The Visitor Information Center is on your right in the second block after you turn. It is housed in the caboose of an old log train on display in front of the Post Office. Great American Pizza Factory and Deli is opposite the Post Office.

Nita's Restaurant is on the left, and Heinie's Broiler is on the right between Third St. and Fourth St. Ming Tree Cafe is in the next block on the left. Price Setter Supermarket is two blocks to the left, at Fifth and Cota.

Marv's Exxon Station, Hallmark Hotel and Timbers Restaurant are on the right between Sixth and Seventh St. Safeway Supermarket is two blocks to the right at Seventh and Franklin.

CITY CENTER
TOURIST INFO
POST OFFICE
FAST FOOD

RESTAURANT
SUPERMARKET

GAS
RESTAURANT
LODGING
SUPERMARKET

At the next street after you turn right (Front Street) State Highway 3 North goes to the left, continues two more blocks to Pine street, and turns right again as it leaves Shelton.

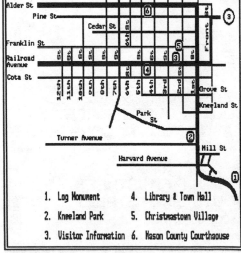

MAP 3-6
Shelton City Center

1. Log Monument
2. Kneeland Park
3. Visitor Information
4. Library & Town Hall
5. Christmastown Village
6. Mason County Courthouse

Railroad Ave. becomes Shelton-Matlock Rd. and (1.6 miles from First St.) joins Highway 101.	C-STORE GAS RESTAURANT BOWLING	Pit Stop 24 Hr. Grocery, Gas, Beer, Wine and Dining Shelton Recreation-Bowl & Pub
Capital Restaurant and Lounge Denny's Texaco	RESTAURANT GAS	
FRANKLIN STREET	2.7 2.2	FRANKLIN STREET
Safeway Supermarket is to the left at 7th & Franklin. Banner and Burnett Chevron Dairy Queen	SUPERMARKET GAS FAST FOOD	
CEDAR STREET PINE STREET	2.8 2.1 GAS PROPANE	Mac's Shell CEDAR STREET Auto Service PINE STREET
ALDER STREET	2.9 2.0	ALDER STREET
Turn left into Alder Street to rejoin Highway 101 at the north end of Shelton.	LODGING	The City Center Motel is in S. First Street on your right just past Alder Street.
Bennett's Photo Center	C-STORE FAST FOOD PHOTO CENTER	Mickey's Deli and Mamma Ella's Pizza and Spaghetti are both on your right after you turn into Alder Street.
		SOUTH SECOND STREET
SOUTH THIRD STREET SOUTH FOURTH STREET MASON COUNTY COURTHOUSE	3.0 1.9	SOUTH THIRD STREET SOUTH FOURTH STREET
SOUTH FIFTH STREET SOUTH SIXTH STREET	3.1 1.8	SOUTH FIFTH STREET SOUTH SIXTH STREET
SOUTH SEVENTH STREET SOUTH EIGHTH STREET	3.2 1.7	SOUTH SEVENTH STREET SOUTH EIGHTH STREET

	SOUTH	NORTH	
B STREET	3.6	1.3	NORTH THIRTEENTH A STREET STREET B STREET

Alder Street becomes Old Olympic Highway North at the top of the hill, at A street.

	HOSPITAL		

Turn right into B Street for Mason General Hospital. After three blocks turn left into N. 13th St. The hospital is then 0.4 miles on the left. I St. also goes to the Hospital.

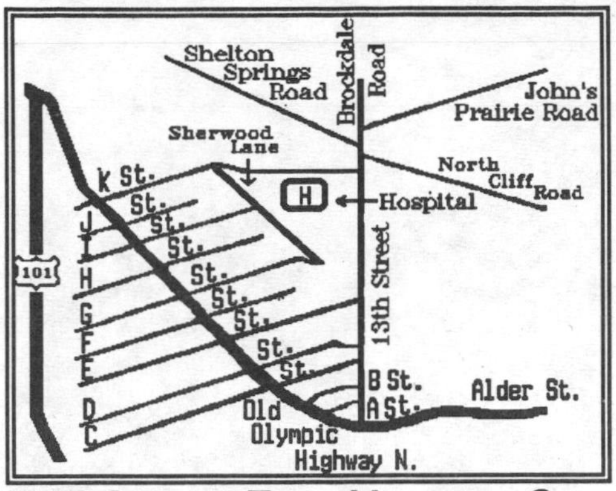

MAP 3-7 To Mason Gen. Hospital

	SOUTH	NORTH	
C STREET D STREET	3.8	1.1	C STREET D STREET
E STREET	3.9	1.0	E STREET
A & W Family Restaurant	FAST FOOD		Taco Time
F STREET	4.0	0.9	F STREET
	RV PARK		The Pines Trailer Park
	RESTAURANT		Hacienda Mexican Restaurant
	C-STORE		Kwik Shop Food Mart
			G STREET
G STREET			
H STREET I STREET	4.1	0.8	H STREET I STREET

	HOSPITAL		

Mason General Hospital is six blocks to the right at I Street and Sherwood Lane.

	SOUTH	NORTH	
B & N Mobil Self Serve Gas	4.2	0.7	Jackpot Food Mart - Gas
	C-STORE	GAS	
J STREET			J STREET

	SHELTON DISTANCE FROM HIGHWAY 101	
	SOUTH	NORTH

K STREET	Olympic Gateway Shopping Center	4.3	0.6		K STREET
Dragon Palace Chinese Rest.		RESTAURANT			
McDonalds		FAST FOOD			
101 Passage Chalet Restaurant		4.4	0.5		
		RESTAURANT			
NORTHVIEW CIRCLE (Loop)		4.5	0.4		
Super 8 Motel		LODGING			
White Spot Tavern		TAVERN			
NORTHVIEW CIRCLE (Loop)		4.6	0.3		
Super 8 Motel		LODGING		Ma and Pa's Steakhouse	
Burgermaster		FAST FOOD		Pizano Pizza	
Skippers Fish and Chowder		RESTAURANT			

SOUTH	OLYMPIA	4.9	0.0	NORTH	PORT ANGELES
🛡101 Mile 345.2				🛡101 Mile 345.2	

SHELTON - SKOKOMISH VALLEY

Our narrative returns to mile 350.2 of Highway 101, the point where we departed for Shelton on the Old Olympic Highway.

	HIGHWAY 101			
	MILES from I-5	MILE NUMBER		
GOLDEN PHEASANT ROAD	17.1	350.2	NORTH OLD OLYMPIC ③ HIGHWAY S.	SHELTON BREMERTON
Divided Highway Ends	17.3	350.0	Divided Highway Ends	

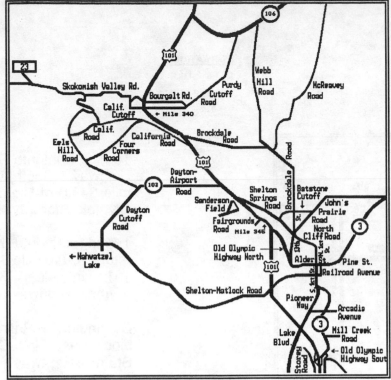

MAP 3-8   SHELTON - SKOKOMISH VALLEY

HIGHWAY 101

MILES	MILE
from	NUMBER
I-5	

18.3 349.0   Entrance Ramp - NO LEFT TURN

Did you notice how quickly that mile went past? I reckon it was 0.2 miles from the end of the divided highway, mile 350.0, to mile 349 at the entrance ramp.

Where there are differences between actual mileages and mileposts I have adjusted my mileages to reflect those shown on the mileposts.

SHELTON-MATLOCK ROAD MATLOCK
Lake Nahwatzel Recreation Area

20.3 347.0

SHELTON-MATLOCK ROAD SHELTON

Matlock via Nahwatzel Lake Recreation Area is to your left after you exit. The Park-n-Ride is to the left, beside Highway 101, on the north side of Shelton-Matlock Road.

CITY CENTER
FAST FOOD
RESTAURANT
GAS LODGING
PARK-N-RIDE
NAT'L HISTORIC
SITES
VISITORS INFO

The City Center and services are to the right. Shelton-Matlock Road becomes Railroad Avenue in Shelton. The services are shown on page 33 under the Railroad Avenue heading.

Railroad Ave. intersects First St. 1.6 miles from the Shelton-Matlock Road exit. At First St. turn either right or left to return to Highway 101.

37

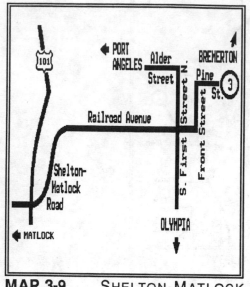

Turning right into S. First St. (State Highway 3 South) will return you to mile 349.0 of Highway 101 via Old Olympic Highway South.

Turning left into N. First St. will return you to mile 345.2 of Highway 101 via Alder Street and Old Olympic Highway North.

Continuing on Railroad Ave. for one block past First St. puts you on State Highway 3 North to Bremerton.

MAP 3-9   SHELTON-MATLOCK ROAD

22.1 345.2   OLD OLYMPIC HIGHWAY N.   SHELTON

HOSPITAL   Shelton's services are discussed
GAS PROPANE   beginning on page 31.
RV PARK LODGING
C-STORE TAVERN
RESTAURANT
FAST FOOD

22.3 345.0
MILEPOST

FAIRGROUNDS ROAD   22.5 344.8
MASON COUNTY FAIRGROUNDS

AIRVIEW WAY   22.8 344.5
SANDERSON FIELD AIRPORT

23.3 344.0   SHELTON SPRINGS ROAD

RESTAURANT   Shelton Springs Road will take you
C-STORE   south, back into Shelton.
PHONE

Cottage Cafe
Airport Deli

SANDERSON WAY   23.5 343.8
Port of Shelton Industrial Park

HIGHWAY 101

MILES   MILE
from NUMBER
I-5   ——

23.8 343.5

WEST DAYTON AIRPORT ROAD

(102) Lake Nahwatzel Resort
    (10 miles)

Washington Correction Center
State Patrol Academy

OLYMPIC MOUNTAINS

25.3 342.0   **OLYMPIC MOUNTAINS**

You get your first really good view of the Olympic Mountains from here. Clouds are often draped over their shoulders like a shawl when there is wet weather.

CALIFORNIA ROAD

25.5 341.8

This gravel road eventually joins Skokomish Valley Road.

25.9 341.4   **BROCKDALE RD   WEBB HILL**

Brockdale Road takes you back south to Shelton.

PAVED TURNOUT

26.8 340.5   **TURNOUT EAGLE POINT ROAD**

This looks like it may have at one time been a picnic area or campground, but it is no longer maintained.

Eagle Point Rd. actually starts from a large, flat, gravel area behind the row of trees at the edge of the turnout.

TURNOUT

27.1 340.2

27.3 340.0   **TURNOUT**
MILEPOST

SKOKOMISH VALLEY ROAD

27.6 339.7   **PURDY CUT-OFF ROAD UNION**

State Salmon & Trout Hatchery
Olympic National Forest
Brown Creek Campground
Forest Trails

Purdy Cut-Off Road joins State Hwy. 106 to Union and Bremerton in about two miles.

FS ROAD 23 S. FORK SKOKOMISH

DISTANCE FROM

HIGHWAY 101

Brown Creek Naturè Trail (877) . . . . 15.7 Miles
Lower South Fork Skokomish Trail (873) . . . . 17.0 Miles
Dry Creek Trail (872) . . . . 22.2 Miles
Upper South Fork Skokomish Trail (873) . . . . 24.5 Miles
Church Creek Trail (870) . . . . 24.5 Miles
Spoon Creek Falls Trail (885) . . . . 36.4 Miles

Finally we are getting near the forest and the hiking trails. I was beginning to get a bit impatient. The Highway 101 story continues to unfold from this point (Mile 339.7) on page 50 in Chapter 4.

Skokomish Valley Road offers a pleasant drive through a farming valley to Forest Service Road (FSR) 23, the main arterial road in this part of the Olympic National Forest. FSR 23 winds and twists it way for 33.1 miles through some of the most spectacular scenery in the National Forest. Although the area is heavily logged, even the clear-cuts have their own special beauty. Ultimately, FSR 23 meets FSR 22 near Lake Wynoochee.

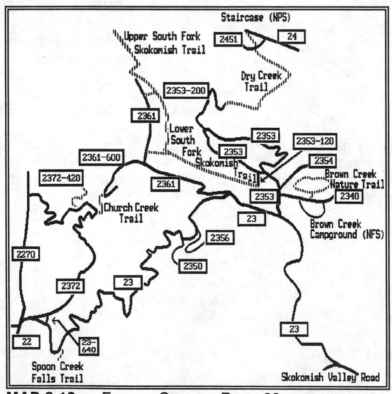

MAP 3-10   FOREST SERVICE ROAD 23

FS ROAD 23

MILES   MILE
from NUMBER
101 _____

0.0 0.0 HATCHERY	The Washington Salmon and Trout Hatchery is on your right just after you turn into Skokomish Valley Road.

Skokomish Valley Road goes on from here for a bit more than a mile to a dead end.

5.6 0.0
FSR 23

FSR 23 begins on the right at mi. 5.6 of Skokomish Valley Rd.

FSR 23 starts as a narrow paved road going uphill. At mile 1.1 the road surface becomes well maintained gravel for 1.5 miles, then the pavement resumes. Although we have not entered the National Forest yet, its beginning to feel like forest.

8.8 3.2
CAMP GOVEY
RANGER STATION

At mile 3.2 of FSR 23 you come to Camp Govey and the National Forest Service Ranger Station, both on your right. The Ranger Station marks the entrance to the Olympic National Forest.

At one time, Camp Govey was probably a major logging camp, but it now seems to be just a maintenance depot.

SCENIC TURNOUT

14.4 8.9
ONE LANE ROAD

SCENIC TURNOUT

The oncoming traffic has right-of-way at this short section of one lane road. There are scenic turnouts at both ends of the one lane section.

23	SPIDER LAKE
2361	LAKE WYNOOCHEE

UPPER S. FORK SKOKOMISH TRAIL
CHURCH CREEK TRAIL
SPOON CREEK TRAIL

FSR 23 forks at mile 9.3. Bear left on the well maintained gravel to remain on FSR 23.

14.9 9.3
ROAD FORKS

To: BROWN CREEK CAMPGR. 2353

BROWN CREEK NATURE TRAIL
LOWER S. FORK SKOKOMISH TRAIL DRY CREEK TRAIL

We leave FSR 23 here for a brief exploration of FSR 2353, the paved road to the right. Description of FSR 23 continues on page 44.

15.5 -
ONE LANE BRIDGE

BROWN CREEK CAMPGROUND 2340
Traffic from the other side of the bridge has right of way.

BROWN CREEK CAMPGROUND

Brown Creek Campground is a beautiful campground situated beside the crystal-clear South Fork Skokomish River. The roads leading to it are not marked on most maps. The campground itself *is* shown, with no roads close to it. This fact and its distance from Highway 101 keeps it delightfully uncrowded most of the time.

It has 19 camping sites (trailers 21 feet maximum), picnic tables, fire rings, potable water and vault toilets. You are right on the river for fishing, and the Brown Creek Nature Trail leaves from the campground. There are two camping sites before the entrance to the camping area loop, and another three sites past the exit with direct access to the road.

Just past the last campsite on the right, but before you reach a concrete bridge, there is a road going off to the left. Keep to the left at the fork shortly after you turn and you will come to a horse camp that was developed, and is maintained by a local riding club. On the way you will see a couple of sites that are quite adequate for either a small RV or camping. If you go right at the fork, you come to a very pleasant campsite near Brown Creek.

To go to Brown Creek Campground, turn hard right at the north end of the one way bridge in FSR 2353. The road is officially FSR 2340 (I think), but you probably won't see any signs to this effect. You may in fact see a sign that calls it FSR 2202, its number two number-changes back. If you read "Hard Right" to mean into the gravel road furthest to your right, that goes downhill, you should have no problems. In two tenths of a mile you will be at the campground entrance.

BROWN CREEK NATURE TRAIL
(0.8 Miles Long)
Trail 877

Brown Creek Nature Trail has little elevation change and circles a small beaver pond (beaver bog?) just north of the campground. The trail has several entrances. The easiest one to find, although it is not marked, leaves from just behind the hand operated water pump about midway between the entrance and the exit to the campground. The trees here are all draped with moss, making you feel like you are in the rain forests on the other side of the mountains.

LOWER SOUTH FORK SKOKOMISH TRAIL
(8.9 Miles Long)
Trail 873

The Lower South Fork Skokomish Trail has moderate elevation changes. After giving you a chance near Church Creek Shelter to cut over to FSR 2361 (0.2 miles north of FSR 2361-600) it goes to Camp Harps, where you can join FSR 2361 via an old road. Upper South Fork Skokomish Trail is at the end of FSR 2361, half a mile north of the Camp Harps exit.

Distances and elevations from the FSR 2353-120 trailhead are:

FSR-2353-120, mile 0.4	0.0 Miles	900 Feet
Camp Comfort	4.3 Miles	630 Feet
Cedar Creek Trail	4.7 Miles	650 Feet
(0.5 miles long, 250 feet elevation loss)		

Church Creek . . . . 6.7 Miles   900 Feet
Church Creek Shelter Trail . . . . 6.8 Miles   900 Feet
   (0.3 miles long, 300 feet elevation loss)

Camp Harps Shelter . . . . 8.5 Miles   1000 Feet
FSR 2361, mile 3.5 . . . . 8.9 Miles   1100 Feet

To get to the Lower South Fork Skokomish Trail, return to the end of the one lane bridge. This time, stay on FSR 2353 which goes to the left when you are coming from Shelton. Go 1.1 miles to FSR 2353-120 on the left. (FSR 2353 forms a loop, so keep left as you pass the other end of it just before you reach FSR 2353-120.) The trailhead is at the end of FSR 2353-120, 0.4 miles from FSR 2353.

CEDAR CREEK TRAIL
(0.5 Miles Long)

Cedar Creek Trail (elevation loss 250 feet) has been abandoned by the forest service and is not maintained. It provides access to Lower South Fork Skokomish Trail from mile 1.1 of FSR 2361 (1000 feet elevation). It ends at the river which must be forded to reach the Lower South Fork Skokomish Trail. It is dangerous to cross the river until late summer.

CHURCH CREEK SHELTER TRAIL
(0.3 Miles Long)
Trail 870

Church Creek Shelter Trail (elevation loss 300 feet) takes you to Church Creek Shelter (900 feet), which is across the river from mile 6.8 of Lower South Fork Skokomish Trail. It starts from an unmarked road (1200 feet) that goes to the right at mile 4.1 of FSR 2361. Note that the shelter is on the west side of the river which must be forded to reach the S. Fork Skokomish Trail. Some maps show it on the east side. The crossing can be dangerous until late summer.

DRY CREEK TRAIL
(7.3 Miles Long)
Trail 872

Dry Creek Trail originates near Staircase in the Olympic National Park where the last 1.3 miles of it is known as Shady Lane. From the FSR 2353-200 trailhead there is an elevation gain of 450 feet to the pass, then an elevation loss of nearly 3,000 feet to the Shady Lane trailhead. I mention the trail here for those who have a second car to leave at this end, and those who don't mind a steep uphill return journey.

Distances from this trailhead and elevations are:

FSR 2353-200, mile 2.0 . . . . 0.0 miles   3200 feet
Pass . . . . 0.7 miles   3650 feet
District Boundary . . . . 1.4 miles   3000 feet
Creek Crossing . . . . 3.2 miles   600 feet

Dry Creek	6.3 miles	800 feet
Roadway Begins	7.1 miles	750 feet
FSR 2451, mile 0.4	7.4 miles	750 feet

To get to the FSR 2353-200 trailhead when headed north from the South Fork Skokomish bridge, stay on FSR 2353 which goes to the left. Follow it for 4.7 miles to FSR 2353-200. (FSR 2353 forms a loop, so keep left as you pass the other end of it just before you reach FSR 2353-120.) Turn left into FSR 2353-200, and go for 2 miles to the Trailhead at the end of the road.

Here we return to mile 9.3 of FSR 23, its junction with FSR 2353. This time we will follow FSR 23 to the left towards the trailheads accessible from FSR 2361.

FS ROAD 23

MILES from 101	MILE NUMBER

23 / 2361 — SPIDER LAKE / LAKE WYNOOCHEE	14.9	9.3	2353
UPPER S. FORK SKOKOMISH TRAIL CHURCH CREEK TRAIL SPOON CREEK TRAIL			To: BROWN CREEK CAMPGROUND BROWN CREEK NATURE TRAIL LOWER S. FORK SKOKOMISH TR. DRY CREEK TRAIL
23 / 2356 / 22 — SPIDER LAKE / LAKE WYNOOCHEE	19.2	13.6	2361
			UPPER S. FORK SKOKOMISH TRAIL CHURCH CREEK TRAIL

UPPER SOUTH FORK SKOKOMISH TRAIL
(7.0 Miles Long)
Trail 873

Upper South Fork Skokomish Trail has an elevation gain 2,800 feet. It will take you into the Olympic National Park, through Sundown Pass to Graves Creek Trail.

At Tumble Creek there is a lovely cascade. There are some campsites at Upper Skokomish Crossing. The trail deteriorates at the National Park boundary and continues to climb to Camp Riley. After Camp Riley you cross several streams, and climb the ridge to Sundown Pass for a glimpse of Mount Olympus. A half mile beyond the pass, the trail intersects Graves Creek Trail (8.6 miles long, elev. gain 4,000 feet). Turn right for Six Ridge Pass, or left for Graves Creek and the East Fork of the Quinault River.

Distances from this trailhead and elevations are:

FSR 2361, Mile 5.5	0.0 Miles	1300 Feet
Tumble Creek	1.2 Miles	1700 Feet
Upper Skokomish Crossing	1.5 Miles	1700 Feet
Startup Creek	3.3 Miles	1800 Feet

```
Olympic National Park Boundary  . . . . . .  4.4 Miles  2700 Feet
Camp Riley  . . . . . . . . . . . . . . . . . . . .  4.7 Miles  3000 Feet
Sundown Pass . . . . . . . . . . . . . . . . .  6.5 Miles  4100 Feet
Graves Creek Trail, mile 7.2  . . . . . . . .  7.0 Miles  3800 Feet
        (8.6 miles long, 4000 feet elevation gain)
```

To get there, follow FSR 23 to its junction with FSR 2361 at mile 13.6, where you turn right. To reach the trailhead go 5.5 miles on FSR 2361 to the end of the road. You will pass FSR 2361-600 on your left 3.5 miles from FSR 23. Accesses to Lower South Fork Skokomish trailheads are at 3.7 miles (Church Creek Shelter) and 5.0 miles (Camp Harps Shelter), both on your right.

CHURCH CREEK TRAIL
(3.5 Miles Long)
Trail 871

Church Creek Trail (elevation gain 1,650 feet) takes you to Upper Satsop Lake. Be aware that Satsop Lake grows and shrinks a lot, and never really gets large enough to make you sure that it is a lake rather than a pond. Distances from this trailhead and elevations are:

```
FSR 2361-600, mile 2.0  . . . . . . . . . . .  0.0 miles  1500 feet
Crest of Divide . . . . . . . . . . . . . . . . .  2.0 miles  3150 feet
Upper Satsop Lake . . . . . . . . . . . . . . .  3.2 miles  2200 feet
FSR 2372, mile 5.6  . . . . . . . . . . . . . .  3.5 miles  2300 feet
```

The trailhead can be reached by turning left to stay on FSR 23 at the fork at mile 9.3. Then, follow FSR 23 to its junction with FSR 2361 at mile 13.6 where you turn right. Go 3.5 miles on FSR 2361 to FSR 2361-600 where you turn left. The trailhead is then two miles from FSR 2361.

We now return to FSR 23 at Spider Lake, the next major landmark after mile 13.6, the point at which we left it.

	FS ROAD 23	
	MILES	MILE
	from	NUMBER
	101	
2356 SPIDER LAKE	21.8	16.2
2350 SPIDER LAKE	22.1	16.5

There is level space for camping to your left, right at the end of Spider Lake.

45

After you pass Spider Lake there are several turnouts where you can stop to take photographs of the panoramic valleys. This area is being heavily logged, but even the geometric patterns of the clearcuts are pretty in the distance. The tracks that radiate from where the logs are skidded up to the road form huge sunbursts, that are attractive in their own way.

29.4	24.0	**HAIRPIN TURN**

Take care to follow FSR 23 all the way around to your right. Another road, FSR 2368, goes south from bottom of the turn.

32.9 27.3

Here, you have spectacular views of two valleys from a ridge between them.

SPOON CREEK FALLS TRAIL   36.4 30.8

SPOON CREEK FALLS TRAIL
(0.2 Miles Long)
Trail 885

This trail is 0.2 miles long according to the Forest Service, and one kilometer long according to the sign at the trailhead. It has an elevation change of only 100 feet so it is a pleasant walk whatever its length. The trailhead is 100 yards east of the bridges on the south (left) side of the road. There is a small pull-out for parking.

37.3 31.7   `23-640`

Shortcut to FSR 2372 and the Satsop Guard Station.

37.9 32.3   **SATSOP LAKES**   `2372`
ANDERSON BUTTE TRAIL
CHURCH CREEK TRAIL
FSR 2372-420 - Abandoned

Shortly after you join FSR 2372 from FSR 23, FSR 2372-020 goes to your left. Follow it about 3 miles until it is no longer drive-able. There you find the remains of Anderson Butte Trail (0.3 miles long, 558 feet elevation gain).

FS ROAD 23

MILES   MILE
from NUMBER
<u>101</u>   ____

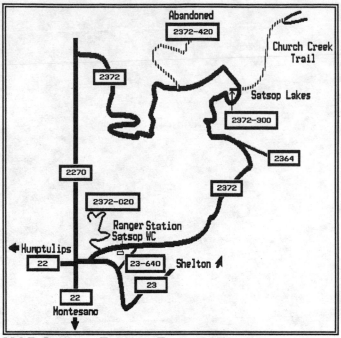

MAP 3-11   FOREST ROAD 2372

The Satsop Lakes end of Church Creek Trail is 5.6 miles from FSR 23 on FSR 2372. It is on your right almost directly opposite FSR 2372-300. It is also very overgrown and very difficult to find.

If you don't find it, (or even if you do) continue on about a mile and a half to FSR 2372-420 on your right. This is an abandoned road. Climb over the barrier and walk along the old roadway for a couple of easy miles for some absolutely fantastic panoramic views and witness how the forest is reclaiming the road. This trail is not in the guidebooks, so you will probably have it to yourself.

| 22 | LAKE WYNOOCHEE HUMPTULIPS MONTESANO | 38.7 33.1 |

FSR 22 is actually about 200 yards south of where FSR 23 ends. To reach it you turn left here. After you turn left, FSR 22 South continues straight ahead to Montesano and US Hwy. 12. FSR 22 West is to the right and takes you to Coho Campground on Lake Wynoochee, then to Highway 101's western leg, near Humptulips. Highway 22 and its attractions are described in Chapter 13. See page 317.

WYNOOCHEE FALLS   2270
WYNOOCHEE TRAIL
WYNOOCHEE LAKE SHORE TRAIL

These attractions are described in Chapter 13. See page 323.

We have covered the entire length of FSR 23 and Skokomish Valley Road. Let's return to Highway 101 now, and explore the area between Hoodsport and Brinnon.

Mount Lincoln from Staircase Rapids Trail.

CHAPTER 4

HOOD CANAL   N. FORK SKOKOMISH

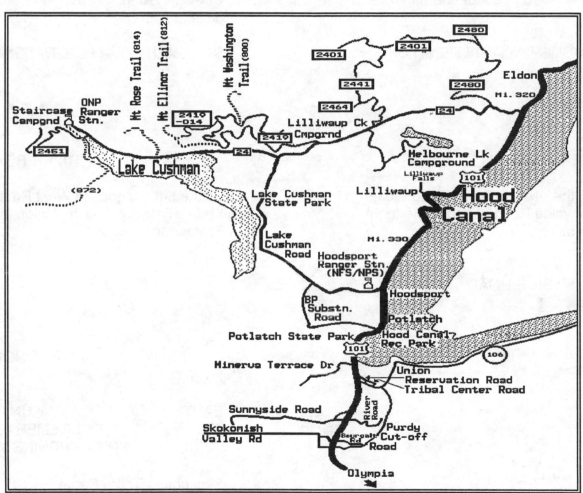

MAP 4-1   HIGHWAY 101 FROM SKOKOMISH VALLEY ROAD TO ELDON

In addition to the information about the roads and trails in the Lake Cushman and Staircase areas, I have included here a brief description of the Kitsap Peninsula for those who want a different perspective from across Hood Canal.

	MILES from I-5	MILE NUMBER	
SKOKOMISH VALLEY ROAD	27.6	339.7	UNION PURDY CUT-OFF ROAD
Purdy Canyon Drive-in Burgers	27.8	339.5 FAST FOOD PHONE	
BOURGALT ROAD	28.2	339.1	BOURGALT ROAD
SKOKOMISH INDIAN RESERVATION	28.4	338.9 SKOKOMISH RIVER	SKOKOMISH INDIAN RESERVATION
TURNOUT	28.7	338.6	
RIVER ROAD	28.9	338.4	RIVER ROAD
SUNNYSIDE ROAD	29.0	338.3	
	29.3	338.0	TURNOUT
	30.3	337.0	EAST UNION

BOURGALT ROAD

Bourgalt Road joins Skokomish Valley Road in about one half mile.

BOURGALT ROAD

To the right, it goes to Purdy Cut-Off Road, about one mile distant.

RIVER ROAD

To the left, River Road joins Sunnyside Road in about one tenth of a mile.

RIVER ROAD

To the right, it goes to West Rd and State Highway 106 to Union and Bremerton.

EAST   UNION
(106)   BREMERTON
          KITSAP PENINSULA

Skokomish Tribal Center
Alderbrook Resort   7 Miles
Twanoh State Park 12 Miles
Belfair State Park 24 Miles

At this point, we make a brief visit to the Kitsap Peninsula. Discussion of Highway 101 continues at mile 337.0 on page 53.

KITSAP PENINSULA

To get a really good look at the Olympic Mountains you need to get out of the forest and far enough away to get some perspective on their grandeur. A right turn here not only gives you that opportunity, but also takes you to the Kitsap Peninsula for a chance to enjoy some of its history and recreational facilities. Both are centered on the salt water that, except for a thin neck of land near Allyn and Belfair, surrounds you there.

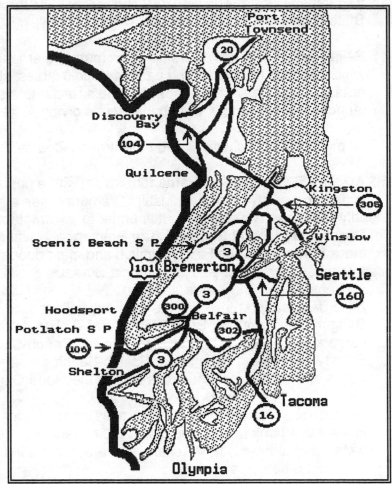

MAP 4-2   KITSAP PENINSULA

VIEWPOINT

At milepost three, be sure to look to your left for a panoramic view of the Olympic Mountains across the Hood Canal. There are a couple of small turnouts on the left if you want to stop and savour the vista. The distance gives you a very different perspective.

UNION

At mile four you come to the small town of Union. Twanoh State Park is another 8.2 miles.

TWANOH STATE PARK

Twanoh State Park has 39 sites (maximum trailer size 35 feet). Nine have hook-ups. The park has picnic tables, kitchen shelters, fire rings, potable water, pay showers, flush toilets, a dump station, a boat launch and a boat dock. It offers fishing, swimming, a beach on the Hood Canal, boating, water skiing, and a hiking trail.

WA-3 BELFAIR

At its 20 mile mark, State Highway 106 ends in a junction with WA-3 at its mile 25 in Belfair. Turn left here for Bremerton, or turn right for Shelton.

WA-300

At mile 26.4 on Highway 3, (1.4 miles from where you joined it) you can turn left into State Highway 300, and follow it for three miles to Belfair State Park.

BELFAIR STATE PARK

Belfair State Park has 180 sites (maximum trailer length 60 feet), of which 47 have hook-ups. The park has picnic tables, shelters, fire rings, potable water, pay showers, flush toilets, a dump station, and a boat launch. It offers fishing, swimming, scuba diving, a beach and boating.

KITSAP COUNTY

At mile 28.3 of Highway 3 you enter Kitsap County.

BREMERTON
MOTHBALL FLEET
SEATTLE FERRY
NAVAL MUSEUM
INFO. CENTER

At mile 35, you come to Bremerton, which, with a population of 36,208, is the largest city on the peninsula. Bremerton has a history as a Navy City that goes back to 1891. It is home to the "Mothball Fleet" and Puget Sound Naval Shipyard. The Bremerton Naval Museum is one block from the Seattle Ferry Terminal and, next door is the Bremerton - Kitsap County Visitor and Convention Bureau.

SILVERDALE
BANGOR
SEABECK

Silverdale, support town for the U.S. Navy Trident Submarine Base at Bangor, is just north of Bremerton on WA-3. Turn to the left at the Silverdale exit, to go to Seabeck and Scenic Beach State Park. Though only 12 miles from Bremerton, Scenic Beach takes you to the magic vistas of the Olympic Mountains across the Hood Canal.

SCENIC BEACH STATE PARK

Scenic Beach State Park has 52 sites (max. trailer length 40 feet). None have hook-ups. It has picnic tables, shelters, fire rings, potable water, pay showers, flush toilets, and a dump station. It offers fishing, swimming, beach, and trails.

WA-305 POULSBO
SUQUAMISH
BAINBRIDGE ISLAND

Continuing north on Highway 3 will take you to State Highway 305, the exit for Poulsbo, Kitsap's Scandinavian city (population 3,453); then to Suquamish, (population 1,400), the Suquamish Indian Museum and Chief Seattle's grave. Bainbridge Island, home of several State Parks and a winery is a bit farther on WA-305. There is a ferry terminal in Winslow, the island's major town. If you're hungry in Winslow, stop at the Streamliner Diner.

To rejoin to Highway 101, return to Poulsbo and turn to the right at the junction with WA-3 and follow it north seven more miles to the Hood Canal Floating Bridge. The road becomes WA-104 at the floating bridge. It takes you fifteen miles, back to mile 285.0 of Highway 101.

Leaving the Kitsap Peninsula, we will return now to the point at which we left Highway 101, mile 337.0.

HIGHWAY 101		
MILES from I-5	MILE NUMBER	
30.3	337.0	EAST UNION
	(106)	BREMERTON
		KITSAP PENINSULA
30.5 C-STORE GAS	336.8	Jackpot Food Mart
30.6 C-STORE GAS	336.7	Twin Totems Texaco Grocery
30.7	336.6	RESERVATION ROAD
		Reservation Road joins Tribal Center Road and WA-106 to Bremerton in 0.6 miles.

MINERVA TERRACE DRIVE | 31.1 PROPANE | 336.2 | Home Gas Propane

Twana Social Club
   Public Card Room   CARD ROOM

VALLEY DRIVE   31.2   336.1

TURNOUT   31.3   336.0

          31.7   335.6   HOOD CANAL

HOOD CANAL

You are now getting your first look at Hood Canal. On your right is Annas Bay and The Great Bend.

You're right. It doesn't look much like a canal. That is because it is not a canal. It's not narrow enough or dirty enough, and it runs into the lump of land at Belfair that makes Kitsap a peninsula rather than an island.

Hood Canal is one of those anomalies of geographic nomenclature that every now and then saddle places with names that don't even faintly resemble their physical attributes. In 1792, when he was out in this neck of the woods discovering things for England, Capt. George Vancouver called it Hood's Channel after the Right Honourable Lord Hood, a popular naval hero. By the time it was transferred from his journal to his book, it had become Hood's Canal — probably a typographical error. The "'s" disappeared when the U.S. Geographical Board struck the possessive from all our maps.

HIGHWAY 101

MILES from I-5	MILE NUMBER
31.8	335.5

SLOW VEHICLE TURNOUT

A line of five vehicles is illegal. Slow Vehicle Turnouts are provided where road conditions prevent other traffic from safely overtaking slow vehicles. It is illegal to park in most of them.

POTLATCH STATE PARK

The campground is to your left.

32.2	335.1
STATE PARK	
PHONE	

POTLATCH STATE PARK

The day-use area is to your right.

POTLATCH STATE PARK

Potlatch State Park has 37 campsites (maximum site length 60 feet). Sites 1-18 have hook-ups. There are flush toilets, pay showers, a dump station and a picnic shelter. Attractions include scuba diving, crabbing, clamming and fishing. There is beach access and floats are maintained in Hood Canal.

If you are a light sleeper, you should be aware that the campground has a dense growth of trees that accumulate rain into huge globs of water that make a resounding boom when they hit the top of your RV or tent.

Minerva Beach RV Park

32.3 335.0
MILEPOST
RV PARK PROPANE

The Minerva Beach RV Park has 37 sites with hookups, flush toilets, pay showers, laundry, recreation hall, heated pool, propane, boat launch and a boat dock.

HARVEY TERRACE DRIVE

32.5 334.8

HURLEY HILL ROAD
Burger World

32.6 334.7
FAST FOOD

32.7 334.6
BOAT LAUNCH
REST ROOMS
PHONE

HOOD CANAL RECREATIONAL PARK

This day-use area is provided by Tacoma City Light.

POWERHOUSE ROAD
Cushman No.2 Hydroelectric Plant

32.8 334.5

32.9 334.4
LODGING
RESTAURANT

Canal Side Resort-Motel

POWERHOUSE ROAD

33.1 334.2

BPA SUBSTATION ROAD

33.2 334.1

POTLATCH ROAD

LEAVING SKOKOMISH INDIAN RESERVATION — ENTERING POTLATCH

33.3 334.0
C-STORE GAS
PROPANE

Potlatch Chevron Food Mart and Car Wash

TURNOUT

33.4 333.9

TURNOUT

33.5 333.8

POTLATCH ROAD

33.7 333.6
LEAVE POTLATCH

34.0 333.3

TURNOUT

34.3 333.0
ENTER HOODSPORT

SLOW VEHICLE TURNOUT

HOODSPORT BUSINESS DISTRICT

Trailers - RV Park Hoodsport Winery Kit & Kaboodle on the Canal (Gifts, Souvenirs, Cards)	34.6 332.7 RV PARK RESTAURANT WINERY GIFT SHOP	Skipper John's Seafood
OLD MILL HILL ROAD	35.3 332.0 RESTAURANT PROPANE	Hoodsport Marina
Treasure Chest - Gifts Hoodsport Restaurant Canal Room Lounge Coin Laundry Bob's Hoodsport Texaco Service Hood Canal Grocery, Gas, Diesel	35.4 331.9 GIFT SHOP RESTAURANT LOUNGE GAS	Hoodsport Mall Antiques & Gifts (Say Hi to Erlyn for me).
HOODSPORT SCHOOL HILL ROAD A free RV park is on the right, 75 feet after turning left into Hoodsport School Hill Road. Model T Tavern	35.5 331.8 FREE RV PARK RESTAURANT STORE SUPERMARKET LIQUOR TAVERN	Sugar Shack Restaurant Nickels Mercantile & Liquor Hoodsport Market Fuddy Duddy's Restaurant

LAKE CUSHMAN ROAD

The Post Office and the information center are in Hoodsport Road, on your right after you turn left from Highway 101.

The information center is operated jointly by the National Forest Service and the National Park Service, and well worth visiting.

Let's turn left now, into Lake Cushman Road, and follow it to its end at Forest Service Road 24. Description of Highway 101 continues from mile 331.7 on page 59.

35.6 331.7
POST OFFICE
PHONE
INFO CENTER

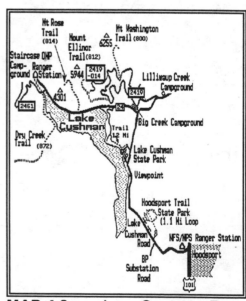

MAP 4-3   LAKE CUSHMAN ROAD

LAKE CUSHMAN

Lake Cushman Road is also known as Hoodsport Road. It will take you on a scenic journey through private and state lands before it ends at its junction with FSR 24, the main Forest Service arterial road in this area. There are several excellent campgrounds operated by the Washington State Parks and Recreation Commission; the Washington Department of Natural Resources; the National Park Service and the National Forest Service that are accessible from Lake Cushman Road and FSR 24. There is also easy access to some excellent hiking trails, including Mount Ellinor Trail which allows you to drive almost all the way to the top.

In the distance chart below, I have included distances to campgrounds and trailheads on FSR 24 as well as those on Lake Cushman Road. Full discussion of the FSR 24 items appears under the FSR 24 heading which begins on page 61.

	DISTANCE FROM HIGHWAY 101
Lake Cushman State Park	7.1 Miles
Olympic National Forest Boundary	9.3 Miles
Lilliwaup Creek Campground	11.5 Miles
Melbourne Lake Campground	15.1 Miles
Big Creek Campground	9.4 Miles
Olympic National Park Boundary	14.7 Miles
Staircase Campground	15.7 Miles
Mount Ellinor Trail	15.5 Miles
Mount Washington Trail	17.6 Miles
Big Creek Trail	9.4 Miles
Mount Rose Trail	12.0 Miles
Shady Lane	15.7 Miles
Staircase Rapids Trail	15.7 Miles
Wagonwheel Lake Trail	15.7 Miles
North Fork Skokomish Trail	15.7 Miles

As you leave Hoodsport you start up a fairly steep grade that lasts for 1.9 miles before it flattens out. Lake Cushman Road is paved all the way to the National Forest boundary.

LAKE CUSHMAN RD

DISTANCE FROM HIGHWAY 101	FROM FSR 24	
3.0	9.3	HOODSPORT TRAIL STATE PARK
PICNIC AREA		(1.1 Mile Loop)

LAKE CUSHMAN RESORT   4.6   4.7

Not only do you get a good view of the lake here, but you can also see (right to left) Mount Washington, Mount Ellinor and Copper Mountain. If you look closely, you will see a good likeness of George Washington's profile defined in the peaks of Mount Washington.

6.1 3.2
VIEWPOINT

Lake Cushman State Park

7.1 2.2
STATE PARK
RANGER STATION
CAMPGROUND

LAKE CUSHMAN STATE PARK

The entrance to Lake Cushman State Park is on the left, one mile past the viewpoint. After you turn, you will see the ranger's residence on your left. A small road and a phone are on your right. The small road leads to another residence, the maintenance depot and the ranger station office.

The campground has 81 sites, of which 30 have full hook-ups. The sites with hook-ups are those with numbers that are preceded by a "T" (e.g. T12) located at the beginning and end of the loop of campsites. The maximum site length is 60 feet. There are pay showers, flush toilets, a dump station, fire rings, picnic tables, a kitchen shelter and potable water.

Attractions include access to Lake Cushman for swimming fishing and boating. There is a boat launch, a dock, and marked hiking trails. The boat launch area is a pretty good place to get an unobstructed view of the mountains.

The entrance to the Upper Camp area of Lake Cushman State Park, which has group facilities, is on your left 0.6 miles past the entrance to the campground.

Lake Cushman Road and the pavement end at FSR 24, the boundary of the national forest. Big Creek and Staircase Campgrounds are to the left. There is a ranger station at Staircase.

9.3 0.0
OLYMPIC NAT'L
FOREST BOUNDARY
FSR 24

To the right are Highway 101, the access roads to Mt. Ellinor and Mt. Washington Trails and the DNR campgrounds at Lilliwaup Creek and Melbourne Lake.

FSR 24 begins 8.8 miles to the east as Jorsted Creek Road. It leaves Highway 101 just north of Jorsted Creek which is six miles north of Lilliwaup or 2.3 miles south of Eldon.

For now, lets return to Highway 101 at Hoodsport, and discuss FSR 24 from its beginning when we reach the Highway 101 end of it. If you just can't wait, discussion of FSR 24 begins on page 61.

	HIGHWAY 101		
	MILES from I-5	MILE NUMBER	
LAKE CUSHMAN ROAD	35.6	331.7	
Hood Canal Burgers & Seafood Drive-in			
First Olympic Bank			
FINCH CREEK ROAD NORTH HILL ROAD	35.7	331.6	Hood Canal Salmon Hatchery Maple's Gifts
Hoodsport Antique & Gift Shop			
	35.8	331.5	Sunrise Motel Resort
	35.9 LEAVE HOODSPORT	331.4	
Glen Ayr RV Park has 57 sites with hookups, flush toilets, showers, laundry, propane, recreation hall, swimming, fishing, golf and a spa house.	36.6 RV PARK	330.7	
	36.7	330.6	Gallery of Fine Arts & Crafts
	37.3 MILEPOST	330.0	Holiday Beach - Private
SUSAN AVENUE	37.5	329.8	SLOW VEHICLE TURNOUT
VIRGINIA STREET	37.6	329.7	
Rest a While RV Park	38.3 RV PARK PHONE GROCERY GAS GIFTS MARINA	329.0	
Rest a While has 107 sites (92 with hookups), flush toilets, pay showers, propane, store, laundry, Rec. hall, swimming, fishing, boat dock and launch.			

	MILES from I-5	MILE NUMBER	
Dew Drop Inn Family Cafe	38.3	329.0	
Guest House Motel		RESTAURANT	
		LODGING	
TERRACE ROAD	38.5	328.8	
	39.3	328.0	CANAL VIEW ROAD
		ENTER LILLIWAUP	
LILLIWAUP POST OFFICE	39.8	327.5	
Lilliwaup Motel Grocery	39.9	327.4	
		FOOD GAS	
LILLIWAUP STREET		LODGING	
Lilliwaup Falls			
	40.0	327.3	
		LILLIWAUP RIVER	
	41.1	326.2	SLOW VEHICLE TURNOUT
			Public Beach
	42.3	325.0	
		MILEPOST	
EAGLE CREEK ROAD	42.5	324.8	
Eagle Creek Saloon	42.6	324.7	
		TAVERN	
SHAR LANE	43.1	324.2	SHADY LANE
PARADISE DRIVE	43.2	324.1	TURNOUT
	43.8	323.5	SLOW VEHICLE TURNOUT
COLONY SURF	44.0	323.3	
	44.3	323.0	SLOW VEHICLE TURNOUT
Jorsted Creek Campground	45.6	321.7	Seafresh Seafood Market
(Members Only)			
	45.9	321.4	
		JORSTED CREEK	
24 JORSTED CREEK ROAD	46.0	321.3	

FS ROAD 24
LAKE CUSHMAN STAIRCASE

	DISTANCE FROM HIGHWAY 101
MELBOURNE LAKE CAMPGROUND	8.0 Miles
LILLIWAUP CREEK CAMPGROUND	6.6 Miles
OLYMPIC NATIONAL FOREST	7.1 Miles
BIG CREEK CAMPGROUND	8.9 Miles
OLYMPIC NATIONAL PARK	14.2 Miles
STAIRCASE CAMPGROUND	15.2 Miles
MOUNT ELLINOR TRAIL	11.8 Miles
MOUNT WASHINGTON TRAIL	13.9 Miles
BIG CREEK TRAIL	8.9 Miles
MOUNT ROSE TRAIL	11.5 Miles
SHADY LANE	15.2 Miles
STAIRCASE RAPIDS TRAIL	15.2 Miles
WAGONWHEEL LAKE TRAIL	15.2 Miles
NORTH FORK SKOKOMISH TRAIL	15.2 Miles

FS Road 24 passes through mostly state lands, skirting the southern boundary of the national forest, until just past Lilliwaup Creek Campground. From there, you see mostly national forest lands until you reach the Olympic National Park boundary. There are many excellent trails to hike, mountains to climb, campgrounds, and man-made Lake Cushman along the way. The description of Highway 101 continues at mile 321.3 on page 74 in Chapter 5.

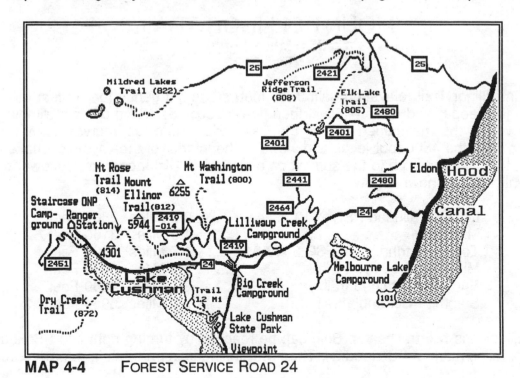

MAP 4-4   FOREST SERVICE ROAD 24

MELBOURNE LAKE CAMPGROUND   5.5   9.9
(DNR)

The Melbourne Lake Campground is maintained by the Washington Department of Natural Resources. It has 5 campsites (maximum trailer length 21 feet). None have hook-ups. There are picnic tables and vault toilets. Potable water is not available.

To reach the campground, turn left from FSR 24 at the 5.5 mile mark into an un-numbered road. Follow this road for 1.8 miles and turn left again. Continue for another 0.7 miles to the campground, which is situated beside Lake Melbourne.

LILLIWAUP CREEK CAMPGROUND AND   6.6   8.8
PICNIC AREA (DNR)

The Lilliwaup Creek Camp and Picnic Area, is maintained by the Washington Department of Natural Resources. It has 13 campsites (maximum trailer size 21 feet). None have hook-ups. It has potable water, vault toilets and a picnic area. The campground is beside Lilliwaup Creek in FSR 24, on your right.

7.2   8.2   **2419**   BIG CREEK ROAD

MOUNT ELLINOR TRAIL
MOUNT WASHINGTON TRAIL

MOUNT ELLINOR TRAIL
(3.0 Miles Long)
Trail 812

The Mount Ellinor Trail (elevation gain 3144 feet) starts out gently for the first mile, grows increasingly steeper and more difficult, then finally becomes real mountain climbing at the tree line where the maintained part of the trail ends. There are marvelous views of the Cascades from the 4500 foot level, and views of the interior of the Olympics make it worth the effort to finish the climb to the summit on a clear day. Distance from the lower trailhead and elevations are shown below:

```
Lower Trailhead FSR 2419, mi.4.6  . . . . 0.0 Miles  2800 Feet
Milepost 1 . . . . . . . . . . . . . . . . . . . . . 1.0 Miles  3100 Feet
To Upper trlhd., end FSR 2419-014 . . . . 1.7 Miles  3600 Feet
Milepost 2 . . . . . . . . . . . . . . . . . . . . 2.0 Miles  3860 Feet
End of maintained trail . . . . . . . . . . . . 2.4 Miles  4500 Feet
Summit - Scramble trail  . . . . . . . . . . . 3.0 Miles  5944 Feet
```

Mount Ellinor has two trailheads. Both can be reached by turning right into FS Road 2419 at the 7.2 miles mark of FS Road 24. The lower trailhead is on the left, 4.6 miles from FSR 24.

For those who are short on time, the upper trailhead shortens the hike by 1.5 miles. It is reached by continuing on FSR 2419 for 1.6 miles past the lower trailhead, then turning left into FSR 2419-014 and driving another one mile to its end.

MOUNT WASHINGTON TRAIL
(2.0 Miles Long)
Trail 800

Mount Washington Trail has an elevation gain of 3255 feet to the summit. The maintained trail ends at a saddle below the base of Mount Washington's east face. From here, there is an unmaintained scramble trail to the top.

Mount Washington is the highest point on a ridge overlooking Lake Cushman. It was named for its resemblance to George Washington's profile. The summit is his chin. There are good views of Hood Canal, Puget Sound and Mount Rainier from the summit. Distances from the trailhead and elevations are:

Trailhead, FSR 2419 mile 6.7	0.0 Miles	3000 Feet
End of Maintained Trail	1.1 Miles	3800 Feet
Summit	2.0 Miles	6255 Feet

The trailhead can be reached by turning right into FSR 2419 from the 7.2 mile mark of FSR 24. Continue on FSR 2419 for 6.7 miles to
the trailhead is on the left.

FS ROAD 24	
MILES	MILES
from	from
101	END

LAKE CUSHMAN ROAD	8.8	6.6	
	8.9	6.5	BIG CREEK CAMPGROUND (NFS)

Big Creek Campground is on your right just after you pass Lake Cushman Road on your left. It is maintained by the National Forest Service, and has 23 sites (maximum trailer size 22 feet), with no hook-ups. There are picnic tables, fire rings, and vault toilets. It is located beside Big Creek and offers fishing, swimming and a hiking trail.

BIG CREEK NATURE TRAIL
(1.3 Miles Long)
Trail 827

The Big Creek Nature Trail has very little change in elevation as it forms a loop that circles the campground. Its main attraction is the diversity in the vegetation that it passes through. The trail starts (or finishes) on either side of the entrance road just after you enter the campground.

11.1 4.3
VIEWPOINT

CUSHMAN FALLS

Cushman Falls is on the right, 2.3 miles from Lake Cushman Rd. Cushman Falls was named for Albert Cushman who came to the area in 1890 after seeing Lake Cushman on a map. There is a turnout just past the falls to enable you to stop for photos of Lightning Peak on the other side of Lake Cushman.

11.5 3.9

MOUNT ROSE TRAIL

Take the road on the right to the trailhead for Mount Rose Trail. On the left is a picnic table, and fire ring on the beach.

MOUNT ROSE TRAIL
(4.8 MILES LONG)
Trail 814

Mount Rose Trail,with its 3,550 feet elevation gain) is extremely steep, and gets quite difficult after the first two miles, where maintenance stops. For those who are prepared to put a bit of effort into it, one can continue for another 2.6 miles to the summit, and get views of Lake Cushman, Prospect Ridge, Dow Mountain and Mount Ellinor. Distances from the trailhead and elevations are:

Trailhead, FSR 24 mile 11.5	0.0 Miles	750 Feet
End of abandoned road	0.2 Miles	800 Feet
National Forest Boundary	0.4 Miles	1000 Feet
Milepost 1	1.0 Miles	1300 Feet
Bench - Trail turns right	2.0 Miles	2600 Feet
Saddle	3.5 Miles	3900 Feet
Summit	4.8 Miles	4300 Feet

2451 LIGHTNING PEAK ROAD   14.0   1.4

When the water level in Lake Cushman is low, you can see huge stumps which, because of the logging technology of the time, were left when the lake filled after the dam was built in 1920. Some of them are 50 to 60 feet tall, and the timber is still good. Tacoma City Light has made arrangements to have the stumps removed by logging companies. Divers cut the stumps near their bases at the bottom of Lake Cushman. The logs are then hauled ashore with draglines.

| OLYMPIC NATIONAL PARK | 14.2 | 1.2 | OLYMPIC NATIONAL PARK |

As you enter the Olympic National Park, two tenths of a mile past the junction with FSR 2451, the road surface becomes blacktop.

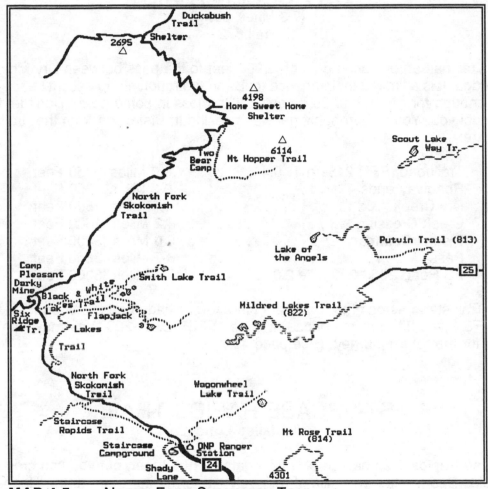

MAP 4-5   NORTH FORK SKOKOMISH TRAIL

| STAIRCASE CAMPGROUND (ONP) | 15.4 | 0.0 | ONP RANGER STATION |

Staircase Campground has 63 campsites (maximum trailer length 16 feet). None of them have hook-ups. There are picnic tables, fire rings, potable water and both flush and vault toilets. There is a phone near the entrance, across from the ranger station. The North Fork Skokomish River offers good fishing, and several marvelous hiking trails originate here.

SHADY LANE TRAIL
(1 Mile Long)
Trail 872

Shady Lane Trail was part of Dry Creek Trail until it was cut by FSR 2451. It passes a tunnel that was abandoned by prospectors after they had gouged out fifteen or twenty feet of the cliff. This area is a good example of old growth. It starts from a clearing across the bridge from the ranger station, and takes you to FSR 2451. It continues as Dry Creek Trail on the other side of FSR 2451.

DRY CREEK TRAIL
(7.3 Miles Long)
Trail 872

Dry Creek Trail has an elevation gain of 2,900 feet to the pass between Dry Mountain and Prospect Ridge. It is a limited maintenance trail, and the rough steep ascent keeps the traffic down well enough for the trail to be carpeted with moss in some parts. Don't let the name Dry Creek fool you. You will probably get wet crossing it. Distances from the trailhead and elevations are:

Trailhead, FSR 2451 mile 0.4	0.0 Miles	750 Feet
Roadway ends	0.3 Miles	750 Feet
Dry Creek	1.1 Miles	800 Feet
Creek Crossing	4.2 Miles	1600 Feet
District Boundary	6.0 Miles	3200 Feet
Pass	6.7 Miles	3650 Feet
FS Road 2353-200 mile 2.0	7.4 Miles	3000 Feet

Dry Creek Trail starts across the road from the end of Shady Lane Trail on FSR 2451, 0.4 miles from FS Road 24 near the bridge. It ends at FSR 2353-200. You may want to leave a car there for the return journey. (See page 43.)

STAIRCASE RAPIDS TRAIL
(3.5 Miles Long)

The Staircase Rapids Trail has an elevation gain of 1,000 feet, but you can cross the river on the Rapids Bridge after one mile of relatively flat terrain to return to the Ranger Station on North Fork Skokomish Trail in a two mile loop. There is another opportunity to return when the trail forks just past Four Stream. The right fork goes to Upper Skokomish Crossing, 2.2 miles from the trailhead, making a five mile loop. Distances from the trailhead are:

Trailhead, Staircase Ranger Station	0.0 Miles	800 Feet
Copper View Camp	1.7 Miles	1000 Feet
Four Stream (Keep Left at Fork)	2.2 Miles	1000 Feet
National Forest Boundary	3.2 Miles	1800 Feet
End of Trail	3.5 Miles	1800 Feet

The Trail starts across the bridge from the Ranger Station.

WAGONWHEEL LAKE TRAIL
(2.9 Miles Long)
Trail 819

Although Wagonwheel Lake Trail is steep, with a 3,250 feet elevation gain, the trail is in good condition. Whoever named Wagonwheel Lake must have had an awfully bumpy riding wagon if the wheels were as oval as the lake. Distances and elevations are:

Trailhead, Staircase Ranger Station	0.0 Miles	900 Feet
Trail levels in meadow	2.5 Miles	4000 Feet
Wagonwheel Lake	2.9 Miles	4150 Feet

The trail starts from the parking lot behind the Ranger Station. There is a scramble trail going up the ridge beyond the lake.

NORTH FORK SKOKOMISH TRAIL
(15.6 Miles Long)

The North Fork Skokomish Trail has a 3,900 feet elevation gain. It begins behind the Ranger Station and goes to the Duckabush Trail near Camp Duckabush. Except for the first few miles, this trail follows the route taken by O'Neil in 1890. If you happen to be here in the winter or spring you will have the pleasure of witnessing the incongruity of deep snow in a rain forest type environment.

There are several other trails which start from the North Fork Skokomish Trail. The lengths and elevation changes of the other trails are shown in parentheses below their names. I encourage you to hike as many of these trails as you can make time for, as each has its own special charm. Don't forget to obtain backcountry permits at the park ranger station if you are planning to stay on the trails in the National Park overnight.

Distance from Staircase and elevation of landmarks along the North Fork Skokomish Trail are:

Trailhead, Staircase Ranger Station	0.0 Miles	800 Feet
Path to Rapids Bridge	1.0 Miles	900 Feet
Upper Skokomish Crossing	2.2 Miles	900 Feet
Mt. Lincoln Way Trail	2.4 Miles	1090 Feet
(2.6 mi. long, elevation gain 2300 ft.)		
Spike Camp	3.7 Miles	1475 Feet
Flap Jack Lakes Trail	3.7 Miles	1475 Feet
(5.6 mi. long, elevation gain 3525 ft.)		
Black & White Lakes Tr.	5.5 Miles	1500 Feet
(2.0 mi. long, elevation gain 2975 ft.)		
Six Ridge Trail (Left)	5.9 Miles	1475 Feet
(9.6 mi. long, elevation gain 3080 ft.)		
Camp Pleasant	6.7 Miles	1600 Feet
Camp Nine Stream	9.6 Miles	2000 Feet

```
Two Bear Camp . . . . . . . . . . . . . . . . . 11.6 Miles  3800 Feet
Camp Lookabout . . . . . . . . . . . . . . 12.4 Miles  4300 Feet
Mt. Hopper Way Trail . . . . . . . . . . . . 12.7 Miles  4500 Feet
     (2.0 mi. long, elevation gain 500 ft.)

First Divide  . . . . . . . . . . . . . . . . . . 12.9 Miles  4700 Feet
Home Sweet Home Shelter . . . . . . . . 13.5 Miles  4200 Feet
Duckabush Trail . . . . . . . . . . . . . . . 15.6 Miles  2700 Feet
     (22.2 mi. long, elevation gain 4500 ft.)
```

MOUNT LINCOLN WAY TRAIL
(2.6 Miles Long)

Mount Lincoln Way Trail (2300 feet elevation gain), although no longer maintained, is still in pretty good shape. It starts from mile 2.4 of North Fork Skokomish Trail (1100 feet), and climbs about half way to the top of Mount Lincoln (5868 feet). The trail gradually disappears after 2.6 miles, in an old burn at about the 3400 feet mark. One can press on, but the summit of Mount Lincoln can be reached a lot more easily from Flapjack Lakes Trail.

FLAPJACK LAKES TRAIL
(5.6 Miles Long)

Flapjack Lakes Trail (3525 feet elevation gain) starts from mile 3.7 of North Fork Skokomish Trail, and continues for a mile and a half beyond Flapjack Lakes to a point overlooking the beginnings of the Hamma Hamma River on the Gladys Divide between Mount Gladys (5600 feet) and Mount Cruiser (6104 feet). It is an easy hike to the top of Mount Gladys from the end of the trail, for views of Mount Anderson to the north and Mount Olympus to the northwest.

Distances and elevations along the trail are:

```
N. Fork Skokomish Tr., mi. 3.7 . . . . . . . 0.0 Miles  1475 Feet
Madeline Creek Bridge, camp . . . . . . . . 2.0 Miles  2100 Feet
Smith Lake Trail (left) . . . . . . . . . . . . . 3.6 Miles  3500 Feet
     (2.1 Miles Long, 700 feet elevation gain)

Flapjack Lakes . . . . . . . . . . . . . . . . . . 4.1 Miles  3900 Feet
Gladys Divide, end of trail . . . . . . . . . . 5.6 Miles  5000 Feet
```

SMITH LAKE TRAIL
(2.1 Miles Long)

Smith Lake Trail (700 feet elevation gain) goes to the left from mile 3.6 of Flapjack Lakes Trail at Donahue Creek. It takes you to an old abandoned mine and a path to Black and White Lakes before continuing on to Smith Lake. In season, there is a profusion of delicious huckleberries along the trail. In the higher reaches there are good views of several nearby mountains. The trail ends at Smith Lake where there are views of a "silver forest" to the north. There are two camps at the lake. One is near the outlet and the other is on the north side of the lake.

Distances and elevations along the trail are:

```
Flapjack Lakes Tr., mile 3.6  . . . . . . . . . 0.0 Miles  3500 Feet
Black & White Mine  . . . . . . . . . . . . . . 1.2 Miles  4200 Feet
Black & White Lakes Way Trail  . . . . . . . 1.3 Miles  4475 Feet
    (2.0 Miles Long, 2975 feet elevation gain)

Trail forks. Keep left.  . . . . . . . . . . . . . 1.6 Miles  4550 Feet
Smith Lake. Trail ends  . . . . . . . . . . . . 2.1 Miles  3970 Feet
```

BLACK & WHITE LAKES WAY TRAIL
(2.0 Miles Long)

Black and White Lakes Way Trail (2975 feet elevation gain) leaves North Fork Skokomish Trail to the right at mile 5.5 opposite Big Log Camp (1500 feet). Its only purpose is to provide the connection for a loop trail to hikers to Smith Lake and Flapjack Lakes. The trail is steep, rough and in poor condition. It ends at mile 1.3 of Smith Lake Trail (4475 feet).

SIX RIDGE TRAIL
(9.6 Miles Long)

Six Ridge Trail (3080 feet elevation gain) is a real challenge, even for experienced hikers. The 3080 feet elevation gain is deceptive because of all the steep ups and downs. It goes to the left from North Fork Skokomish Trail at mile 5.9, just after you cross the bridge over the North Fork Skokomish River. Camp Pleasant is to the right. The trail passes through a primitive campsite beside the river just after the start. In the high country, the snowfields don't disappear until late summer. Beyond McGravey Lakes the trail deteriorates until it reaches Six Ridge Pass. Several of the interior mountains, including Mount Olympus, can be seen from Six Ridge Pass. Beyond the pass the trail is known as Graves Creek Trail. Graves Creek Trail trailhead is at the end of South Shore Quinault Road. (See page 312 in Chapter 12.

Distances and elevations along the trail are:

```
N. Fork Skokomish Tr., mile 5.9  . . . . . . 0.0 Miles  1475 Feet
Top of Six Ridge, campsite . . . . . . . . . . 4.9 Miles  4400 Feet
Mount Olson Trail (Right) . . . . . . . . . . . 5.4 Miles  4400 Feet
    (8.5 miles long, 3750 feet elevation loss)

Camp Belview . . . . . . . . . . . . . . . . . . . 6.4 Miles  4100 Feet
McGravey Lakes . . . . . . . . . . . . . . . . . 8.5 Miles  4000 Feet
Six Ridge Pass . . . . . . . . . . . . . . . . . . 9.6 Miles  4560 Feet
```

MOUNT OLSON TRAIL
(8.5 Miles Long)

Mount Olson Trail (3750 feet elevation loss) is a great high country trail. Since it originates from Six Ridge Trail which is notorious for its rigor, there is far less traffic than that on most of the other high country trails in the Olympics. It starts out on the crest of Six Ridge, giving you clear views down to both Six Stream and Seven Stream. Although the trail loses 3650 feet in elevation before its end at East Fork Quinault River near O'Neil Creek, it gains 500 feet before it starts its descent. The trail is not maintained beyond Lake Success, and it is often hard to find. It also becomes difficult to differentiate the trail from numerous game trails that are sometimes blazed. Experienced cross-country hikers will probably find it easier to abandon the trail. The trail ends at the East Fork Quinault River near its junction with O'Neil Creek. O'Neil Creek Camp on the Enchanted Valley Trail is on the other side of the river. (See Chapter 12, page 310.) There is no bridge, and crossing can be dangerous until mid summer.

Distances and elevations along the trail are:

Six Ridge Trail, mile 5.4	0.0 Miles	4400 Feet
Lake Success (camp on west side)	3.0 Miles	4200 Feet
Saddle on E. side of Mt. Olson	4.5 Miles	4800 Feet
E. Fork Quinault, trail ends	8.5 Miles	1150 Feet

MOUNT HOPPER TRAIL
(2.0 Miles Long)

Mount Hopper Trail (500 feet elevation gain) is not maintained on a regular basis. It starts from mile 12.7 of North Fork Skokomish Trail (4540 feet) just below First Divide. It has a lot of ups and downs that are not included in the 500 feet elevation gain shown above. There are excellent views of Mount Skokomish (6434 feet) and Skokomish Glacier along the way to the trail's ends at Fisher's Pass (5040 feet). From Fisher's Pass, you can follow the south ridge for about an hour to the top of Mt. Hopper (6114 feet) and superb views in all directions.

Beyond the end of the trail, you can continue for another four miles to a pass (5250 feet) on the slopes of Mount Stone overlooking the source of Hamma Hamma River. At about three miles beyond the end of the trail, you will pass a directional arrow that has been formed with rocks.

Distances and elevations along the trail are:

N. Fork Skokomish Tr., mi. 12.7	0.0 Miles	4540 Feet
Fisher's Pass, end of trail	2.0 Miles	5040 Feet
Great Stone Arrow	5.0 Miles	5350 Feet
Pass on west side of Mt. Stone	6.0 Miles	5250 Feet

We will now return to Highway 101 at mile number 321.3, the point at which we left it to explore Forest Service Road 24 and the Staircase Area.

Mount Cruiser from the end of Hamma Hamma Road.

CHAPTER 5

HAMMA HAMMA, DUCKABUSH and DOSEWALLIPS

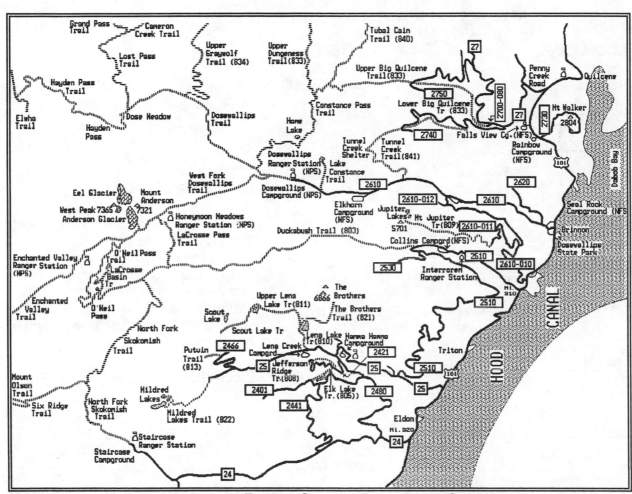

MAP 5-1   HIGHWAY 101 FROM FOREST SERVICE ROAD 24 TO QUILCENE

Although the roads that run beside the Hamma Hamma, Duckabush and Dosewallips Rivers are short, they get you into the mountains very quickly. The peaks look deceptively close, but the steep trails on this side of the peninsula make you earn your reward — some of the best views anywhere in the Olympics. The excellent vistas include Mount Olympus and the Bailey

73

Range; the Strait of Juan de Fuca, Hood Canal and Puget Sound; and the Cascades from Mount St. Helens in the south to Mount Baker in the north. Let's continue now on Highway 101.

| | HIGHWAY 101 | | |
	MILES from I-5	MILE NUMBER	
24 JORSTED CREEK ROAD	46.0	321.3	
SOUTHBOUND SLOW VEHICLE TURNOUT	46.4	320.9	
	47.1	320.2	SLOW VEHICLE TURNOUT
	OYSTER FARM		Hama Hama Oyster Farm & Seafood
SOUTHBOUND SLOW VEHICLE TURNOUT	47.2	320.1	
ELDON LANE	47.3	320.0	
	MILEPOST		
	HAMMA HAMMA R.		
LON WEBB ROAD	47.8	319.5	
Mark Northwest Carvings	GIFT SHOP		
	48.1	319.2	Hungry Bear Cafe
	RESTAURANT GIFT SHOP		This cafe serves large portions of good food. If time permits, it's worth a stop even if you are not hungry, just to see the stuffed bears, bear pictures, teddy bears, bear cartoons, and other bear paraphernalia. They also have a small gift shop.
	48.2	319.1	Eldon Store
	C-STORE PHONE GAS DIESEL		
	48.3	319.0	
	LEAVING ELDON		
	48.8	318.5	
	WAKETICKEH CRK.		
25 HAMMA HAMMA ROAD	49.4	317.9	SLOW VEHICLE TURNOUT HIDDEN COVE LANE Hidden Cove Resort

FS ROAD 25   HAMMA HAMMA

	DISTANCE FROM HIGHWAY 101
OLYMPIC NATIONAL FOREST	4.8 Miles
NFS RANGER STATION	5.6 Miles
HAMMA HAMMA CAMPGROUND	6.0 Miles
LENA CREEK CAMPGROUND	7.8 Miles
JEFFERSON RIDGE TRAIL	8.2 Miles
ELK LAKE TRAIL	8.2 Miles
LENA LAKE TRAIL	7.7 Miles
PUTVIN TRAIL	12.0 Miles
MILDRED LAKES TRAIL	13.2 Miles

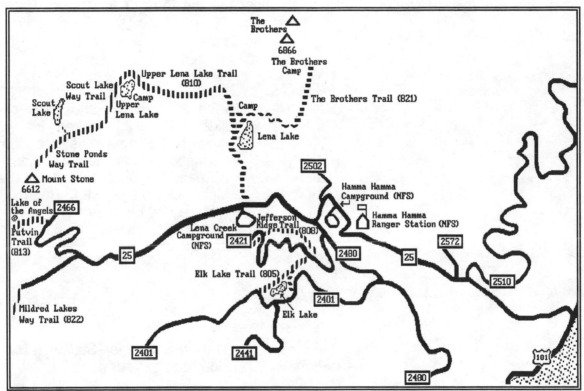

MAP 5-2   FOREST SERVICE ROAD 25 - HAMMA HAMMA ROAD

Although Hamma Hamma Road is only a bit more than 13 miles long, it provides some stunning mountain views, and access to The Brothers and Mount Skokomish Wilderness Areas. In addition to the two Forest Service campgrounds in FSR 25, there are 29 maintained campsites surrounding Lena Lake, a very pleasant 3.5 mile hike from the road.

Those who wish to continue on Highway 101 may turn to mile 317.9 on page 83.

0.0 13.2

FSR 25 starts as a two lane, paved road with a fairly steep grade.

1.0 12.2

After the first mile, the grade levels out, and, although the pavement continues, the roadway narrows to one lane with turnouts.

1.4 11.8

You get a fantastic view of the mountains here. Sometimes they have clouds draped on their shoulders like a shawl, or gathered on one shoulder like the toga of an ancient Roman Senator.

2.3 10.9

2510

FSR 2510 twists and turns considerably as it makes its way through the mountains to become Duckabush Road just west of the trailhead for Duckabush trail. (See Map 5.3, page 86.) Return to Highway 101 is faster and saves a lot of wear and tear on both vehicle and driver.

4.8 8.4
ENTER NATIONAL
FOREST

5.6 7.6
RANGER STATION

The NFS Ranger Station is on a side road to your right.

HAMMA HAMMA CAMPGROUND (NFS)

6.0 7.2

NFS CAMPGROUND

At the six mile mark you come to the Hamma Hamma Campground on your left between the road and the Hamma Hamma River. It has 15 campsites (maximum trailer size 21 feet), picnic tables, fire rings, potable water and pit toilets.

6.3 6.9 |2502|

Three tenths of a mile past the Hamma Hamma Campground FSR 2502, (Cabin Creek Road) branches to the right.

|2480| JEFFERSON RIDGE TRAIL   6.4 6.8 |25|
        ELK LAKE TRAIL

Here you come to a T intersection. FSR 2480 goes to the left. FSR 2480 continues on to FSR 24 after it passes FSR 2421, the access road for the Elk Lake and Jefferson Ridge Trails.

FSR 25 goes to the right here, and the road surface becomes well maintained gravel.

At this point we will explore to the south by turning left into FSR 2480. The listing of FSR 25 continues on page 78.

Three tenths of a mile after you turn into FSR 2480, turn right into FSR 2421 and follow it for 1.5 miles. This was the end of FSR 2421, but the road has now been extended. Both Jefferson Ridge Trail and Elk Lake Trail trailheads are located here. Jefferson Ridge Trail is to the right, and Elk Lake Trail goes to the left at the trail register.

JEFFERSON RIDGE TRAIL
(2.9 Miles Long)
Trail 808

The Jefferson Ridge Trail is a limited maintenance trail, and has been erased in places by abandoned logging roads and clearcuts. At one point, on a skid road, it has a grade of 65%. Those who persist to the top however, will be rewarded with one of the broadest and most beautiful views in the Olympics.

Distances and elevations of landmarks are:

Trailhead, FSR 2421 mile 1.5	0.0 Miles	1000 Feet
National Forest Boundary	0.1 Miles	1100 Feet
Trail obliterated, follow skid road. Grade 65%	1.7 Miles	2800 Feet
Trail resumes	1.9 Miles	3200 Feet
Clearcut	2.2 Miles	3400 Feet
Trail ends	2.9 Miles	3800 Feet

ELK LAKE TRAIL
(2.0 Miles Long)
Trail 805

The Elk Lake Trail branches to the left from the main Jefferson Ridge Trail at the trail register. Although this trail is relatively flat, it has limited maintenance, and there is an overflow channel crossing near the FSR 2401 (South) trailhead that is difficult in winter. After one mile, the trail forks, with the left branch leading to the FSR 2401 (South) trailhead. The right branch continues along the north shore of Big Elk Lake, then follows Jefferson Creek to FSR 2401 (West). There is a pit toilet and campsites are scattered around the lake near the FSR 2401 (South) trailhead. Distances and elevations along the trail are:

FSR 2421 (East) Trailhead	0.0 Miles	1100 Feet
Fork — Right for FSR 2401 (West)	1.2 Miles	1100 Feet
FSR 2401 (West) Trailhead	2.0 Miles	1200 Feet

OR

FSR 2421 (East) Trailhead	0.0 Miles	1100 Feet
Fork — Left for FSR 2401 (South)	1.2 Miles	1100 Feet
Boulder-filled overflow channel	1.25 Miles	1100 Feet
FSR 2401 (South) Trailhead	1.5 Miles	1200 Feet

The renumbering of the Forest Service roads gets a little confusing here. The section of road currently numbered FSR 2401 between FSR 2480 and the junction where FSR 2441 heads south was formerly considered to be part of FSR 2441, and FSR 2401, coming in from the west ended there. The renumbering has FSR 2401 continuing east, past the present end of FSR 2441, to FSR 2480.

The FSR 2401 South and West trailheads can be reached by continuing on FSR 2480 south of the FSR 2421 junction for 1.9 miles to FSR 2401, where you turn right. The Elk Lake Parking area and the FSR 2401 (South) trailhead are in FSR 2401 about 2.5 miles from FSR 2480. FSR 2401 continues (past FSR 2441 on your left a half mile further on), to the FSR 2401 (West) trailhead.

Alternatively, the FSR 2401 trailheads can be reached from FSR 24 as follows: Follow FSR 24 for 1.3 miles from Highway 101 to FSR 2480 and turn right. Continue for 5.5 miles to FSR 2401 and turn left for the south and west trailheads. Continue straight ahead on FSR 2480 for the east trailhead.

We will return now to FSR 25 at its junction with FSR 2480 at mile 6.4.

	FS ROAD 25		
	MILES	MILES	
	from	from	
	101	END	
2480 JEFFERSON RIDGE TRAIL ELK LAKE TRAIL	6.4	6.8	**25**

FSR 25 becomes well maintained gravel here.

7.7 5.5

LENA   CREEK   CAMPGROUND
(FSR)

LENA LAKE TRAIL
UPPER LENA LAKE TRAIL
SCOUT LAKE TRAIL
THE BROTHERS TRAIL

Lena Creek Campground is on the left, just west of the parking area for Lena Lake Trail. It has frontage on the Hamma Hamma River. There are 21 campsites (maximum trailer length 16 ft.) with picnic tables, fire rings, vault toilets and potable water from a hand-pump well.

LENA LAKE TRAIL
(3.5 Miles Long)
Trail 810

The trailhead for the Lena Lake Trail is on your right. As you look at the trail, there is a vault toilet on your right. The trail has been recently renovated, with lots of switchbacks added in the really steep bits. A beautifully maintained trail with easy grades has its price though. In summer it is as crowded as a city street. Fortunately, the trails beyond Lena Lake are not so well maintained, and steeper, so one can regain relative solitude as soon as he passes the lake.

There are 29 campsites with fire rings and pit toilets at Lower Lena Lake. The Forest Service is re-vegetating the southwest corner of Lena Lake, and has closed several campsites. To handle the summer traffic, they have developed ten backcountry sites on the north end of the lake. Distances and elevations on the Lena Lake Trail are as follows:

Trailhead, FSR 25 mile 7.7 . . . . 0.0 Miles   660 Feet
First wood stringer bridge . . . . 1.9 Miles 1600 Feet
Second wood stringer bridge . . . . 2.6 Miles 1800 Feet
Upper Lena Lake Trail (Left) . . . . 2.8 Miles 2100 Feet
　　(4.0 Miles Long, 2450 Feet Elevation Gain)

Lena Lake . . . . 3.1 Miles 1800 Feet
The Brothers Trail . . . . 3.5 Miles 1900 Feet
　　(4.5 Miles Long, 5000 Feet Elevation Gain)

UPPER LENA LAKE TRAIL
(4.0 Miles Long)
Trail 811

The trailhead for Upper Lena Lake Trail is 2.8 miles from FSR 25 on the Lena Lake Trail (Trail 810). Beyond Lower Lena Lake the trails are not so well maintained, and steeper. You can fill out a National Park Registration form at the National Park Boundary if you plan to stay overnight. Don't forget that motor vehicles, firearms, and pets are prohibited on the National Park trails. Campfires are not allowed past Lower Lena Lake either, so you should bring a stove. Use the campsites on the north shore, to assist the re-vegetation project. The two Lena Lakes are very different, so be sure to include time for both if you can. Upper Lena Lake Trail has a profusion of wildflowers at higher altitudes. Glorious sunsets electrify the ridge to the west of the lake.

Distances and elevations are:

```
Lena Lake Trail, mile 2.8  . . . . . . . . . . . 0.0 Miles  2100 Feet
Junction - Old trail  . . . . . . . . . . . . . . 0.4 Miles  2150 Feet
Olympic National Park Boundary . . . . . . 1.2 Miles  2550 Feet
Lena Creek Crossing  . . . . . . . . . . . . . 4.0 Miles  4550 Feet
Scout Lake Trail . . . . . . . . . . . . . . . . . 4.0 Miles  4550 Feet
    (3.0 Miles Long, 900 Feet Elevation Gain)
```

SCOUT LAKE WAY TRAIL
(3.0 Miles Long)

Scout Lake Trail is more a path than a trail, as it is not maintained. Still, it is in pretty good shape and offers some excellent views. It starts from the west shore of Upper Lena Lake.

Distances and elevations are:

```
Upper Lena Lake Tr., mile 4.0 . . . . . . . . 0.0 Miles  4550 Feet
    (Lena Creek Crossing)
Scout Lake Pass  . . . . . . . . . . . . . . . . 1.7 Miles  5150 Feet
Deerheart Lake  . . . . . . . . . . . . . . . . . 2.2 Miles  4970 Feet
Stone Ponds Way Trail  . . . . . . . . . . . . 2.6 Miles  4500 Feet
    (1.2 miles long, 400 feet elevation gain)

Scout Lake  . . . . . . . . . . . . . . . . . . . . 3.0 Miles  4250 Feet
```

STONE PONDS WAY TRAIL
(1.2 Miles Long)

Stone Ponds Way Trail (400 feet elevation gain) goes from Scout Lake to Stone Ponds. For the first 0.4 miles after leaving the south end of the lake, the trail coincides with Scout Lake Trail. The two trails separate at 0.4 miles, with Stone Ponds Trail heading south toward Mount Stone. Beyond the end of the trail, one can continue another 1.6 miles to St. Peter's Gate and Lake of the Angels. From there Putvin Trail will take you back to Boulder Creek Road, mile 1.2. Boulder Creek Road is closed 0.8 miles from FSR 25.

Distances and elevations along the trail are:

```
Scout Lake  . . . . . . . . . . . . . . . . . . .  0.0 Miles  4500 Feet
Scout Lake Tr. branches right  . . . . . . .  0.4 Miles  4500 Feet
Stone Ponds Pass  . . . . . . . . . . . . . .  1.0 Miles  4900 Feet
Stone Ponds, trail ends  . . . . . . . . . .  1.2 Miles  4600 Feet
Saint Peter's Gate  . . . . . . . . . . . . . .  2.0 Miles  5900 Feet
Lake of the Angels  . . . . . . . . . . . . . .  2.8 Miles  4900 Feet
```

THE BROTHERS TRAIL
(3.0 Miles Long)
Trail 821

The Brothers (6866 Feet), with its two peaks, is one of the most conspicuous landmarks in the eastern Olympics. The Brothers Trail starts from Lower Lena Lake, 3.5 miles from FSR 25 on the Lena Lake Trail. It is maintained on a limited basis only, for the first three miles. Hikers and climbers should be not only experienced, but, wary on this trail. This is especially so past the end of the maintained trail, as it becomes quite dangerous for the neophyte.

For those planning to ascend to the summit, The Brothers Camp, at the end of the maintained trail will accommodate 12 tents. Although the actual climb is better termed "strenuous" than "difficult", the mountain has claimed lives. There is high avalanche risk on The Brothers Trail until quite late in spring, so check with the Ranger Station in Hoodsport before you set out on an early climb. The trail begins at the junction of Lower Lena Lake and East Fork of Lena Creek near the northwest corner of the Lake. Distances and elevations are:

```
Lena Lake Trail, mile 3.5  . . . . . . . . . . .  0.0 Miles  1900 Feet
Camp  . . . . . . . . . . . . . . . . . . . . . . . .  1.5 Miles  2300 Feet
Camp  . . . . . . . . . . . . . . . . . . . . . . . .  1.9 Miles  2450 Feet
The Brothers Camp, end of trail  . . . . . .  3.0 Miles  3100 Feet
Summit of The Brothers  . . . . . . . . . . .  4.5 Miles  6866 Feet
```

We will now return to FSR 25, Hamma Hamma Road at its mile 7.7.

	FS ROAD 25		
	MILES from 101	MILES from END	
LENA CREEK CAMPGROUND (NFS)	7.7	5.5	LENA LAKE TRAIL UPPER LENA LAKE TRAIL THE BROTHERS TRAIL
PICNIC AREA	8.1 LENA CREEK	5.1	PICNIC AREA
Here there is a sign on the left noting the trailhead of the Paul W. Tirrell Memorial Trail. The trail is 0.2 miles long, and ends at a small pond.	9.8	3.4	

FS ROAD 25

MILES from 101	MILES from END
10.0	3.2

MILEPOST

10.2 3.0
MAPLE CREEK

12.0 1.2
BOULDER CREEK

Putvin Historical Marker

"Near here is the grave of Carl Putvin, pioneer, trapper and explorer. Born Sept. 4, 1892. Died January 10, 1913". The path here leads to Putvin Trail trailhead in FSR 2466.

12.2 1.0   **2466** BOULDER CREEK ROAD
PUTVIN TRAIL

FSR 2466 is on the right 0.2 miles past the Putvin marker. It is closed 0.8 miles from FSR 25 because of washouts.

PUTVIN TRAIL
(3.8 Miles Long)
Trail 813

You must walk 0.4 miles along the road to the trailhead, 1.2 miles from FSR 25. This is a steep, limited maintenance trail, and after 0.9 miles the trail divides into several unmaintained way trails that take you to the slopes of Mount Skokomish, and the ridge between Mount Skokomish and Mount Stone. Although it is pretty hard going, the hike up to the ridge (5250 Feet) gives you magnificent views of the Olympic peaks, including Mount Olympus, to the west. To the east you can look across Hood Canal and Puget Sound to the Cascades, dominated by Mount Rainier. In late summer a profusion of fresh huckleberries compensates you for the arduous journey. Beyond the ridge, one can go cross country to the Mount Hopper Way Trail.

Distances from the trailhead and elevations are:

Trailhead, FSR 2466 mile 1.2	0.0 Miles	2120 Feet
Alpine Meadows	0.7 Miles	3100 Feet
Whitehorse Creek Camp, left	1.0 Miles	3360 Feet
Lake of the Angels, trail ends	3.0 Miles	3100 Feet

FS ROAD 25		
MILES	MILES	
from	from	
101	END	

Just past Whitehorse Creek an unmarked road branches to the left.

	12.4	0.8

WHITEHORSE CRK.

	13.1	0.1	Toilet, set back from road.

MILDRED LAKES WAY TRAIL

	13.2	0.0

END OF FSR 25

FSR 25 crosses the Hamma Hamma River on a high concrete bridge, then suddenly ends in a turnaround. The river cascades under the bridge and the steep, craggy mountains, Skokomish, Henderson, Cruiser, Pershing and Jefferson Peak encircle you so closely that you feel you can almost reach out and touch them.

MILDRED LAKES WAY TRAIL
(5.5 Miles Long)
Trail 822

The Mildred Lakes Way Trail is a very difficult hike. It starts from the turnaround at the end of FSR 25 after you cross the Hamma Hamma River. The trail was created by the footprints of hikers, and is not maintained. Beyond Huckleberry Creek the path is steep and difficult to follow, and some of the log "bridges" are definitely not for the squeamish. The trail's bad reputation does mean though, that quite often you will have the trail to yourself. Distances and elevations are:

```
Trailhead  . . . . . . . . . . . . . . . . . . . . . . 0.0 Miles  1678 Feet
Creek crossing, 2 campsites  . . . . . . . . 2.4 Miles  3000 Feet
First lake, campsites  . . . . . . . . . . . . . 4.9 Miles  3850 Feet
End of Trail, 2nd lake, campsites  . . . . . 5.5 Miles  3900 Feet
```

The lake at the end of the trail is the largest subalpine lake in the Olympics. The third lake is a bit north of the second, and off from the trail. From the second lake, you can see Mount Lincoln and Mount Cruiser with the jagged Sawtooth Ridge, only one mile away, stretching between them.

We will now return to Highway 101 where we left it, at mile number 317.9, and head for the Duckabush area.

HIGHWAY 101		
MILES	MILE	
from	NUMBER	
I-5	___	

25	HAMMA HAMMA ROAD	49.4	317.9	SLOW VEHICLE TURNOUT HIDDEN COVE LANE

	HIGHWAY 101		
	MILES from I-5	MILE NUMBER	
Mike's Campground	49.7	317.6	
		RV PARK	
	49.8	317.5	Mike's Beach Resort
	C-STORE PHONE		
	LODGING		
	BOAT LAUNCH		
SOUTHBOUND SLOW VEHICLE LANE	50.2	317.1	
	50.3	317.0	SLOW VEHICLE TURNOUT
	LODGING		
			Peterson's Cabin Camps
	50.7	316.6	SLOW VEHICLE TURNOUT
	51.0	316.3	Camp Robinswold
	52.0	315.3	RV Parking, Self Contained Only
	RV PARK		
BEACON POINT DRIVE	52.1	315.2	Beacon Point Resort
	52.2	315.1	TRITON HEAD DRIVE
	52.3	315.0	
	MILEPOST		
HINES ROAD	52.4	314.9	WEBSTER LANE
	52.7	314.6	
	ENTER JEFFERSON COUNTY		
	52.9	314.4	Triton Cove Trailer Court
	RV PARK		
	53.0	314.3	FOREST DRIVE
WILLIAMS COURT	53.2	314.1	Triton Cove Oyster Farms
	OYSTER FARM		
SOUTHBOUND SLOW VEHICLE TURNOUT	53.5	313.8	
	53.7	313.6	
	FULTON CREEK		

FULTON CREEK ROAD	53.8 313.5	
SEAMOUNT DRIVE	54.0 313.3	
	54.9 312.3	SLOW VEHICLE TURNOUT Private Picnic Shelter
	55.4 311.9	SLOW VEHICLE TURNOUT
CANAL VIEW STREET	56.5 310.8	CANAL LANE
SOUTHBOUND SLOW VEHICLE TURNOUT Twin Eagles RV Park, Self Contained Only	57.0 310.3 RV PARK	
	57.1 310.2 DUCKABUSH RIVER	
2510 DUCKABUSH ROAD	57.3 310.0 MILEPOST	

FS ROAD 2510 DUCKABUSH ROAD

	DISTANCE FROM HIGHWAY 101
OLYMPIC NATIONAL FOREST	3.7 Miles
INTERROREM GUARD STATION	3.7 Miles
COLLINS CAMPGROUND	5.1 Miles
INTERROREM NATURE TRAIL	3.7 Miles
RANGER HOLE TRAIL	3.7 Miles
DUCKABUSH TRAIL	6.1 Miles

FS Road 2510 (formerly FSR 2515) starts out as a paved, two lane road. It takes you along beside the Duckabush River, through privately owned properties with neat holiday homes and state-owned lands to the Olympic National Forest. The National Forest begins at the Interrorem Guard Station, the first building in the National Forest, built in 1906. The road then continues on to the trailhead of the Duckabush Trail. Although the mountains here are somewhat lower than those further north, the Duckabush Trail passes through some of the loveliest alpine meadows in the Olympics on its way to O'Neil Pass.

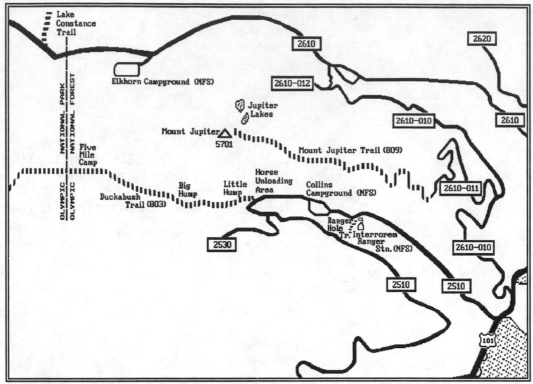

MAP 5-3   FOREST SERVICE ROAD 2510 - DUCKABUSH ROAD

FS Road 2510 has been re-numbered from its old number, 2515, but the some of the old signs remain. Those who wish to continue on Highway 101 can turn to mile number 310.0 on page 90.

FS ROAD 2510	
MILES	MILES
from	from
HWY 101	Tr 803

INTERROREM GUARD STATION
INTERROREM NATURE TRAIL
RANGER HOLE TRAIL

3.7	2.4
ENTER NATIONAL	
FOREST	
PAVEMENT ENDS	

Interrorem has a picnic area and there is a toilet on the right, near the trailhead. No overnight camping.

RANGER HOLE TRAIL
(0.8 Miles Long)
Trail 824

The trailhead for the Ranger Hole Trail and the Interrorem Nature Trail is to the right, in front of Interrorem Guard Station. Ranger Hole is the fishing hole on the Duckabush River at the end of the trail. It was used by the Ranger who lived at Interrorem in the early days of the National Forest. It is a picturesque spot where a rapid plunges into a deep, bubbling pool.

INTERROREM NATURE TRAIL
(0.5 Miles Long)
Trail 804

The Interrorem Nature Trail goes off to the left from the Ranger Hole Trail to form a loop east of it. It passes through a forest of large second growth trees, and stumps of the original trees, some of which are seven or eight feet thick.

FS ROAD 2510		
MILES	MILES	
from	from	
HWY 101	Tr 803	
3.8	2.3	Here the road becomes one lane with turnouts.

COLLINS CAMPGROUND EXIT — 4.9 1.2

COLLINS CAMPGROUND (NFS) — 5.1 1.0

The Collins Campground, with frontage on Duckabush River, has 14 sites (maximum trailer length 15 feet) with picnic tables, fire rings, vault toilets and potable water from a hand-pump well.

After you pass Collins Campground you will notice the huge moss-covered boulders which are liberally sprinkled about.

2510

FSR 2510 continues across the Duckabush River for another three tenths of a mile, where it forks. FSR 2530 goes to the right. FSR 2510 bends sharply left to head back to the east along the south bank of the Duckabush River for several miles before turning south to join FSR 25 (Hamma Hamma Road) in about 14 miles.

6.0 0.1

HORSE UNLOADING AREA

The horse unloading area for the Duckabush Trail has a large parking lot, hitching rail, two horse pens and a third that has fallen into disrepair. There is also a clearly marked path up to the trailhead.

6.1   0.0

2510-011

Immediately after the exit to the horse unloading area, FSR 2515-011 branches to the right to take you to the trailhead for the Duckabush Trail.

Don't believe the sign at the beginning of FSR 2510-011 that says that it is .01 miles to the trailhead. It is in fact one tenth of a mile up a fairly steep grade to a large car park and toilet near the trailhead.

DUCKABUSH TRAIL
(22.2 Miles Long)
Trail 803

The Duckabush Trail gains 4,550 feet in elevation as it climbs to O'Neil Pass on the Grand Divide in the National Park. There are a lot of ups and downs along the way though, and obstacles like Big Hump help preserve the solitude of the early parts of the trail. There has been no logging here since early in the century, so even the second growth forests in the first few miles are impressive. One encounters a broad variation in the vegetation and terrain as he passes to the higher altitudes, where snow and ice often prevail until late in the summer. The solitude also increases your chances of observing the wildlife, especially after you cross into the National Park. Motor vehicles, firearms and pets are prohibited on the National Park trails. If you are planning to stay in the park overnight, backcountry permit forms are available at the trailhead in the National Forest. Although the trail is maintained in summer, the climb over Big Hump is steep and loose rock, and erosion west of Big Hump makes travel difficult for stock. Distances and elevations of landmarks are:

Trailhead, FSR 2510 mile 6.1	0.0 Miles	400 Feet
Little Hump	1.2 Miles	900 Feet
Duckabush River	2.4 Miles	700 Feet
Big Hump	3.5 Miles	1700 Feet
Duckabush River	4.8 Miles	1100 Feet
Five Mile Camp	5.3 Miles	1200 Feet
National Park Boundary	6.1 Miles	1300 Feet
Ten Mile Camp	10.0 Miles	1500 Feet
LaCrosse Pass Trail	15.8 Miles	2677 Feet
(6.5 miles long, elevation gain 2900 feet)		

Camp Duckabush	17.5 Miles	2700 Feet
N. Fork Skokomish Trail	17.6 Miles	2700 Feet

(15.6 miles long, elevation gain 3900 feet)

Marmot Lake	21.1 Miles	4350 Feet
LaCrosse Basin Trail	21.1 Miles	4350 Feet

(1.5 miles long, elevation gain 550 feet)

O'Neil Pass	22.2 Miles	4950 Feet

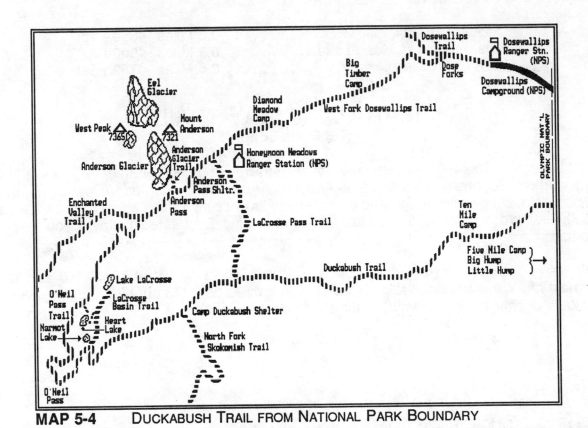

MAP 5-4   DUCKABUSH TRAIL FROM NATIONAL PARK BOUNDARY

After O'Neil Pass the Duckabush Trail becomes the O'Neil Pass Trail (7.4 miles long, 1,750 feet elevation gain) which leads to the Enchanted Valley Trail (18.9 miles long, 3850 feet elevation gain), giving you access to the Quinault area.

LACROSSE PASS TRAIL
(6.5 Miles Long)

The LaCrosse Pass Trail connects the Duckabush Trail to the West Fork Dosewallips Trail near Honeymoon Meadows. The pass itself provides striking views of the snow and ice on the rugged mountains. Distances and elevations are:

Duckabush Trail, mile 15.8	0.0 Miles	2677 Feet
LaCrosse Pass	3.0 Miles	5566 Feet
West Fork Dosewallips Trail	6.5 Miles	3627 Feet

LACROSSE BASIN TRAIL
(1.5 Miles Long)

LaCrosse Basin Trail (550 feet elevation gain) crosses a patch of fantastic subalpine meadow that is often crusted with snow and frozen lakes until late summer. It starts on the Duckabush Trail near Marmot Lake, and takes you to Heart Lake and Lake LaCrosse. There is a steeply descending trail starting from Heart Pass (Heart Lake Way Trail, 0.5 Miles Long, 900 feet elevation loss) which provides a strenuous short-cut to Anderson Pass.

Distances and elevations for LaCrosse Basin Trail are:

Duckabush Trail, mile 21.1	0.0 Miles	4350 Feet
Side path left to Heart Lake	0.5 Miles	4900 Feet
Lake LaCrosse	2.4 Miles	4750 Feet

HEART LAKE WAY TRAIL
(0.5 Miles Long)

Heart Lake Way Trail (900 feet elevation loss) starts from the ridge north of Heart Lake (5170 feet), and cuts four miles off the hike to Anderson Pass and Enchanted Valley for the hardy. This unmaintained trail is rough and very steep in its descent to mile 3.8 of O'Neil Pass Trail (4300 feet). You will miss a pleasant walk overlooking Enchanted Valley if you take the shortcut.

Let's resume our northward journey now. We return to Highway 101 at mile 310.0, and follow it almost four miles to Dosewallips Road. The four miles doesn't count an arduous diversion to Mount Jupiter along the way for some incredible scenery.

		HIGHWAY 101		
		MILES from I-5	MILE NUMBER	
2510	DUCKABUSH ROAD	57.3	310.0	
		57.4	309.9	ROBINSON ROAD
2610-010		57.8	309.5	

MOUNT JUPITER ROAD
To: MT. JUPITER TRAIL - 6.4 mi.

Mount Jupiter Road appears as FSR 2620 on older maps.

MOUNT JUPITER TRAIL
(7.5 Miles Long)
Trail 809

Mount Jupiter Trail is also known as Jupiter Ridge Trail. It has 3600 feet elevation gain, and offers unparalleled views of the Olympics, the Cascades, and even the Coast Range in

British Columbia to those who are prepared to put in the effort. The effort is not just on the trail. The road leading to the trailhead is steep, winding, rough and, in places, difficult to find. Forest Service literature doesn't say "Trailers Prohibited". It says "Trailers Impossible".

To reach the trailhead, located at the end of FSR 2610-011 (Formerly FSR 2620-011) you turn left from Highway 101 into FSR 2610-010 (Formerly FSR 2620). Follow FSR 2610-010 for 3.7 miles to FSR 2610-011 on the left.

(FSR 2610-010 continues for another four and a half miles to join Dosewallips Road, FSR 2610, near Wilson Creek, but it is much easier to get there by returning to Highway 101 rather than persisting on this shocking road.)

FSR 2610-011 is 2.7 miles long. There is a four way intersection 0.5 miles after you join FSR 2610-011. FSR 2610-011 goes to the right at the intersection. Unless you have four wheel drive, you may wish to park here rather than driving to the trailhead, as the road has deep ruts and large bogs that are difficult to pass in wet weather.

Carry plenty of water. There is none on the trail, and after you leave the lower forests, precious little shade. Plan to spend some time at the summit enjoying the cool breeze, listening to the muffled sounds of nature and absorbing the panoramic vistas that are probably the absolute best of any in the peninsula. In the Olympics, Mount Constance and The Brothers command your attention, with hazy glimpses of Seattle's tall buildings in the distance beyond Hood Canal and Puget Sound. The Cascades are visible from Mount Adams and Mount St. Helens in the south. Mount Rainier's looming presence is relatively close by. In the north you can see Mount Baker. On a really clear day, one can see Canada's Coast Range. Distances and elevations along the trail are:

Trailhead, FSR 2610-011 mi. 2.7	0.0 Miles	2000 Feet
National Forest Boundary	1.0 Miles	2850 Feet
Duckabush Valley overlook	3.6 Miles	3300 Feet
Summit of Mount Jupiter	7.1 Miles	5701 Feet
Scramble to Jupiter Lakes	7.5 Miles	4500 Feet

HIGHWAY 101

MILES from I-5	MILE NUMBER	
57.9	309.4	BLACK POINT ROAD
STATE PARK		PLEASANT HARBOR STATE PARK
(Day Use Only)		BLACK POINT GAME RESERVE
		Black Point Resort
58.4	308.9	Pleasant Harbor Marina
59.1	308.2	PLEASANT HARBOR ROAD
59.3	308.0	
ENTER BRINNON		

Dosewallips Grocery, Gas
(Closed due to fire)

59.7   307.6

60.2   307.1   Geoduck Tavern
TAVERN

DOSEWALLIPS STATE PARK   60.3   307.0   DOSEWALLIPS STATE PARK
CAMPGROUND   STATE PARK   BEACH ACCESS (DAY USE)

DOSEWALLIPS STATE PARK

Dosewallips State Park is situated on 514 acres with both Dosewallips River and Hood Canal frontage. It has good views of Mount Walker and Mount Constance. There are 128 campsites (maximum trailer length 36 feet). Forty of the sites (Numbers 1 through 40) have full hook-ups. Other facilities include picnic tables, fire rings, potable water, pay showers, flush toilets and a public boat launch nearby. Boats can be moored at Pleasant Harbor Marine State Park, two miles south. A restaurant, liquor store, post office, general store and service station are located one half mile north of the park.

60.6   306.7
DOSEWALLIPS
RIVER

Flock In Trailer Park   60.8   306.5

Flock in Trailer park has 23 sites,   RV PARK
all with full hook-ups. It has picnic   RESTAURANT
tables, a recreation hall, flush toilets GIFT SHOP
and showers. Halfway House Rest-   POST OFFICE
aurant, a gift shop, a Post Office   LIQUOR STORE
and a liquor store are adjacent and
a general store, and service station
are across the road.

BRINNON LANE   60.9   306.4   Brinnon General Store Chevron
GAS   PROPANE
C-STORE

2610   DOSEWALLIPS ROAD   61.2   306.1
LODGING

Bayshore Motel

FS ROAD 2610 DOSEWALLIPS ROAD

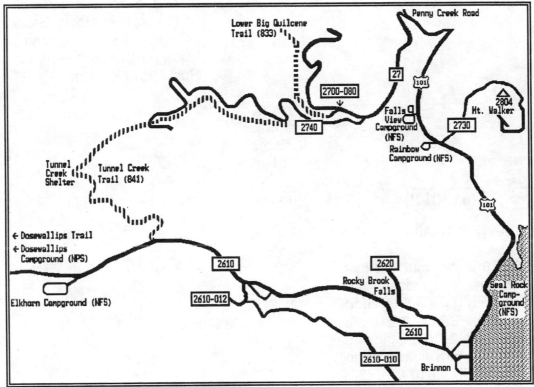

MAP 5-5   FOREST SERVICE ROAD 2610 - DOSEWALLIPS ROAD

Those who wish to continue on Highway 101 may turn to mile 306.1 on page 104.

Dosewallips Road goes to the left, leaving Highway 101 just north of Brinnon. Just after you turn into it, you will see a sign advising you that Dosewallips Ranger Station, Campground and Trailhead are 14.3 miles away. I'm not sure that my observation will add much to plate tectonics theory, but my reckoning shows them having slipped a little further away than that. I reckon that the ranger station and the trailhead to the Dosewallips Trail, on the far side of the campground, are 14.9 miles from Highway 101.

0.0   14.9

The two lane road starts out paved, passing several pleasant looking homes on developed streets in the first half mile or so.

1.0   13.9   ROCKY BROOK ROAD   2620
(Formerly FSR 2621)

3.0   11.9   ROCKY BROOK FALLS

ROCKY BROOK

There is a bridge just past milepost 3, and a turnout west of it. The bridge crosses Rocky Brook. If time permits, take a refreshing break by following the path on your right to Rocky Brook Falls.

5.5   9.4

ENTER NATIONAL

FOREST

2610-010   2610-011   5.9   9.0

MOUNT JUPITER TRAIL

FSR 2610-010 is on your left just past Wilson Creek. It crosses the Dosewallips then goes left to head back to the east. FSR 2610-010 will take you to FSR 2610-011 in 4.5 miles. There you turn right and go to the end of FSR 2610-011 (2.7 Miles) to the trailhead for Mt. Jupiter Trail. After it leaves the National Forest, the road is terrible. It is much easier to go back to Highway 101 and join FSR 2610-010 at mile number 309.5 if you are going to hike the Mount Jupiter Trail. (See page 90 for details of the roads and the fantastic views from Mount Jupiter.)

94

6.8   8.1
BEGIN ONE LANE
GRAVEL ROAD

8.9   6.0

TUNNEL CREEK TRAIL

You will see parking for Tunnel Creek Trail (7.3 miles long, 4,500 ft. elevation gain) before you see the trailhead, which is just beyond the parking area. You would have to be a dedicated masochist to carry a pack from this end. The views from the ridge are probably worth it, but you can save a lot of wear and tear by leaving a car here and starting from the FSR 2740 trailhead. FSR 2740 is reached via Penny Creek Road just south of Quilcene, and FSR 27. See page 110 for description of the trail and access roads.

ELKHORN CAMPGROUND (NFS)

10.6   4.3

Elkhorn Campground is nestled back in the old growth trees on your left. Many campsites face the Dosewallips, which becomes quite broad here. There are 20 sites (maximum trailer length 21 feet) with picnic tables, fire rings, vault toilets and potable water from a hand-pump well. The campsites are large and spaced well apart.

After you leave Elkhorn, the road becomes steeper and narrower, and there is a sign which says, "ROAD NOT SUITABLE FOR TRAILERS". Although there is only one hill, just past Dosewallips Falls, that is steep enough, and narrow enough to be troublesome, I don't recommend towing a trailer past Elkhorn unless you are very proficient at reversing down a steep narrow road if the hill should happen to stop you. Vans and small motor homes should not encounter any difficulty if they are in good mechanical condition. If they do have trouble, at least they are a lot easier to coax back down the hill in reverse.

12.9   2.0
ENTER NATIONAL
PARK

13.1   1.8   LAKE CONSTANCE TRAIL
CONSTANCE CREEK   MOUNT CONSTANCE

LAKE CONSTANCE TRAIL
(2.0 Miles Long)

Lake Constance Trail is extremely steep (elevation gain 3250 feet) and primitive, but you have a good chance of being rewarded with sightings of mountain goats and marmots which are relatively abundant in this area. Experienced climbers may wish to continue past Lake Constance to climb Mount Constance (7743 Feet), the tallest peak in the Eastern Olympics. It is mostly rocky crags and piles of talus, and the climb gets a bit sticky just before you reach the top. You have to decide whether to crab-walk along a tiny ledge; cross a steep, open snowfield; or to turn back when you are so close to success. Distances and elevations along the trail are:

Trailhead	0.0 Miles	1400 Feet
Half Acre Rock	1.0 Miles	3200 Feet
Lake Constance	2.0 Miles	4650 Feet

Unfortunately, camping at Lake Constance is by reservation only, and the lake water is polluted.

DOSEWALLIPS FALLS   13.2   1.7

Dosewallips Falls cascade down several steps where the river is confined in a narrow, steep canyon. The steep hill that I mentioned earlier is next, and, after you level out again, you will see a road leading toward the river on your left. It goes to a horse unloading area.

UPPER JUMPOFF   13.4   1.5
OLD DOSEWALLIPS TRAIL
    (abandoned)

OLD DOSEWALLIPS TRAIL
(1.5 Miles Long)

Old Dosewallips Trail (500 feet elevation loss) a fragment of a trail which started at Elkhorn Campground before the road was extended. The trail has not been maintained in many years and is hard to locate. It starts from the south side of the river just above Dosewallips Falls at Upper Jumpoff. There is no bridge, and it is dangerous to ford the river when it is clouded by glacial silt. At mile 0.3 it passes Muscott Basin Trail on the right, then proceeds for 1.5 miles to FSR 2610 about 0.2 miles after entering the national forest.

MUSCOTT BASIN TRAIL
(2.1 Miles Long)

Muscott Basin Trail (1200 feet elevation gain) goes to the right from Old Dosewallips Trail, 0.3 miles from Upper Jumpoff. The Dosewallips River must be forded, a task that is quite dangerous when the river is clouded by glacial silt. The trail is not maintained and littered with lots of large windfalls. There is a primitive trail to the south side of the river near Dosewallips Campground at mile 1.0., but it is in worse shape than Muscott Basin Trail. The trail ends after 2.1 miles at Muscott Creek. Bits of the old trail can be found for another mile by determined hikers who are prepared to force a path through the thickets.

FS ROAD 2610

	MILES from 101	MILES from END	
DOSEWALLIPS CAMPGROUND (NPS)	14.7 CAMPGROUND	0.2	DOSEWALLIPS CAMPGROUND (NPS)

The Dosewallips Campground with 33 sites (maximum trailer length 21 feet), none with hook-ups, has picnic tables, fire rings, potable water and flush toilets. It is located beside the Dosewallips River. Although there are lots of trees, the campground is large enough to include some broad open areas to drive away the gloom of the dense forest.

	14.9 END OF FSR 2610 DOSEWALLIPS TRAIL	0.0	RANGER STATION (NPS)

RANGER STATION (NPS)

The Dosewallips Trail begins on the west side of the campground near the Ranger Station.

DOSEWALLIPS TRAIL
(15.4 Miles Long)

The Dosewallips Trail (4,250 feet elevation gain) climbs gradually over most of its length until you approach Hayden Pass. It crosses dozens of streams on its way to the source of the Dosewallips River. One of the contributors to the Dosewallips is Silt Creek, which adds the silty melt from Eel Glacier on Mount Anderson. Most of the year the Dosewallips remains clear enough see the bottom so it can be safely forded. On the warms days of summer, however, the melt makes it into a raging torrent, and the silt obscures the slippery rocks and deep holes. When the bottom is obscured, it should be approached with extreme caution. There are many opportunities to enjoy the fragrance and color of the wildflowers, and the sweetness of the berries in late summer in the higher open areas along the trail. In addition to the excellent sample of the interior Olympics vegetation, you may be lucky enough to spot an elk, or even a bear at Soda Springs. The wildlife is attracted to the minerals in the seep water here.

Distances and elevations of points along the trail are as follows:

Trailhead, FSR 2610 mile 14.9	0.0 Miles	1600 Feet
Dose Forks	1.4 Miles	1800 Feet
West Fork Dosewallips Trail	1.4 Miles	1800 Feet
(9.1 Miles Long, 2560 Feet Elevation Gain)		
Soda Springs	2.0 Miles	1970 Feet
Constance Pass Trail - Right	2.5 Miles	2182 Feet
(8.5 Miles Long, 4300 Feet Elevation Gain)		
Camp Marion	8.3 Miles	3400 Feet
Graywolf Trail - Right	9.2 Miles	3660 Feet
(12.9 Miles Long, 4000 Feet Elevation Gain)		
Bear Camp Shelter	11.0 Miles	3850 Feet
Dose Meadow	12.8 Miles	4450 Feet
Lost Pass Trail - Right	12.8 Miles	4450 Feet
(2.8 Miles Long, 5100 Feet Elevation Gain)		
Camp Number Three	14.5 Miles	5300 Feet
Hayden Pass	15.4 Miles	5847 Feet

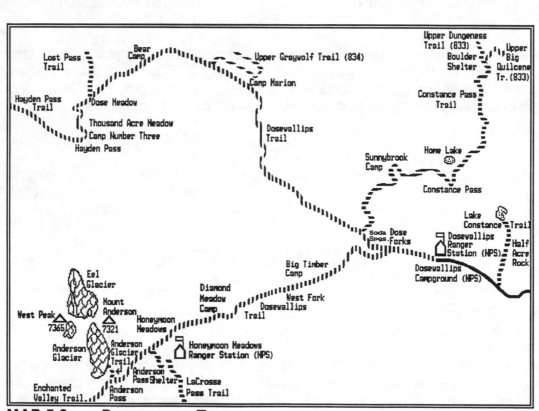

MAP 5-6   DOSEWALLIPS TRAIL

Camp Number Three is a great camp. Most people don't know it is there, and it cannot be seen from the trail so it is often unoccupied. It is hidden above the trail north of a small stream. It is an excellent base for exploring Thousand Acre Meadow, where in late summer you can gather superb huckleberries. Beyond Hayden Pass the trail becomes Hayden Pass Trail and continues on to the Elwha River. The pass is cold and grim, but it gives you excellent views of both valleys — the gentler slopes of the Elwha to the west and the glacier-scooped Dosewallips to the east.

WEST FORK DOSEWALLIPS TRAIL
(9.1 Miles Long)

At Dose Forks, 1.4 miles from the trailhead of Dosewallips Trail, West Fork Dosewallips Trail (2,560 feet elevation gain) starts on your left and goes to Anderson Pass. There it continues as Enchanted Valley Trail (18.2 Miles Long, 3850 Feet Elevation Gain). Enchanted Valley Trail starts from Graves Creek at the end of South Shore Quinault Road. Anderson Glacier Trail (0.7 Miles Long, 700 Feet Elevation Gain) also starts at Anderson Pass, and is a good approach for Eel Glacier and the summits of Mount Anderson. There is a shelter just before Anderson Pass, often referred to as "Camp Siberia" because of the cold winds that sweep down from the nearby glaciers. It is, however, a much better base for climbing Mount Anderson than Flypaper Pass. Flypaper Pass, with an elevation of 6500 feet is always cold, and usually wet.

Distances and elevations along West Fork Dosewallips Trail are:

Dose Forks	0.0 Miles	1800 Feet
West Fork Dosewallips	0.9 Miles	1800 Feet
Big Timber Camp	2.7 Miles	2300 Feet
Diamond Meadow Camp	5.3 Miles	2692 Feet
Honeymoon Meadows	7.5 Miles	3527 Feet
LaCrosse Pass Trail (Left)	7.6 Miles	3627 Feet
(6.5 Miles Long, 3000 Feet Elevation Gain)		
Anderson Pass Shelter	8.3 Miles	4100 Feet
Anderson Pass	9.1 Miles	4464 Feet

ANDERSON GLACIER TRAIL
(0.7 Miles Long)

Anderson Glacier Trail gains 700 feet as it takes you to Anderson Glacier. The glaciers on Mount Anderson are the largest in the Olympics. There are excellent views here, and there is a reasonably good campsite near a small pond beside the lateral moraine. A lake has formed between the glacier and the moraine that is filled with huge chunks of ice. This is also the route to the summits of Mount Anderson. The mountain should be attempted by experienced climbers only, especially the West Peak (7365 Feet), which is steeper and more difficult than the main peak (7321 Feet) or East Peak (6200 Feet).

CONSTANCE PASS TRAIL
(8.5 Miles Long)

The Constance Pass Trail (4,300 feet elevation gain) is called Home Lake Trail, Trail 893, in Forest Service literature. Although this primitive trail climbs without mercy for half its distance, its even surface makes the hike a lot easier than you might expect. At the crest of Del Monte Ridge, you can strike out cross country along the ridge to Gunsight Pass (6350) and Mount Mystery (7631 Feet). Constance Pass marks the end of Del Monte Ridge and the grade down to Boulder Shelter is much gentler. The trail ends at Boulder Shelter in the National Forest at a junction with Upper Dungeness Trail (See page 142) and Upper Big Quilcene Trail (See Page 114).

Distances and elevations along the trail are:

Dosewallips Trail, Mile 2.5	0.0 Miles	2182 Feet
Spring	2.0 Miles	3600 Feet
Sunnybrook Camp	2.5 Miles	5000 Feet
Campsite	3.5 Miles	5650 Feet
Crest of Del Monte Ridge	4.0 Miles	6500 Feet
Constance Pass	5.0 Miles	5850 Feet
Home Lake	5.4 Miles	5350 Feet
National Forest Boundary	7.6 Miles	4850 Feet
Boulder Shelter	8.5 Miles	4950 Feet

LOST PASS TRAIL
(2.8 Miles Long)

At Dose Meadows, 12.8 miles from the trailhead of Dosewallips Trail, Lost Pass Trail (2000 feet elevation gain) climbs sharply to the right, and takes you to Cameron Pass. You will encounter every kind of wildflower imaginable in the broad expanses beyond the beginnings of Lost River. At Three Sons Camp you get good views of Mount Olympus, Mount Anderson, Bailey Range and the Low Divide. You will see the Strait of Juan de Fuca in the distance beyond the Cameron Basin when you reach Cameron Pass. For unrestricted views in all directions, it is an easy stroll to a peak (6733 Feet) just west of the pass. The trail continues past Cameron Pass as Cameron Creek Trail which starts at Three Forks, the junction of the Lower and Upper Graywolf Trails.(See pages 154 and 156 respectively.)

Distances and elevations along Lost Pass Trail are:

Dosewallips Trail - Dose Meadows	0.0 Miles	4450 Feet
Lost Pass	0.9 Miles	5500 Feet
Three Sons Camp	1.7 Miles	5400 Feet
Cameron Pass	2.8 Miles	6450 Feet

We now return to mile 306.1 of Highway 101, and proceed to explore Quilcene and its surroundings.

Storm Clouds over Fallsview Campground on Highway 101.

CHAPTER 6

BIG and LITTLE QUILCENE, SEQUIM BAY

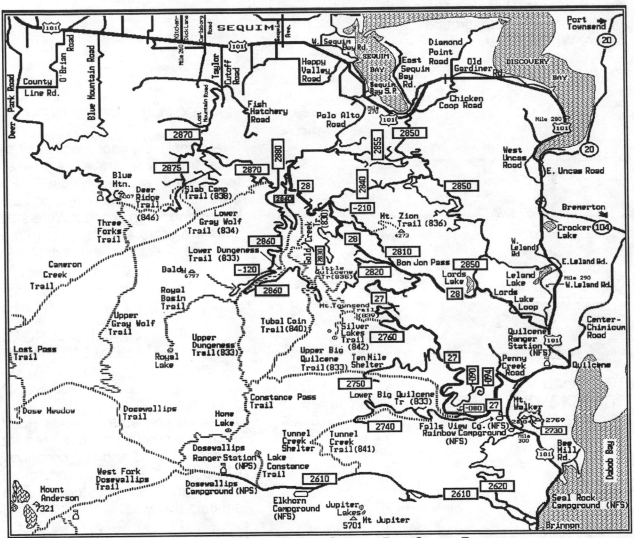

MAP 6-1 HIGHWAY 101 FROM BRINNON TO SEQUIM BAY STATE PARK

There are two arterial roads that cut across the national forest in this area, FSR 27 and FSR 28. Both begin well away from Highway 101, keeping the traffic on the trails to a minimum. Several high vantage points accessible both by road and by trail provide excellent views. You will also see the patchwork designs of the considerable logging activity in the area.

103

We now return to Highway 101 at mile number 306.1 where we left it.

2610	DOSEWALLIPS ROAD	61.2 306.1

2620	ROCKY BROOK ROAD	61.3 306.0
		LEAVING BRINNON

FSR 2620 takes you past a junction with FSR 2610, and eventually returns you to Highway 101 south of Rainbow Campground and Mount Walker.

SMALL TURNOUT

62.1   305.8

61.9   305.4
CAMPGROUND

SEAL ROCK CAMPGROUND (NFS)

Seal Rock Campground has 35 sites (maximum trailer length 21 feet), none with hook-ups. There are picnic tables, fire rings, potable water and flush toilets. Waterside sites are more expensive than the sites not directly on the water.

62.3   305.0
MILEPOST

63.0   304.3

SEAL ROCK ROAD
SMALL TURNOUT

TOG ROAD
BRINNONWOLD ROAD

63.8   303.5
RV PARKING
BOAT LAUNCH

HJELVICS ROAD

Just after you enter Hjelvics Road there is a privately owned area for launching boats and self-contained RV parking. Payment should be made at Hjelvics store before entering the area.

63.9   303.4
C-STORE GAS
HARDWARE STORE

Hjelvics Grocery
& Shell Station

At this point we say goodbye to Hood Canal. The road turns inland until we reach Discovery Bay off the Strait of Juan De Fuca. At Discovery Bay, Highway 101 begins a gradual curve to the west and we begin to see the Olympic Mountains from an entirely different perspective.

64.1	303.2	WAWA POINT ROAD
		Camp Parsons Boy Scout Camp
		BEE MILL ROAD
		WHITNEY POINT
		STATE SHELLFISH LABORATORY

64.3	303.0	Cove Grocery & Unocal 76
C-STORE PHONE		Cove RV Park
GAS PROPANE		
RV PARK		

64.5	302.8	SLOW VEHICLE TURNOUT
64.8	302.5	TURNOUT

TURNOUT

65.7	301.6	MOUNT WALKER ROAD

This is not the road to the top of Mt. Walker. See mile 299.8.

The Store

This looks like a fascinating curiosity shop, but it has never been open when I passed.

66.3	301.0	
ANTIQUE SHOP		

66.6	300.7	BUCKHORN ROAD

67.3	300.0	Dodee's Trading Post
MILEPOST		Antiques & Collectibles
ANTIQUE SHOP		

2620 ROCKY BROOK ROAD
UPPER TUNNEL CREEK ROAD

67.4	299.9

FSR 2620 writhes its way to FSR 2610, Dosewallips Road, then continues to Highway 101 near the FSR 2610 junction.

67.5   299.8 | 2730 | WALKER MOUNTAIN ROAD

MOUNT WALKER VIEWPOINT - 5 Mi.
MOUNT WALKER TRAIL   - 0.3 Mi.

After passing the trailhead for Mt. Walker Trail, FSR 2730 goes on to the top of Mt. Walker.

TRAILS ON HIGHWAY 101

MOUNT WALKER TRAIL
(2.0 Miles Long)
Trail 894

Mount Walker is the only peak facing the Puget Sound with a road all the way to its summit. For the more energetic there is also Mount Walker Trail (2.0 miles long, 2,000 feet elevation gain), a very pleasant uphill hike to the north viewpoint (2804 Feet). The trailhead is on your right, 0.3 miles after you turn into Walker Mountain Road.

By car, the north viewpoint is to the left when Walker Mountain Road forks near the top. From the north viewpoint you can see several peaks in the Olympics; all the nearby communities from Quilcene to Port Townsend; the Hood Canal Floating Bridge; and Mount Baker in the Cascades. The south viewpoint (2759 Feet), is located at the end of the right branch of FSR 2730, 0.5 miles from the north viewpoint. From the south viewpoint you can see Mount Rainier; Seattle; Tacoma; Bangor Submarine Base; Bremerton; and Bainbridge Island.

RAINBOW CAMPGROUND (NFS)
RAINBOW CANYON TRAIL

67.6   299.7

CAMPGROUND

Rainbow Campground has 9 sites (none large enough for trailers and no hook-ups). It has picnic tables, fire rings, a hiking trail, potable water and pit toilets.

RAINBOW CANYON NATURE TRAIL
(0.5 Miles Long)
Trail 892

Rainbow Canyon Trail (125 feet elevation gain on the return journey) leaves from the northwest corner of Rainbow Campground. It is a delightful walk in a tall stand of Douglas Fir, past a nice waterfall on Elbo Creek, down to a bend in the Big Quilcene River where the canyon walls are covered in ferns and vine maple.

	MILES from I-5	MILE NUMBER
SOUTHBOUND SLOW VEHICLE TURNOUT	67.8	299.5
TURNOUT	67.9	299.4
TURNOUT	68.4	298.9
	68.5	298.8	TURNOUT
TURNOUT	68.7	298.6
FALLSVIEW CAMPGROUND (NFS) FALLSVIEW LOOP TRAIL FALLSVIEW CANYON TRAIL	69.0 CAMPGROUND	298.3

Fallsview Campground has 35 sites (21 feet maximum trailer length), none with hook-ups. It has picnic tables, fire rings, potable water and pit toilets.

There are two trails starting from the Fallsview Campground parking lot. Both are suitable for inexperienced hikers. To reach them, you turn left immediately after entering the campground. When the road forks to become a one way loop, turn right. Shortly, the road curves to the left, taking you to a parking area for the trails.

FALLSVIEW LOOP NATURE TRAIL
(0.1 Mile Long)
Trail 848

Fallsview Loop Trail (0.1 mile long) is on your right. It is a short loop to two viewpoints. On the opposite side of a steep narrow canyon, you will see a beautiful waterfall plunging about 150 feet into the Big Quilcene River. The second viewpoint is the more spectacular of the two. The viewpoints are fenced and there are cozy picnic tables sequestered in the foliage nearby.

FALLSVIEW CANYON TRAIL
(0.6 Miles Long)
Trail 868

From the parking area, Fallsview Canyon Trail is on your left. It goes down to a point where the Big Quilcene River smashes into a large rock that diverts its course. Although the trail is a bit steep, there are wooden handrails. At the bottom, near the river, the trail goes over a plank bridge to your left, following the river. At the end of the maintained trail, a narrow track continues up the hillside but becomes difficult to find, and finally disappears in 0.3 miles.

	HIGHWAY 101		
	MILES from I-5	MILE NUMBER	
	69.4	297.9	
	LEAVE OLYMPIC NATIONAL FOREST		
TURNOUT	69.6	297.7	
HIDDENDALE DRIVE	69.9	297.4	
TURNOUT	70.4	296.9	
QUILCENE HATCHERY ROAD QUILCENE NATIONAL FISH HATCHERY	70.6 BIG QUILCENE R.	296.7	
TURNOUT	70.8	296.5	
SOUTHBOUND SLOW VEHICLE TURNOUT	70.9	296.4	
FOREST LANE	71.0	296.3	
	71.1	296.2	DUTCH LANE SLOW VEHICLE TURNOUT
via PENNY CREEK ROAD	71.2	296.1	

FS ROAD 27   BIG QUILCENE

	DISTANCE FROM HIGHWAY 101
TUNNEL CREEK TRAIL	11.2 Mi.
LOWER BIG QUILCENE TRAIL	5.3 Mi.
UPPER BIG QUILCENE TRAIL	15.5 Mi.
MOUNT TOWNSEND TRAIL	14.6 Mi.
FOREST SERVICE ROAD 28	17.5 Mi.
BON JON PASS	18.8 Mi.

MAP 6-2   FOREST SERVICE ROAD 27, BIG QUILCENE RIVER

FSR 27 begins at the National Forest boundary, 3.3 miles from Highway 101. It is paved for most of its length, and its distance from Highway 101 helps to reduce the traffic on the trails. The fact that Penny Creek Road has no street sign, and the Forest Service's recent re-numbering of the roads add to your solitude on the trails. You will however, see a lot of logging trucks, as there is extensive logging in this area.

To reach the beginning of FSR 27 from northbound Highway 101, turn left at mile 296.1 into Penny Creek Road. Be alert for the turn, as there was no sign marking it last time I passed there. If you miss the turn and have to come back, Penny Creek Road is 0.9 miles west of the Quilcene Forest Service Ranger Station.

Penny Creek Road starts out as a two lane paved road. You will see a street sign 0.4 miles after you leave Highway 101 at a fork in front of a stable and a two story farmhouse. The road on the left goes to the National Fish Hatchery. To go to FSR 27 stay to the right and follow Penny Creek Road for another mile (1.4 miles from Highway 101), until it forks again. At this fork, both roads become one lane with turnouts and have a gravel surface.

Penny Creek Road goes to the right at the fork. You should go to the left. The road to the left is not marked, but there is a sign indicating that Big Quilcene and Mount Townsend Trails are 14 miles to the left. You should turn left and go another 1.9 miles (3.3 miles from Highway 101) to the beginning of FSR 27 and the Olympic National Forest boundary. Although the roadway continues to be one lane with turnouts, the pavement resumes here, and it is clearly marked FSR 27.

Those who wish to continue on Highway 101 may turn to mile 296.1 on page 117.

FS ROAD 27	
MILE	MILES
NUMBER	from
	FSR 28

0.0	17.5

ENTER OLYMPIC
NATIONAL FOREST

2700-042   0.4   17.1

2700-170   0.8   16.7

2740   1.2   16.3

TUNNEL CREEK TRAIL - 6.7 Miles

TUNNEL CREEK TRAIL
(7.3 Miles Long)
Trail 841

Tunnel Creek Trail (2,450 feet elevation gain to Tunnel Creek Ridge) is well maintained, but it has a rough tread past Harrison Lake. The trail has a 20% maximum grade when it is hiked from this trailhead. From the Dosewallips Road (FSR 2610) end, the average grade is 40% for the first three miles. Unless you have a compelling reason to do otherwise, you should hike this trail from this end. Many hikers park a car at the Dosewallips Road trailhead to avoid the steep return journey. There is a campsite just across the road from the Dosewallips trailhead, so one can stop overnight and start the return journey fully rested. You will encounter fantastic views of several peaks on this trail. The view of Mount Constance's barren, vertical east face is unobscured as you come within two miles of it. From Tunnel Creek Ridge you will be able to see the Cascades, Hood Canal and Puget Sound when the weather is clear. Distances and elevations along the trail are as follows:

FSR 2740 Trailhead	0.0 Miles	2600 Feet
Tunnel Creek Shelter	2.7 Miles	3750 Feet
Harrison Lake (Campsite)	3.7 Miles	4750 Feet
Gamm Creek	6.2 Miles	2750 Feet
FSR 2610 Trailhead	7.3 Miles	500 Feet

The FSR 2740 trailhead is 6.7 miles from FSR 27. There is a primitive campsite on the right, just after you cross the Big Quilcene River Bridge 1.8 miles from FSR 27. The campsite is at the end of a lane leading down to the river to the left of the road-level parking area. There are two forks in FSR 2740 before you reach the trailhead. FSR 2740-060 goes to the right and steeply uphill at mile 3.4 of FSR 2740 and FSR 2740-110 goes to the right at mile 4.7

The sign marking the trailhead, on the right at mile 6.7, is set back some distance from where FSR 2740 makes a sharp bend to the left. A primitive road leads down to the creek just in front of the trailhead.

The FSR 2610 trailhead is nine miles west of mile 306.1 of Highway 101.

We now return to mile 1.2 of FSR 27.

FS ROAD 27	
MILE NUMBER	MILES from FSR 28

2740

TUNNEL CREEK TRAIL ·

1.2   16.3

2700-080

LOWER BIG QUILCENE TRAIL
BIG QUILCENE CAMP

1.6   15.9

Big Quilcene Camp is 0.4 miles to the left, at the end of FSR 2700-080. There are two campsites with fireplaces and picnic tables and a stylish vault toilet with a Mansard roof. You will hear the river softly murmuring far below. At night, the soft glow in the valley to the east looks like an extraterrestrial's space ship that may arrive at any moment. The glow is, in fact, reflected light pollution from Quilcene, more than six miles away.

LOWER BIG QUILCENE TRAIL
(6.0 Miles Long)
Trail 833

The Lower Big Quilcene Trail (1,300 feet elevation gain, 25% maximum grade) follows the Big Quilcene River to FSR 2750 where it has an unmarked trailhead near Ten Mile Shelter and the Upper Big Quilcene Trail trailhead. This trail gives you a close-up look at logging. You will see old second growth that almost appears to be virgin forest when seen in the distance. You will also see the desolation of recent clear cuts. Between the two extremes you pass through a "partial cut" where the desolation is softened by the many trees that were left standing. The ground in the partial cut is still heaped with slash, and chutes, where the logs were dragged uphill to the road, still cut the trail from time to time. The trail is well maintained, but the bridges are not all safe for motorbikes. Distances and elevations are:

Big Quilcene Campground	0.0 Miles	1300 Feet
Access Trail from FSR 2740	0.7 Miles	1300 Feet
Path to Bark Shanty Camp	2.4 Miles	1500 Feet
Path to Camp Jolley	4.5 Miles	2000 Feet
FSR 2750, Ten Mile Shelter	6.0 Miles	2500 Feet

There are three places to begin this hike. To reach the best, turn left from FSR 27 into FSR 2700-080 at mile 1.6, and follow it for 0.4 miles to its end at Big Quilcene Camp. The trail starts from the west end of the campground, and is a continuation of the road, which was once known as Bark Shanty Road. It was closed many years ago, and Mother Nature has laid such a thick carpet of vegetation over it in the intervening years that is often difficult to imagine that it was ever anything but deep forest.

Second choice, if Big Quilcene Camp is fully occupied, is to go back to FSR 27, turn right and go four tenths of a mile back to FSR 2740. Turn right again into FSR 2740 and follow it 1.8 miles to a primitive camp on the west side of the Quilcene River Bridge. On your right, you will see a small road leading down to the river to the left of a parking area. You can camp here overnight, and in the morning walk back up FSR 2740 the way you came until you see a chain link fence and a sign marking the Big Quilcene Watershed on your right. Directly opposite the sign, on your left, is an abandoned road that will take you one tenth of a mile up to intercept the Lower Big Quilcene Trail at mile 0.7. You turn left at the junction, and, in a few minutes, you will confirm that you are on the right track when you see a weather beaten sign marking the Municipal Watershed for the City of Port Townsend.

The third option is to start from the upper trailhead, 4.7 miles from FSR 27 on FSR 2750, near Ten Mile Shelter and the trailhead for Upper Big Quilcene Trail. (See page 113)

We will now return to FSR 27 at mile 1.6, the junction with FSR 2700-080.

FS ROAD 27	
MILE	MILES
NUMBER	from
	FSR 28
1.6	15.9

2700-080

LOWER BIG QUILCENE TRAIL
BIG QUILCENE CAMP

VIEWPOINT

2.7   14.8

Here you will see a large flat area, on your left. This is a good place for photographs of the snowy ridge to the west.

3.5   14.0

2700·090

BIG QUILCENE RIDGE LOOKOUT

BIG QUILCENE RIDGE LOOKOUT

You should not miss this lookout. Apart from the fantastic view, you will marvel at the way this one lane gravel road clings precariously to the side of the mountain. The road looks awfully narrow, and the distance that you would free-fall before you hit anything in the gorge below is likely to make you feel a little uneasy. I met a log truck as I came down and we were able to pass between turnouts with little difficulty. Deer, scampering up the mountain side and bounding across the road, didn't seem to notice the steepness.

You will pass FSR 2700-091 1.3 miles from FSR 27. Two miles from FSR 27, FSR 2700-090 continues straight ahead to a logging site.

FSR 2700-094 takes you to the right, up the hill in an ever decreasing corkscrew, to a turn-around at the top. The top is 2.5 miles from FSR 27. The view is spectacular, with the Cascades to the east, and the Olympics to the west.

4.0   13.5

2700·100

2750

7.5   10.0

UPPER BIG QUILCENE TRAIL
LOWER BIG QUILCENE TRAIL
TEN MILE SHELTER

Ten Mile Shelter is set back from the road on the right, 4.7 miles from FSR 27. It is nestled among the trees and not visible from the road until you are directly in front of it, just west of Wet Weather Creek. There is a fire ring in front of the shelter and a vault toilet a short distance behind it.

UPPER BIG QUILCENE TRAIL
(6.7 Miles Long)
Trail 833

The Upper Big Quilcene Trail (3,500 feet elevation gain, 30% maximum grade) takes you to the cold winds of Marmot Pass and a junction with Tubal Cain Trail. It then continues on, to join Constance Pass Trail (a.k.a. Home Lake Trail) and the Upper Dungeness Trail at Boulder Shelter. This trail offers you a good look at the high country meadows that are awash with wildflowers in the summer, and close-up looks at Buckhorn and Iron Mountains. Parts of these mountains come right down to the trail — as boulders in the avalanches that can occur until late spring. Distances and elevations along the trail are:

FSR 2750, Ten Mile Shelter	0.0 Miles	2500 Feet
Path to Shelter Rock Camp (Left)	2.6 Miles	3650 Feet
Camp Mystery	4.6 Miles	5400 Feet
Marmot Pass, Tubal Cain Trail	5.3 Miles	6000 Feet
(8.8 miles long, 3,000 feet elevation gain)		
Boulder Shelter	6.7 Miles	4950 Feet
Constance Pass Trail	6.7 Miles	4950 Feet
(8.5 miles long, 4,300 feet elevation gain)		
Upper Dungeness Trail	6.7 Miles	4950 Feet
(6.3 miles long, 2,450 feet elevation gain)		

To reach the trailhead, turn left into FSR 2750 at mile 7.5 of FSR 27. Go 4.7 miles on FSR 2750 to Ten Mile Shelter and the trailhead, both on the right, just beyond Wet Weather Creek. The unmarked trailhead for Lower Quilcene Trail is on your left, opposite the sign for the Upper Big Quilcene Trail.

We will now return to mile 7.5 of FSR 27.

	FS ROAD 27	
	MILE	MILES
	NUMBER	from
		FSR 28

2750
UPPER BIG QUILCENE TRAIL
LOWER BIG QUILCENE TRAIL
TEN MILE SHELTER

              7.5   10.0

2760
MOUNT TOWNSEND TRAIL

              10.5   7.0

MOUNT TOWNSEND TRAIL
(6.3 Miles Long)
Trail 839

In June and July, the Mount Townsend Trail (2,780 feet elevation gain, 30% maximum grade) takes you through a marvelous display of rhododendrons on the way to the summits of Mount Townsend. The summits are really only the high points of a rather flat portion of the ridge. The trail divides, with the south summit to your right and the north summit to your left. The trails rejoin beyond the summits. The south summit is at an elevation of 6280 feet, and the north summit is at 6212 feet. They offer excellent vistas of many of the most impressive mountains in the Olympics. When you have satisfied your appetite for the nearby mountains, turn 180 degrees to look at Puget Sound, Discovery Bay and the Cascades. Sometimes you can see all the way to Mount St. Helens, and make out the faint outlines of Seattle. Large birds often come here to practice their wheeling and soaring on Mount Townsend's strong winds. Distances and elevations along the trail are:

FSR 2760 Trailhead	0.0 Miles	2850 Feet
Sink Lake Shelter	0.5 Miles	3000 Feet
Old FSR 2700-190 Trailhead	1.0 Miles	3250 Feet
Path to Camp Windy	3.6 Miles	5300 Feet
Silver Lakes Trail (Left)	4.0 Miles	5650 Feet
(2.5 Miles Long, 250 Feet Elevation Loss)		
Summit Ridge, Trail Divides	5.0 Miles	6250 Feet
(Main Trail Left, North Summit Right)		
Little Quilcene Trail	6.3 Miles	5275 Feet
(4.2 Miles Long, 1100 Feet Elevation Gain)		

The trailhead for this hike is in FSR 2760. To reach it, turn left at mile 10.5 of FSR 27, into FSR 2760. The trailhead is on your right, 0.8 miles from FSR 27. There is a long turnout, on the left just before you reach the trailhead, that will accommodate several cars if it is not full with logging equipment. There is parking for one car at the trailhead.

There is another trailhead at the end of FSR 2700-190, if it has not been closed. FSR 2700-190 is a very rough and narrow road hewn out of the side of the mountain 1.2 miles past FSR 2760, at mile 11.7 of FSR 27. After you turn left, you will find the trailhead 0.7 miles from FSR 27.

SILVER LAKES TRAIL
(2.5 Miles Long)
Trail 839

Four tenths of a mile past Camp Windy on the Mount Townsend Trail, Silver Lakes Trail (250 feet elevation loss) goes to the left. It takes you to the larger of the two lakes. Both lakes have trout, and there is a path around the larger one. There are huge boulders scattered about the surrounding meadow. Diving Rock, at the southeast corner of the lake is sometimes used by swimmers in summer. Another path takes you to a campsite north of the lake, then about a quarter of a mile beyond the campsite to the other lake.

We now return to mile 10.5 of FSR 27.

2760

MOUNT TOWNSEND TRAIL

10.5 7.0

2700·190

MOUNT TOWNSEND TRAIL

11.7 5.8
PAVEMENT ENDS

A second trailhead for Mount Townsend Trail is at the end of this narrow, rough road, 0.7 miles from FSR 27.

12.0 5.5   **2700·212**

2700·220

16.5 1.0   **2700·330**

28   BON JON PASS   17.5 0.0   LORDS LAKE   **28**
To: MOUNT ZION TRAIL   END OF FS ROAD 27
To: LITTLE QUILCENE TRAIL

2800·080

FSR 27 ends here at its junction with FSR 28, 1.3 miles south of Bon Jon Pass. FSR 28 starts at the end of Palo Alto Road, 7.6 miles from Highway 101 east of Sequim, and goes 14.5 miles to Lord's Lake Loop Road, 3.4 miles from Highway 101 north of Quilcene.

Mount Zion Trail (1.8 miles long, 1325 feet elevation gain) and Little Quilcene Trail (4.2 miles long, 1075 feet elevation gain) are somewhat isolated from the other trails that use Palo Alto Road and FSR 28 for access.

To reach Mount Zion Trail from here, proceed 1.3 miles to Bon Jon Pass on FSR 28. At Bon Jon Pass, turn right into FSR 2810, and follow it for 2.0 miles to the trailhead on your right. There is a parking area on your left, just across the road from the trailhead. (See page 120 for discussion of this trail and its access via Lords Lake Loop Road.)

To reach the Little Quilcene Trail from here go 1.6 miles to the left (0.3 miles beyond Bon Jon Pass) on FSR 28 to FSR 2820 on your left. Follow FSR 2820 for 4.0 miles to the trailhead on your right. The trailhead is at 4200 feet elevation, and often gets snow late in the spring that makes the road treacherous in places. Details on Little Quilcene Trail begin on page 120.

We now return to Highway 101 at mile 296.1 just south of Quilcene.

	HIGHWAY 101		
	MILES from I-5	MILE NUMBER	
PENNY CREEK ROAD	71.2	296.1	
PETE BECK ROAD	71.4	295.9	PETE BECK ROAD
	71.5	295.8	GLENLOGIE ROAD
DEEMA SMACKMAN ROAD DEEMA SMACKMAN MEMORIAL FIELD Timber House Lounge and Rest.	71.7 RESTAURANT LOUNGE RV PARK	295.6	Tranquilscene RV & Trailer Park
QUILCENE RANGER STATION (NFS)	72.1 RANGER STATION LODGING	295.2	Maple Grove Motel

QUILCENE BUSINESS DISTRICT

JEFFERSON COUNTY CAMPGROUND	72.3 MILEPOST 295 CAMPGROUND RESTAURANT PHONE GAS	295.0	Loggers Landing Restaurant Texaco Service Station

The Jefferson County Campground in Quilcene has 12 campsites (no hook-ups), picnic tables, fireplaces, a picnic shelter, a water tap and vault toilets.

WASHINGTON STREET

ROBERTS ROAD

OLD CHURCH ROAD COUNTRY MARKET FAIR	72.4 2nd HAND SHOP TAVERN POST OFFICE	294.9	Whistling Oyster Tavern POST OFFICE
	72.5 2nd HAND SHOP	294.8	RODGERS STREET Second Hand Palace is behind the Post Office in Rodgers St. Quilcene Cafe (closed)

ROSE STREET   ROSE STREET

Chevron Service Station	72.6 294.7	SCHOOL
	GAS LIQUOR	
HERBERT STREET		
Liquor Store		
Peninsula Foods	72.7 294.6	Shell Service Station
	C-STORE	
BOWEN STREET	GAS DIESEL	CENTER CHIMACUM ROAD
	BANK	PORT LUDLOW
		INDIAN ISLAND
		U.S. Bank

Traffic here is less congested than in most towns. I once saw a deer ambling across the highway in front of the bank at the 9:00 A.M. rush hour.

WASHINGTON STREET	72.8 294.5	
	BOOK STORE	
Mary's Used Books & Videos	VIDEOS	
COLUMBIA STREET	72.9 294.4	COLUMBIA STREET
WALKER ROAD	73.1 294.2	Mary's Village Store/Texaco
	GAS PROPANE	
	C-STORE PHONE	
QUILCENE CEMETERY ROAD	73.2 294.1	
SHADY LANE		
OLD STATE HIGHWAY	73.5 293.8	
Granny's Antiques Collectibles	73.7 293.6	
Furniture and Glassware	LITTLE QUILCENE	
	RIVER	
WILD WOOD ROAD	LEAVE QUILCENE	
	ANTIQUE SHOP	
	74.1 293.2	Second Time Around Antique Shop
	ANTIQUE SHOP	(a.k.a. Juel's Jenuine Junque)

	HIGHWAY 101 MILES from I-5	MILE NUMBER	
RICE'S LAKE ROAD	74.3	293.0	RICE'S LAKE ROAD
28 via LORDS LAKE LOOP ROAD	74.5	292.8	

BON JON PASS
OLD LELAND VALLEY ROAD

Lords Lake Loop and Old Leland Valley Road both start here. Lord's Lake Loop is to the left of Old Leland Valley Road.

FS ROAD 28 LITTLE QUILCENE

DISTANCE FROM
HIGHWAY 101

BON JON PASS . . . . 8.6 Miles
MOUNT ZION TRAIL . . . . 10.7 Miles
LITTLE QUILCENE TRAIL . . . . 13.0 Miles
HIGHWAY 101, MILE 267.4 . . . . 25.4 Miles

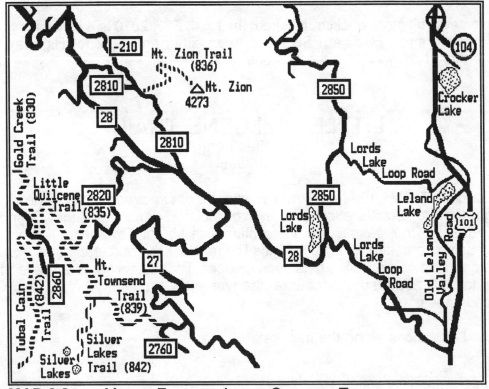

MAP 6-3   MOUNT ZION AND LITTLE QUILCENE TRAILS

Mount Zion Trail and Little Quilcene Trail are somewhat isolated from the other trails that use Palo Alto Road near Sequim and FSR 28 for access. Although both trails can be reached from the Dungeness Valley end of FSR 28, most people leave Highway 101 here, taking Lord's Lake Loop for 3.3 miles to the Lords Lake end of FSR 28. It is then another 5.3 miles to Bon Jon Pass on FSR 28. From Bon Jon Pass, Mount Zion Trail is two miles to the right on FSR 2810. The trailhead is on the right and a parking area is across the road on the left.

To get to Little Quilcene Trail from Bon Jon Pass, continue on FSR 28 for another 0.3 miles beyond Bon Jon Pass, where you turn left into FSR 2820. The trailhead is on the right 4.0 miles from FSR 28. There is a small parking area near the trailhead.

The road that goes to the right at Lords Lake is FSR 2850. It meanders for 13 miles before returning you to mile 271.3 of Highway 101 at the south end of Sequim Bay. (See page 127.)

MOUNT ZION TRAIL
(1.8 miles Long)
Trail 836

Even from the road, before you get to the trailhead, there are excellent views of snowy peaks and sheer rock faces. There are also views of large clear-cuts. The Mount Zion Trail (1,325 feet elevation gain, 15% maximum grade) is not as difficult as you envision when you see the "Mount" in its name. From the trailhead at 2950 feet, it climbs steadily, but not steeply, all the way to the top. There are campsites at the top where the trail comes out in to the open, but be sure to bring water. The trail takes you through lovely stands of rhododendrons which bloom in June and July. The views from the summit (4273 feet) include the Olympic peaks, the Strait of San Juan de Fuca, Mount Baker and Puget Sound.

If you want to see a bit more backcountry from the road, FSR 2810 is a loop road that returns to FSR 28 at both ends. Back at FSR 28 you can either turn right for Highway 101 near Sequim or left for Highway 101 near Quilcene.

LITTLE QUILCENE TRAIL
(4.2 Miles Long)
Trail 835

The Little Quilcene Trail (1,100 feet elevation gain, maximum grade 35%) starts off in a clear cut, then goes on to provide excellent views of Mount Townsend, Puget Sound and the Cascades. After the trail passes the intersection with Mount Townsend Trail its condition deteriorates as you proceed along Dirty Face Ridge. Near the end, each time you complain about the steepness of the trail, it gets even steeper. The last mile has a grade of 35%, as it descends to FSR 2860, so expect to re-discover every problem you have ever had with your toes and knees.

Distances and elevations along the trail are:

FSR 2820 Trailhead	0.0 Miles	4200 Feet
Little River Summit	0.9 Miles	4800 Feet
Mt. Townsend Trail (Left)	2.0 Miles	5275 Feet
FSR 2860 Trailhead	4.2 Miles	3400 Feet

Be prepared for bad weather here. My first attempt at hiking the Little Quilcene Trail was frustrated by snow in May. If bad weather blocks your progress by car, FSR 2800-080 has been closed 0.8 miles from FSR 28, and provides a good parking place whilst you proceed on foot. I was fascinated by the bad weather. The road flattens out near a pass about two thirds of the way to the trailhead. You can witness the precipitation being wrung out of the clouds as they pass from one valley to the other.

Let's return now to Highway 101, and continue our northward journey.

	HIGHWAY 101		
	MILES from I-5	MILE NUMBER	
28 via LORDS LAKE LOOP ROAD BON JON PASS OLD LELAND VALLEY ROAD	74.5	292.8	
	74.9	292.4	SLOW VEHICLE TURNOUT
TURNOUT	75.1	292.2	
SOUTHBOUND SLOW VEHICLE TURNOUT	76.4	290.9	
LELAND CUTOFF LAKE LELAND - PUBLIC FISHING	77.2	290.1	
	77.3	290.0 MILEPOST	
WEST LELAND VALLEY ROAD LELAND LAKE CAMPGROUND & BOAT LAUNCH (Jefferson County)	78.3 RV PARKING CAMPGROUND BOAT LAUNCH	289.0	EAST LELAND VALLEY ROAD

As you turn left into W. Leland Valley Road there is a small, adults only RV Park for self-contained units on the right.

Leland Lake Campground and Boat Launch, operated by Jefferson County, is 0.3 miles from the intersection. The boat launch and dock are to your right, and the campground is to your left. The campground is located on a grassy knoll and, in contrast to the dark forest, has a feeling of spaciousness.

There are 22 sites (no hook-ups), picnic tables, fireplaces and pit toilets. There is a sign near a hand pump stating: "WATER UNSAFE TO DRINK". Firewood is available from the campground host.

SNOW CREEK ROAD	78.7	288.6	
BOULTON ROAD	79.3	288.0	
WEST LELAND VALLEY ROAD	79.4	287.9	EAST LELAND VALLEY ROAD
WEST LELAND VALLEY ROAD	80.3	287.0	
	81.0 BOAT LAUNCH	286.3	CROCKER LAKE BOAT LAUNCH

This boat launch is operated by Jefferson County. There are pit toilets at the south end of the parking lot. Public fishing is allowed. The area is closed from 10 PM to 4 AM.

Snow Creek Ranch Campsites (self contained)	81.3 RV PARKING	286.0	
	81.6	285.7	FULLER ROAD

(104) EAST   HOOD CANAL BRIDGE   KITSAP PENINSULA   BREMERTON   SEATTLE FERRY   82.3 MILEPOST   285.0

This is not an error. You do turn left to go east on WA 104.

WEST UNCAS ROAD   83.3   284.0

122

MILES from I-5	MILE NUMBER	
83.6	283.7	EAST UNCAS ROAD
84.0	283.3	
84.3	283.0	DISCOVERY BAY
84.5	282.8	EAST UNCAS ROAD
84.6	282.7	ⓨ PORT TOWNSEND

TURNOUT

DISCOVERY BAY

EAST

NATIONAL HISTORIC DISTRICT
WHIDBEY ISLAND FERRY
HOSPITAL

PORT TOWNSEND

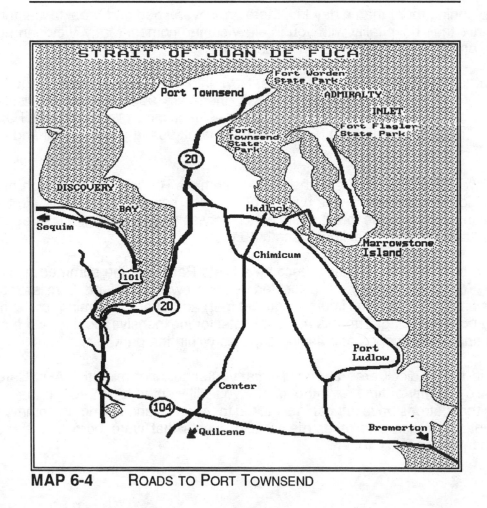

MAP 6-4   ROADS TO PORT TOWNSEND

You are only 13 miles from Port Townsend, and if you can fit a day into your schedule to see this marvelously well preserved Victorian seacoast town, you will find it well worth the effort.

Port Townsend was named by Captain George Vancouver in 1792 and settled by Alfred Plummer and Charles Bachelder in 1851. It prospered as the main port of entry into Puget Sound well into the 1880's when the population reached 7,000.

When the intercontinental railroads started creeping across the prairies, then crossed the Rocky Mountains, everyone in Port Townsend geared up for acceleration of the area's rapid growth in anticipation of being named the Northwest rail terminus. Planning was based on population forecasts of at least 20,000 when the railroad came. Developers started building more Victorian mansions uptown, and erecting elegant stone and brick commercial buildings downtown as they dreamed of Port Townsend's participation in the railroad boom. The dreams of grandeur faded in 1890 when the railroads chose Seattle for the terminus and the shipping boom shifted to the other side of Puget Sound.

In 1976 the downtown waterfront area and the residential area on the bluff overlooking it were designated a National Historic District. With the inclusion of Fort Worden, it has also been designated a National Landmark. Stop at the Tourist Information Office maintained by the Chamber of Commerce at 2437 Sims Way (State Highway 20) on your way into Port Townsend for a Historic Tour Map with comments on over 70 historic homes, buildings and other attractions in the city. Forty of the buildings in the downtown area have been included in the National Register of Historic Places.

If you are planning more than a day trip, there are several bed and breakfast establishments that will share their hospitality with you in old Victorian homes. Many Victorian hotel rooms and apartments are also available on a casual basis.

Twenty-four of the homes along Officers Row in Fort Worden State Park have been converted into tourist accommodation. In all, there are 99 buildings on display at Fort Worden, the high point being the commandant's residence. Fort Worden State Park also has 50 RV sites (maximum length 50 feet) all with full hook-ups, a youth hostel and conference facilities.

There are two more State Parks in the area which have RV facilities, although neither have hook-ups. Old Fort Townsend was built in 1859,and is now included in Old Fort Townsend State Park. In addition to the fort, it offers beach access and clamming. It is three miles south of town and has 40 sites (maximum length 40 feet).

Fort Flagler, built in 1898, has also become a State Park. It is the summer music camp for the Seattle Youth Symphony. It is located on Marrowstone Island 8 miles northeast of Hadlock. It has 116 sites (maximum length 50 feet) and offers clamming, crabbing, salmon fishing and bottom fishing. There is a youth hostel for inexpensive lodging and a concession store sells snacks, groceries and fishing supplies within the park.

If you are in the Hadlock area at dinner time, you should not miss the Ajax Cafe in Lower Hadlock. Allow plenty of time for it though, as you will want to look through the hundreds of mementos that patrons have left behind, tacked to the walls and ceiling, to commemorate the engagements, divorces and other memorable events that were born in the magic of an evening spent at the Ajax Cafe.

If you can tear yourself away from the lovely shops (many); museums (4); restaurants (more than 20); golf courses (3); tennis courts (16); and historical attractions of Port Townsend, we will continue our journey.

We now return to Highway 101 at mile 282.7 near the south end of Discovery Bay.

	HIGHWAY 101		
	MILES from I-5	MILE NUMBER	
Fat Smitty's Restaurant	84.6 RESTAURANT	282.7	㉒ EAST PORT TOWNSEND
			NATIONAL HISTORIC DISTRICT WHIDBEY ISLAND FERRY HOSPITAL
Bud's Tire Shop Collectibles	84.7 TIRE SHOP COLLECTIBLES	282.6	
WEST UNCAS ROAD	84.8	282.5	
	84.9 C-STORE GAS SEAFOOD	282.4	Discovery Bay Groceries/Shell
	85.3	282.0	MILL POINT ROAD
	85.4	281.9	TURNOUT
Discovery Bay Tavern	85.5 TAVERN	281.8	
	85.6 LEAVING DISCOVERY BAY	281.7	
	85.7	281.6	OLD GARDINER HIGHWAY
TURNOUT	85.9	281.4	
	86.3	281.0	SLOW VEHICLE TURNOUT

	HIGHWAY 101		
	MILES from I-5	MILE NUMBER	
HOLLAND DRIVE DISCOVERY BAY VILLAGE	86.8 RESTAURANT LOUNGE	280.5	OLD GARDINER HIGHWAY Discovery Bay Rest. & Lounge
TURNOUT	87.3 MILEPOST	280.0	
	87.4	279.9	BRODERS ROAD
SOUTHBOUND SLOW VEHICLE TURNOUT	87.6	279.7	
	88.6	278.7	SLOW VEHICLE TURNOUT
	88.9	278.4	OLD GARDINER HIGHWAY
	89.3 HISTORICAL MARKER	278.0	HISTORICAL MARKER Near here Captain George Van- couver made his first camp May 2, 1792.
	90.4 MEMB. RV PARK HISTORICAL SIGN	276.9	Discovery Bay Resort (Naco West Membership RV Park)
	90.8 ENTER GARDINER	276.5	
GARDINER CEMETERY ROAD	91.0	276.3	GARDINER BEACH ROAD
	91.3 C-STORE	276.0	BMT'S Gardiner Store
	91.4	275.9	OLD GARDINER HIGHWAY
	91.5	275.8	OLD GARDINER HIGHWAY
	91.7 LEAVE GARDINER	275.6	
	92.3 MILEPOST	275.0	
	92.5	274.8	OLD GARDINER ROAD
CHICKEN COOP ROAD	92.6 JEFFERSON CTY.- CLALLAM CTY. BOUNDARY RV PARK	274.7	DIAMOND POINT ROAD (COUNTY LINE ROAD) DIAMOND POINT RECREATION AREA

DIAMOND POINT RECREATION AREA

Don't be misled by the sign that says Diamond Point next right. Old Gardiner Road actually rejoins Highway 101 (yet again) immediately before Diamond Point Road, making it the second right. On some maps the first mile of Diamond Point Road is shown as County Line Road.

You will pass Diamond Point RV Park and Campground on your left about a quarter of a mile before you reach the access road to it, three miles from Highway 101. To reach the entrance, turn left into the access road, then left again into Industrial Parkway. It offers full hook-ups, a boat ramp, a laundry, propane and a mini-grocery.

Although the RV park seems to be the only commercial enterprise devoted to tourists, it is a very pleasant drive to continue past the airport for another half mile to the end of Diamond Point Road at a T intersection with Beach Drive, Beach Drive is a loop around Diamond Pond with views of the Strait of Juan de Fuca and the entrance to Discovery Bay.

	HIGHWAY 101		
	MILES from I-5	MILE NUMBER	
GUILES ROAD	93.1	274.1	KNAPP ROAD
	93.7	273.6	PIERCE ROAD

Here you will get a view of the Olympic Mountains from the North. It is very different from the view that you have enjoyed from the East up until now.

	94.3	273.0	OLD BLYN HIGHWAY SLOW VEHICLE TURN OUT
SOUTHBOUND SLOW VEHICLE TURNOUT	94.4	272.9	
	94.6	272.4	BLYN ROAD
CHICKEN COOP ROAD ZACCARDO ROAD	95.6	271.7	
	95.9 ENTERING BLYN	271.4	
`2850` WOODS ROAD	96.0 RV PARK	271.3	BLYN CROSSING S. SEQUIM BAY RECREATION AREA S. Sequim Bay RV Park

FSR 2850 (13 miles Long) runs along beside Jimmycomelately Creek for two and a half miles to FSR 2855 on the left. FSR 2855 (4 miles long) joins Palo Alto Road near Louella Guard Station.

This short access road takes you over the old railroad right of way to Old Blyn Highway. Turn right for East Sequim Bay Road and Travis Spit.

FSR 2850 then goes on to FSR 2840 on the left in another two and a half miles. FSR 2840 (5 miles long) takes you to FSR 28 near Bear Mountain. Beyond FSR 2840, FSR 2855 goes about eight miles to FSR 28 at Lords Lake.

Turn left, pass a large holding area for logs on your right, then, 0.5 miles from Highway 101, you see the entrance to South Sequim Bay RV Park. It has 24 full hook-up sites and 5 sites without hook-ups (maximum length 45 feet). Attractions are fishing, crabbing and clamming.

Past the RV Park, go West on Old Blyn Highway for 0.2 miles to rejoin Highway 101 at mile 270.5.

SOPHUS ROAD
DUNGENESS TAVERN

96.3   271.0

TAVERN

CORRIEA ROAD

96.7   270.6

96.8   270.5

OLD BLYN HIGHWAY
S. SEQUIM BAY RECREATION AREA

97.0   270.3

TURNOUT

97.3   270.0

MILEPOST

97.8   269.5

Sequim Bay General Store

C-STORE PHONE
GAS PROPANE

97.9   269.4

DAWLEY ROAD

LOUELLA ROAD
Louella Road, in 0.9 miles, takes you to Palo Alto Rd., the main access to the Sequim area trails in the national forest. If you are towing, note that Louella Road is very steep as you approach Palo Alto Rd. The national forest is to the left at Palo Alto Road.

98.0   269.2

The area is described beginning at mile 267.4 on page 133.

**SEQUIM BAY STATE PARK
RANGER STATION**

98.3   269.0
CAMPGROUND
PHONE
RANGER STATION

SEQUIM BAY STATE PARK
PHONE DAY USE CAMPGROUND

Sequim Bay State Park has 86 campsites (maximum trailer size 20 feet). The 26 sites which have hook-ups are to the left immediately after you enter the park. There are picnic tables, fire rings, potable water, pay showers and flush toilets. The facility comprises 90 acres, with boat launch, boat dock, playground, swimming, tennis courts and a hiking trail.

At this point we will turn into the state park for a good night's rest before we continue on to Palo Alto Road and Sequim in Chapter Seven.

Dungeness Valley from Forest Service Road 2860.

CHAPTER 7

DUNGENESS AND GRAY WOLF

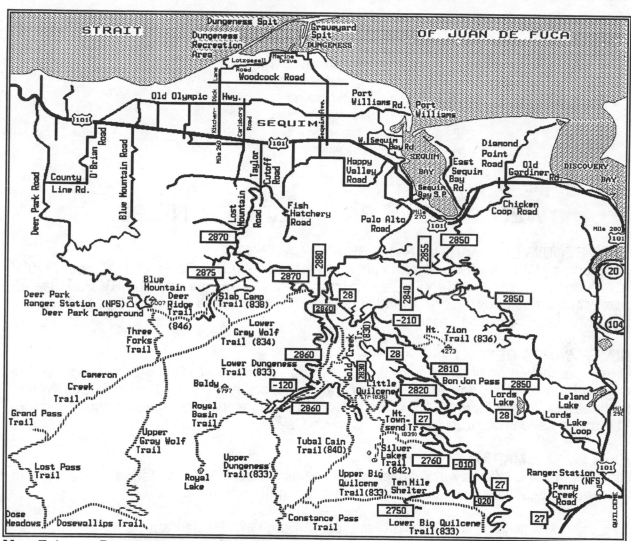

Map 7-1   DUNGENESS AND GRAY WOLF VALLEYS

Although FSR 28 is the main Forest Service arterial road in this area, most of the major trailheads are on FSR 2860 which starts from mile 1.0 of FSR 28. The only trails that are reached more or less directly from FSR 28 are Mount Zion Trail and Little Quilcene Trail near

Bon Jon Pass (See page 119.). They are usually accessed from the Lords Lake end of FSR 28. There are several trailheads on FSR 2870 and FSR 2875 which can be reached from either FSR 2860 or from Taylor Cutoff Road and Lost Mountain Road.

	HIGHWAY 101		
	MILES from I-5	MILE NUMBER	
SEQUIM BAY STATE PARK RANGER STATION	98.3 CAMPGROUND PHONE	269.0	SEQUIM BAY STATE PARK PHONE DAY USE CAMPGROUND (See page 129.)
	98.7	268.6	BARKER ROAD
	98.8 CABINS RV PARK CAMPING C-STORE PICNIC AREA RESTAURANT RESTROOM PHONE FISHING TACKLE MARINA	268.5	WEST SEQUIM BAY ROAD WEST SEQUIM BAY RECREATION AREA

WEST SEQUIM BAY RECREATION AREA

WEST SEQUIM BAY MARINA, RV PARK AND CAMPING
Eight tenths of a mile after you turn right into West Sequim Bay Road, you will see Sequim Bay Marina on your right. Sequim Bay Marina RV Park is on your left. The RV Park has 43 sites with full hook-ups. There are 50 tent sites. The facility has flush toilets, pay showers, a laundry and a recreation room.

SILVER SANDS RESORT
At the intersection of West Sequim Bay Road and Whitefeather Way, one mile from where you left Highway 101, you will see Silver Sands Resort. It is run by the same people that operate Sequim Bay Marina and RV Park. It offers cottages fully equipped for housekeeping. All of them have unobstructed views of Sequim Bay.

JOHN WAYNE MARINA
Three tenths of a mile beyond Whitefeather Way is the John Wayne Marina. It is a modern structure on beautifully landscaped grounds offering the following:

Tackle Box & Boat Brokerage	True Grits Restaurant
Transient Moorage	Bosun's Locker Supplies
Nelson Electronics	Fuel Dock, Picnic Area
Sequim Bay Yacht club	Rest Rooms and Telephones

If you continue west on West Sequim Bay Road for another three miles you will rejoin Highway 101 at the City Limit of Sequim. This narrative however, shall now return to the point at which we left Highway 101, MILE 268.5.

	98.8	268.5

WEST SEQUIM BAY ROAD

28 via PALO ALTO ROAD

	99.9	267.4

To: 2860

OLYMPIC NATIONAL FOREST

FSR 28, FSR 2860 DUNGENESS

DISTANCE FROM
HIGHWAY 101

FS ROAD 28	7.6 Miles
OLYMPIC NATIONAL FOREST	7.6 Miles
DUNGENESS FORKS CAMPGROUND	8.7 Miles
GRAY WOLF TRAIL	10.1 Miles
BON JON PASS	16.8 Miles
MOUNT ZION TRAIL	14.2 Miles
LITTLE QUILCENE TR. (FSR 2820 Trailhead) . . .	20.5 Miles
HIGHWAY 101, MILE 292.8	25.4 Miles
FSR 2860	8.6 Miles
EAST CROSSING CAMPGROUND	10.6 Miles
GOLD CREEK TRAIL	11.6 Miles
LOWER DUNGENESS TRAIL	12.6 Miles
UPPER MAYNARD BURN TRAIL	19.9 Miles
LOWER DUNGENESS TRAIL (Upper Trailhead) .	19.8 Miles
UPPER DUNGENESS TRAIL	19.8 Miles
GOLD CREEK TRAIL (Upper Trailhead)	23.5 Miles
TUBAL CAIN TRAIL	23.5 Miles
LITTLE QUILCENE TR. (FSR 2860 Trailhead) . . .	23.5 Miles

We have only been back on Highway 101 for half a mile and here we go off again on another big excursion. Palo Alto Road takes you to two of the nicest campgrounds in the Olympic National Forest, and gives you access to most of the trails in the Sequim area. Because they are somewhat distant from the highway, these campgrounds and trails are seldom crowded.

When Palo Alto Road enters the national forest, it becomes FSR 28. It takes you to Bon Jon Pass, and then to the Quilcene area trails via FSR 27. The Quilcene area trails are discussed beginning at mile 296.1 of Highway 101 on page 108, and mile 292.8 on page 119.

There is also access, via FSR 2870, from this area to the trails further west that are usually reached from Taylor Cut-off and Lost Mountain Road. These trails are discussed at mile 262.0 of Highway 101 on page 151.

Description of Highway 101 resumes at mile 267.4 on page 146.

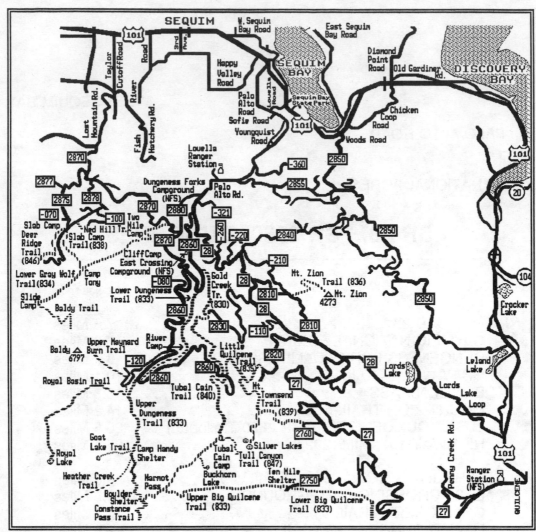

Map 7-2   DUNGENESS VALLEY

<table>
<tr><td></td><td colspan="2">PALO ALTO ROAD</td></tr>
<tr><td></td><td>MILES</td><td>MILES</td></tr>
<tr><td></td><td>from</td><td>to</td></tr>
<tr><td></td><td>HWY 101</td><td>FSR 28</td></tr>
<tr><td></td><td>0.0</td><td>7.6</td></tr>
<tr><td></td><td colspan="2">HIGHWAY 101</td></tr>
<tr><td>MARSHALL ROAD</td><td>0.4</td><td>7.2</td></tr>
<tr><td>OLD LOG CABIN</td><td>1.3</td><td>6.3</td></tr>
<tr><td>SHARP CURVE TO THE LEFT</td><td>1.5</td><td>6.1</td></tr>
<tr><td>LOUELLA ROAD</td><td>2.2</td><td>5.4</td></tr>
</table>

Louella Rd. goes 0.9 miles to
Highway 101, mile 269.2.

134

PALO ALTO ROAD

	MILES from HWY 101	MILES to FSR 28	
	2.3	5.3	SOFIE ROAD
	3.1	4.5	YOUNGQUIST ROAD

Youngquist Road is sometimes shown on maps as Old Palo Alto Road. It forks near its end, in about a mile, and both branches rejoin Palo Alto Road.

	MILES from HWY 101	MILES to FSR 28	
	4.1	3.5	YOUNGQUIST ROAD
	4.2	3.4	YOUNGQUIST ROAD
OLD LOG CABIN	5.3	2.3	
2800-360	5.5	2.1	
	5.6	2.0 PAVEMENT ENDS	
2855	6.4	1.2	
To: JIMMYCOMELATELY ROAD			
DON SCHMITH ROAD	6.5	1.1	
	6.6	1.0	ROAD TO LOUELLA GUARD STATION
SHARP TURN TO THE LEFT	7.0	0.6	
	7.2	0.4	REMAINS OF OLD LOG CABIN
	7.4	0.2	SHARP TURN TO THE RIGHT
28	7.6 0.0 END OF PALO ALTO ROAD OLYMPIC NATIONAL FOREST CAMPGROUND		2880 DUNGENESS FORKS CAMPGROUND(NFS) To: GRAY WOLF TRAIL

28

Palo Alto Road forks here. FSR 28 begins to your left. It goes 9.2 miles to Bon Jon Pass, and gives access to Little Quilcene Trail in FSR 2820, and Mt. Zion Trail in FSR 2810. (See page 119.)

2880 DUNGENESS FORKS CAMPGROUND(NFS)
To: GRAY WOLF TRAIL

FSR 2880 goes to the right again 0.3 miles after leaving Palo Alto Road and FSR 28. It becomes one-lane with turnouts. A warning sign states "Narrow Road Not Recommended for Trailers or Motor Homes". The road is narrow and quite steep, with several tight curves.

Unless your RV is only a small one, East Forks Campground (2.0 miles farther, on FSR 2860) is a better choice than Dungeness Forks. Alternatively, the other end of FSR 2880 joins FSR 2870 2.5 miles from its jct. with FSR 2860. That end is not so steep. Dungeness Forks Campground (also known as Two Forks Campground) is in FSR 2880, 1.1 miles from the end of Palo Alto Road It is on the right just after the bridge over the Dungeness. The Dungeness and Gray Wolf Rivers merge here. Campsites are too small for trailers. There are picnic tables, potable water, fireplaces, and vault toilets.

Continue on FSR 2880 for 0.8 mi. past the campground to FSR 2870, turn right and go 0.6 mi. to the trailhead for the Lower Gray Wolf Trail.

FS ROAD	28
MILE	MILES
NUMBER	from
	HWY 101
7.6	0.0
START FSR 28	
8.2	0.6
8.6	1.0

2800-321

2880

2860

To: E. CROSSING CAMPGR.

Most of the major trails in the Dungeness Valley start from FSR 2860, a gravel, one-lane road. We turn right here to explore them.

Description of FSR 28 continues at mile 1.0 on page 145.

0.0   8.6

START FSR 2860

When you pass sections of the road with steep slopes above you, you should be alert for debris from rock slides in the roadway.

1.0   9.6

MILEPOST

If you are squeamish about high places, try not to look over the edge on your right for the next couple of miles. The valley is quite beautiful, but no guard rail makes it seem a long way down.

2.0   10.6

CAMPGROUND

EAST CROSSING CAMPGROUND (NFS)

The entrance to East Crossing Campground is easy to miss. It sneaks in from your right just as your attention is absorbed in negotiating a curve to your left.

There are nine campsites (max. trailer size 16 feet), picnic tables, fireplaces, potable water and pit toilets. The campground is on the river, so you won't have far to go to catch a few fish.

When you rejoin FSR 2860, the road runs along beside the Dungeness River and you will catch glimpses of little rapids and hear the rushing water all the way to the Gold Creek Trail trailhead.

GOLD CREEK TRAIL

3.0   11.6

GOLD CREEK TRAIL
(6.4 Miles Long)
Trail 830

You will see the trailhead for the Gold Creek Trail (elevation gain 2,050 feet, maximum grade 20%) on your left just before you cross a bridge over the Dungeness River. On your right is space for parking three or four cars, and a couple of primitive campsites down by the river.

The limited maintenance and steepness of this trail means that you will usually have it to yourself all the way to the upper trailhead near the Tubal Cain Trail trailhead at mile 14.9 of FSR 2860.

Distances and elevations are:

```
Trailhead, FSR 2860 mile 3.0 . . . . . . . . 0.0 Miles   1250 Feet
Gold Creek Shelter . . . . . . . . . . . . . . . . 0.2 Miles   1220 Feet
End of FSR 2830 . . . . . . . . . . . . . . . . . 2.8 Miles   2500 Feet
Tubal Cain Tr.(Upper trailhead) . . . . . . . 6.4 Miles   3300 Feet
        (8.8. Miles Long, Elevation Gain 2,700 feet)
```

The trail passes through an area that is still recovering from a past fire, then a clearcut at about 2.4 miles that gives you unobstructed views up and down the Dungeness Valley. A bit further on, you pass near the end of FSR 2830 on your left. It comes in from FSR 28. You cross another clearcut at about mile five, from which you can see FSR 2860 and the peaks around Royal Basin in the distance.

We now return briefly to mile 3.0 Of FSR 2860.

	FS ROAD 2860	
	MILE	MILES
	NUMBER	from
		HWY 101
GOLD CREEK TRAIL	3.0	11.6
LOWER DUNGENESS TRAIL	4.0	12.6

LOWER DUNGENESS TRAIL
(5.8 Miles Long)
Trail 833

The Lower Dungeness Trail (elevation gain 850 feet, maximum grade 15%) is neither marked nor maintained, so it is mainly used by fishermen and hunters. It is very easy to miss the trailhead unless you keep a sharp lookout for it. It is located on the left side of the road at a point where the road makes a sharp turn to the right. Although you probably won't be able to see the trail until you stop and look back in the trees, there is a wide turnout on the left with enough space to park two small cars just as you make the sharp turn. Your best bet is to watch your odometer for almost exactly one mile from Gold Creek Trail trailhead. The upper trailhead is located at mile 11.2 of FSR 2860, across the road from the Upper Dungeness Trail trailhead.

The trail goes high above the river through old growth and second growth timber before coming to an open area that provides magnificent views — up to 180 degrees near Three O'Clock Ridge — of the valley. Descending, the trail crosses several streams before reaching the shelter at River Camp at 4.3 miles. Past River Camp, the trail follows the river before emerging on FSR 2860 just north of the Upper Dungeness Trail (6.4 miles long, 3500 feet elevation gain).

Distances and elevations along the Lower Dungeness Trail are:

```
Trailhead, FSR 2860 (mile 4.0) . . . . . . . 0.0 Miles  1650 Feet
Path to FSR 2860 (mile 7.9) . . . . . . . . 2.5 Miles  2650 Feet
    (0.5 Miles Long, 400 Feet Elevation Gain)

River Camp Shelter . . . . . . . . . . . . . . 4.3 Miles  2100 Feet
Trailhead, FSR 2860 (mile 11.2) . . . . . . 5.8 Miles  2500 Feet
```

We now return to mile 4.0 of FSR 2860, the point at which we left it.

FS ROAD 2860	
MILE NUMBER	MILES from HWY 101

LOWER DUNGENESS TRAIL 4.0 12.6

4.9 13.5

2870

To: DUNGENESS FORKS CAMPGROUND
(Alternate Route)
GRAY WOLF TRAIL

It is 2.5 miles to FSR 2880 via FSR 2870. FSR 2880 goes to Dungeness Forks Campground, 0.8 mi. from FSR 2870 on the left.

Lower Gray Wolf Trail trailhead is in FSR 2870, 0.6 mi. beyond FSR 2880, on the left, a bit past the Gray Wolf bridge. Details on this trail appear on page 154.

5.0 13.6
MILEPOST

5.4 14.0

2860-080

Path to Lower Dungeness Trail. 7.9 16.7
(0.5 miles long)

8.0 16.6
MILEPOST

9.6 18.2

2860-120

MAYNARD BURN TRAILS

FSR 2860-120 has no sign, and it is closed 1.7 miles from FSR 2860 because of washouts and rock slides. There is a large flat parking area just before you reach the closure barrier.

The views on these unmarked and unmaintained way trails, especially the Upper Maynard Burn Trail, are worth the effort. Your first challenge however, is to find them. I missed both of them on my first pass, so I will try to make my directions as clear as possible.

LOWER MAYNARD BURN WAY TRAIL
(0.5 Miles Long)

The Lower Maynard Burn Trail starts 1.2 miles past the place where you left your vehicle (2.8 miles from FSR 2860). You will see a large turnout on the left that would have been adequate for three or four cars when the road was open. There is a large rock in the middle of the road just before you reach it and a sharp switchback to the right just after it. The turnout is the last one to appear whilst the downhill side of the mountain is to your left. The trail starts from about the middle of the turnout. The trail has been narrowed by vegetation near the road but it becomes much clearer when you reach the trees.

The Lower Maynard Burn Trail is 0.4 miles long, and joins the Royal Basin Trail (See page 142) 0.1 miles after it leaves the Upper Dungeness Trail at mile 1.0.

UPPER MAYNARD BURN WAY TRAIL
(1.9 Miles Long)
(3.5 Miles to Summit of Baldy)

The Upper Maynard Burn Way Trail (2,000 feet elevation gain — 2,800 feet elevation gain to the summit of Baldy) starts on your left, 1.7 miles from the parking area (3.4 miles from FSR 2860) and is even more difficult to see at its beginning. It goes uphill quite steeply across a barren rock slide and you won't feel sure that you have found it until you get to the trees. There the steepness continues, but the trail becomes clear. It starts from a small drainage ditch that has been dug across the road just before a sharp curve in the road to the left. The end of the closed road is 0.3 miles beyond the beginning of the trail. If you see the end of the road, or a stand of trees in the distance that has been flattened by an avalanche, you have missed the trail. Another clue is a large rock in the middle of the road just before the trailhead, and another just after.

The search, and the arduous hike will be amply justified when you see the fantastic views from the 6,000 foot mark of Baldy. The views from the summit are great too, if you want to press on. Although the trail ends at the 6000 foot level, a trail is not needed to go on to the false summit at the 6500 feet level, or the true summit at 6797 feet. The true summit is 3.5 miles from the trailhead.

Distances and elevations along the trail are as follows:

Trailhead . . . . 0.0 Miles 4000 Feet
Lookout Point . . . . 1.2 Miles 5250 Feet
End of Trail . . . . 1.9 Miles 6000 Feet
Summit of Baldy . . . . 3.5 Miles 6797 Feet

We now return to mile 9.6 of FSR 2860.

FS ROAD   2860

MILE NUMBER	MILES from HWY 101	

| 9.6 | 18.2 | |

2860-120
MAYNARD BURN WAY TRAILS

| 9.7 | 18.3 |

PANORAMIC VIEWS

Because of regenerating clearcuts below, you have unobstructed views of the Dungeness Valley along here. You can see the serpentine road clinging to the face of the slope on the other side. In summer the snow capped peaks complement clusters of white daisies that wave to you from the roadside.

| 10.0 | 18.6 |

MILEPOST

| 11.1 | 19.7 |

MUELLER CREEK

| 11.2 | 19.8 |

LOWER DUNGENESS TRAIL

There is parking space here for four or five vehicles. There is a vault toilet near the road, and a few primitive campsites near the point where the Lower Dungeness Trail emerges from the trees. See page 138 for a description of this trail.

UPPER DUNGENESS TRAIL

The sign marking the Upper Dungeness Trail is on your left just before you cross Dungeness River. There is a parking space here. A car park for 25 or 30 cars is just across the bridge on the right.

UPPER DUNGENESS TRAIL
(6.4 Miles Long)
Trail 833

The Upper Dungeness Trail (elevation gain 3,500 feet, maximum grade 20%) starts out over more or less level ground. It passes a salt lick at 1.6 miles where you often catch sight of deer and other wild animals. This trail offers a bit of everything. Deep forest, flowery meadows, rocky ridges, icy glaciers, racing streams and an occasional mountain goat are seen as you hike to Boulder Shelter.

Distances and elevations along the trail are as follows:

Trailhead . . . . 0.0 Miles 2500 Feet
Royal Basin Trail . . . . 1.0 Miles 2800 Feet
    (7.0 miles long, 2900 feet elevation gain)

Salt Lick . . . . 1.6 Miles 2800 Feet
Dungeness River Log Bridge . . . . 2.4 Miles 3500 Feet
Camp Handy Shelter (Path) . . . . 3.2 Miles 3100 Feet
Heather Creek Trail (Right) . . . . 3.5 Miles 3250 Feet
    (4.0 miles long, 825 feet elevation gain)

Boulder Shelter . . . . 6.3 Miles 4950 Feet

Boulder Shelter marks the end of the Upper Dungeness Trail. The trails that continue are the Constance Pass Trail (a.k.a. Home Lake Trail) to your right, and Big Quilcene Trail to your left. Constance Pass Trail (8.5 miles long, 4300 feet elevation gain), is discussed on page 100, and the Big Quilcene Trail (6.7 miles long, 3,500 feet elevation gain) is discussed on page 114. If you want to see a bit more of the high country, Marmot Pass is only 1.4 miles from Boulder Shelter on the Big Quilcene Trail.

Further, the Tubal Cain Trail (8.8 miles long, 2700 feet elevation gain) ends at Marmot Pass. Enjoy the relics from the old mines, and return to mile 14.9 of FSR 2860, only 3.7 miles from the Upper Dungeness trailhead. (See page 143.)

ROYAL BASIN TRAIL
(7.0 Miles Long)
Trail 832

The Royal Basin Trail (2900 feet elevation gain, maximum grade 20%) starts from mile 1.0 of the Upper Dungeness Trail near the point where Royal Creek merges with the Dungeness River. It passes into the National Park, then back out again before it finally re-enters the National Park and heads for Royal Lake and Deception Glacier. Deer, marmots, elk and mountain goats are frequently sighted, especially in the National Park sections of the trail. Experienced climbers may wish to continue on to Mount Deception and the beautiful Deception Basin. The Needles, west of the Royal Basin provides some good opportunities for rock climbing, even though the tilted pillow lava is a bit crumbly.

Distances and elevations along the trail are:

Upper Dungeness Trail, Mile 1.0 . . . . . . 0.0 Miles 2800 Feet
Lower Maynard Burn Trail (Right) . . . . . 0.1 Miles 2800 Feet
National Park Boundary . . . . 3.5 Miles 4100 Feet
Royal Lake . . . . 6.0 Miles 5130 Feet
Deception Glacier Camp . . . . 7.0 Miles 5700 Feet

142

HEATHER CREEK TRAIL
(4.0 Miles Long)

Although Heather Creek Trail (elevation gain 825 feet) is not marked or maintained, it is in very good shape. It goes to the right from mile 3.6 of Upper Dungeness Trail, 0.3 miles beyond Camp Handy. It more or less follows Heather Creek to the National Park boundary. You pass the remains of a couple of old cabins, one complete with a rubbish heap, along the way. There is another cabin, with no roof, near the end of the trail at Heather Creek Camp.

Distance and elevations along the trail are:

Upper Dungeness Trail, Mile 3.5	0.0 Miles	3175 Feet
Heather Creek (no bridge)	2.0 Miles	3260 Feet
Old Hunters Camp	2.9 Miles	3475 Feet
Heather Creek Camp	4.0 Miles	4000 Feet

We now return to mile 11.2 of FSR 2860.

	FS ROAD 2860	
	MILE NUMBER	MILES from HWY 101
LOWER DUNGENESS TRAIL	11.2 19.8	UPPER DUNGENESS TRAIL
	13.6 22.2 SILVER CREEK	
GOLD CREEK TRAIL LITTLE QUILCENE TRAIL	14.9 23.5	TUBAL CAIN TRAIL

Gold Creek Trail (6.4 mi. long, 2050 feet elevation gain — See page 137.) ends on your right, opposite the entrance to the car park for Tubal Cain Trail. It runs along above the road for about 50 yards.

The Little Quilcene Trail (4.2 miles long, 1100 feet elevation gain — See page 120.) comes up on the left just past the entrance to the car park.

TUBAL CAIN TRAIL
(8.8 Miles Long)
Trail 840

Tubal Cain Trail (2,700 feet elevation gain, 15% maximum grade) starts from the south end of the car park. Near the start, on your left, just off the trail, is a shelter, a fire ring, and plenty of flat ground for camping. On your right as you face the open end of the shelter, there is a trail which goes up to the road and emerges just across from the Little Quilcene Trail trailhead. There are also a couple of small camp sites nestled in the trees beside Silver Creek.

This trail has many relics left from the days early in this century, when miners tried to extract enough copper and manganese from Tubal Cain and Tull City to justify the risk of avalanches and fire. The elements finally won the battle when the snows of 1911's severe storms drove the miners away. Although it looks extremely tempting, one should resist the urge to explore the mine itself. Floods and avalanches over the years since the mine was abandoned have made the old mine shafts very dangerous.

The Strait, Mt. Baker and the peaks of Canada's Coast Range can be seen from the high vantage points on the trail. You will also enjoy wildflowers in the meadows and sub-alpine forests. As the terrain grows more hostile, you will see glaciers and bizarre rock formations created in a cataclysmic geological era.

Distances and elevations along the trail are:

FSR 2860, Mile 14.9	0.0 Miles	3300 Feet
Tull Canyon Trail (Left)	3.2 Miles	4150 Feet
(0.7 miles long, 850 feet elevation gain)		
Tubal Cain Camp	3.6 Miles	4350 Feet
Buckhorn Lake Trail (Left)	5.5 Miles	5300 Feet
(0.5 miles long, 150 feet elevation loss)		
Buckhorn Pass	7.0 Miles	5900 Feet
Marmot Pass	8.8 Miles	6000 Feet

Buckhorn Lake Way Trail is unmarked, and appears to be the main trail, so be alert unless you really want to go to the lake. After Buckhorn Pass at 7.0 miles you climb to an altitude of 6,300 feet for some fantastic views both to the north and to the south before descending to Marmot Pass and the Upper Big Quilcene Trail (6.5 miles long, 3,500 feet elevation gain).

TULL CANYON TRAIL
(0.7 Miles Long)
Trail 847

Tull Canyon Trail is short and steep (850 feet elevation gain). It leaves the Tubal Cain Trail at mile 3.2. Near the start, you come to an old miner's tunnel, then a short distance later the trail forks. The left branch takes you to a small valley, where wreckage of a plane that crashed in 1941 is scattered. The right branch takes you to a camp and an old cabin on the site of old Tull City.

BUCKHORN LAKE WAY TRAIL
(0.5 Miles Long)
Trail 845

Buckhorn Lake Way Trail (elevation loss 150 feet) starts from mile 5.5 of the Tubal Cain Trail (See page 144). The trail is not marked, but you should have no trouble finding it. It is so obvious that it is often mistaken for the main trail. There are a couple of campsites along the way, that are preferable to the one at the lake itself.

We now return to mile 1.0 of FSR 28, where we turned into FSR 2860.

	FS ROAD 28		
	MILE NUMBER	MILES from HWY 101	

Left	MILE NUMBER	MILES from HWY 101	Right
	8.6	1.0	2860 EAST CROSSING CAMPGROUND (NFS)
2840			
2800-210	11.7	4.1	
2810 MOUNT ZION TRAIL (See page 120 for description.)	13.2	5.6	
	13.7	6.1	2830 GOLD CREEK TRAIL (See page 137 for description.)
	14.9	7.3	2800-110
	16.5	8.9	2820 LITTLE QUILCENE TRAIL (See page 120 for description.)
2810 MOUNT ZION TRAIL (See page 120 for description.)	16.8 9.2 BON JON PASS		
	18.0	10.4	QUILCENE AREA TRAILS 27
2850	22.1 14.5 END OF FSR 28		LORDS LAKE LOOP ROAD

Lords Lake Loop Road takes you 3.3 mi. to mile 292.8 of Highway 101. The distance from mile 267.4 to mile 292.8 is 25.4 mi. via FSR 28.

We now return to mile 267.4 of Highway 101, at Palo Alto Road.

	HIGHWAY 101	
	MILES MILE	
	from NUMBER	
	I-5 ___	

PALO ALTO ROAD

99.9   267.4

100.0   267.3
RV PARK LODGING
RESTAURANT
MARINA

WHITEFEATHER WAY
JOHN WAYNE MARINA
SILVER SANDS RESORT
SEQUIM BAY MARINA & RV PARK

These attractions are discussed at mile 268.5 of Highway 101, W. Sequim Bay Rd., on page 132.

HAPPY VALLEY WAY

100.3   267.0

100.5   266.8

KEELER ROAD

100.7   266.6

LOFGRIN ROAD

SIMDARS ROAD

101.0   266.3

SOUTH RHODEFER ROAD

101.7   265.6

NORTH RHODEFER ROAD

Lamplighter Original Mexican Restaurant

101.9   265.4
RESTAURANT

WEST SEQUIM BAY ROAD
WASHINGTON HARBOR ROAD
WEST SEQUIM BAY RECREATION AREA

The attractions at West Sequim Bay are discussed at mile 268.5 of Highway 101 on page 132.

Washington Harbor Road goes to the right 0.7 miles from Highway 101. It is a bit of a disappointment. It is 1.3 miles long and ends before you reach the water, at a locked gate. A sign identifies it as the gate to Battelle Research Area.

STILL ROAD
Neuharth Winery

101.9   265.4
WINERY
PARK
ENTER SEQUIM
POP. 3,180

BLAKE ROAD
CARRIE BLAKE PARK

The winery is only a quarter of a mile from the highway and it is well worth a stop to taste their wines. They press grapes grown in Eastern Washington.

In a field near the entrance to Carrie Blake Park is a grove of old growth satellite dishes and television antennas. There is also a Convention Center, built by the Lions Club, in the park.

SEQUIM BUSINESS DISTRICT

HIGHWAY 101

MILES   MILE
from NUMBER
I-5 _____

Treat's Second Hand and Pottery Studios	102.2	265.1	TOURIST INFORMATION BOOTH 101 Outpost C-Store, Exxon

SOUTH BROWN ROAD

NORTH BROWN ROAD
To: PORT WILLIAMS
MARLYN NELSON COUNTY PARK

To reach Port Williams, turn right into N. Brown Road and go for 1.1 miles to Port Williams Road. Turn right again. Port Williams Road ends in 2.2 miles at Marlyn Nelson Park, a lovely beach with nice views across the water to Mount Baker in the Cascade Mountains.

Though overnight parking is not permitted, the park has tables, boat launch and vault toilets.

Vern's Seafood and Chowder
Driftwood Cache Gifts, Antiques
SuperValu 24 Hour Foods, Phones
Crazy Eric's Restaurant, Phone
The Glass House Stained Glass

Great House Motel
Sequim Chamber of Commerce
Olympic Lanes Bowl, Beer, Pizza
Northwestern National Bank
   (Access from Dunlap Avenue)

102.3	265.0	DUNLAP AVENUE

PIONEER MEMORIAL PARK   102.4   264.9   GOVAN AVENUE

Creamery Square Center
   Moon Palace Restaurant
   Antique Shop
   Liquor Store
   Hog Sisters Pizza

Traylor's Restaurant

SOUTH SUNNYSIDE AVENUE   102.5   264.8   NORTH SUNNYSIDE AVENUE
To: POST OFFICE

Lehman's Mark & Pack Supermarket (Access from Etta St. via S. Sequim Avenue.)

Texaco Service Station, Phone
Bakery and Tea Room
Sundown Saloon
Anthony's Tea Coffee and Spices
Gull Service Station

| SOUTH SEQUIM AVENUE | 102.6   264.7 | NORTH SEQUIM AVENUE |

SEAFIRST BANK
  (1/2 Block South on the left)

SCENIC DRIVE
DUNGENESS SCHOOL HOUSE
DUNGENESS RECREATION AREA
NAT'L WILDLIFE REFUGE

SEQUIM - DUNGENESS MUSEUM
  (1 Block N, 1/2 block W.
  on the left)

Sequim Gallery
(1 Block North on right)

Ristorante Pelligrino
(1/2 Mile North on left)

3 Crabs Rest. & Fish Market
(5.4 Miles North at the beach)

SEQUIM-DUNGENESS VALLEY SCENIC DRIVE

Sequim Avenue is the beginning of a 12.7 mile Scenic Drive that takes you through the flat, irrigated farms of The Dungeness Valley to the Dungeness Recreation Area, then back to mile 260.0 of Highway 101. The road is marked with distinctive "Scenic Drive" signs.

After leaving Sequim, Sequim Avenue becomes Sequim-Dungeness Way which goes to the right at the 4.6 mile mark. The scenic drive continues straight on Marine Drive. Sequim-Dungeness Way takes you past the Dungeness Tavern and the Groveland Dungeness Cottage Bed and Breakfast, in the small community of Dungeness which was founded in 1851. Eight tenths of a mile from where you left the scenic drive, at the end of the road, is Three Crabs Restaurant, Fish Market and Souvenir Shop. From the end of the road, and from Three Crabs Road to the right, you get excellent views of Mount Baker and the Cascades across the Strait of Juan de Fuca.

Back on the Scenic Drive, three tenths of a mile past the point where Sequim Dungeness Way went off to the right, is the picturesque Dungeness School House.

The scenic drive then follows the coast on Marine Drive past the Juan de Fuca Cottages and Dungeness Bay Motel which are 6.9 miles from Highway 101. Marine Drive then bends inland to the left. At 7.9 miles you turn right into Lotzgesell Road which will take you to the Dungeness Recreation Area. The entrance to the Dungeness Recreation Area is Voice of America Road, 9.4 miles from Highway 101 on the Scenic Drive.

Turning into Voice of America Road, you will find a horse unloading area, then several little turnouts into secluded picnic areas before you reach the campground, six tenths of a mile from Lotzgesell road. There are 65 sites, none with hook-ups. Potable water is available, and there are flush toilets, a dump station, pay showers and fireplaces. Firewood is offered for sale.

Seven hundred yards from the campground entrance is the Dungeness National Wildlife Refuge on the seven mile long Dungeness Spit which ends at the Dungeness Light. Over 275 species of birds have been catalogued on the spit.

Going back to Lotzgesell Road, it is only another two tenths of a mile, to your right, to Kitchen-Dick Lane, where you turn left. You follow Kitchen-Dick Lane for 3.1 miles to rejoin Highway 101 at mile 360.0. Sequim is to the left and Port Angeles is to the right.

We will now return to mile 264.7 of Highway 101, the intersection with Sequim Avenue where we left for the Scenic Drive.

	HIGHWAY 101 MILES from I-5	MILE NUMBER	
SOUTH SEQUIM AVENUE	102.6	264.7	**NORTH SEQUIM AVENUE**

SOUTH SEQUIM AVENUE	NORTH SEQUIM AVENUE
U.S. Bank	Ice Cream Shoppe
Sunshine Cafe	Sirrah Collectibles
Sweet Tooth Pastry	SEAL STREET
Great Northwest Savings	Sequim Cleaners & Laundromat
	Unocal 76 Service Station

SOUTH SECOND AVENUE	102.7	264.6	**NORTH SECOND STREET**

SOUTH SECOND AVENUE	NORTH SECOND STREET
Chevron Service Station	D & L Grocery & Deli
Country Cottage Antique Mall	Clay & Fiber+ Crafts Gallery
Anne's Sequim Antiques	

SOUTH THIRD AVENUE	102.8	264.5	**NORTH THIRD AVENUE**

SOUTH THIRD AVENUE	NORTH THIRD AVENUE
Oak Table Cafe	Sundowner Motel
(1/2 Block south on left)	The Bandit's Pizza Parlor
Antiques	
(1 Block south on right)	
Gil's New and Used Stuff	

SOUTH FOURTH AVENUE	102.9	264.4	**NORTH FOURTH AVENUE**

SOUTH FOURTH AVENUE	NORTH FOURTH AVENUE
Antiques 'n' Things	Payless Drug Store
Burger Boy Restaurant	

SOUTH FIFTH AVENUE	102.9 264.4	**NORTH FIFTH AVENUE**

SOUTH FIFTH AVENUE

Eclipse Cafe
(1 Block South on right)

Interwest Savings Bank

Landmark Mall
  El Cazador Mexican Restaurant

Sequim Village Center
  Safeway
  Fricks Drug Store
  Tarcisio's Italian Restaurant
  Laundromat
  Sam's Restaurant
  1st Federal Savings and Loan

Phones: E. side of Safeway,
        northeast corner of
        parking lot.

NORTH FIFTH AVENUE

Tom Tom Grocery, Deli, Chevron
Idle Wheels Mobil Home Park
(O'niters welcome, Laundry)

SEVENTH AVENUE   103.1 264.2

Eric's Auto/RV Repair, Propane
(1 Block South on right)

McDonalds
Town Tavern

Maytag Laundromat

Sequim West Motel, Restaurant &
RV Park

103.3 264.0   **BRACKETT STREET**

Mil-Key C-Store, Shell Gas

Jackpot Food Mart Deli & Gas

Red Ranch Inn, Coffee Shop &
Restaurant

SOUTH DEMMING ROAD   103.4 263.9   **NORTH DEMMING ROAD**
                                LEAVE SEQUIM

Nolan's Fast Service Restaurant

104.2 263.1   **PRIEST ROAD**

RIVER ROAD	104.3	263.0	
		MILEPOST	
	105.1	262.2	
		DUNGENESS RIVER	
TAYLOR CUT-OFF ROAD	105.3	262.0	GILBERT ROAD

To: LOST MOUNTAIN ROAD

FS ROAD 2870   GRAY WOLF

	DISTANCE FROM HIGHWAY 101
LOST MOUNTAIN ROAD	2.6 Miles
FS ROAD 2870	5.2 Miles
LOWER GRAY WOLF TRAIL	11.5 Miles
FSR 2880	12.1 Miles
DUNGENESS FORKS CAMPGROUND	12.9 Miles
FS ROAD 2875	6.0 Miles
SLAB CAMP	9.6 Miles
SLAB CAMP TRAIL	9.6 Miles
DEER RIDGE TRAIL	9.6 Miles
FS ROAD 2860	14.6 Miles

Taylor Cut-Off Road takes you 2.6 miles to Lost Mountain Road, which, in turn, takes you another 2.6 miles to FSR 2870, the access road for the Slab Camp Trails and the Lower Gray Wolf Trail. Both roads are paved, although the pavement on Lost Mountain Road ends just past the point where you turn into FSR 2870.

The Upper Gray Wolf Trail and the Cameron Creek Trails, which start at the end of Lower Gray Wolf Trail, are also discussed in this section. Both of these trails can be reached more quickly from Deer Park (See page 163.) or Slab Camp (See page 152.) if you are pressed for time.

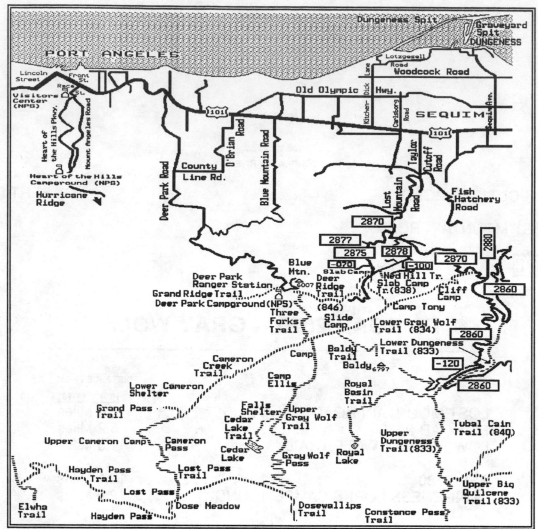

Map 7-3   FS ROAD 2870 GRAY WOLF VALLEY, SLAB CAMP

FS ROAD	2870	
MILE	**MILES**	
NUMBER	from	
	HWY 101	

LOST MOUNTAIN ROAD   0.0   5.2   LOST MOUNTAIN ROAD

Rifle Range   0.5   5.7

                                                          0.8   6.0

2875

SLAB CAMP   SLAB CAMP TRAIL
DEER RIDGE TRAIL

Slab Camp is 3.6 mi. from FSR 2870, on the right. FSR 2875-090 passes through the campground. It has a vault toilet and five or six large campsites with fire rings and benches.

NED HILL TRAIL
(1.2 Miles Long)

Ned Hill Trail goes to an old abandoned fire lookout. The lookout was probably abandoned because of the second growth trees which have obscured the view. The trail is steep, gaining 900 feet over its 1.2 miles. It is included here only because I see, on the newer Forest Service maps, that a road, FSR 2878-100 has been built to the summit (3450 feet). Although I have not been to the summit since the road was built, its construction implies that loggers may have opened up a nice view.

It is difficult to find the trailhead. The best way to find it is to drive exactly 0.3 miles on FSR 2878, and look to your right for a large pile of rocks that spill down to the edge of the road. Climb the rockpile to the obvious bare spot on the left at the top, and sharp eyes will be able to pick out the start of the trail.

DEER RIDGE TRAIL
(5.0 Miles Long)
Trail 846

Deer Ridge Trail (2950 feet elevation gain, 35% maximum grade)starts from the south end of the road that forms a loop through Slab Camp (FSR 2875-090). The trail runs along beside the road for a while then climbs steadily (15-20% average grade) up Deer Ridge to Blue Mountain and Deer Park Campground (NPS). There are many panoramic vistas along the way, providing excellent views of the Strait, the Cascades, the Olympic Peaks and the Gray Wolf Valley. The trail passes within a few feet of the largest known shore pine at mile 3.9.

Distances and elevations along the trail are:

FSR 2875, Slab Camp	0.0 Miles	2540 Feet
Path to FSR 2875	1.3 Miles	3250 Feet
View Rock	1.5 Miles	3200 Feet
Water Seep	1.7 Miles	3300 Feet
Spring	2.0 Miles	3600 Feet
National Park Boundary	3.6 Miles	4750 Feet
3 Forks Trail(Rt. to Deer Park)	5.0 Miles	5360 Feet
(4.5 miles long, 3300 feet elevation loss)		
Deer Park Road	5.2 Miles	5400 Feet

SLAB CAMP TRAIL
(2.5 Miles Long)
Trail 838

Slab Camp Trail (1100 feet elevation loss, 30 % maximum grade) starts from the east side of FSR 2875, opposite the campground. It descends to the Lower Gray Wolf Trail, shortening the hike to Camp Tony by three miles. The most of the time, the trail is on an ice age moraine, and you will get good views of the meadows on Baldy near the start of the trail.

Distances and elevations along Slab Camp trail are as follows:

```
FSR 2875, Slab Camp .............0.0 Miles  2540 Feet
Duncan Flat (Path to camp) ........2.1 Miles  1500 Feet
Gray Wolf Crossing .............2.2 Miles  1440 Feet
Lower Gray Wolf Tr., Mi. 4.9 ........2.5 Miles  1650 Feet
        (9.8 miles, 1250 feet elevation gain)
```

We will return now to mile 0.8 of FSR 2870, where we will turn right and resume our journey to Lower Gray Wolf Trail.

```
                    FS ROAD  2870

                 MILE     MILES
                 NUMBER   from
                 _____    HWY 101
```

	0.8	6.0	2875
2870-030	1.3	6.5	2878

(This is the other end of the road to Ned Hill Trail.)

2870-050	1.8	7.0	
	3.8	9.0	2870-150
	5.2	10.4	2870-180

LOWER GRAY WOLF TRAIL
(Old Trailhead - 1.2 Miles)

6.3   11.5   LOWER GRAY WOLF TRAIL

One can complete a loop, returning to mile 267.4 of Highway 101 via Palo Alto Road, by continuing east beyond the Gray Wolf Trail trailhead on FSR 2870.

There are two routes. The shorter route (10.1 miles) is to continue for 0.6 miles to FSR 2880; turn left and go 1.9 miles (past Dungeness Forks Campground) on FSR 2880 to Palo Alto Road. It is then 7.6 miles to Highway 101 via Palo Alto Road.

If the very steep climb from the campground to Palo Alto Road worries you, you can continue east on FSR 2870 for 3.1 miles to its end at FSR 2860; turn left and go 4.9 miles on FSR 2660 (past East Crossing Campground) to FSR 28; turn left again and go 1.0 miles on FSR 28 to Palo Alto Road. This route adds 6.5 miles (total 16.6 miles to Highway 101) to the journey, but it avoids the steep hill.

LOWER GRAY WOLF TRAIL
(9.8 Miles Long)
Trail 834

The Lower Gray Wolf Trail (elevation gain 1250 feet, maximum grade 15%) starts from a large parking lot, 0.1 miles north of the concrete bridge over the Gray Wolf River. Apparently the route of the trail has been changed in recent years, as I had great difficulty in reconciling the differences in distances and elevations that I found in the various maps and other materials available to me. Disparities still existed after taking into account the 1986 Olympic National Park boundary adjustment. In the finish, I had to accept what ever seemed the most reasonable figures on a segment by segment basis. I apologize if you find my figures to be inaccurate. If it is any consolation, my reckoning comes up with the shortest overall distance to the end of the trail.

The trail has its ups and downs, but never gets very steep. The slopes that the trail traverses do get quite steep, however. Several types of rock are exposed along the way. There are a couple of places with narrow rock ledges that must be negotiated carefully. It is an awfully long drop if you mis-step.

Distances and elevations along the trail are as follows:

FSR 2870 Trailhead	0.0 Miles	950 Feet
Path to FSR 2870-180 (0.3 mi.)	1.8 Miles	1150 Feet
Two Mile Camp	1.8 Miles	1150 Feet
Cliff Camp	3.5 Miles	1200 Feet
Log Stringer Bridge	4.2 Miles	1350 Feet
Camp Tony Shelter	4.9 Miles	1600 Feet
Slab Camp Trail	4.9 Miles	1600 Feet
(2.5 miles long, 1100 feet elevation loss)		
Slide Camp	7.2 Miles	2150 Feet
Baldy Trail	7.2 Miles	2150 Feet
(3.0 miles long, 3550 feet elevation gain)		
Trail Forks, Lower Gray Wolf Ends	9.8 Miles	2125 Feet
Upper Gray Wolf Trail (Left)	9.8 Miles	2125 Feet
(12.9 miles long, 1475 feet elevation gain)		
Cameron Creek Trail (Right)	9.8 Miles	2125 Feet
(11.3 miles long, 2650 feet elevation gain)		

BALDY TRAIL
(3.0 Miles Long)

The unmarked and unmaintained Baldy Trail (3550 feet elevation gain) climbs endlessly up the north slope of Baldy to a point about 1100 feet below the summit. Hiking five miles from Slab Camp before the start of Baldy Trail makes the trail seem even steeper and longer. By the time you reach the end of the trail the wind literally screams, and it is often bitterly cold, even in summer. The vistas one encounters here though, always give encouragement to press on the extra mile to the summit, where the views get even better.

Distances and elevations for the Baldy Trail are:

Slide Camp (Lower Gray Wolf Tr.)	0.0 Miles	2150 Feet
National Park Boundary	2.0 Miles	4500 Feet
End of Trail	3.0 Miles	5700 Feet
North Summit	3.5 Miles	6600 Feet
Summit	4.0 Miles	6797 Feet

UPPER GRAY WOLF TRAIL
(12.9 Miles Long)

The Upper Gray Wolf Trail (4,000 feet elevation gain) begins at the junction of the Lower Gray Wolf Trail and the Cameron Creek Trail. Although this junction can be reached by hiking the full length of the Lower Gray Wolf Trail, starting from Slab Camp shortens the hike by about 2.5 miles. Shorter still, Three Forks Trail, from Deer Park to mile 0.3 of Cameron Creek Trail, brings you to the start of the Upper Gray Wolf Trail in a total distance of 4.7 miles.

The trail passes through an area that has been swept by avalanches and you will probably see patches of snow, even in late summer, before you get to Gray Wolf Pass. As you reach Gray Wolf Pass you will have spectacular views of most of the major peaks in the Olympics. Even Mount Olympus and Lost Mountain will come into view if you scramble on the talus a bit. The pass is flat, and would be a great camp if it weren't so cold and windy. As you descend from the pass to the south slope, the warm sunshine returns.

Distances and elevations along the trail are as follows:

Trailhead, ... 0.0 Miles 2125 Feet
Cameron Creek Trail . . . . 0.0 Miles 2125 Feet
    (11.3 miles long, 4350 feet elevation gain)

Lower Gray Wolf Trail . . . . 0.0 Miles 2125 Feet
    (9.8 miles long, 1250 feet elevation gain)

Nameless Camp . . . . 1.0 Miles 2450 Feet
Camp Ellis . . . . 2.7 Miles 2900 Feet
Falls Shelter . . . . 5.4 Miles 3900 Feet
Cedar Lake Way Trail . . . . 5.4 Miles 3900 Feet
    (3.0 miles long, 1380 feet elevation gain)

Gray Wolf Pass . . . . 9.5 Miles 6150 Feet
Dosewallips Trail(Mile 9.2) . . . . 12.9 Miles 3600 Feet
    (15.4 miles long, 4250 Feet elevation gain)

CEDAR LAKE WAY TRAIL
(3.0 Miles Long)

Cedar Lake Way Trail (elevation gain 1380 feet) takes you from Falls Shelter at mile 5.4 of the Upper Gray Wolf Trail to Cedar Lake, a large sub-alpine lake that is stocked with rainbow trout. The trail starts from behind the shelter at Falls Shelter. Although there is no trail, one can return to the Upper Gray Wolf Trail by climbing to Gray Wolf Pass. If you go that way, look for the large ice blocks that float in one of the lakes you pass, even at the end of summer. There are excellent views of Mount Deception (7788 feet), Mount Mystery and the Needles. There is a good campsite at the northwest end of the lake.

CAMERON CREEK TRAIL
(11.3 Miles Long)

The Cameron Creek Trail (4350 feet elevation gain) begins at the junction of the Lower Gray Wolf Trail and the Upper Gray Wolf Trail. Although this junction can be reached by hiking the full length of the Lower Gray Wolf Trail, most people start from Deer Park, hiking Three Forks Trail (4.5 miles long, 3300 feet elevation loss), to mile 0.3 of Cameron Creek Trail.

The trail passes through avalanche-created meadows in the high country, and often becomes hard to find in the rocks and snow fields near Cameron Pass. The views at Cameron Pass get even better if you hike to the peak you see to the west. You can see Mount Olympus, the Bailey Range and the Low Divide.

Distances and elevations along the trail are as follows:

Trailhead, ... 0.0 Miles 2125 Feet
Lower Gray Wolf Trail . . . . 0.0 Miles 2125 Feet
    (9.8 miles long, 1250 feet elevation gain)

Upper Gray Wolf Trail . . . . 0.0 Miles 2125 Feet
    (12.9 miles long, 4025 feet elevation gain)

Three Forks Trail . . . . 0.3 Miles 2100 Feet
    (4.5 miles long, 3300 feet elevation loss)

Lower Cameron Shelter . . . . 5.3 Miles 3800 Feet
Grand Pass Trail . . . . 7.6 Miles 4200 Feet
    (8.0 miles long, 1950 feet elevation loss)

Upper Cameron Camp . . . . 10.0 Miles 5400 Feet
Lost Pass Trail . . . . 10.0 Miles 5400 Feet
    (2.8 miles long, 2000 feet elevation gain)

We will now return to mile 262.0 of Highway 101, and follow it to Kitchen-Dick Lane, the western end of the Dungeness Scenic Drive.

HIGHWAY 101		
MILES	MILE	
from	NUMBER	
I-5		

TAYLOR CUT-OFF ROAD To: LOST MOUNTAIN ROAD ☐2870	105.3	262.0	GILBERT ROAD
	105.4	261.9	Rainbow's End RV Park

This RV Park has 37 sites with hook-ups and 15 tent sites. It has tables, fireplaces, laundry, showers and flush toilets, Firewood is offered for sale.

	HIGHWAY 101		
	MILES from I-5	MILE NUMBER	
SLOW VEHICLE TURNOUT	105.8 RESTAURANT	261.5	MILL ROAD Flipper's Restaurant
	105.9 STORE	261.4	Sunny Farms Country Store
HOOKER ROAD Casoni's Restaurant	106.1 RESTAURANT C-STORE GAME FARM	261.2	CARLSBORG ROAD Jean's Mini Mart, Deli, Cafe & Exxon Gas To: Olympic Game Farm
	106.6	260.7	JOSLIN ROAD
SOUTH BOYCE ROAD	106.8	260.5	NORTH BOYCE ROAD
KIRK LANE	107.3 MILEPOST	260.0	KITCHEN-DICK LANE

**DUNGENESS SCENIC DRIVE
DUNGENESS RECREATION AREA
NATIONAL WILDLIFE REFUGE**

See mile 264.7 of Highway 101 on page 148 for a description of these attractions.

Just past Kitchen-Dick Lane, on your left, is Sunshine RV Park. Let's stop there for the night, and continue on to Deer Park and Hurricane Ridge in Chapter 8.

Vista from the end of Deer Park Road near the Summit of Blue Mountain.

CHAPTER 8

DEER PARK HURRICANE RIDGE PORT ANGELES

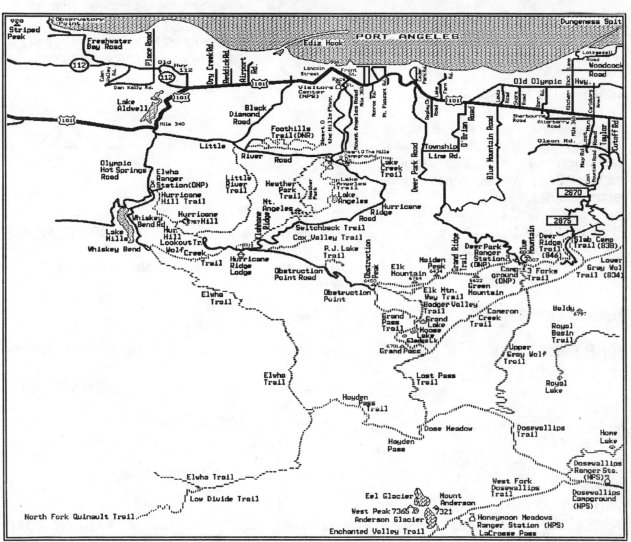

MAP 8-1   DEER PARK, HURRICANE RIDGE AND PORT ANGELES

With a few exceptions, we now leave the National Forest until we get near the end of our Highway 101 Olympic Odyssey. Most of the time that we spend on the hiking trails and interior roads will be in the National Park now. You will notice many differences between the National Forest and the National Parks. Some of the differences are quite subtle, such as the sudden appearance of wild creatures who have been emboldened by the prohibition of firearms in the park and the absence of motorized vehicles and pets on the trails. Other differences are not so subtle; the absence of clearcuts and logging trucks for example.

We will start out at mile 260.0 of Highway 101, and head west for our first stop, at Deer Park in the Olympic National Park.

	HIGHWAY 101		
	MILES from I-5	MILE NUMBER	
KIRK ROAD	107.3 MILEPOST	260.0	KITCHEN-DICK ROAD
			DUNGENESS SCENIC DRIVE
			DUNGENESS RECREATION AREA
			DUNGENESS NAT'L WILDLIFE REFUGE
			SEQUIM VALLEY AIRPORT
Sunshine RV Park	107.5 RV PARK	259.8	

Sunshine RV Park has 58 sites, including 12 drive-throughs. All have hook-ups. Facilities include flush toilets, showers, laundry and recreation hall.

PIERSON ROAD	108.2	259.1	DRYKE ROAD
	108.3 RV REPAIRS	259.0	Jacks RV Repairs entrance.
SHERBOURNE ROAD	109.0	258.3	
BARR ROAD	109.2	258.1	BARR ROAD EXTENSION
	110.2	257.1	SHORE ROAD
	110.4 RESTAURANT	256.9	Depuis Restaurant
	110.7 2nd HAND SHOP	256.6	Vic's Trading Post
BLUE MOUNTAIN ROAD	110.8	256.5	LEWIS ROAD
	110.9 C-STORE GAS	256.4	R Corner Grocery, Texaco

162

	111.6 255.7 RV PARK	Conestoga Quarters RV Park **SEIBERTS CREEK ROAD**

Conestoga Quarters has 34 sites with full hook-ups, including 12 pull-through sites. facilities include showers, flush toilets, recreation hall and a picnic area.

O'BRIEN ROAD KOA Port Angeles	112.2 255.1 RV PARK	**OLD OLYMPIC HIGHWAY**

KOA Port Angeles has 90 sites with hook-ups, including 50 tent sites. The entrance is one block south of Highway 101 on O'Brien Road. It has a dump station, flush toilets, showers, laundry, store, propane, recreation hall and a pool.

SUTTER ROAD	112.8 254.5	
SHORT DRIVE	113.1 254.2	**LAKE FARM ROAD**
BAGLEY CREEK ROAD	113.4 253.9	**NORTH BAGLEY CREEK ROAD**
	113.8 253.5	U-Turn Route
DEER PARK ROAD DEER PARK CAMPGROUND (ONP) BLUE MOUNTAIN GRAND RIDGE TRAIL DEER RIDGE TRAIL THREE FORKS TRAIL	114.2 253.1 OLYMPIC NATIONAL PARK CAMPGROUND	

DEER PARK

Deer Park Road takes you to one of the most delightful spots in the high country of the Olympic National Park. The road climbs over a mile in the journey from Highway 101, and becomes so twisty and narrow that Deer Park is never as crowded as the main attraction in this region, Hurricane Ridge. Although the views are well worth the effort, allow plenty of time for the drive, as the road is a real shocker. The road ends only a few hundred feet short of the summit of Blue Mountain, where the 360° panorama allows you to see Sequim and Port Angeles below and the glaciers of Mount Olympus above.

Moreover, the hike to Obstruction Point on the Grand Ridge Trail is a superb high country walk. When the weather is good, it gives you a better feel for the high country than many trails twice as long and twice as steep.

The description of Highway 101 continues on page 167 at mile number 253.1

	DEER PARK ROAD	
	MILES	MILES
	from	to
	HWY 101	DEER PARK

	MILES from HWY 101	MILES to DEER PARK	
	0.0 HIGHWAY 101	16.2	Sign: "Olympic National Park Deer Park Area 17 miles. Primitive Road For 11 miles" The 17 miles is to the end of the road near the top of Blue Mountain.
	0.2	16.0	PARK n RIDE
	0.4	15.8	WALL STREET
	0.5	15.7	BOARDWALK ROAD
	0.6	15.6	VIEW RIDGE DRIVE
	1.0	15.2	4 SEASONS PARK DRIVE (No Through Traffic) 4 Seasons Park
	4.2	12.0	PELIKAN ROAD
TOWNSHIP LINE ROAD	4.5	11.7	Small sign: "This Road Is Not Suitable for Trailers."
	5.5 PAVEMENT ENDS	10.7	
	8.6 ENTER OLYMPIC NATIONAL PARK	7.6	
	10.0 MILEPOST	6.2	
WIDE TURNOUT	10.6	5.6	
	15.0 MILEPOST	1.2	

164

DEER PARK CAMPGROUND (ONP)
THREE FORKS TRAIL
DEER RIDGE TRAIL
BLUE MOUNTAIN

16.0 0.2

ROAD FORKS

GRAND RIDGE TRAIL
DEER PARK RANGER STATION

The road forks here. The picnic area, campground, Three Forks Trail, Deer Ridge Trail and the summit of Blue Mountain are to the left.

After passing the trailhead for Grand Ridge Trail, on the right about one tenth of a mile from the fork, you will see a large shed on your left. One tenth of a mile past the shed, on your right, is the ranger station. Beyond the ranger station the road curves back to the left to rejoin the main road.

GRAND RIDGE TRAIL
(7.6 Miles Long)

Grand Ridge Trail stays between 5000 and 6500 feet for its entire length. This means that, except for an occasional descent to the tree line, the spectacular views are continuous and unobscured. This trail is, without a doubt, one of the best examples of Olympic high country. Fortunately, the roads at both ends of the trail are absolutely shocking, so it is seldom crowded. One can easily walk to the tops of Maiden Peak (5434 feet) and Elk Mountain (6764 Feet) to get even better views than those from the trail.

Near the Obstruction Point end, the trail offers connections to Cameron Creek Trail via Elk Mountain Way Trail, Badger Valley Trail or Grand Pass Trail, allowing you to return to Deer Park in a long (up to 27 miles) loop if you have plenty of time.

Distances and elevations along the trail are:

Deer Park, near Ranger Station . . . . . . 0.0 Miles 5230 Feet
Saddle . . . . 2.0 Miles 5500 Feet
Grassy Valley . . . . 2.5 Miles 5500 Feet
Roaring Winds Camp . . . . 4.5 Miles 6000 Feet
Elk Mountain Way Trail . . . . 5.6 Miles 6575 Feet
   (1.0 miles long, 1275 feet elevation gain)

Badger Valley Trail . . . . 7.4 Miles 6050 Feet
   (4.5 Miles Long, 2050 Feet elevation loss)

Obstruction Point . . . . 7.6 Miles 6100 Feet

ELK MOUNTAIN WAY TRAIL
(1.0 Miles Long)

This way trail starts 2.0 miles from the Obstruction Point end of Grand Ridge Trail, and offers a short cut to Badger Valley Trail (See page 183). It loses 1275 feet in the one mile hike between Grand Ridge Trail and Badger Valley Trail. It joins Badger Valley Trail 1.0 miles from Obstruction Point (0.8 miles from the Badger Valley Trailhead on the Grand Ridge Trail).

We now return to Deer Park Road to complete our journey to the campground and Blue Mountain.

	DEER PARK ROAD		
	MILES	MILES	
	from	to	
	HWY 101	DEER PARK	
DEER PARK CAMPGROUND (ONP) THREE FORKS TRAIL DEER RIDGE TRAIL BLUE MOUNTAIN	16.0 ROAD FORKS	0.2	GRAND RIDGE TRAIL DEER PARK RANGER STATION
BLUE MOUNTAIN (6007 Feet)	16.2 CAMPGROUND	0.0	DEER PARK CAMPGROUND (ONP) THREE FORKS TRAIL DEER RIDGE TRAIL

The road continues for 0.8 mi. to your left, to a parking area just below the summit of Blue Mountain. The last 0.2 miles of the road has been closed, but you can continue on foot along the roadway to the summit. Alternatively, there is a short trail to your left, starting beside a boulder before you get to the barrier in the road.

From the summit, you get good views of Port Angeles, Vancouver Island, Sequim and snowy peaks of the Olympics, including Mount Olympus.

The road to the Deer Park Campground continues straight ahead from where the Blue Mountain branch goes to the left. The campground has 18 tent sites, potable water, two shelters, a picnic area and vault toilets.

A picnic area is to the left as you enter the campground. Three Forks Trail starts on the far side of a meadow in the picnic area. A path from Three Forks Trail to Blue Mountain is on the left just past the start of the trail. Deer Ridge Trail begins 0.2 miles from the trailhead. See page 153 for details on Deer Ridge Trail.

THREE FORKS TRAIL
(4.5 Miles Long)

Three Forks Trail is an upside down trail, losing 3300 feet over the course of its 4.5 miles to Cameron Creek Trail. The trail ends at a shelter near the point where Cameron Creek, Grand Creek and the upper Gray Wolf Rivers merge into the lower Gray Wolf. Even though there are a lot of switchbacks, your knees and toes will remind you that the trail goes relentlessly downhill. The end of the trail is 0.3 miles west of the junction of the Lower Gray Wolf, Upper Gray Wolf and Cameron Creek trails.

Distances and elevations along the trail are:

Deer Park Picnic Area . . . . 0.0 Miles   5400 Feet
Deer Ridge Trail . . . . 0.2 Miles   5400 Feet
End of Trail, 3 Forks Shelter . . . . 4.5 Miles   2100 Feet

We now return to mile 253.1 of highway 101, and press on to Port Angeles.

HIGHWAY 101

MILES from I-5	MILE NUMBER

DEER PARK ROAD **DEER PARK CAMPGROUND (ONP)**	114.2 253.1 OLYMPIC NATIONAL PARK CAMPGROUND	
	114.4 252.9 RESTAURANT VIEWPOINT	**BUCHANAN DRIVE** **SCENIC VIEW** C'est Si Bon Restaurant
		Immediately after you turn into Buchanan Drive, turn left into Cedar Park Drive. Just behind the C'est Si Bon Restaurant you will see a large parking lot for the viewpoint. There are good views of both Hurricane Ridge and the sea. There are interpretive signs at the west end of the car park.
	115.0 252.3	**MONTGOMERY ROAD** **STRAIT VIEW ROAD**
MORSE CREEK ROAD	115.1 252.2	
	115.5 251.8	**MASTERS ROAD**
	115.6 251.7	**OAKRIDGE DRIVE**
Muncheese Pizza	115.7 251.6 FAST FOOD	
Traylor's Restaurant	115.9 251.4 RESTAURANT	**MYRTLE STREET**

Left	MILES from I-5	MILE NUMBER	Right
MOUNT PLEASANT ROAD Mt. Pleasant IGA Supermarket Mt. Pleasant Village Texaco	116.2 SUPERMARKET GAS MOTEL RV PARK	251.1	Evergreen Motel & Trailer Park MCNUTT STREET LINCOLN AVENUE
WASHINGTON AVENUE Mil-Key Farms C-Store, Shell	116.3 C-STORE GAS FAST FOOD MOTEL	251.0	Pizza Mia Sportsman Motel
SOUTH BAY VIEW AVENUE	116.4	250.9	NORTH BAY VIEW AVENUE
Shirley's Bear and Doll House	116.5 GIFT SHOP	250.8	
BROOK STREET	116.6 TAVERN RV PARK	250.7	Loomis Tavern LEES CREEK ROAD BROOK AVENUE NORTH To Al's RV Park, Lees Creek Rd. Al's RV Park is half a mile north of Highway 101 on Lee's Creek Road. There are 32 sites, all with hook-ups. There are flush toilets, showers and a laundry. Propane is available.
MONROE ROAD	116.8 GAS	250.5	PIONEER ROAD Gasomat Self Serve Gasoline
Peking China Mandarin Food Wonder Bakery Thrift Shop Elmer's Trailer and RV Park Elmer's RV Park (Adults Only) has 11 sites with hook-ups. It has a dump station, flush toilets, showers and a laundry.	117.0 RESTAURANT BAKERY RV PARK C-STORE GAS FAST FOOD SUPERMARKET	250.3	Highway Market and Gas LEWIS (GALES) STREET Plush Pup Sandwiches Mark It Bulk Foods
	117.1	250.2	BAKER STREET
	117.2 BEECH STREET CHESTNUT STREET	250.1	
	117.3 MILEPOST ENTER PORT ANGELES POP. 17,000	250.0	

PORT ANGELES

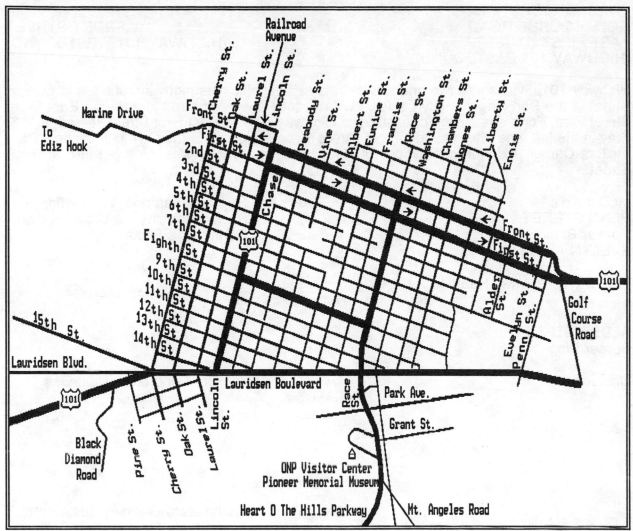

MAP 8-2   PORT ANGELES

Port Angeles is the last large town until we get to Forks, so stock up on hard to find items. Highway 101 divides as you enter Port Angeles. Westbound traffic is shunted to Front Street, and eastbound traffic uses First Street. The two routes come back together in the city center at Lincoln Street.

	HIGHWAY 101	
	MILES	MILE
	from	NUMBER
	I-5	
Super 8 Motel	117.4	249.9
DEL GUZZI DRIVE	MOTEL	
Plaza Shopping Center	SUPERMARKET	
Safeway Supermarket	DRUG STORE	
Roy's Chuck Wagon	RESTAURANT	

| GOLF COURSE ROAD
EAST FIRST STREET
(HIGHWAY 101 EASTBOUND) | 117.5 249.8 | FRONT STREET
(HIGHWAY 101 WESTBOUND) |

Highway 101 divides into two one-way streets at this point. The highway reunites at Lincoln Street in the Port Angeles city center. I will describe the westbound journey on East Front Street here. For a description of eastbound Highway 101, on East First Street see page 185. Stay in the left lane after you join Front Street if you are going to the Olympic National Park Visitors Center and Hurricane Ridge. Access to these attractions is via a left turn at Race Street.

McDonald's PENN STREET Rainier Bank EVELYN AVENUE	117.6 249.7 FAST FOOD BANK	Skippers Seafood & Chowder Baskin Robbins Ice Cream Godfather's Pizza
Frugal's Take Away Seafood	117.7 249.6 FAST FOOD	
ALDER STREET Burger King	117.8 249.5 FAST FOOD	
Chinook Motel	117.9 249.4 ENNIS STREET MOTEL C-STORE GAS	Jackpot Food Mart, Deli, Gas
	118.0 249.3 LIBERTY STREET	
	118.1 249.2 JONES STREET RESTAURANT GAS DELI LAUNDRY	Tanhausers German Restaurant Exxon Gas, Laundromat, Deli
	118.2 249.1 CHAMBERS STREET C-STORE GAS	Shell Gas & C-Store
Budget Host Aircrest Motel	118.3 249.0 WASHINGTON ST. MOTEL	
OLYMPIC NATIONAL PARK VISITORS CENTER PIONEER MEMORIAL MUSEUM HURRICANE RIDGE HEART O THE HILLS CAMPGROUND	118.4 248.9 RACE STREET NATIONAL PARK GAS HOSPITAL	Chevron Service Station HOSPITAL (Go 3 blocks to the right)

HURRICANE RIDGE

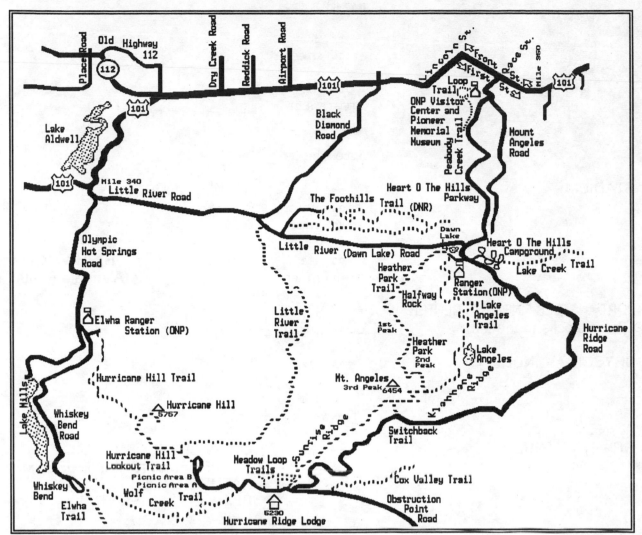

MAP 8-3   HURRICANE RIDGE

We will turn left here to go to the Visitor Center and Museum. Then, we continue on to Hurricane Ridge. The road to Hurricane Ridge has three name changes along the way. It starts on Race Street, which ends at a fork, 0.1 miles past the Visitor Center. We go to the right, on Heart O The Hills Parkway. The road to the left is Mount Angeles Road. Beyond Heart O The Hills Campground, near the entrance to Olympic National Park, the road is known as Hurricane Ridge Road. The mileage figures from Highway 101 are calculated from Front Street (Mile number 248.9) even though eastbound traffic must turn at First Street, and alternate routes for westbound traffic start at Lauridsen Boulevard and at E. Eighth St.

Description of Highway 101 continues at mile 248.9 on Page 184.

171

STADIUM				TENNIS COURTS
	0.0	18.8	FRONT STREET	
	0.1	18.7	FIRST STREET	
	0.2	18.6	SECOND STREET	
STADIUM	0.3	18.5	ERICKSON PARK FOURTH STREET	TENNIS COURTS
	0.6	18.2	EIGHTH STREET	HIGHWAY 101 (Alternate Route)
PORT ANGELES FINE ARTS CENTER (Three blocks to the left)	0.8	18.0	LAURIDSEN BLVD.	
BRYSON AVENUE	0.9	17.9		
	1.0	17.8	PARK AVENUE	
GRANT AVENUE	1.1	17.7		ONP VISITOR CENTER PIONEER MEMORIAL MUSEUM NATURE TRAIL PEABODY CREEK TRAIL

The Visitor Center has the best selection of maps and gifts in the park. There are frequent informative slide shows about the park and Hurricane Ridge.

ONP VISITOR CENTER NATURE TRAIL

There is a loop trail behind the Visitor Center which is cool and green, and amazingly quiet for a trail in the city near busy roads. It is a bit difficult to find unless you know where the trailhead is. The trail is marked by a sign on your right as you enter the first entrance to the parking lot. The first entrance is to the RV parking area. Just the other side of its namesake, Peabody Creek Trail goes to the left. The nature trail goes to the right. Shortly, a path leading to the National Park headquarters goes to the left, and the nature trail goes to the right to return to the Visitor Center parking lot. The loop trail ends about 50 yards to the right of where it started.

PEABODY CREEK TRAIL
(3.0 Miles Long)

This trail starts from the Visitor Center Nature Trail just after you cross Peabody Creek. The nature trail starts on the right as you enter the RV Area of the parking lot.

Peabody Creek Trail, after crossing the creek several times, more or less parallels Heart O The Hills Parkway. At the end of the trail, you can return to the Visitor Center by the road in only 2.3 miles. You might have to push your way through the vegetation for a few yards to get to the road.

We will return to Race Street for its last tenth of a mile, then continue our journey to Hurricane Ridge on Heart O The Hills Parkway.

	RACE STREET		
	MILES from HWY 101	MILES to H. RIDGE	
GRANT AVENUE	1.1	17.7	ONP VISITOR CENTER PIONEER MEMORIAL MUSEUM NATURE TRAIL PEABODY CREEK TRAIL
			ONP VISITOR CENTER - EXIT
MOUNT ANGELES ROAD	1.2 ROAD FORKS	17.6	HEART O THE HILLS PARKWAY
			Take the road to the right for Hurricane Ridge

	HEART O HILLS PWY		
	MILES from HWY 101	MILES to H. RIDGE	
	2.6	16.2	SLOW VEHICLE TURNOUT
	3.2	15.6	SLOW VEHICLE TURNOUT
	5.5	13.3	LOOKOUT
	6.0	12.8	SLOW VEHICLE TURNOUT
	6.1	12.7	LAKE DAWN ROAD (LITTLE RIVER ROAD)

This road is dreadful. Little River and Foothills trails are more easily accessible from the Elwha area. See page 206.

6.4   12.4

ONP ENTRANCE

BOOTH

HEATHER PARK TRAIL
LAKE ANGELES TRAIL

A road to the right, just before the entrance booth for the park, passes a staff residential area before it ends in a parking lot. Lake Angeles Trail is on the left, about halfway to the end of the lot. Heather Park Trail starts from the end.

There is a telephone just past the park entrance.

HEATHER PARK TRAIL
(MOUNT ANGELES TRAIL)
(10.0 Miles Long)

Heather Park Trail, also known as Mount Angeles Trail, offers beautiful vistas on its way to Mount Angeles. Most of the climb gives you unobstructed views through sub-alpine terrain. Near Mount Angeles the trail passes a junction with the Lake Angeles Trail, giving you an opportunity to return to Heart O The Hills in a 12.9 mile loop. Another opportunity to shorten the route is offered after hiking another mile, where Switchback Trail descends 0.6 miles to Hurricane Ridge Road 700 feet below. The lower trailhead of Switchback Trail is 15.8 miles from Highway 101 (Front Street) on Hurricane Ridge Road.

Distances and elevations along the trail are:

Heart O The Hills . . . . 0.0 Miles 1850 Feet
Halfway Rock . . . . 2.3 Miles 3000 Feet
Heather Park . . . . 4.0 Miles 5300 Feet
Heather Pass . . . . 4.5 Miles 5650 Feet
   (Paths to 1st Peak-5740 ft. and 2nd Peak-6025 ft.)

Lake Angeles Trail (Left) . . . . 6.3 Miles 5880 Feet
   (6.5 miles long, 4050 feet elevation gain)

Switchback Trail (Left) . . . . 7.4 Miles 5100 Feet
   (0.5 miles long, 700 feet elevation gain)

Path, Mt. Angeles summit-6454 ft. . . . . . . 7.6 Miles 5100 Feet
Hurricane Ridge Lodge . . . . 10.0 Miles 5230 Feet

LAKE ANGELES TRAIL
(KLAHHANE RIDGE TRAIL)
(6.5 Miles Long)

After leaving from the same parking lot as Heather Park Trail, this trail takes you to Lake Angeles, located in a deep cirque. The steep slopes that surround it and a particularly beautiful island in it will make you wish you had brought more film for your camera. There is also a nice waterfall at its upper end. There are campsites at the northern end. A better camp, if you are planning a moonlight hike to Mount Angeles, is Camp Freezeout 1.2 miles south of the lake. The views of the fairy lights of Port Angeles and Victoria are magic. On a clear night you can even see the lights of the ships in the Strait.

The trail ends at a junction with Heather Park Trail and offers you four options. You can retrace your steps back to Heart O The Hills the way you came. You can turn right to complete the other half of a 12.9 mile loop back to Heart O The Hills on Heather Park Trail. You can turn left, and after one mile, turn left again into Switchback Trail which descends to Hurricane Ridge Road 15.8 miles from Highway 101 (Front Street). Finally, you can turn left and continue 3.6 miles past Switchback Trail to Hurricane Ridge Lodge.

Distances and elevations along the trail are:

Heart O The Hills	0.0 Miles	1840 Feet
Ennis Creek Crossing	1.1 Miles	2750 Feet
Lake Angeles	3.5 Miles	4200 Feet
Camp Freezout	5.0 Miles	5850 Feet
Junction Heather Park Trail	6.5 Miles	5880 Feet

We now return to the end of Heart O The Hills Parkway, and the start of Hurricane Ridge Road near the National Park entrance.

HURRICANE RIDGE RD

MILES from HWY 101	MILES to H. RIDGE	
6.4	12.4	**HEATHER PARK TRAIL**
ONP ENTRANCE		**LAKE ANGELES TRAIL**
6.5	12.3	
CAMPGROUND		
AMPHITHEATER		

HEART O THE HILLS CAMPGROUND
LAKE CREEK TRAIL

There are 105 campsites, (no hookups) including 21 pull-throughs. Maximum length is 21 feet. There are picnic tables, potable water, fire places and flush toilets. There are public showers in Port Angeles at Wm. Shore Memorial Pool, 225 E. 5th Street. In summer, programs are presented in the amphitheater.

175

LAKE CREEK TRAIL
(2 Miles Long)

Lake Creek Trail starts from Loop E of the campground. The main road through the campground bends to the right, and Loop E is the last camping loop on the left. The trailhead is to your right immediately after you turn left into loop E. Don't be misled by this trail's name. There is no lake, so bring your own water. The trail takes you through dense vegetation typical of the lowland forests in this area. It follows Lake Creek for two miles to the National Park Boundary according to Park Service literature. Some trail maps show it continuing over private land to Mount Pleasant Road. Others show it stopping after 1.6 miles, some four tenths of a mile short of the boundary. Since it is fairly level, and only 1.6 miles (or 2.0 miles; or 3.5 miles) long it might be worth an afternoon stroll to find out who is right. The best place to park is the amphitheater parking area between loop A and Loop C, on the left as you enter the campground.

We return to Hurricane Ridge Road now, winding our way ever higher to Hurricane Ridge Lodge.

HURRICANE RIDGE RD		
MILES from HWY 101	MILES to H. RIDGE	
6.5	12.3	HEART O THE HILLS CAMPGROUND LAKE CREEK TRAIL
CAMPGROUND		
AMPHITHEATER		
10.0	8.8	LOOKOUT ROCK

LOOKOUT ROCK

This viewpoint overlooks Port Angeles and the Strait of Juan de Fuca. The town looks like a little model railroad town. The lookout has interpretive signs.

10.1	8.7	
3 SHORT TUNNELS		

TURNOUT — 11.0 7.8

TURNOUT — 11.2 7.6

This turnout has a great view of the Strait of Juan de Fuca.

TURNOUT — 11.6 7.2

Here you get a glimpse of the beautiful snow capped peaks, and little snow patches here and there on the slopes.

	MILES from HWY 101	MILES to H. RIDGE	
	11.9	6.9	There are some interesting rock formations along this stretch of the road.
LONG TURNOUT	12.4	6.4	
VIEWPOINT	12.6	6.2	

This viewpoint has interpretive signs. Blue Mountain is to the east, with Deer Park Road turning and twisting up its steep sides.

| VIEWPOINT | 12.7 | 6.1 | |

This large viewpoint has interpretive signs.

TURNOUT	14.3	4.6	
	14.6	4.2	TURNOUT
TURNOUT	15.5	3.3	
TURNOUT	15.6	3.2	Small Cascade
	15.8	3.0	SWITCHBACK TRAIL

The trail climbs steeply from the right side of the car park.

SWITCHBACK TRAIL
(0.5 Miles Long)

Switchback trail is short and steep. From the parking area you can see a little stream that cascades down from the rocky ridge above. Although the trail looks almost vertical, it is the shortest and fastest way to Mount Angeles. It ends at the Heather Park Trail. There, you can either turn left, and traverse to Hurricane Ridge Lodge in 3.6 miles, or turn right and descend to Heart O The Hills. If you turn right you will have a choice between continuing on the Heather Park Trail, or diverting to the Lake Angeles Trail which branches to the right in one mile. It is about eight miles to Heart O The Hills by either route.

TURNOUT	16.3 2.5	

Here you see grassy sub-alpine meadows above you and on the other side of the valley.

TURNOUT	17.0 1.8	SMALL GRAVEL TURNOUT
TURNOUT	17.1 1.7	SMALL GRAVEL TURNOUT
	18.1 0.7	TURNOUT
TURNOUT	18.2 0.6	

There is a marvelous view of the glacier fields from here.

	18.4 0.4	TURNOUT
OBSTRUCTION POINT ROAD	18.6 0.2	

You probably won't see Obstruction Point Road when you come from this direction. It comes in at an acute angle, and drops off in elevation quite sharply. For safe access to it, continue on into the parking area where you can turn around.

HURRICANE RIDGE LODGE	18.8 0.0 HURRICANE RIDGE	MEADOW LOOP TRAILS HEATHER PARK TRAIL

HURRICANE RIDGE LODGE
(Hurricane Ridge Visitor Center)

Hurricane Ridge is the most accessible viewpoint in the peninsula for the glacier shrouded inner mountains. There is nowhere else that you can see the effects of the geologic upheavals of 20 to 40 million years ago without even leaving your car. It is hard to believe that 50 million years ago these mile-high rocks and crags were lying peacefully at the bottom of the sea.

The ridge stretches for eleven miles, from Hurricane Hill to Obstruction Point. Most visitors to Hurricane Ridge confine their visits to the developed areas surrounding Hurricane Ridge Lodge, and along the paved road to the Hurricane Hill Trail trailhead, where the views are merely spectacular. Although these visitors return home content that they have obtained full value from their trip, I strongly encourage those with the time, to stray a bit further afield. Walk to the summit of Hurricane Hill; or get a much better view of Mount Olympus from Alpine Hill where it is less obscured by the Bailey Range; or study the interesting differences in the plant life along each side of the knife-edge of Sunrise Ridge. Two entirely different habitats exist, only a few feet apart. None of these walks is particularly steep, and part of the Hurricane Hill Trail is paved.

For a change of pace, drive to Obstruction Point for an appreciation of what the roads were like before the construction of the present Hurricane Ridge Road. Obstruction Point Road is a narrow, steep, twisty road with lots of bumps. It must cost the Park Service a fortune to install all the potholes. The plus side of this road is that you get to enjoy some magnificent views (from the comfort of your car) in relative solitude, and gain access to some of the best hiking trails in the high country of the Olympics. Although the road is shocking by comparison to Hurricane Ridge Road, it is safe if you drive slowly and remain alert for other cars from either direction.

Hurricane Ridge Lodge has a misleading name. The ridge is a day-use only area. There is no accommodation at the lodge, and camping is not permitted. Some sources are beginning to refer to it as "Hurricane Ridge Visitor Center". Naturalist programs are presented daily in summer to complement several interesting exhibits. Metal plaques explain the scenery that one observes from the large deck at the back of the center. The center also has a snack bar and a gift shop. Rangers operate an information booth and provide trail information. Two large picnic areas are located about a mile from the lodge toward Hurricane Hill.

MEADOW LOOP TRAILS

These paved trails start in Big Meadow, across the road from the lodge. They begin from each end of the parking area. There is also an access path in the middle of the parking area. The west end of the Cirque Rim Trail is at the western end of the parking area, where the road to Hurricane Hill begins. It follows the rim, to a junction with the middle path, then proceeds to a point about even with the eastern end of the parking area before turning back towards the lodge. Just after the turn, an unpaved trail to Sunrise Ridge goes off to your left. Shortly thereafter, another trail goes to the right, along a line of trees that separate it from the Cirque Rim Trail, to the middle path. As you come out of the trees, a paved trail on your left takes you to Alpine Hill for a better look at Mount Olympus. It is paved for about half the distance to Alpine Hill. It then continues on past the mountain, to intersect the trail mentioned above to Sunrise Ridge. Turn right at this intersection, and you join Heather Park Trail which traverses Sunrise Ridge and Klahhane Ridge to Mount Angeles and Heart O The Hills. See page 174. A left turn will return you to Big Meadow and the lodge. You often see Black Tail Deer, and hear the whistle of marmots nearby on these trails. Wildflowers grow profusely in the open areas along these trails throughout the summer months.

Access to the picnic areas and more trails is by Old Hurricane Ridge Road which goes to the trailhead for Hurricane Hill Trail.

	MILES from H.R.LODGE	MILES to H. HILL TR.	
HURRICANE RIDGE LODGE	0.0	1.2	
	0.2	1.0	PAVED LOOKOUT
WOLF CREEK TRAIL	0.6	0.8	SMALL GRAVEL PARKING AREA

This trail follows the roadbed of the old Hurricane Ridge Rd. It was abandoned when the new road was built. It drops 3750 feet in the 8 miles to Whiskey Bend. Details of the trail are on page 213.

PICNIC AREA - UNIT A	0.9	0.5	

There are paved paths to 30 picnic tables on paved sites. These sites are nestled in the trees, and have great views. There is an amenities building with drinking fountains, water taps and flush toilets. Open fires are not permitted.

PICNIC AREA - UNIT B	1.1	0.2	

This picnic area duplicates the facilities of Unit A above.

HURRICANE HILL LOOKOUT TRAIL HURRICANE HILL TRAIL LITTLE RIVER TRAIL	1.3 END OF ROAD	0.0	The road ends in a parking area loop. Keep to the right as you enter the loop.

See page 211 for a description of Hurricane Hill Trail, and page 208 for a description of Little River Trail.

HURRICANE HILL LOOKOUT TRAIL
(1.4 Miles Long)

Hurricane Hill Lookout Trail is often referred to as Hurricane Hill Trail. In this section I treat the 1.4 miles from the end of the parking area loop to the top of Hurricane Hill as Hurricane Hill Lookout Trail. I consider the 6.4 miles from the top of Hurricane Hill to Whiskey Bend Road behind the Elwha Ranger Station to be Hurricane Hill Trail. The two trails overlap for the last 0.2 miles to the summit of Hurricane Hill.

Hurricane Hill Lookout Trail is paved for its first half mile. It starts out in a meadow that is filled with wildflowers until the end of summer. The huge lump of rock on your right is Mount Angeles. To your left you look down the Elwha Valley. In the distance, you can see the vegetation zones changing from the forests of the lowlands to the meadows of the sub-alpine zone, and finally the snow and ice and bare rocks of the Bailey Range demonstrate the Arctic-alpine zone. At the summit, you have panoramic views from the Strait and the Cascades to the inner peaks of the Olympics.

Distances and elevations along the trail are:

    Parking Area . . . . 0.0 Miles 5000 Feet
    Little River Trail . . . . 0.2 Miles 5125 Feet
        (8.1 miles long, 4225 feet elevation gain)

    Hurricane Hill Trail . . . . 1.2 Miles 5640 Feet
        (6.3 miles long, 5300 feet elevation gain)

    Summit of Hurricane Hill . . . . 1.4 Miles 5757 Feet

We now return to the east end of the Lodge parking area, to start our journey to Obstruction Point.

OBSTRUCTION POINT

Obstruction Point Road starts from the east end of the parking area for Hurricane Ridge Lodge at a fork in the road. The angle between the two roads is so acute, that turns into Obstruction Point Road can only be safely negotiated by eastbound traffic. The road is steep, narrow, twisty and rough, but your efforts are amply rewarded by the beautiful views on the drive, and the trails that the drive gives access to. Although the road looks scary to those of us accustomed to modern freeways, it is quite safe for passenger cars In good mechanical condition. If you remain alert for cars from both directions, and drive at a reasonable speed, before long, you will find that you are enjoying the drive.

	OBSTRUCTION POINT ROAD		
	MILES from H. RIDGE RD.	MILES to OBST. POINT	
HURRICANE RIDGE ROAD	0.0	7.5	Sign: "Obstruction Point 7.8 Mi. Primitive Road. Not Suitable for Trailers." I reckon it is 7.5 miles to Obstruction Point.
COX VALLEY TRAIL	0.6	6.9	

COX VALLEY TRAIL
(2.0 Miles Long)

This unmarked and unmaintained trail starts at an elevation of 4870 feet on the left side of Obstruction Point Road, 0.6 miles from Hurricane Ridge Road. There is a tiny parking area at the trailhead that is easy to miss if no one is parked in it. It is a remnant of the old Morse Creek Trail, but it has deteriorated to the point that it is difficult to follow, and disappears altogether in a meadow two miles from the road, at an elevation of 3600 feet. There is a campsite at the one mile mark.

We will return now to Obstruction Point Road.

	OBSTRUCTION POINT ROAD		
	MILES from H. RIDGE RD.	MILES to OBST. POINT	
COX VALLEY TRAIL	0.6	6.9	
P.J. LAKE TRAIL	3.7	3.8	Sign: NO CAMPING Sign: ROUGH ROAD

P.J. LAKE TRAIL
(1.0 Miles Long)

There is no evidence of a trail near the road, but on your left you can see a clearing. Further investigation discloses an abandoned campground. On the other side of the clearing is a sign marking the trailhead. The trail is an unmaintained way trail, that descends sharply for about a mile to a small glacial lake. There are wide pullouts on both sides of the road for parking.

P.J. LAKE TRAIL	3.7	3.8	
GRAND RIDGE TRAIL	7.5	0.0	GRAND PASS TRAIL
BADGER VALLEY TRAIL	END OF ROAD		
ELK MOUNTAIN WAY TRAIL	OBSTRUCTION PT.		

The road ends at Obstruction Point, 6150 feet elevation, on the slopes of Obstruction Peak in the barren high country. This area is in the rain shadow, so it is quite dry. By mid summer there are only small patches of snow in protected areas. When you look off to the southwest, you can see where all the missing snow is lurking. The snowy peaks and glaciers of the Bailey Range and Mount Olympus sparkle in the distance.

There is a small parking area at the end of the road, where signs mark the trailheads of two trails, Grand Ridge Trail to your left, and Grand Pass Trail to your right. Grand Ridge Trail is a superb high country trail that gives you unobstructed views as it passes though sub-alpine terrain between 5000 and 6500 feet elevation. Details on the Grand Ridge Trail appear on page 165. Elk Mountain Way Trail connects Grand Ridge Trail to Badger Valley Trail. It leaves Grand Ridge Trail two miles from Obstruction Point. Details of Elk Mountain Way Trail are on page 166.

BADGER VALLEY TRAIL
(4.5 Miles Long)

Badger Valley Trail starts from Grand Ridge Trail (the trailhead on your left) 0.2 miles from Obstruction Point. Combining the first 0.8 miles of it with Elk Mountain Way Trail and Grand Ridge Trail makes a nice four mile loop. Badger Valley Trail traverses a shale slope before it drops 2050 feet in elevation by the time you reach Emergency Camp (where fires are permitted). The trail then gains 950 feet before it ends at the Grand Pass Trail west of Grand Lake.

Distances and elevations along the trail are:

Grand Ridge Trail Trailhead . . . . 0.0 Miles 6050 Feet
Elk Mountain Way Trail . . . . 0.8 Miles 5300 Feet
   (1.0 miles long, 1275 feet elevation gain)

Emergency Camp . . . . 2.8 miles 4000 Feet
Grand Lake-Path to S. shore camp . . . . 4.3 Miles 4740 Feet
Grand Pass Trail . . . . 4.5 Miles 4950 Feet
   (8.0 miles long, 1200 feet elevation gain)

GRAND PASS TRAIL
(8.0 Miles Long)

Grand Pass trail starts from Obstruction Point. It is the trailhead on the right. Its elevation loss of 1950 feet to Cameron Creek Trail is a little misleading, as the trail climbs and descends several times along the way. Most of the trail is above the timber line, giving you expansive views. There are three lakes in the Grand Valley that are stocked with trout. An added attraction of Grand Lake, the largest of the three, is beautiful Amalia Falls. There is also an unnamed peak (6701 feet) near Grand Pass that gives you good views of Mount Olympus.

Distance and elevations along the trail are:

Obstruction Point . . . . 0.0 Miles 6150 Feet
Highest Point of Trail . . . . 2.1 Miles 6450 Feet
Badger Valley Trail . . . . 3.8 Miles 4950 Feet
   (4.5 Miles Long 2050 feet elevation gain)

Moose Lake . . . . 4.3 Miles 5075 Feet
Grand Pass . . . . 6.3 Miles 6450 Feet
Cameron Creek Trail . . . . 8.0 Miles 4200 Feet
   (11.3 miles long, 4350 feet elevation gain)

We will now return to mile 248.9 of Highway 101 on Front Street.

There are two alternate routes for westbound Highway 101 that allow you to avoid the city center. The first is Lauridsen Boulevard. Continue past the ONP Visitor Center in Race Street to Lauridsen Boulevard, the second major intersection. Turn left and go 7 blocks to Highway 101 at the junction where Lincoln Street and 14th Street come in from the right and merge with Lauridsen Boulevard. Eighth Street is an official alternate route of westbound Highway 101. You turn left into it from Race Street three blocks north of Lauridsen Boulevard. You will rejoin Highway 101 in seven blocks when you turn left at Lincoln Street.

HIGHWAY 101

MILES   MILE
from   NUMBER
I-5

OLYMPIC NATIONAL PARK
  VISITORS CENTER
PIONEER MEMORIAL MUSEUM
HURRICANE RIDGE
HEART O THE HILLS CAMPGROUND

118.4   248.9
RACE STREET
NATIONAL PARK
GAS
HOSPITAL

Chevron Service Station
HOSPITAL (Turn right, 3 blocks, then right again.)

118.6   248.7
FRANCIS STREET

118.7   248.6
EUNICE STREET

AGGIE'S MOTEL

118.8   248.5
ALBERT STREET
MOTEL

118.9   248.4
VINE STREET

PEABODY STREET

119.0   248.3

HIGHWAY 101 (Westbound)

119.2   248.1
LINCOLN STREET
RESTAURANT
TOURIST INFO
MUSEUM   FERRIES

Red Lion Motel
La Casita Restaurant
Haguewood's Restaurant
CITY PIER
WATERFRONT VISITORS CENTER
FERRY TERMINALS

PORT ANGELES CITY CENTER

Highway 101 goes to the left here. Turn right for a 5 block loop tour of Downtown Port Angeles. Go right on Lincoln Street for one block; left on Railroad Avenue for one block; left on Laurel for two blocks; left on First Street for one block, and rejoin Westbound Highway 101 by turning right into Lincoln Street.

Some of the attractions on this route are listed below in pretty much the same sequence as you will encounter them along the 5 block route. I have also indicated whether they are on the right side of the street or the left.

> City Pier - Restrooms, Marine Lab & Touching Zoo - Right
> Chamber of Commerce Visitors Center - Right
>   (Ask them for directions to the other attractions)
> Coho Ferry Terminal - Right

The Tourist Trap - Gifts and Travel - Left
Olympic Stained Glass - Right
First Street Haven Restaurant - Left
Treehouse Toys - Right

EASTBOUND HIGHWAY 101
(East First Street)
From Lincoln Street to Golf Course Road

Here, Highway 101 divides into two one-way streets. Westbound traffic uses Front Street. Eastbound traffic turns right from Lincoln Street into East First Street, and follows it to Golf Course Road where the two routes rejoin. In the listing below, I have used mile numbers consistent with the Front Street route. Description of Westbound Highway 101 continues from mile 248.1 on page 187.

	EASTBOUND HIGHWAY 101	
	MILES from I-5	MILE NUMBER
	119.2 LINCOLN STREET GAS	248.1	**FIRST STREET (EASTBOUND HIGHWAY 101)** Gull Service Station

We start Eastbound Highway 101 by turning right from Lincoln Street into East First Street.

| | 119.1 CHASE STREET | 248.2 | |

POST OFFICE at 119.0 PEABODY STREET 248.3

Flagstone Motel — 118.9 VINE STREET MOTEL 248.4

Royal Victorian Motel
Handy Spot Groceries
Aggie's Motel, Restaurant
Chevron Service Station
— 118.8 ALBERT STREET MOTEL GENERAL STORE RESTAURANT C-STORE GAS 248.5 — **Swain's General Store**

118.7 EUNICE STREET RESTAURANT 248.6 — **Birney's Restaurant**

Louie's Burgers — 118.6 FRANCIS STREET FAST FOOD MOTEL 248.7 — **Ruffles Motel**

(left side)	MILES from I-5	MILE NUMBER	(right side)
HOSPITAL (Left 3 blocks, then right.) Mobil Service Sta. - Car Wash	118.4	248.9 RACE STREET HOSPITAL FAST FOOD GAS	A & W Family Drive In Kentucky Fried Chicken
Texaco Service Station El Amigo Restaurant The Wreck Tavern	118.3	249.0 WASHINGTON ST. RESTAURANT TAVERN GAS	
	118.2	249.1 CHAMBERS STREET	
Gordy's Pizza & Deli Traveller's Motel	118.1	249.2 JONES STREET FAST FOOD BANK GAS	Northwestern National Bank
Doranian Motel Payless Gas Shell Station	118.0	249.3 LIBERTY STREET MOTEL TAVERN GAS FAST FOOD	The Sub Shop Sunrise Tavern
Chinook Motel	117.9	249.4 ENNIS STREET MOTEL	
Burger King Bushwhacker Prime Rib and Seafood	117.8	249.5 ALDER STREET FAST FOODS RESTAURANT	Its All Greek to Me (Greek food to go)
Rainier Bank	117.6	249.7 EVELYN STREET BANK	
McDonald's	117.6	259.7 PENN STREET FAST FOODS	Wendy's
	117.5	259.8 GOLF COURSE RD.	

This completes the listing for the eastbound section of Highway 101 on East First Street. We now return to Front Street in the city center where we turn left into Lincoln Street to continue our trip, westbound on Highway 101.

HIGHWAY 101 (Westbound)

Hwy. 101 turns left here, from Front Street into Lincoln St.

119.2 248.1	CITY PIER
LINCOLN STREET	WATERFRONT VISITORS CENTER
	FERRY TERMINALS

Gull Service Station - Deli
City Center Trailer Park

119.2 248.1	Gift Shop
FIRST STREET	Elbo Inn Tavern
RV PARK GAS	
TAVERN	

This trailer park (adults only) has 24 sites with hook-ups. It is within walking distance of shopping and ferries. It has a laundry, showers, flush toilets, and a dump station.

CITY LIBRARY
CITY PARK

119.3 248.0	Uptown Motel (Right 1 Block)
SECOND STREET	Safeway Supermarket
THIRD STREET	
MOTEL	
SUPERMARKET	

CLALLAM COUNTY COURTHOUSE
CLALLAM COUNTY MUSEUM

119.4 247.9	Black Kettle Restaurant
FOURTH STREET	
RESTAURANT	

WM. SHORE MEM. SWIMMING POOL
(Left one block on 5th Street)
Public Showers.

119.5 247.8	Texaco Service Station
FIFTH STREET	
POOL SHOWER GAS	

Albertson's Supermarket
Pay n Save Drug Store

119.6 247.7	Chevron Service Station
SIXTH STREET	Gordy's Cafe
SEVENTH STREET	U.S. Bank
SUPERMARKET	
DRUG STORE	
GAS CAFE	

Mobil Service Station
Country Store 2nd Hand Shop

119.7 247.6	Round The Clock Deli, Groceries
EIGHTH STREET	
C-STORE GAS	
2ND HAND STORE	

Drake's U-Bake Pizza

119.8   247.5
NINTH STREET
TENTH STREET
FAST FOOD

119.9   247.4
ELEVENTH STREET

187

	120.0 247.3	
	TWELFTH STREET	

	120.1 247.2	
	THIRTEENTH ST.	

All View Motel	120.2 247.1	FOURTEENTH STREET
Short Stop Exxon & Groceries	LAURIDSEN BLVD.	LAUREL STREET
Walt's Blvd. Texaco & Grocery	MOTEL	
	C-STORE GAS	

Lincoln St. goes to the right as it passes 14th Street and merges with Lauridsen Boulevard coming in from the left.

LAUREL STREET	120.3 247.0	OAK STREET
Arlene's Washington Only	GIFTS WINE	
Gift and Wine Shop		

OAK STREET	120.4 246.9	CHERRY STREET
		WEST FIFTEENTH STREET

BLACK DIAMOND ROAD	120.6 246.7	PINE STREET
	PORT ANGELES	
	CITY LIMITS	

	121.0 246.3	NICHOLAS AVENUE

DOYLE ROAD	121.3 246.0	NEWELL ROAD
EASTBOUND HWY. 101 TRUCK ROUTE	EUCLID AVENUE	

DAVIS ROAD	121.4 245.9	Fairmount Motel Restaurant,
	FAIRMOUNT AVE.	Fairmount Service and Grocery
	MOTEL	
	C-STORE GAS	

	121.5 245.8	Welcome Inn RV & Trailer Court
	RV PARK PROPANE	

Welcome Inn has 100 sites, 53 with hook-ups. 16 are drive-through. It has showers, laundry, flush toilets, a dump station and propane.

	121.6 245.7	BEAN ROAD

BENSON ROAD	121.8 245.5	The Pond Thunderbird Motel
	MOTEL	

122.2	245.1	AIRPORT ROAD
	AIRPORT	FAIRCHILD INTERNATIONAL AIRPORT
122.7	244.6	FEY ROAD
123.0	244.3	REDDICK ROAD
123.5	243.8	DRY CREEK ROAD
124.4	242.9	WEST (112)

CAMERON ROAD

SEKIU
NEAH BAY   MAKAW MUSEUM
SALMON SPAWNING CHANNEL

We will stop here for now, and start off Chapter 9 with a side trip on Washington Highway 112.

Wagner's Grocery and Chevron, and The Junction Tavern are just beyond the point where Highway 112 goes off to the right. Both are on the right as you continue on Highway 101.

The description of Highway 101 continues from mile 242.9 on page 206.

Wetland Clearing from Cape Alava Trail in the Ozette Area of the Olympic National Park.

CHAPTER 9

HIGHWAY 112   ELWHA   LAKE CRESCENT

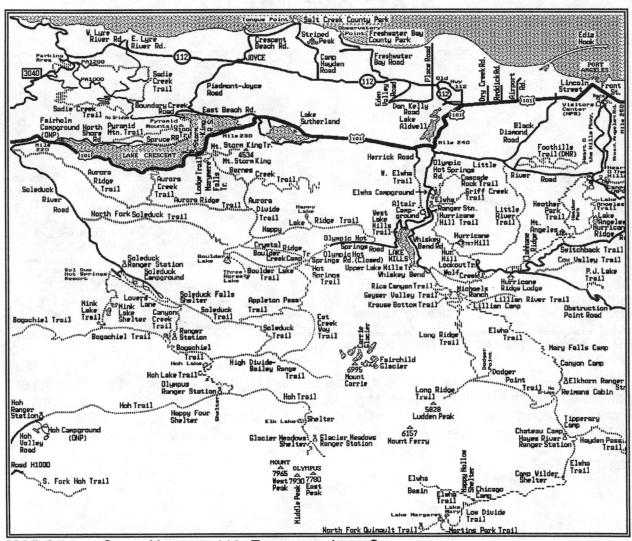

MAP 9-1   STATE HIGHWAY 112, ELWHA AND LAKE CRESCENT

We will now explore State Highway 112 which is mainly served by state and county recreational facilities, rather than the National Forest and National Park facilities that have been the mainstay of our journey until now. Many of the state and county facilities are

191

superb. They are seldom crowded, even in midsummer. Many people come to the Olympic Peninsula with a limited knowledge of the area and spend most of their stay at the centerpieces of Olympic National Park, Hurricane Ridge, and the Hoh River Rainforest.

After our Highway 112 excursion, we will return to Highway 101 to visit the Elwha Area, and its extensive system of trails in the National Park. We then continue on to Lake Crescent. Lake Crescent can be any color from deep blue to emerald green, depending on the time of day and weather conditions. There are frequent scenic lookouts, and picnic areas as Highway 101 writhes along the south shore. Stop for a while, and witness the changes in the lake as you watch.

The description of Highway 101 resumes at mile 242.9 on page 206.

STATE HIGHWAY 112

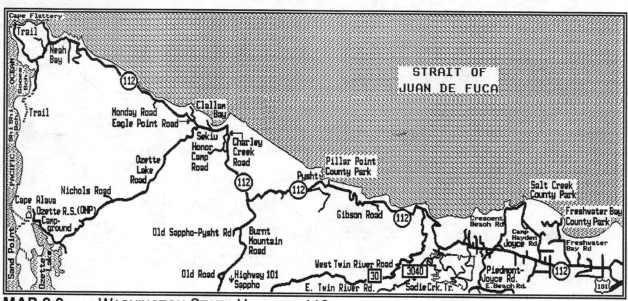

MAP 9-2   WASHINGTON STATE HIGHWAY 112

State Highway 112 starts on your right at mile 242.9 of Highway 101. Since the mileposts are numbered from the Neah Bay end of Highway 112, in the far northwest corner of the Olympic Peninsula, we start at mile number 61.4. The road is paved, and in good condition. It more or less parallels the northern coast, and is seldom more than a few miles from the strait.

HIGHWAY 112

MILES from HWY.101	MILES to NEAH BAY
0.0	61.4
BEGIN HWY. 112	

0.2	61.2	AIRPORT SALMON SPAWNING CHANNEL (2 miles)

OAKERMAN ROAD   0.4   61.0

LOWER DAM ROAD   1.0   60.4   POWER PLANT ROAD
SCENIC VIEW

RV PARK   PHONE
VIEWPOINT

Shady Tree RV Park is to the left immediately after you turn left into Lower Dam Road. The Scenic Viewpoint is to the right.

Shady Tree RV Park has 33 sites with hook-ups, a store, phone, showers and flush toilets.

The scenic view is of the Elwha Valley and the Highway 112 Elwha River bridge. There is a large paved parking area and turn-around loop with 3 pull-through spaces. There are also a couple of fishermen's paths that might bear investigation.

1.4   60.0
MILEPOST

WIDE TURNOUT   1.7   59.7

2.3   59.1   ELWHA RIVER ROAD

DAN KELLY ROAD   2.6   58.8   PLACE ROAD
COLVILLE ROAD

EDEN VALLEY ROAD   3.8   57.6   PETES ROAD

4.1   57.3   TURNOUT

4.7   56.7   OXENFORD ROAD

4.8   56.6

FRESHWATER BAY ROAD
FRESHWATER BAY COUNTY PARK
STRIPED PEAK VISTA AND TRAIL

Seventeen acre Freshwater Bay County Park is 2.5 miles from Highway 112 on Freshwater Bay Road, which is paved. As you enter the park, there is parking for the picnic area, a rubbish bin, and toilets on your right. The paved road continues to a boat launch and parking area for oversized vehicles and trailers. There is more parking near the start of the gravel road that goes to Striped Peak.

STRIPED PEAK VISTA & TRAIL

The gravel road to your left leads to Striped Peak Vista and Trail, 2.0 miles from the picnic area. Keep to your left at forks that look like they may be the main road. Although Striped Peak is not classified as a campground by DNR, there is plenty of level ground, and even a metal fire ring if you continue down the abandoned section of the road near the viewpoint. There is a parking area on your right, and a path along the edge of a cliff overlooking the sea to your left. In summer there are raspberries on the bushes beside the path. At the end of the cliff, to the east, the path descends through the trees to the water. I was unable to find the trail that comes from Salt Creek County Park, so you should probably hike it from the Salt Creek end. That trailhead is to your right, just past the entrance to Salt Creek County Park. (See page 195 below.) The hike is also a little confusing in that Striped peak has two summits. The western summit is at an elevation of 1166 feet, and the eastern summit is at 1018 feet.

We now return to mile 56.6 of Highway 112.

4.8   56.6

FRESHWATER BAY ROAD
FRESHWATER BAY COUNTY PARK
STRIPED PEAK VISTA AND TRAIL

GERBER ROAD   5.3   56.1

	MILES from HWY. 101	MILES to NEAH BAY	
DODGER LANE	5.9	55.5	
VERT ROAD	6.4	55.0	
WASKENKARI ROAD	6.9	54.5	THOMPSON ROAD
	7.2	54.2	JOHNSON ROAD
	7.5 C-STORE GAS TAVERN PHONE CAMPGROUND RV PARK	53.9	CAMP HAYDEN ROAD (CRESCENT BEACH ROAD) SALT CREEK RECREATION AREA

SALT CREEK COUNTY PARK
Salt Creek Inn and Mini-Mart
Carols Crescent Beach Resort

Salt Creek Inn and Salt Creek Mini-Mart are on the northwest corner of the intersection of Highway 112 and Camp Hayden Rd.

Carols Crescent Beach offers day use of the beach. There are hook-ups, showers, laundry and flush toilets. The resort is on your right in Crescent Beach Road, 1.8 miles west of where it branches left from Camp Hayden Road at a fork 3.3 miles from Highway 112.

SALT CREEK COUNTY PARK

Salt Creek County Park is a 196 acre park that was created from Fort Hayden, a World War II harbor defense site. Although the cannons were scrapped years ago, the old bunkers are still there. There are 80 sites (no hook-ups), a public telephone, showers, dump station, picnic tables, kitchen shelters, marine life sanctuary, horseshoe pits, baseball field, and hiking trails.

To get to the park you turn right from Highway 112 into Camp Hayden Road. The road forks 3.3 miles from Highway 112. Camp Hayden Road continues straight (the right branch), and Crescent Beach Road goes off to the left. The park entrance is another 0.2 miles on Camp Hayden Road, 3.5 miles from Highway 112.

About 2.6 miles from Highway 112 you will pass a loop road named Camp Hayden Park Road. Its other end is 0.6 miles farther on. Neither of these roads is the correct one for the park entrance.

The trailheads for the trails to the cove (1.1 miles), and to Striped Peak (2.4 miles) are located in a small road to your right just past the entrance to the park. There are two beach trails. One leaves from the parking area at the northwest corner of the bunkers. The other starts from Crescent Beach Road just past the turn-off for the park. There are two small parking areas before you reach the trailhead, and a toilet at the trailhead. There are also several short trails to the tidepools on Tongue Point.

We now return to mile 54.1 of Highway 112.

	HIGHWAY 112		
	MILES from HWY. 101	MILES to NEAH BAY	
	7.5 C-STORE TAVERN CAMPGROUND RV PARK	53.9 GAS PHONE	CAMP HAYDEN ROAD (CRESCENT BEACH ROAD) SALT CREEK RECREATION AREA
			SALT CREEK COUNTY PARK Salt Creek Inn Salt Creek Mini-Mart Carols Crescent Beach
GRAUL-RAMAPO ROAD	7.7	53.7	
	8.4	53.0	NORDSTROM ROAD
DEMPSEY ROAD	8.7	52.7	
BISHOP ROAD	9.2	52.2	
MILLER ROAD	9.5	51.9	TURNOUT
	9.9 ENTERING JOYCE	51.5	
Chevron Service Station	10.4 GAS LAUNDROMAT C-STORE	51.0 GIFTS	Joyce Depot Laundromat CRESCENT BEACH ROAD Joyce General Store
Family Kitchen Cafe	10.5 RESTAURANT GAS POST OFFICE	50.9	Unocal 76 Service Station POST OFFICE
The End Zone Fast Foods	10.7 FAST FOODS	50.7	
PIEDMONT-JOYCE ROAD PIEDMONT RECREATION AREA LAKE CRESCENT EAST BEACH	11.1	50.3	AGATE BEACH ROAD

196

	from	to
	11.0	50.4
LEAVING JOYCE		
	11.4	50.0
MILEPOST		
WYE ROAD	12.2	49.2
	12.4	49.0

SCHMITT ROAD
WHISKEY CREEK RECREATION AREA
Whiskey Creek Beach

Whiskey Creek Beach is a private resort with cabins and 40 tent sites in addition to 11 self-contained RV sites. The RV sites have potable water and sewer hook-ups, but no electricity. There are tables, a laundry and a boat launch.

To get there, turn left into Schmitt Road. Continue north on the gravel road when the paved road goes to the left.

GOSSETT ROAD	12.9	48.5
HOWARD ROAD	13.9	47.5

FARRINGTON ROAD

WATER LINE	14.6	46.8

REYNOLDS ROAD

	14 9	46.5
CAMPGROUND		

EAST LYRE RIVER ROAD
LYRE RIVER CAMPGROUND (DNR)

Lyre River Campground has 11 sites (maximum trailer length 20 feet). Some are on the river bank, nestled in among the maples alders and conifers There is potable water, a shelter and pit toilets.

To reach the campground, turn left into E. Lyre River Rd. Go 0.4 miles and turn left into a gravel road that leads down to the river and the campground.

197

15.2	46.2
LYRE RIVER	

Road to north segment of Sadie Creek Trail   15.5   45.9

15.6	45.8
RV PARK	
RESORT	

WEST LYRE RIVER ROAD
LYRE RIVER RECREATION AREA
Lyre River Park
Harrison Beach

Lyre River Park is 0.5 miles to the right on W. Lyre River Road There are 60 hook-up sites and 15 tent sites, some with electricity. There are picnic tables, pay showers, dump station, flush toilets, laundry, recreation room, store, propane and a boat ramp. Clallam Transit buses stop at the office.

Harrison Beach resort is next door to Lyre River Park. They rent cabins, mobile homes and trailers complete with cooking utensils, dishes and cutlery.

3040 (EAST TWIN RIVER ROAD) SADIE CREEK TRAIL (DNR)

18.8   42.6

To reach Sadie Creek Trail, turn left into FSR 3040 which starts in an open area created by a recent clearcut. Go 0.1 miles to a small road on your right. Turn right and go another 0.1 miles to a parking area. The trailhead is on your left just before you reach the parking area. There is an unloading platform, and, at the far north end of the parking area there is a toilet.

SADIE CREEK TRAIL
(18.1 Miles Long)
Department of Natural Resources

Sadie Creek Trail (elevation gain 2100 feet) is a hidden treasure. It is not shown on most maps, so you may have the entire trail to yourself. My curiosity was piqued when I saw the southern segment of it, with no access roads marked, on a quad of Lake Crescent. The 18.1 mile loop includes 4.6 miles along made roads. The northern segment is a relatively flat, easy walk. The southern segment is more difficult. Near the start of the southern segment, a series of switch backs climbs to 2400 feet with no let-up. From there you climb more gradually for about half a mile to the highest point on the trail, 2731 feet. There, the worst is over with a long traverse before you descend to DNR Road PA1000 near Boundary Creek.

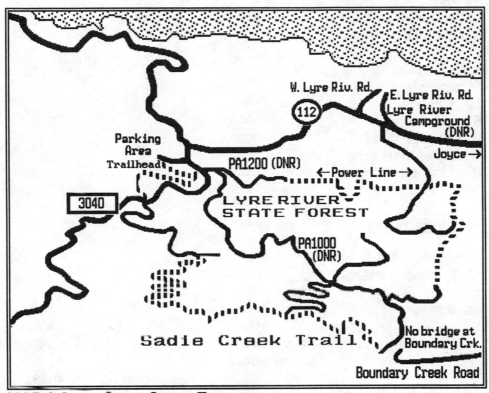

MAP 9-3 SADIE CREEK TRAIL

Assuming a counter-clockwise hike to put the more difficult southern segment first, distances and elevations along the way are as follows:

Parking Area . . . . 0.0 Miles 600 Feet
Path to DNR PA1000 & FSR 3040 jct. . . . 0.2 Miles 600 Feet
Cross FSR 3040 to primitive road . . . . . . 1.6 Miles 800 Feet
Trail resumes (Switchbacks start) . . . . . . 2.6 Miles 200 Feet
Junction primitive road (left) . . . . 8.3 Miles 2050 Feet
Southern end of DNR PA1000 . . . . 10.1 Miles 700 Feet
Primitive road (right) . . . . 11.1 Miles 900 Feet
Trail resumes . . . . 12.1 Miles 750 Feet
Road to Hwy 112 left, Trail right . . . . . . 13.2 Miles 300 Feet

Power Line (Trail turns west)	13.8 Miles 250 Feet
Cross Road to Highway 112	14.1 Miles 450 Feet
East end of DNR PA1200	16.3 Miles 800 Feet
Junction DNR PA1000 (turn right)	17.7 Miles 650 Feet
Cross FSR 3040, then turn right	17.9 Miles 600 Feet
Parking Area	18.1 Miles 600 Feet

We will now return to mile 42.6 of Highway 112.

<table>
<thead>
<tr><th colspan="2">HIGHWAY 112</th></tr>
<tr><th>MILES</th><th>MILES</th></tr>
<tr><th>from</th><th>to</th></tr>
<tr><th>HWY. 101</th><th>NEAH BAY</th></tr>
</thead>
<tbody>
</tbody>
</table>

3040 (EAST TWIN RIVER ROAD)
SADIE CREEK TRAIL (DNR)

18.8   42.6

FSR 3040, after passing Sadie Creek Trail, ultimately makes its way through the National Forest, and ends at Snider Rd., 0.5 mi. from Klahowya Campground (NFS) on Highway 101. The road deteriorates markedly for the last 5 miles.

30   (WEST TWIN RIVER ROAD)

22.3   39.1

FSR 30 goes to mile 208.1 of Highway 101, 3.5 miles west of Klahowya Campground (NFS). It is paved for the last 8 miles.

29.0   32.4
RV PARK PROPANE

Jim Creek Silver King Resort

The resort is 0.5 miles north of Highway 112. It has water and electricity hook-ups, picnic tables, store, pay showers, flush toilets, a dump station. There is also a boat launch and a boat dock.

31.2   30.2
COUNTY PARK

PILLAR POINT ROAD
PILLAR POINT COUNTY PARK

Pillar Point County Park is 0.5 miles north of Highway 112, on Pillar Point Road. It has 37 sites (no hook-ups), a picnic shelter, boat launch and flush toilets.

	32.2 29.2	**PYSHT**

The road leaves the coast until we reach Clallam Bay.

BURNT MOUNTAIN ROAD   37.8 23.6   **HIGHWAY 112**
To: CLALLAM BAY

Sappho, on Highway 101, is 10 mi. south on Burnt Mountain Rd.

HONOR CAMP ROAD   43.0 18.4

44.4 17.0   **CLALLAM BAY SPIT PARK**
CLALLAM BAY

Clallam Bay Spit is a 33 acre, day use only, beach park operated jointly by Clallam County and the State Park Commission.

There are several RV Parks, resorts and other tourist services in the Sekiu-Clallam Bay area. The list below includes an outline of major facilities offered by the RV Parks.

SEKIU AND CLALLAM BAY

RV PARKS   (Unless otherwise noted, all have hook-ups, showers, flush toilets and boat launch facilities.)

NAME and LOCATION	PHONE	SITES	DUMP STN.	LP GAS	STORE	LAUNDRY	CAFE
Sam's Trailer and RV Hwy 112 in Clallam Bay	963-2402	20	YES			YES	
Coho Resort and RV Hwy. 112 1 Mi. East of Sekiu	963-2333	64	YES			YES	YES
Surfside Resort Hwy 112 East edge of Sekiu	963-2723	24	YES				YES
Curley's Resort and RV Hwy. 112 in Sekiu	963-2281	12	YES		YES	YES	

RV PARKS (Continued)

NAME and LOCATION	PHONE	SITES	DUMP STN.	LP GAS	STORE	LAUNDRY	CAFE
Rice's Resort 0.2 Mi. North on Main Street, then 0.1 Mi. West on Rice Street	963-2300	16	YES				
Olson's Resort 0.5 Mi. North on Main Street	963-2311	35			YES		YES
Bayview Mobil and RV Airport Road, 1st Road West of Sekiu	963-2750			YES			
Trettevik's Hwy. 112 8 Mi. West of Sekiu	963-2688	26		YES			

RESTAURANTS & LOUNGES
CLALLAM BAY

Breakwater Inn	963-2428
Fishmonger's Kitchen	963-2600
Morgan's Drive In	963-2644
Clallam Bay Inn	963-2759
Smuggler's Inn	963-2521
Spring Tavern	963-2855

RESTAURANTS AND LOUNGES
SEKIU

The Cove	963-2321

OTHER SERVICES
CLALLAM BAY

Baker's Mobil & Mini-Mart	963-2392
Gary's Pay & Save Gas	963-2485
Baker's IGA	963-2392
Clallam Bay Inn Motel	963-2759
Smuggler's Inn Motel	963-2521

OTHER SERVICES
SEKIU

The Cove Motel	963-2321
Ray's Grocery & Gas	963-2604
Sekiu Trading Post	963-2344
Herb's Motel	963-2346
Straitside Motel	963-2604

We return now to mile 17.0 of Highway 112.

HIGHWAY 112

MILES from HWY. 101	MILES to NEAH BAY
44.4	17.0

CLALLAM BAY

46.8	14.6

SEKIU

OZETTE ROAD   49.1 12.3
OLYMPIC NAT'L PARK-OZETTE AREA
RANGER STATION
OZETTE LAKE
OZETTE CAMPGROUND (ONP)
ERICKSONS BAY CAMPGROUND (ONP)
CAPE ALAVA TRAIL
SAND POINT TRAIL

Ozette Campground is 20 miles from Highway 112 on Ozette Rd. It has 12 sites (no hook-ups), potable water, flush toilets, fireplaces, tables, phone and a boat launch.

Ericksons Bay Campground is a boat-in campground on the west bank of Ozette Lake. There are 15 campsites.

The Olympic National Park includes 57 miles of Pacific Ocean coastline. One can walk the entire length of it if he is extremely careful about tides. There are trails at the more dangerous spots, but a tide table is essential, even for a short hike. The two trails mentioned below can be connected into a 9.3 mile loop trail by walking along the beach for the three miles between them.

The trailhead for both of the trails is behind the ranger station in a shelter that has an interesting interpretive display. The trails start out as a single path. Just past the bridge over the Ozette River, Cape Alava Trail branches off to your right.

CAPE ALAVA TRAIL
(3.3 Miles Long)

The northern trail, Cape Alava Trail, takes you 3.3 miles through a spongy wetland. The trail is flat, and most of the time you walk on a wooden walkway. Cape Alava is the western-most point in the contiguous United States. Unfortunately, the archeological dig at Cape Alava has been closed. The artifacts recovered from the 500 year old village are on display at the Makah Museum in Neah Bay. To the north along the beach, there is a trail to get you around Point of Arches (1.0 miles long), and another for the last 1.3 miles along Shi Shi Beach to the Makah Indian Reservation boundary. That trail continues into the reservation to meet the road to Neah Bay near Portage Head and Anderson Point. To the south, you can walk along the beach for three miles, to the southern trail, Sand Point Trail. There are 56 Indian petroglyphs along the way.

SAND POINT TRAIL
(3.0 Miles Long)

Sand Point Trail, the southern trail, has less wetland than Cape Alava Trail, but you still come across sections of wooden walkway where the ground gets a bit soft. When you reach the beach, you can go south for 0.6 miles to a primitive trail on your left that goes 1.9 miles to Ozette Lake. It ends south of Ericksons Bay. The Norwegian Memorial commemorating the seamen who perished in an early 1900s shipwreck is on the beach 7.4 miles beyond the trail to Ozette Lake. If you are really adventurous, pushing on to Rialto Beach 15.6 miles south of Sand Point is a very rewarding hike along the coast.

We will now return to mile 12.3 of Highway 112.

	HIGHWAY 112	
	MILES	MILES
	from	to
	HWY. 101	NEAH BAY

OZETTE ROAD 49.1 12.3
OLYMPIC NAT'L PARK-OZETTE AREA
RANGER STATION
OZETTE LAKE
OZETTE CAMPGROUND (ONP)
ERICSONS BAY CAMPGROUND (ONP)
CAPE ALAVA TRAIL
SAND POINT TRAIL

61.4 0.0
ENTER
MAKAH INDIAN
RESERVATION
HWY. 112 ENDS

Although we have reached mile 0.0 of Highway 112 by my reckoning, 3.5 miles remain before we reach the town of Neah Bay. The road makes you drive a little bit slower here, so that you can enjoy the seascapes.

64.9
NEAH BAY

NEAH BAY

The main attraction in Neah Bay (apart from the great fishing) is the Makah Cultural and Research Center also known as the Makah Museum. It houses the artifacts discovered at a centuries old Makah village that was uncovered by tidal erosion in 1970. Ozette village had been preserved by a sudden mudslide, and the artifacts give us a glimpse of the daily life of the Indians of 500 years ago. The fascinating displays in the museum include a full-scale replica of a 15th century Indian longhouse.

At the western edge of town, the road forks, and the road signs point both ways to Cape Flattery. This is because the road makes a loop. The road is much better if you turn left. It is paved as far as Makah Air Force Station. It is 8.5 miles to the trailhead of a 0.5 mile trail to a high bluff overlooking Tatoosh Island and its lighthouse. This is the northwestern-most corner of the contiguous United States. Whales are often sighted from March until May each year. The trail has a rough tread, and roots reach out and grab your ankles at times. But, it is an easy hike and worth the effort required to keep the errant roots at bay.

If you turn left at the Air Force Station and cross the Waatch River bridge instead of continuing on to Cape Flattery, you find yourself en route to the Shi Shi Beach Trail mentioned above under Cape Alava Trail on page 203. After you cross the Waatch River, keep to your right on the road that goes to Hobuck Beach. Continue past Hobuck Beach, cross the Sooes River and proceed to the trailhead at the end of the road near Anderson Point. Spur trails go to Anderson Point and Portage Head.

It is seven miles from Neah Bay to the end of the road, and the trail to Shi Shi Beach is three miles long. The seclusion of this pristine wilderness beach makes the ten mile journey from Neah Bay seem more like a thousand miles from the stresses of civilization. Stay to watch the sun set if you can.

As was the case with Sekiu-Clallam Bay, there are several RV Parks, resorts and other tourist services in the Neah Bay area. The list below includes an outline of major facilities offered by the RV Parks.

RV PARKS   (Unless otherwise noted, all have hook-ups, showers, flush toilets and boat launch facilities.)

NAME and LOCATION	PHONE	SITES	DUMP STN.	LP GAS	STORE	LAUNDRY	CAFE
Neah Bay Resort Hwy. 112, 3 Mi. East	645-2288	38	YES	YES	YES		YES
MJ & Co. In Town	645-2789	21	YES		YES		
Morton's (No Hook-ups) Hwy. 112 In Town	645-2250	50					
Thunderbird Resort & RV Hwy. 112 In Town	645-2450	45		YES		YES	
Tyee Motel and RV Hwy. 112 In Town	645-2223	40	YES	YES		YES	
The Village Cabins & RV Hwy. 112 In Town, Bayview Ave.	645-2659	32	YES				
Westwind Resort Hwy. 112 In Town	645-2751	26				YES	
Snow Creek Resort (No Hook-ups) Hwy. 112, 3 Mi. East of Town	645-2284	16					

RESTAURANTS	& LOUNGES
Makah Cafe	645-2476
Waterfront Cafe	645-2212
Windsong Cafe	645-2534

OTHER SERVICES

Tryon's Union 76 Station	645-2387
Washburn's Gen. Merchandise	645-2211
Big Salmon Fishing Resort	645-2374
Far West Fishing Resort	645-2270
Ocean Shores Motel	1-800-562-9748
Silver Salmon Resort	645-2388

We return now to mile 242.9 of Highway 101.

HIGHWAY 101

MILES from I-5	MILE NUMBER	
124.4	242.9	STATE HWY 112 WEST SEKIU NEAH BAY MAKAH MUSEUM
124.5 C-STORE	242.8 GAS	Wagner's Grocery and Chevron
124.6	242.7 TAVERN	The Junction Tavern
124.8	242.5	
125.9	241.4	**TURNOUT**
126.9	240.4	**TURNOUT**
127.3	240.0 MILEPOST	
127.7 RESORT GAS	239.6 RV PARK PROPANE	Elwha Resort & Texaco

HANSEN ROAD

OLYMPIC HOT SPRING ROAD
OLYMPIC NAT'L PARK. ELWHA AREA
LITTLE RIVER (DAWN LAKE) ROAD
LITTLE RIVER TRAIL

We turn left here to explore the
Little River and The Foothills Trails,
and then return to the Elwha Area
of Olympic National Park.

Elwha Resort has 4 RV sites with
full hook-ups. Other facilities are
pay showers, flush toilets, picnic
area, store, propane, gas, boat
launch and a cafe. They also have
rental boats and offer raft trips on
the Elwha and West End Rivers.

ELWHA

We will leave Olympic Hot Springs Road immediately after we join it, to go to the trailheads
on Little River Road. Little River Road is signed Dawn Lake Road at its other end, near the
National Park entrance at Heart O The Hills. It is 7.4 miles long, and becomes quite rough

and narrow beyond its intersection with Black Diamond Road. You will save lots of wear and tear on your vehicle (and its driver) by going to its two trails from this end. At the intersection with Black Diamond Road, Little River road makes a 90° right turn and its surface becomes gravel. The paved road that continues is Black Diamond Road.

We then return to Olympic Hot Springs Road, and follow it to Whiskey Bend Road. After a diversion to the trailheads for Elwha Trail and Wolf Creek Trail at the end of Whiskey Bend Road, we return again to Olympic Hot Springs Road and follow it to its end. The Elwha Valley has a long and interesting history. Most of today's Elwha Trail follows the route established by the Press Party Expedition of 1889-90. Stop at the ranger station before you set out on any hikes. There are displays there that document a lot of the efforts that were expended around the turn of the century in subduing the surrounding wilderness.

Description of Highway 101 resumes at mile 239.6 on page 224.

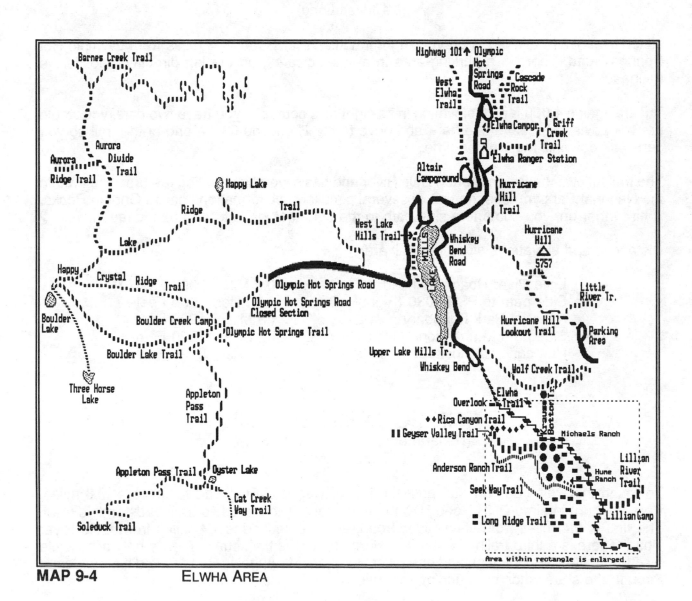

MAP 9-4   ELWHA AREA

OLYMPIC HOT SPRINGS RD.

MILES	MILES
from	to
HWY. 101	END OF ROAD

0.0   10.0

HIGHWAY 101

LITTLE RIVER ROAD
 (DAWN LAKE RD)   0.2   9.8
LITTLE RIVER TRAIL
THE FOOTHILLS TRAIL

LITTLE RIVER TRAIL
(8.1 Miles Long)

Little River Trail trailhead is on your right in Little River Road, 3.4 miles from Olympic Hot Springs Road. There is a parking area in a small clearing on the left directly opposite the trailhead.

The trail gains 4,000 feet in elevation in its eight mile course. If you have two cars, you would be well advised to leave one here and drive to the Hurricane Ridge end of the trail so you can walk downhill most of the time.

The trail follows the South Branch Little River and has several interesting features. Just within the National Park you see the first of several peculiar rock formations called Gnome Rocks. A bit further on, you come to a side path to the right that leads to an abandoned mine.

Distances and elevations along the trail are:

Little River Road Trailhead	0.0 Miles	900 Feet
Side path to FSR 3030 (Right)	0.1 Miles	900 Feet
National Park Boundary	1.3 Miles	1200 Feet
Side path to abandoned mine	1.9 Miles	1350 Feet
Hurricane Hill Lookout Trail	8.1 Miles	5125 Feet

THE FOOTHILLS TRAIL
(Department of Natural Resources)
(8.7 Miles Long)

To reach this trail, you continue past the Little River Trail Trailhead for another 0.8 miles. Here you turn left into DNR Road H1000 (unmarked). There are two trailheads on this road. The first is 0.4 miles from Little River Road, and the second is 1.4 miles from Little River Road. There is a third trailhead at the eastern end of the trail, but it is really only accessible by off-road vehicles (ORV's), and one must start from Mt. Angeles Road to find it meandering through the state lands surrounding the trail.

The trail was apparently built primarily as a place for people to exercise their ORV's as the views are not particularly interesting, and there are a lot of mudholes when it is wet. It is laid out in a figure of eight with a long tail at each end. The total mileage of the trail is 7.3 miles, but some parts must be repeated if you want to complete all sections of it.

We now return to Olympic Hot Springs Road.

OLYMPIC HOT SPRINGS RD.		
MILES	MILES	
from	to	
HWY. 101	END OF ROAD	
1.6	8.4	TURNOUT

MADISON FALLS TRAIL

2.0	8.0	
ENTER OLYMPIC		
NATIONAL PARK		

This trail is a short hike that is graded and paved for wheel chairs. It leads to a lovely waterfall. There is a parking area on the left, just south of the entrance booth to the park.

SERVICE ROAD

2.4	7.6	Parking area for a short fisherman's trail to the river.
2.7	7.3	TURNOUT (Overlooking the river)

CASCADE ROCK TRAIL

2.9	7.1	

There is no place to park near the trailhead for Cascade Rock Trail. There is a large parking area on the right 0.2 miles further on, at the Elwha Campground Amphitheater.

CASCADE ROCK TRAIL
(2.0 Miles Long)

Cascade Rock Trail (elevation gain 1400 feet) starts out by turning south to parallel Elwha Campground. It divides shortly after the start. The trail goes uphill, to the left. The path to the right goes to a kitchen shelter in the campground. A bit further on, a short path goes to the right, to a lookout with a good view of the Elwha Valley and the mountains beyond. The trail goes downhill to the left.

Distances and elevations along the trail are:

Olympic Hot Springs Rd. mile 2.9	0.0 Miles	400 Feet
Cascade Rock viewpoint	1.5 Miles	1000 Feet
Olympic National Park Boundary	1.8 Miles	1400 Feet
End of trail. View of Madison Ck.	2.0 Miles	1800 Feet

CASCADE ROCK TRAIL	2.9	7.1	
EXIT TO ELWHA CAMPGROUND	3.0	7.0	
ENTRANCE TO ELWHA CAMPGROUND ELWHA CAMPGROUND LOOP TRAIL	3.1	6.9	AMPHITHEATER

Go to the right upon entering the campground. Go past a walk-in campsite parking, and follow the road's curve to the left to a kitchen shelter. Elwha Campground Loop Trail is to your right, behind the shelter. It is 0.7 miles long and mostly flat. The path on the left goes to Cascade Rock Trail. If the parking spaces near the shelter, are all occupied, you can park at the amphitheater parking area across the road from the campground.

The campground has 41 sites (no hook-ups), fire grates, tables, flush toilets and a kitchen shelter. The Park Service presents naturalist programs in summer.

	3.5	6.5	Private Road - No Camping
RANGER STATION (ONP) TOILETS PHONE GRIFF CREEK TRAIL	3.9 RANGER STATION PHONE	6.1	ONP STAFF RESIDENCES

The trailhead for Griff Creek Trail is not readily apparent. If you walk to the back of the cabin to the sign directing you to the toilets, you will see the trailhead to your left. Be sure to stop and look at the displays in the ranger station.

GRIFF CREEK TRAIL
(2.8 Miles Long)

Griff Creek Trail (elevation gain 2900 feet) climbs continuously for its entire length. You go from an elevation of 390 feet at the ranger station to 3300 feet at the end of the trail. There are reputed to be only 35 switchbacks, but it seems more like 3500. There are several opportunities to enjoy vistas of Griff Creek Valley, and Hughes Creek Valley across the Elwha. You can also get glimpses of Lake Mills. The trail deteriorates after two miles, and disappears into rocky pinnacles at 2.8 miles. At the end there are good views of Unicorn Peak (5100 feet) and Griff Peak (5120 feet) in the Elwha River Range.

	OLYMPIC HOT SPRINGS RD.	
	MILES from HWY. 101	MILES to END OF ROAD
PICNIC AREA WHISKEY BEND ROAD	4.0	6.0

Here we will turn left and explore Whiskey Bend Road and the trails that depart from it, and from the Elwha Trail. The Olympic Hot Springs Road listing continues on page 219.

WHISKEY BEND ROAD

Whiskey Bend Road is a pleasant drive on a well maintained, one-lane, gravel road. On the way to the trailheads at Whiskey Bend you pass Lake Mills, and two or three streams form cascades as they pass under the road.

	WHISKEY BEND ROAD	
	MILES from HOT SPGS. RD.	MILES to END OF RD.
SMALL UNMARKED ROAD HURRICANE HILL TRAIL	0.2	4.2

You go about 100 yards on this small road to Hurricane Hill Trail on the right.

HURRICANE HILL TRAIL
(6.3 Miles Long)

Hurricane Hill Trail (elevation gain 5350 feet) is another of those long steep challenges. The effort is probably worthwhile, because of the long beautiful vistas after you climb out of the trees. If the elevation gain of more than a mile doesn't appeal to you, and you have two cars, leave one here, and hike back to it from the Hurricane Hill Lookout Trail's parking Area. This way you can get the views, with a lot less effort. The first few miles of the trail are forested, so the contrast is accentuated when the panoramic views spring up from nowhere as you come to the meadows.

Near the end of the trail, you get a great look at the interior mountains, including glacier crusted Mount Olympus, and Mount Anderson in the Bailey Range. Hurricane Hill Trail combines with Hurricane Hill Lookout trail for its last 0.2 miles. See page 180 for a description of Hurricane Hill Lookout Trail.

Distances and elevations along the way are:

Near Whiskey Bend Rd, Mile 0.2	0.0 Miles	400 Feet
Stream	1.0 Miles	1500 Feet
Meadow	3.8 Miles	3000 Feet
Large Meadow	5.0 Miles	5000 Feet
Elwha Overlook	5.4 Miles	5400 Feet
Hurricane Hill Lookout Trail	6.1 Miles	5640 Feet
Hurricane Hill Summit	6.3 Miles	5757 Feet

WHISKEY BEND ROAD

	MILES from HOT SPGS. RD.	MILES to END OF RD.	
SMALL UNMARKED ROAD HURRICANE HILL TRAIL	0.2	4.2	
	1.2	3.2	TURNOUT TO GLINES CANYON DAM There is parking here for two cars, and another small space a bit farther south.
	4.0	0.4	UPPER LAKE MILLS TRAIL There is a wide turnout here to provide parking for the trail.

UPPER LAKE MILLS TRAIL
(0.4 Miles Long)

The trail descends 400 feet in 0.4 miles to a camp near where Wolf Creek enters the lake. A bit upstream from the lake, Wolf Creek dives off a high bluff. Its fall is only broken once before it reaches the level of the lake with a roar. Although Lake Mills is beautiful, the waterfall is the real reason for this hike.

We return to Whiskey Bend Road now.

	4.0 0.4	UPPER LAKE MILLS TRAIL
WOLF CREEK TRAIL	4.4 0.0	ELWHA TRAIL
	END OF ROAD	

RICA CANYON TRAIL	1.2 Miles
KRAUSE BOTTOM TRAIL	1.6 Miles
LONG RIDGE TRAIL	1.9 Miles
LILLIAN RIVER TRAIL	4.1 Miles
DODGER POINT TRAIL	12.8 Miles
HAYDEN PASS TRAIL	16.8 Miles
LOW DIVIDE TRAIL	25.6 Miles
N. FORK QUINAULT TR.	28.7 Miles
N. FORK QUINAULT RD.	44.6 Miles

As you approach the end of the parking area loop at the end of Whiskey Bend Road, the trailhead on your right is to Elwha Trail. The one to the left is to Wolf Creek Trail. There are toilets to the left as you start out on the Elwha Trail. There is an unloading platform for stock, a hitching rail and a small pen for stock near the start of Wolf Creek Trail. The parking area loop is long and wide, with plenty of room to park horse trailers.

WOLF CREEK TRAIL
(8.0 Miles Long)

Wolf Creek Trail (elevation gain 3800 feet) follows the route of what was once the road to Hurricane Ridge. The road has been closed for 30 years, and it is a good example of how quickly nature takes the land back from man. The route is often used by skiers in winter because of the long downhill run from Hurricane Ridge. It starts out from Whiskey Bend in a densely forested area which pretty well obscures the beautiful vistas that are offered once you get above the trees. Although the steepness of the trail makes you earn your vistas, they seem to get better with every step you take. To avoid the steep climb, you may want to leave a car here at Whiskey Bend, and start from the Hurricane Ridge end. That trailhead is 0.6 miles west of Hurricane Ridge Lodge.

ELWHA TRAIL
(25.6 Miles Long)

The Elwha Trail has an elevation gain of only 1550 feet. The Elwha River and the glaciers that preceded it have gouged out a long deep valley that connects with North Fork Quinault Valley in the south via Low Divide. Low Divide (3662 feet) is the lowest pass that one can use to cross the Olympics. If you decide to go to North Fork Quinault Road, most of the time you will be following in the footsteps of the Press Party on their expedition of 1889-90. The early parts of the Elwha Trail, and the Geyser Valley trails still display evidence of the turn of the century attempts to settle the area. Another delightful feature of Elwha Trail is its solitude. Casual hikers seldom venture past Michaels Ranch. Moreover, as you go deeper and deeper into the interior, you notice something is missing. After a while you work out that when you left the casual hikers behind, you also left behind the candy wrappers and cigarette ends that some of the less considerate casual hikers discard along many popular trails.

Distances and elevations along the trail are as follows:

Whiskey Bend Road . . . . 0.0 Miles 1198 Feet
Path to Elk Overlook-0.1 Mi. Long . . . . . 0.9 Miles 1300 Feet
Rica Canyon (Goblin Gates) Trail . . . . . 1.2 Miles 1300 Feet
    (0.5 miles long, 600 feet elevation loss)

Krause Bottom Trail (Right) . . . . 1.6 Miles 1200 Feet
    (1.6 miles long, 300 feet elevation gain)

Long Ridge Trail (Right) . . . . 1.9 Miles 1150 Feet
    (13.3 miles long, 4100 feet elevation gain)

Michaels Ranch Cabin . . . . 1.9 Miles 1150 Feet
Lillian River Trail (Left) . . . . 4.1 Miles 1480 Feet
    (3.1 miles long, 400 feet elevation gain)

Camp Lillian . . . . 4.7 Miles 1273 Feet
Mary Falls Camp . . . . 8.7 Miles 1300 Feet
Canyon Camp . . . . 10.3 Miles 1400 Feet
Elkhorn Shelter & Ranger Station . . . . 11.3 Miles 1450 Feet
Cross Lost River . . . . 12.5 Miles 1500 Feet
Riemans Cabin . . . . 12.7 Miles 1450 Feet
Elwha River Ford . . . . 12.8 Miles 1451 Feet
Dodger Point Trail (Right) . . . . 12.8 Miles 1451 Feet
    (5.8 miles long, 4300 feet elevation gain)

Tipperary Camp . . . . 15.5 Miles 1400 Feet
Chateau Camp . . . . 16.1 Miles 1600 Feet
Hayes River Ranger Station . . . . 16.5 Miles 1650 Feet
Hayden Pass Trail (Left) . . . . 16.8 Miles 1700 Feet
    (8.4 miles long, 4200 feet elevation gain)

Camp Wilder . . . . 20.6 Miles 1885 Feet
Chicago Camp . . . . 25.6 Miles 2185 Feet
Low Divide Trail (Left) . . . . 25.6 Miles 2185 Feet
    (3.1 miles long, 1400 feet elevation gain)

Happy Hollow Shelter . . . . 26.3 Miles 2400 Feet
End of Trail . . . . 28.4 Miles 2700 Feet

Although the trail ends in the meadows of Elwha Basin, the experienced and hardy can continue another 3 miles to Dodwell-Rixon Pass (4750 Feet). Be careful in late summer, as the Elwha Snowfinger is riddled with ice caves then.

RICA CANYON TRAIL
(0.5 Miles Long)

Rica Canyon Trail (600 feet elevation loss) is also known as Goblin Gates Trail. The name "Goblin Gates" was bestowed by more imaginative members of the Press Party who saw faces in the rock formations in the canyon walls. Just beyond the junction with the Geyser Valley Trail to the left, the trail ends at a deep pool in the river where the river churns violently before it continues on its journey to the sea. You can get a better look at the whirlpool from the Anderson Ranch Trail. (See page 216.)

GEYSER VALLEY TRAIL
(0.8 Miles Long)

Geyser Valley Trail has some ups and downs, but, for the most part it is flat. The trail starts from Rica Canyon Trail near its end, 0.5 miles from Elwha Trail. It runs parallel to the river, and connects Rica Canyon Trail to Krause Bottom Trail. There are no geysers. It seems the "geysers" that Press Party heard when they named the valley were, in fact, the drumming of the grouse that live in the valley.

KRAUSE BOTTOM TRAIL
(1.6 Miles Long)

Krause Bottom Trail is relatively flat. It loses 350 feet on its way to its junction with Geyser Valley Trail. It then gains most of it back by the time you reach its end just west of Michaels Ranch. Near Humes Ranch cabin, you will see remnants of the fruit orchards that were planted in the early 1900's. There are good camp sites near the cabin. There is a way trail from Hume's cabin to mile 1.0 of Long Ridge Trail near the bridge over the Elwha. This half mile long path has a very nice campsite just beyond Idaho Creek.

Distances and elevations along the way are:

Elwha Trail, Mile 1.5	0.0 Miles	1150 Feet
Geyser Valley Trail (Right)	0.4 Miles	800 Feet
(0.8 miles long)		
Path to Elwha campsite (Right)	0.7 Miles	800 Feet
Humes Ranch, path to campsites	1.1 Miles	900 Feet
Long Ridge Trail:		
Mi. 0.2 W. of Michaels Ranch	1.3 Miles	1100 Feet
or Mi. 1.0 Near Elwha Bridge	1.6 Miles	900 Feet

LONG RIDGE TRAIL
(13.3 Miles Long)

Long Ridge Trail (elevation gain 4100 feet) climbs Long Ridge to Dodger Point Trail. It merges with Dodger Point Trail for half a mile, then an abandoned 1.3 mile segment of the trail goes to the base of Ludden Peak (5828 feet).

An interesting 27.7 mile loop can be made by continuing on Dodger Point Trail to a ford of the Elwha River just beyond Riemans cabin on the Elwha Trail. You then return to Michaels Ranch on the Elwha Trail. Be sure to check on the condition of the river before you set out, as the ford can be dangerous if attempted during a period of high water.

Distances and elevations along the trail are:

Mile 1.9 Elwha Trail	0.0 Miles	1150 Feet
Krause Bottom Trail (Left)	0.2 Miles	1100 Feet
(1.6 miles long, 300 feet elevation gain)		
Way Path to Humes Ranch (Left)	1.0 Miles	900 Feet
Bridge over Elwha	1.2 Miles	900 Feet
Anderson Ranch Trail (Left)	1.3 Miles	900 Feet
2.0 miles long, 200 feet elevation gain)		
Seek Way Trail (Left)	2.0 Miles	1700 Feet
(0.7 miles long, 900 feet elevation loss)		
Meadow (Cave west of trail)	10.0 Miles	4900 Feet
Dodger Pt. Tr.(Dodger Pt. Left)	11.5 Miles	5200 Feet
(5.8 miles long, 4300 feet elevation gain)		
Dodger Point Tr.-Elwha Tr. Left	12.0 Miles	5000 Feet
End of Trail	13.3 Miles	5000 Feet

There was once a plan to extend the trail across Bailey Range. Although that plan has been abandoned in the interest of preserving the wilderness nature of the Bailey Range, it still makes a good cross-country hike for the experienced hiker with appropriate equipment.

Here we will discuss the two trails that start from Long Ridge Trail before returning to those that start from the Elwha Trail.

ANDERSON RANCH TRAIL
(2.0 Miles Long)

Anderson Ranch Trail (elevation gain 200 feet) was badly damaged by a flood some years ago, but there is a scramble path to get you past the worst damage early in the hike. Crossing Long Creek, 1.1 miles from Long Ridge Trail can be a bother in times of high water, especially in early spring. At the end of the trail you get an excellent view of the whirlpool at Goblin Gates. There is a campsite just upstream from Goblin Gates.

SEEK WAY TRAIL
(0.7 Miles Long)

This way trail came about as an alternative to Anderson Ranch Trail. After the flood destroyed parts of Anderson Ranch Trail, the Park Service put up a sign instructing hikers trying to reach Goblin Gates to "Seek Way Trail". In contrast to Anderson Ranch Trail, this trail has a lot of steep ups and downs. It starts from mile 2.0 of Long Ridge Trail, at an elevation of 1700 feet, and descends some 800 feet to the river. After 0.7 miles the trail ends at Long Creek which must be forded if you want to press on to Anderson Ranch and Goblin Gates. Crossing Long Creek can be dangerous in times of high water.

We now return to the description of trails starting from Elwha Trail.

LILLIAN RIVER TRAIL
(3.1 Miles Long)

Lillian River Trail (elevation gain 400 feet) starts at mile 4.1 of the Elwha Trail. It begins as a moderate climb, then flattens out along the 2000 feet contour until it descends gradually to Lillian River. About half way through the hike you begin to get good views up and down the valley. There is a campsite at the end of the trail.

DODGER POINT TRAIL
(5.8 Miles Long)

Dodger Point Trail (elevation gain 4300 feet) starts from the west side of the Elwha River at mile 12.8 of Elwha Trail. Check with the Park Service to be sure that the river can be forded before you start your hike. Fording the Elwha can be quite dangerous at times. Dodger Point Trail connects Elwha Trail and Long Ridge Trail, enabling you to make a 27.8 mile loop from Michaels Ranch.

Dodger Point because of its central location, offers one of the best 360° panoramic views in the peninsula. One can see most of the major peaks in the Olympics, Mount Rainier, the Elwha Valley and the Strait of Juan de Fuca.

Distances and elevations along the way are:

Mile 12.8 of Elwha Trail	0.0 Miles	1451 Feet
Enter Clearing	3.7 Miles	4200 Feet
Long Ridge Trail	4.8 Miles	5000 Feet
(13.3 miles long, 4100 feet elevation gain)		
Ludden Peak is to the left. To the right,		
the trails merge for 0.5 miles.		
Long Ridge Trail (left)	5.3 Miles	5200 Feet
Dodger Point, end of trail	5.8 Miles	5753 Feet

HAYDEN PASS TRAIL
(8.4 Miles Long)

Hayden Pass Trail (elevation gain 4200 feet) connects the Elwha Trail to the Dosewallips Trail (15.4 miles long, 4250 feet elevation gain. See page 97.) These three trails can be combined for a 40.6 mile hike from Dosewallips campground to Whiskey Bend Road. By combining Dosewallips Trail with Hayden Pass Trail, Elwha Trail, Low Divide Trail and North Fork Quinault Trail you get a 42.3 mile hike from Dosewallips Campground to North Fork Quinault Road.

Because of the long steep ascent, Hayden Pass Trail is usually approached from the Dosewallips end. The trail begins 0.3 miles east of the Hayes River Ranger Station. At Hayden Pass, Sentinel Peak (6592 feet) and Sentinel's Sister (6301 feet) offer you an easy climb. Mount Fromme (6655 feet) and Mount Claywood (6893 feet) are relatively easy climbs too, and you have the added reward of picturesque Claywood Lake.

Distances and elevations along the trail are:

Elwha Trail, mile 16.8	0.0 Miles	1700 Feet
Frog Lake Creek	5.0 Miles	4700 Feet
Bone Camp	6.5 Miles	5300 Feet
Hayden Pass	8.4 Miles	5847 Feet

Beyond Hayden Pass the trail becomes Dosewallips Trail.

LOW DIVIDE TRAIL
(3.1 Miles Long)

Low Divide Trail (1400 feet elevation gain) leaves the Elwha Trail at mile 25.6 near Chicago Camp. There are two lovely sub-alpine lakes, Lake Mary and Lake Margaret, on your right before you reach the trail to Martins Park.

It connects Elwha Trail to North Fork Quinault Trail (15.9 miles long, 3100 feet elevation gain). The three trails together add up to a pleasant 44.6 mile hike across the interior of the Olympics, with a lot of beautiful scenery en route.

Distances and elevations along the trail are:

Elwha Trail, Mile 25.6	0.0 Miles	2185 Feet
Martins Park Trail (Left)	2.3 Miles	3600 Feet
(2.3 miles long, 1050 feet elevation gain)		
Low Divide Rngr.Stn. Trail Ends	3.1 Miles	3602 Feet

The trail continues beyond the Ranger Station as North Fork Quinault Trail. (See page 303.

MARTINS PARK TRAIL
(2.3 Miles Long)

Martins Park Trail (elevation gain 1050 feet) starts from mile 2.3 of Low Divide Trail, near the southern end of Lake Margaret. It takes you through a delightful meadow on its way to Martins Lakes. There is a campsite between the two lakes. You will often see marmots, and occasionally a bear, on this trail.

Distances and elevations along the trail are:

> Low Divide Trail, mile 2.3 . . . . 0.0 Miles 3600 Feet
> Lower Basin of Martins Park . . . . 1.0 Miles 4000 Feet
> Upper Basin . . . . 1.9 miles 4300 Feet
> Trail Ends at Martins Lakes . . . . 2.3 Miles 4650 Feet

We now return to mile 4.0 of Olympic Hot Springs Road. After all these trails, a soak in the hot springs will sure feel good.

	OLYMPIC HOT SPRINGS RD.		
	MILES	MILES	
	from	to	
	HWY. 101	END OF ROAD	
WHISKEY BEND ROAD	4.0	6.0	
	4.3	5.7	**ALTAIR CAMPGROUND (NPS)** **WEST ELWHA TRAIL**
	ELWHA RIVER		
	CAMPGROUND		

ALTAIR CAMPGROUND (NPS)
WEST ELWHA TRAIL

Altair Campground has 29 sites (no hook-ups), maximum trailer length 18 feet. It has potable water, tables, fire grates, and flush toilets. Naturalist programs are presented in summer. The campground is set back from the road. The entrance road is at the south end of the bridge. The Elwha Raft Tours start from this campground.

WEST ELWHA TRAIL
(3.0 Miles Long)

West Elwha Trail (elevation gain 200 feet) parallels the river as it traverses the lower levels of a steep hillside. The trailhead is difficult to find in the maze of twisty little camp trails. The signs that say "Trail" are not much help either, as most merely point at more twisty little paths that surround the campground. To get to the trail with the least bother, drive to the raft launch area, and stand in the first parking space on your right after you pass it. Look straight ahead. You will see a path going uphill at the outer edge of the campground. It crosses under two fallen trees, bears a bit to the left, then a bit to the right. That is the trail. You will see a sign that says "Trail" when you get there. It appears that all the trails that are marked by signs eventually end up at this point.

The trail crosses Hughes Creek at 1.5 miles from the campground, and the National Park Boundary at 2.6 miles. It then crosses private land to the end of Herrick Road at 3.0 miles. The end of Herrick Road is 1.3 miles from Highway 101. It is the first road on your right after you cross the Elwha on Highway 101.

4.3	5.7	ALTAIR CAMPGROUND (NPS)
ELWHA RIVER		WEST ELWHA TRAIL

SIGN: WARNING - No Trailers
Beyond This Point - DEAD END

| 5.1 | 4.9 | WIDE TURNOUT |

Private Road - Authorized Vehicles
Only - No Camping   5.1   4.9

TURNOUT - River Overlook   5.3   4.7
Chained Driveway - Authorized
Vehicles Only

GLINES CANYON DAM   5.5   4.5
ROAD TO BOATRAMP
WEST LAKE MILLS TRAIL

Olympic Hot Springs Road forms an
S-bend here. The gravel road to the
boatramp is on the left past the
houses near the dam.

WEST LAKE MILLS TRAIL
(2.0 Miles Long)

The road to the boatramp is 0.2 miles long, and ends in a parking area. There are picnic tables and toilets nearby. One of the Park Service sign writers has a sense of humor. At the trailhead there is a sign that says Boulder Creek 2.0; End of Trail 1.9. West Lake Mills Trail ends suddenly at a high precipice above the point where Boulder Creek empties into the lake. I am sure that more than one inattentive hiker has taken an unplanned dive from the end of the trail. For the most part this trail is a series of gentle ups and downs near the shore of the lake. There is a viewpoint and a campsite near the end of the trail.

OBSERVATION POINT   7.9   2.1

| 8.6 | 1.4 | HAPPY LAKE RIDGE TRAIL |

HAPPY LAKE RIDGE TRAIL
(10.0 Miles Long)

As the road curves to the left there is a large turnout on the right in front of the trailhead. It would probably hold two or three cars. You might get another one or two on the other side of the road in an "unofficial" turnout.

Happy Lake Ridge Trail (elevation gain 3250 feet) climbs to Happy Lake Ridge where it becomes a long traverse, finally ending at Boulder Lake. There are good views of Mount Olympus and Mount Carrie. They seem to rise up from nowhere. When you get to the north side of the ridge, you can see Port Angeles and Mount Baker. There is a campsite at the south end of Happy Lake.

Distances and elevations along the way are:

Olympic Hot Springs Road Mi.8.6 . . . . . 0.0 Miles 1750 Feet
Crest of Happy Lake Ridge . . . . 3.0 Miles 4500 Feet
Path to Happy Lake-0.5 mi. long . . . . . . 4.5 Miles 5300 Feet
Aurora Divide Trail . . . . 7.5 Miles 5000 Feet
    (5.6 miles long, 3450 feet elevation gain)

End of Trail . . . . 10.0 Miles 4400 Feet
Boulder Lake Trail . . . . 10.0 Miles 4400 Feet
    (2.8 Miles long, 2000 feet elevation gain)

Boulder Lake Trail will take you to the Boulder Creek Campground where you are only half a mile from the hot springs, or 2.4 miles from the end of Olympic Hot Springs Road.

We now return briefly to Olympic Hot Springs Road, and follow it to its end.

OLYMPIC HOT SPRINGS RD.

MILES	MILES	
from	to	
HWY. 101	**END OF ROAD**	
8.6	1.4	HAPPY LAKE RIDGE TRAIL
10.0	0.0	
ROAD CLOSED		

Although the road continues for another 2.2 miles to the parking area for Boulder Creek Campground and Olympic Hot Springs, It has been closed to vehicular traffic because of washouts and rockslides. There is no parking at the end of the road and the turn-around near the barrier is narrow. The "No Trailers" sign near Altair Campground becomes clear now. After turning around at the end of the road you can park along the edge of the road if your vehicle is not too wide. Although I don't think there is any official name, I shall refer to this section of the road as Olympic Hot Springs Road Trail. At the barrier there is a sign with the following information:

Appleton Pass Trailhead	2.2	High Divide	13.8
Hot Springs Campground	2.2	Sol Duc Ranger Station	17.0
Hot Springs	2.4	Olympus Ranger Station	22.7
Boulder Lake	5.9	Hoh Ranger Station	31.7
Appleton Pass	7.7		

OLYMPIC HOT SPRINGS ROAD TRAIL
(2.2 Miles Long)

The elevation gain between the point where the road is closed and the parking area for the hot springs and the campground is only 375 feet, so it is quite an easy stroll. The steepest part is probably the 0.2 miles uphill from the parking area to Boulder Creek Campground.

About half a mile from the campground there is a short road to your right as you walk toward the campground. If you follow the road, and the primitive trail that starts when the road finishes you will see evidence of a small settlement that has long since disappeared. At the end of the trail is a rubbish heap that will probably give some future archaeologist raptures.

When you reach the parking area, the path to the right goes to the campground. The path leading away from the western end of the parking area goes to the bridge over Boulder Creek that takes you to the hot springs.

Boulder Creek Campground has 50 sites. There are flush toilets, potable water, picnic tables and fire rings. You should use the food cache bars, as bears are often spotted in this area. As you enter the campground, the loop designated Camp Area 2 is to your right. The toilets and water spigot are in the area between Camp Area 2 and the loop that forms Camp Area 1. Crystal Ridge Trail starts from the northeast corner of the campground (Area 2). When the road forks just beyond the toilets to form the Area 1 loop, keep to the left for a short trail that descends to the bridge over Boulder Creek that goes to the hot springs.

Past the trail descending to the hot springs, you will find the trailhead for Appleton Pass Trail, which leads to Boulder Lake Trail. It is at the western extreme of the loop that forms Area A, near a backcountry station.

OLYMPIC HOT SPRINGS TRAIL
(0.5 Miles Long)

Olympic Hot Springs Trail starts at the western end of the old parking area. After about one tenth of a mile you come to a junction with the trail coming down from the campground. There is toilet on your right, and a bridge to your left. The trail crosses the bridge, and takes you to several small pools that were made by building small dams on thermal seeps. The deepest is about two feet deep, and the hottest is 138° F. The warm pools really feel great after a long day hiking.

The springs were once the main feature of a resort, but all the buildings have been gone for many years. The Park Service points out the fact that the impounded pools frequently fail water quality standards for public bathing, and that you use them at your own risk.

CRYSTAL RIDGE TRAIL
(3.0 Miles Long)

Crystal Ridge Trail has an elevation gain of 2700 feet, and has been abandoned for many years. It goes from the northeast corner of Boulder Creek Campground to Happy Lake Ridge Trail, 1.5 miles east of its junction with Boulder Lake Trail. It is a steep trail, and the last half of it is difficult to find. The last half no longer appears on the quads, so it is now, for all practical purposes, a cross-country hike.

APPLETON PASS TRAIL
(7.8 Miles Long)

Appleton Pass Trail (elevation gain 2850 feet) connects the Olympic Hot Springs area to the Soleduck Trail. The trailhead is at the southwestern corner of Camp Area #1 in Boulder Creek Campground. The highlight of this hike is Boulder Creek Falls. After a long drop into a large pool it continues to fall in a series of cascades. The views in the high country along this trail are excellent. There are campsites at both Lower and Upper Boulder Creek Falls, and at Appleton Pass.

Distances and elevations along the way are:

Boulder Creek Campground . . . . 0.0 Miles 2200 Feet
Boulder Lake Trail . . . . 0.6 Miles 2350 Feet
    (2.8 miles long, 2050 feet elevation gain)

Path to Lower Boulder Crk. Falls . . . . . . 1.5 Miles 2500 Feet
Path to Upper Boulder Crk. Falls . . . . . . 1.7 Miles 2400 Feet
Cat Creek Way Trail . . . . 5.2 Miles 5050 Feet
    (4.5 miles long, 800 feet elevation loss)

Appleton Pass . . . . 5.2 Miles 5050 Feet
Cross Rocky Creek . . . . 7.4 Miles 3400 Feet
Soleduck Trail . . . . 7.8 Miles 3100 Feet
    (8.5 miles long, 3350 feet elevation gain)

BOULDER LAKE TRAIL
(2.8 Miles Long)

Boulder Lake Trail (elevation gain 2050 feet) connects Appleton Pass Trail to Happy Lake Ridge Trail, then turns south for one tenth of a mile to Boulder Lake. There is a path that continues past the end of the trail for about three quarters of a mile to Three Horse Lake, and experienced hikers may want to traverse to Appleton Pass. Boulder Peak (5600 feet) is nearby, and offers great views of Mount Olympus, Mount Carrie and the strait. The ascent is more of a steep hike than a climb, and well worth the effort.

Distances and elevations along the way are:

Appleton Pass Trail mile 0.6 . . . . 0.0 Miles 2350 Feet
Halfway Creek . . . . 1.1 Miles 3200 Feet
Happy Lake Ridge Trail . . . . 2.7 Miles 4400 Feet
    (10.0 miles long, 3250 feet elevation gain)

Boulder Lake . . . . 2.8 Miles 4350 Feet

CAT CREEK WAY TRAIL
(4.5 Miles Long)

Cat Creek Way Trail (Elevation gain 1250 feet) goes through the high country from Appleton Pass to High Divide. The views of Mount Carrie, Mount Olympus and Mount Tom are mostly unobstructed. Only the ends of this trail show on most maps. This is indicative of the way the trail sometimes disappears and is often confused with game trails. Deer, elk and the occasional bear are seen on this trail.

Distances and elevations along the way are:

Appleton Pass	0.0 Miles	5050 Feet
Oyster Lake	0.2 Miles	5170 Feet
Spread Eagle Pass	2.0 Miles	5400 Feet
Cat Creek Basin Campsites	4.0 Miles	4250 Feet
High Divide - Bailey Range Trail	4.5 Miles	4500 Feet

We now return to mile 239.6 of Highway 101, and make our way to Lake Crescent.

	HIGHWAY 101 MILES from I-5	MILE NUMBER	
OLYMPIC HOT SPRING ROAD OLYMPIC NAT'L PARK ELWHA AREA LITTLE RIVER (DAWN LAKE) ROAD LITTLE RIVER TRAIL	127.7 RESORT GAS	239.6 RV PARK PROPANE	Elwha Resort & Texaco
	128.1 BOAT RAMP RV PARK PICNIC TABLES	239.2	**LAKE ALDWELL ROAD** INDIAN CREEK RECREATION AREA Indian Creek Camp
HERRICK ROAD End of West Elwha Trail	128.5	238.8	
	129.2	238.1	TURNOUT
	129.7 INDIAN CREEK	237.6	
	131.8 MOTEL CAFE	235.5 RV PARK	Indian Valley Motel & RV Park Granny's Cafe
SOUTH SHORE ROAD LAKE SUTHERLAND	132.6	234.7	TURNOUT
	132.6 INDIAN CREEK	234.7	
LONGFELLOW ROAD	133.8	233.5	

HIGHWAY 101		
MILES	MILE	
from	NUMBER	
I-5		
134.1	233.2	Timberlane Restaurant
	RESTAURANT	
	STORE TAVERN	

LAKE SUTHERLAND ROAD   134.7 232.6

FISHER COVE ROAD   135.3 232.0   **EAST BEACH ROAD**
LAKE CRESCENT
E. BEACH SWIMMING & PICNIC AREA
Log Cabin Resort
SPRUCE RAILROAD TRAIL

LAKE CRESCENT

To get our first looks at lake Crescent, we turn right here to look into the attractions on East Beach Road. East Beach Road is sometimes referred to as Piedmont Road or Piedmont-Joyce Road. Piedmont is the name of the locality surrounding Log Cabin Resort, and Joyce is a community on State Highway 112 about four miles to the north.

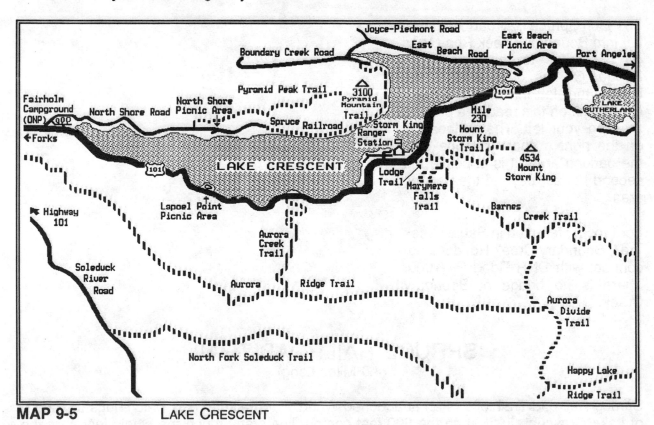

MAP 9-5   LAKE CRESCENT

225

TURNOUT	0.0	4.0

	0.7	3.3

ENTER OLYMPIC

NATIONAL PARK

EAST BEACH SWIMMING AND PICNIC AREA	0.8	3.2

Log Cabin Resort	3.2	0.8

CABINS MARINA

STORE RV PARK

MOTEL

RESTAURANT

GAS

This privately operated resort has motel rooms, cabins, marina, store, gas, laundry and an RV Park (40 sites with hook-ups). There are flush toilets and pay showers. There is a roped swimming area and paddle boats are available.

BOUNDARY CREEK ROAD TO SPRUCE RAILROAD TRAIL	3.2	0.8	JOYCE ROAD

To reach Spruce Railroad Trail, turn left into Boundary Creek Road, and go 0.7 miles to the Lyre River Bridge. On the other side of the bridge, turn left into a gravel road. Go 0.1 mi. on this road to a parking area on your left. The trailhead is on the right a short distance past the parking area. It is opposite the second house, beyond the parking area.

For those interested in Sadie Creek Trail, Boundary Creek Rd. does not connect with DNR Road PA-1000. There is no bridge at Boundary Creek.

SPRUCE RAILROAD TRAIL
(4.0 Miles Long)

Spruce Railroad Trail follows an abandoned World War I railroad bed which hugs the shore of Lake Crescent. It sticks to the 600 feet contour line pretty much the whole length of the trail. It is a designated bike trail. It has excellent views of the lake and the nearby peaks.

226

Distances along the trail are as follows:

Boundary Creek Rd. spur Parking Area	0.0 Miles
Devils Point	1.1 Miles
Little Creek	1.5 Miles
2nd Tunnel	2.9 Miles
North Shore Road	4.0 Miles

We now return to mile 232.0 of Highway 101, and continue on to Storm King Ranger Station on the other side of Lake Crescent.

HIGHWAY 101

	MILES from I-5	MILE NUMBER	
FISHER COVE ROAD	135.3	232.0	EAST BEACH ROAD
TURNOUT	135.8	231.5	
	136.0	231.3	LAKE CRESCENT
	ENTER OLYMPIC NATIONAL PARK		TURNOUT
	136.1	231.2	TURNOUT
	136.4	230.9	SCENIC TURNOUT
	137.3	230.0	
	MILEPOST		
	137.7	229.6	SCENIC VIEWPOINT
TURNOUT	137.8	229.5	TURNOUT
	139.1	228.2	TURNOUT
	139.4	227.9	STORM KING RANGER STATION
	RANGER STATION		PICNIC AREA BOAT LAUNCH
	PICNIC AREA		BARNES POINT
	BOAT LAUNCH		Lake Crescent Lodge
	LODGE		BARNES CREEK TRAIL
	RESTAURANT		MOUNT STORM KING TRAIL
			MARYMERE FALLS TRAIL
			To: AURORA DIVIDE TRAIL

Just after you leave Highway 101 there is a 4-way intersection: Turn right to the picnic area, toilets and ranger station; left to the lodge; and go straight ahead to the boat launch. Description of Highway 101 continues at mile 227.9 on p. 229.

The trails in this area of Crescent Lake all branch from Barnes Creek Trail. Its trailhead is located at the edge of a clearing to your right as you come out of the ranger station cabin. There are displays in the cabin.

BARNES CREEK TRAIL
(9.4 Miles Long)

As soon as you leave the clearing, the path forks, with the left branch going down close to the shore of Lake Crescent. The two paths rejoin just before you cross under Highway 101 into another clearing. Shortly after you re-enter the forest, 0.3 miles from the Ranger Station, the trail coming from Lake Crescent Lodge (0.4 miles long) comes in from the right. One tenth of a mile after that, near a large boulder, Mount Storm King Trail goes off to the left, then Marymere Falls Trail goes to the right in another tenth of a mile. The trail is not maintained beyond the junction with Aurora Divide Trail, and sometimes the trail is hard to find on the remainder of the hike.

Distances and elevations along Barnes Creek Trail are:

```
Storm King Ranger Station  . . . . . . . . . .  0.0 Miles   600 Feet
Mount Storm King Trail - Left  . . . . . . . .  0.3 Miles   700 Feet
    (2.8 miles long, 3565 feet elevation gain)

Marymere Falls Trail - Right  . . . . . . . . .  0.4 Miles   750 Feet
    (0.2 miles long, 250 feet elevation gain)

Dismal Draw Camp  . . . . . . . . . . . . . .  3.5 Miles  1700 Feet
Aurora Divide Trail - Right . . . . . . . . . .  3.9 Miles  1500 Feet
    (5.6 miles long, 3450 feet elevation gain)

Lizard Head Creek . . . . . . . . . . . . . . .  6.1 Miles  1830 Feet
Old camp . . . . . . . . . . . . . . . . . . . .  6.8 Miles  2075 Feet
Fork (Right Branch ends 100 yds) . . . . .  9.1 Miles  4800 Feet
Lookout Dome  . . . . . . . . . . . . . . . . .  9.4 Miles  5090 Feet
```

MOUNT STORM KING TRAIL
(2.8 Miles Long)

Mount Storm King Trail has an elevation gain of 3565 feet, and it warns you by making the first step sharply uphill. Most of the other steps on this trail are uphill too. It takes you to a high vantage point on Mount Storm King where the views make the effort worthwhile. After the first 1.7 miles the trail gets quite steep and indistinct. Many casual hikers may want to end their hikes there. At the end of the trail, experienced hikers may want to forge ahead to the summit of Mount Storm King at 4534 feet.

Distances and elevations along the trail are:

```
Barnes Creek Tr, Mile 0.3 . . . . . . . . . . .  0.0 Miles   700 Feet
Trail deteriorates  . . . . . . . . . . . . . . .  1.7 Miles  2600 Feet
Promontory  . . . . . . . . . . . . . . . . . . .  2.8 Miles  4265 Feet
```

MARYMERE FALLS TRAIL
(0.2 Miles Long)

Marymere Falls Trail starts from mile 0.4 of Barnes Creek Trail, and is mostly flat until you reach Barnes Creek. It begins to climb just the other side of the bridge, and gains 250 feet by the time you reach the higher overlook. There is a low overlook that is accessible by wheelchair. The trail to the higher overlook is wide, and made into steps with handrails at the steeper parts. The waterfall is ninety feet high and quite close to the overlooks, so bring the wide angle lens for your camera.

AURORA DIVIDE TRAIL
(5.6 Miles Long)

Aurora Divide Trail (3450 feet elevation gain) connects Barnes Creek Trail and Aurora Ridge Trail to Happy Lake Ridge Trail. It leaves the Barnes Creek Trail 3.9 miles from Storm King Ranger Station. When the trail ends at Happy Lake Ridge Trail, turn right to go to Boulder Creek Campground near Olympic Hot Springs via Boulder Creek Trail and Appleton Pass Trail. A left turn at Happy Lake Ridge Trail will take you to Olympic Hot Springs Road 8.6 miles from Highway 101.

Distances and elevations along Aurora Divide Trail are:

Barnes Creek Trail, mile 3.9	0.0 Miles	1500 Feet
Campsite	3.2 Miles	4200 Feet
Aurora Ridge Trail	3.6 Miles	4750 Feet
Happy Lake Ridge Trail	5.6 Miles	4950 Feet

We will now return to mile 227.9 of Highway 101, and try to find the trailhead for Aurora Creek trail.

HIGHWAY 101

MILES from I-5	MILE NUMBER	
139.4	227.9	STORM KING RANGER STATION
RANGER STATION		PICNIC AREA BOAT LAUNCH
PICNIC AREA		Lake Crescent Lodge
BOAT LAUNCH		
LODGE		
RESTAURANT		
139.7	227.6	
BARNES CREEK		
140.1	227.2	TURNOUT
140.5	226.8	TURNOUT
140.8	226.5	TURNOUT

	HIGHWAY 101		
	MILES	MILE	
	from	NUMBER	
	I-5		
	141.0	226.3	PAVED TURNOUT

PAVED TURNOUT
This is a good place to leave your car whilst you hike Aurora Creek Trail.

141.8   225.5

VIEWPOINT
This large paved turnout provides unobscured views of Lake Crescent. It is also a good place to leave your car whilst you hike Aurora Creek Trail.

AURORA CREEK TRAIL

142.0   225.3

AURORA CREEK TRAIL
(2.5 Miles Long)

The trailhead for Aurora Creek Trail (3500 feet elevation gain) is often overgrown with vegetation, and the park service has done an excellent job of making the small sign blend in with the scenery. Furthermore, there is no parking area (not even a turnout) directly in front of the trailhead. There is a small turnout just west of the trailhead, but it is a narrow gravel area on a sharp curve. You will probably rest easier if you park in one of the large paved turnouts at mile 225.5, and walk the last 0.2 miles. Walking on this narrow curvy section of road is not, however, without its own risk.

The trailhead is on your left as you head west on Highway 101. This is one of the steepest trails in the Olympics. The only break you get is if you take the small sidepath at mile 1.7 (2400 feet elevation) down to the creek for water.

The views are not particularly good because of the dense gloomy forest. The lack of good views is probably a benefit, as it allows you to concentrate your full attention on climbing up the trail to Aurora Ridge Trail. Aurora Ridge Trail is described in Chapter 10 in the Soleduck section. (See page 238.)

We return now to mile 225.3 of Highway 101, and continue to North Shore Road.

	HIGHWAY 101		
	MILES	MILE	
	from	NUMBER	
	I-5		
AURORA CREEK TRAIL	142.0	225.3	
TURNOUT	142.5	224.8	
	142.6	224.7	PAVED TURNOUT
	142.9	224.4	TURNOUT

143.6	223.7	**LA POEL PICNIC GROUND (ONP)**
PICNIC GROUND		**(NOT SUITABLE FOR TRAILERS)**

There is a short bit of paved road to a 0.4 mile loop road through the picnic ground. Most sites have individual parking spaces, tables and fire rings. The narrow gravel road descends sharply through the old growth forest to the lake before returning to Highway 101.

144.0	223.3	**TURNOUT**
144.3	223.0	**TURNOUT**
144.5	222.8	**TURNOUT**
145.2	222.1	**TURNOUT**

TURNOUT

146.1	221.2	Fairholm General Store
C-STORE		
GAS PHONE		There is a parking area behind the store.

146.4	220.9	**NORTH SHORE ROAD**
BOAT LAUNCH		**FAIRHOLM CAMPGROUND (ONP)**
CAMPGROUND		**NORTH SHORE PICNIC AREA (ONP)**
PICNIC AREA		**FAIRHOLM NATURE TRAIL**
		PYRAMID PEAK TRAIL
		SPRUCE RAILROAD TRAIL

We turn right here and explore North Shore Road. The description of Highway 101 continues at mile 220.9 on page 236.

0.0	4.8	
START OF ROAD		
4.7	0.1	**BOAT LAUNCH**
		DUMP STATION

4.6 0.2 CAMPGROUND	

FAIRHOLM CAMPGROUND (ONP)

Fairholm Campground's 87 campsites (No hook-ups) are in a maple grove on the shore of the lake. It has flush toilets, a dump station, a boat ramp, fire grates, tables, and a swimming beach. In summer, Rangers present naturalist programs.

The road is not suitable for trailers beyond the campground.

FAIRHOLM CAMPGROUND NATURE TRAIL
(0.7 Miles Long)

This short loop trail gains about 100 feet in elevation, and is a quite pleasant stroll through the forest. It starts from the left side of North Shore Road, 0.3 miles from Highway 101, just beyond the entrance to the campground. It ends a few hundred feet north of the campground in North Shore Road.

4.2   0.6
PAVEMENT ENDS

3.3   1.5   **CAMP DAVID JR**

Camp David Jr. is a 9 acre recreation camp run by Clallam County. (Reservations Only)

PYRAMID PEAK TRAIL   1.6   3.2

There is a small turnout on the right, opposite the trailhead. The parking area for N. Shore Picnic Area, 0.1 miles farther on North Shore Road, is a better place to park.

PYRAMID PEAK TRAIL
(3.5 Miles Long)

Pyramid Peak Trail (2400 feet elevation gain) is uphill all the way to the top of Pyramid Mountain. It passes a clearcut that comes precisely to the National Park boundary. You can see the Strait of Juan de Fuca through the clearcut. There are excellent views from the summit.

Distances and elevations along the trail are:

North Shore Road, Mile 3.1 . . . . 0.0 Miles   700 Feet
June Creek . . . . 1.4 Miles 1070 Feet
Summit of Pyramid Mountain . . . . 3.5 Miles 3100 Feet

NORTH SHORE ROAD		
MILES	MILES	
from	to	
HWY. 101	**ROAD END**	

| 1.5 | 3.3 | **NORTH SHORE PICNIC AREA** |

This is a delightful place on the edge of the lake. It seems to have been a campground at one time. There is a dock for access by water. There are toilets, uphill on your right as you come from the parking area.

| 0.0 | 4.8 | |
| END OF ROAD | | |

Spruce Railroad Trail starts at the end of the road, where there is a narrow turn-around. See page 226 for a description of Spruce Railroad Trail.

Now let's return to Fairholm Campground to rest up for our adventures in the Soleduck Area of the park in Chapter 10.

Sand Point Beach at the end of the North Beach Wilderness Hike in the Ozette Area of the Olympic National Park.

CHAPTER 10

SOLEDUCK FSR 29 BEACH HIKES FSR 2932

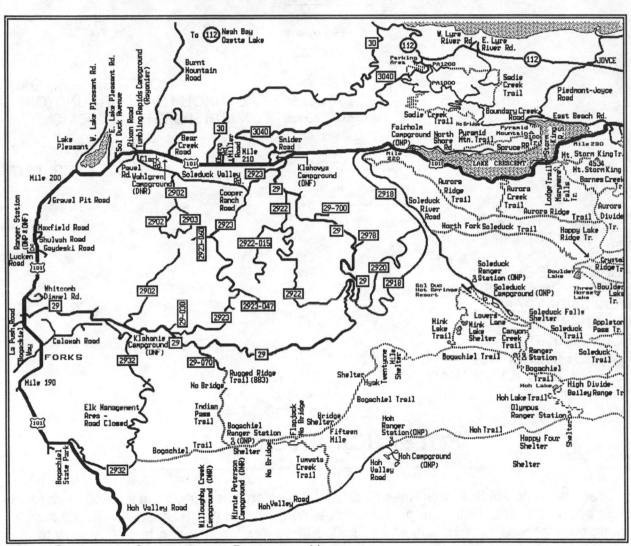

10-1 SOLEDUCK, CALAWAH AND BOGACHIEL VALLEYS

Soleduck (often spelled Sol Duc) River Road was completely rebuilt in 1987 and 1988. The wide, smooth, paved road now makes driving its entire 12.6 mile length a pleasure. Access to several rapids, has been preserved, so you can see for yourself why the river is named Soleduck, or, in English, "sparkling water".

After we return to Highway 101, we pass through several small communities before the highway turns gradually to the south. The highway follows the path of the Soleduck River. It crosses the river several times before leaving it north of Forks. Forks is the last large town until you reach Hoquiam, 104 miles south.

Near Forks we divert to the Mora-Rialto Beach area of Olympic National Park, and investigate the beach trails that start from La Push Road near the Quileute (often spelled Quillayute) Indian Reservation. A few miles south of Forks, we find Bogachiel State Park, and the access road to the 32.7 mile Bogachiel Trail.

We now continue our journey at mile 220.9 of Highway 101, near Fairholm Campground, the point at which we left the description of Highway 101 in Chapter 9.

HIGHWAY 101

MILES from I-5	MILE NUMBER		
146.4	220.9		NORTH SHORE ROAD
BOAT LAUNCH			FAIRHOLM CAMPGROUND (ONP)
CAMPGROUND			NORTH SHORE PICNIC AREA (ONP)
PICNIC AREA			
147.3	220.0		TURNOUT
MILEPOST			

SOLEDUCK RIVER ROAD   148.0   219.3
Sol Duc Hot Springs Resort

AURORA RIDGE TRAIL
NORTH FORK SOLEDUCK TRAIL
MINK LAKE TRAIL
LOVERS LANE
SOLEDUCK TRAIL
CANYON CREEK TRAIL
SEVEN LAKES BASIN TRAIL
HIGH DIVIDE-BAILEY RANGE TRAIL

SOLEDUCK RIVER ROAD

The reconstruction of Soleduck River Road makes exploration of this area a much easier and more enjoyable task. There are paved turnouts near several of the Soleduck River's beauty spots; easy access to waterfalls and secluded lakes; and challenging trails that lead to the high country in the interior. One can even hike to the summit of Mount Olympus via Canyon Creek Trail which connects with Bogachiel, Hoh Lake and Hoh River Trails. The park service was constructing an interpretive center near the park's entrance booth in Soleduck River Road. It may now be completed. Several other interpretive centers are planned. Description of Highway 101 resumes at mile 219.3 on page 245.

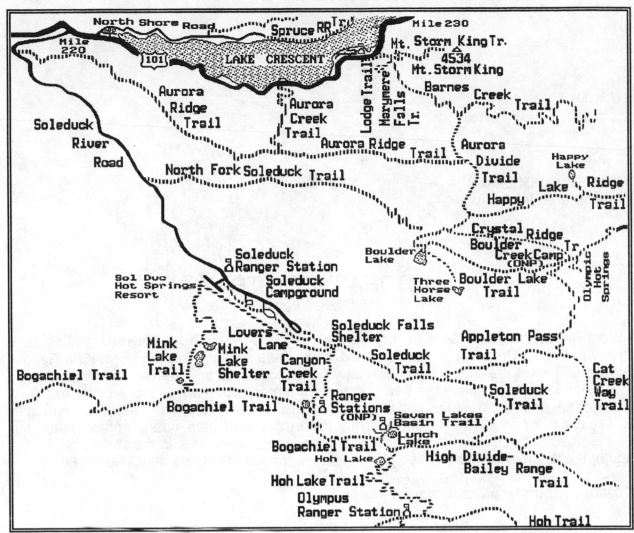

10-2 SOLEDUCK AREA

SOLEDUCK RIVER ROAD

MILES from HWY. 101	MILES to ROAD END	
0.0	12.6	HIGHWAY 101
0.2	12.4	OLYMPIC NAT'L PARK INFO. CENTER (Under construction)
0.3	12.3	OLYMPIC NAT'L PARK ENTRANCE BOOTH

TURNOUT — 1.3 — 11.3

2.3 — 10.3
SERVICE ROAD

AURORA RIDGE TRAIL — 2.5 — 10.1
(Parking area for 6 cars)

AURORA RIDGE TRAIL
(15.5 Miles Long)

Aurora Ridge Trail (3600 feet elevation gain) takes you along the ridge between the Soleduck Valley and Lake Crescent to Aurora Divide Trail. There you turn left for Storm King Ranger Station on Lake Crescent, or right for Happy Lake Ridge Trail and the Elwha Area. Although the trail never climbs above the tree line, there are many open areas that provide excellent views of the nearby mountains and the North Fork Soleduck Valley. This valley has managed to escape the ravages of logging and fire, and therefore, more nearly approximates the unmarred vistas seen by the early explorers than most other sites in the Olympics. To the south, the glaciers on Mount Olympus sparkle as though they were sprinkled with glitter.

Distances and elevations along the trail are:

Soleduck River Road, Mile 2.5 . . . . 0.0 Miles 1150 Feet
Path to Eagle Lakes (0.6 mi.long) . . . . . 5.6 Miles 3700 Feet
Sourdough Camp . . . . 8.5 Miles 4550 Feet
Aurora Creek Trail . . . . 10.6 Miles 4100 Feet
    (2.5 miles long, 3500 feet elevation gain)

Aurora Spring . . . . 11.6 Miles 4450 Feet
Aurora Divide Trail . . . . 15.5 Miles 4750 Feet
    (5.6 miles long, 3450 feet elevation gain)

2.9 — 9.7 — TURNOUT

4.8 — 7.8 — TURNOUT

5.4 — 7.2
BRIDGE

6.1 — 6.5 — TURNOUT

6.6 — 6.0 — TURNOUT

238

7.1	5.5	**SALMON CASCADES**

There is a short path leading from the parking area to the river, where you can view the cascades from a rock overhang. There are toilets near the start of the path, on the left.

7.4	5.5	**TURNOUT**

NORTH FORK SOLEDUCK TRAIL

8.2	4.4	Trailhead Parking for 6 cars.

There is no sign at the road marking the trailhead. There is a trail register and some back country registration forms up the steps to your left.

NORTH FORK SOLEDUCK TRAIL
(10.5 Miles Long)

North Fork Soleduck Trail (2850 feet elevation gain) follows the North Fork Soleduck River through dense forest for about half its length. When the river turns south, the trail follows one of its major tributaries and continues in a more or less easterly direction to North Fork Soleduck Shelter. Beyond the shelter the trail, although it is not maintained, goes on for another mile and a half where it ends. From there it is about one mile (cross country) over fairly steep ground to Happy Lake Ridge. Since this trail doesn't really connect with other trails, it is often overlooked and seldom has much traffic.

Distances and elevations along the trail are:

Soleduck River Road, Mile 8.2	0.0 Miles	1450 Feet
N. Fork Soleduck Log Bridge	1.0 Miles	1500 Feet
Riverside Camp	2.9 Miles	1750 Feet
Frying Pan Camp	3.0 Miles	1700 Feet
Trail leaves N. Fork Soleduck	5.5 Miles	2100 Feet
Cross to S. side of tributary	6.0 Miles	2300 Feet
N. Fork Soleduck Shelter	9.0 Miles	2900 Feet
End of trail	10.5 Miles	4300 Feet

We return now to mile 8.2 of Soleduck River Road.

	MILES from HWY. 101	MILES to ROAD END	
NORTH FORK SOLEDUCK TRAIL	8.2	4.4	Trailhead Parking for 6 cars.
	8.5	4.1	TURNOUT
TURNOUT	8.7	3.9	TURNOUT
	8.9	3.7	TURNOUT
TURNOUT	9.4	3.2	
	9.8	2.8	TURNOUT
	10.0	2.6	TURNOUT
	10.4	2.2	SERVICE ROAD
ONP RANGER STATION	10.8	1.8	TURNOUT
	10.9 RESORT HOT SPRINGS RESTAURANT	1.7 RV PARK	SOLEDUCK CAMPGROUND TRAIL Sol Duc Hot Springs Resort MINK LAKE TRAIL LOVERS LANE

After you turn right into the short road to the resort, there is a sign on your left marking the Campground Trail. It goes through both loops of the campground, then continues for a total length of 2.1 miles. It joins Soleduck Trail 0.1 miles from its trailhead at the end of the road.

The resort has cabins, motel rooms, and an RV Park with hook-ups. There is a restaurant in the lodge. Use of the hot spring mineral pools is available at daily rates for those not staying in the resort.

MINK LAKE TRAIL
(4.3 Miles Long)

Mink Lake Trail (2450 feet elevation gain) starts from the northwest corner of the resort grounds, just to the left of a barricaded gravel service road. After you enter the resort, continue straight to a T intersection on the western edge of the grounds. Turn right and continue until you see the gravel road mentioned above. There is a parking area just beyond the gravel road on your left.

The trail starts in a second growth forest, then climbs through virgin forest to the sub-alpine zone. The trail ends at a junction with Bogachiel Trail at Little Divide. Little Divide should not be confused with Low Divide, the pass that connects the Elwha Area to the Quinault Area.

Distances and elevations along the trail are:

Sol Duc Hot Springs Resort . . . . 0.0 Miles 1679 Feet
Mink Lake (path to shelter left) . . . . 2.5 Miles 3104 Feet
Bogachiel Trail at Little Divide . . . . 4.3 Miles 4130 Feet
(32.7 miles long, 4850 feet elevation gain)

LOVERS LANE
(2.8 Miles Long)

Lovers Lane branches to the left from Mink Lake Trail a few hundred yards from its start near the northwest corner of the resort grounds. After you enter the resort, continue straight to a T intersection on the western edge of the grounds. Turn right, and continue until you see a barricaded gravel service road. The trailhead is on your left just before you reach the road. There is a parking area just beyond the gravel road on your left.

This trail is quite flat, with an elevation gain of only 250 feet as it follows the western bank of the river. It crosses three streams on log bridges with handrails, and has good views of the river and a small waterfall near its end. It ends in a junction with Canyon Creek Trail 0.1 miles from its beginning at Soleduck Falls on the Soleduck Trail. Soleduck River Road is 0.8 miles from Soleduck Falls via Soleduck trail.

Distances and elevations along the trail are:

Sol Duc Hot Springs Resort . . . . 0.0 Miles 1679 Feet
Canyon Creek Trail . . . . 2.8 Miles 1930 Feet
(3.1 miles long, 1620 feet elevation gain)

We return now to mile 10.9 of Soleduck River Road.

SOLEDUCK RIVER ROAD		
MILES	MILES	
from	to	
HWY. 101	ROAD END	
10.9	1.7	SOLEDUCK CAMPGROUND TRAIL Sol Duc Hot Springs Resort
11.0	1.6	RV Campground

11.1	1.5	Amphitheater Parking Area (A water tap and walk-in camping are at the south end of the parking area.)
11.2 CAMPGROUND	1.4	SOLEDUCK CAMPGROUND (ONP) **Area A**

This campground has 84 sites (no hook-ups). Facilities include flush toilets, potable water, tables, fire grates and a dump station. There are naturalist programs in summer. Sol Duc Hot Springs Resort has hot spring swimming pools, a restaurant and a small store.

11.5	1.1	SOLEDUCK CAMPGROUND (ONP) **Area B**
12.6	0.0	END OF ROAD SOLEDUCK TRAIL

SOLEDUCK TRAIL
(8.4 Miles Long)

The trailhead for Soleduck Trail is at the end of Soleduck River Road, which ends in a large parking loop. There is a horse unloading dock, a hitching rail, and plenty of parking for stock trailers near the trailhead. There is a toilet on your left just after the trail begins.

Soleduck Trail (3100 feet elevation gain) takes you through Soleduck Park, one of the best examples of sub-alpine terrain in the Olympics, on its way to the High Divide - Bailey Range Trail. Its proximity also makes it a good base camp for cross country excursions in the Bailey Range. The views of the Pacific, Cat Creek Ridge, Hoh Valley, Mount Olympus and the Bailey Range are all spectacular. Though it doesn't seem possible, the views improve as you penetrate deeper into the interior.

Distances and elevations along the trail are:

```
      End of Soleduck River Road . . . . . . . . . 0.0 Miles  1950 Feet
      Soleduck Campground Trail (Right) . . . . 0.1 Miles  2000 Feet
          (2.1 miles long, 50 feet elevation gain)
      Canyon Creek Trail (Right) . . . . . . . . . . 0.8 Miles  2000 Feet
          (3.1 miles long, 1620 feet elevation gain)
```

242

Soleduck Falls, Shelter . . . . 0.8 Miles 1925 Feet
Appleton Pass Trail . . . . 4.9 Miles 3100 Feet
    (7.8 miles long, 2850 feet elevation gain)

Upper Soleduck Camp . . . . 5.3 Miles 3150 Feet
Log over Soleduck and Bridge Ck. . . . . 5.5 Miles 3300 Feet
Cross Bridge Creek . . . . 6.5 Miles 3800 Feet
Bridge Creek Camp . . . . 7.7 Miles 4500 Feet
Heart Lake . . . . 8.1 Miles 4750 Feet
High Divide-Bailey Range Trail . . . . 8.4 Miles 5050 Feet

CANYON CREEK TRAIL
(3.1 Miles Long)

Canyon Creek Trail (1620 feet elevation gain) begins on the Soleduck Trail at Soleduck Falls, 0.8 miles from the end of Soleduck River Road. Mist from the waterfall sprays over a picturesque, wooden footbridge at the beginning of the trail. Lovers Lane, a flat 2.8 mile stroll to Sol Duc Resort begins just south of the bridge. You get another waterfall when the trail bridges Canyon Creek one mile from Soleduck Falls. The vegetation along the trail is prolific, with berries, ferns grasses and wildflowers everywhere. The trail is quite popular, and the park service has had to restrict camping at Deer Lake.

Distances and elevations along the trail are:

Soleduck Trail at Soleduck Falls . . . . . . 0.0 Miles 2000 Feet
Lovers Lane . . . . 0.1 Miles 1930 Feet
    (2.8 miles long, 250 feet elevation gain)

Bridge over Canyon Creek . . . . 1.0 Miles 2378 Feet
Deer Lake (Ranger Station on left)2.9 Miles 3525 Feet
Bogachiel Trail, Mile 28.4 . . . . 3.1 Miles 3550 Feet
    (32.7 miles long, 4850 feet elevation gain)

Seven Lakes Basin Trail and High Divide-Bailey Range Trail both start from the Bogachiel Trail which is discussed on page 260 below. Because of the distances involved, most people gain access to these trails from Soleduck River Road. For example, Seven Lakes Basin Trail is 31.8 miles from the trailhead of Bogachiel Trail, but only 7.3 miles from Soleduck River Road via Soleduck Trail, Canyon Creek Trail and Bogachiel Trail. Hoh Lake Trail, which starts at a three-way junction with Bogachiel Trail and High Divide-Bailey Range Trail, is discussed on page 271, as it is more closely related to the Hoh and Mount Olympus areas.

SEVEN LAKES BASIN TRAIL
(0.9 Miles Long)

Seven Lakes Basin Trail (500 feet elevation loss) begins at mile 31.8 of Bogachiel Trail, 3.4 miles east of its junction with Canyon Creek Trail. There are at least a dozen lakes in the basin, and its 1600 acres is crisscrossed with little way trails between them. The basin has heavy snowfall in winter, and the lakes often don't thaw until July. The main trail takes you to the north side of Lunch Lake, where there is a spur to Clear Lake, and the beginning of a way trail to the eastern portion of the basin. There is a Ranger Station on a knoll above Lunch Lake to your left as you come from Bogachiel Trail.

Distances and elevations along the trail are:

```
Bogachiel Trail, mile 31.8 . . . . . . . . . . . 0.0 Miles  4900 Feet
Round Lake Spur Tr.(0.2 mi. long) . . . . . 0.5 Miles  4450 Feet
Clear Lake Spur Tr.(0.3 mi. long)  . . . . . 0.9 Miles  4400 Feet
```

HIGH DIVIDE - BAILEY RANGE TRAIL
(6.2 Miles Long)

High Divide - Bailey Range Trail loses 1084 feet in elevation from the top of Bogachiel Peak to its low point near the head of Cat Creek, then gains 610 feet of it back before it ends. The panoramic views along this trail are among the best in the peninsula. The sunsets and sunrises are marvelous. You can see the entire northwest corner of the peninsula from the top of Bogachiel Peak (5474 feet) which is only a few hundred yards from the trail. The view from Bogachiel Peak is so spectacular that one feels somewhat disappointed that the good view came so early in the hike. But soon it is matched by views of Mount Olympus, Bailey Range and the Bogachiel, Hoh and Soleduck Valleys in rapid succession. This trail is one of those that continuously reminds you of the reasons you go hiking, and justifies all the pain and suffering.

Access to High Divide - Bailey Range trail is easiest from the end of Soleduck River Road. The trailhead is 32.7 miles from the trailhead of Bogachiel Trail, but only 8.2 miles from Soleduck River Road via Soleduck Trail, Canyon Creek Trail and Bogachiel Trail.

Distances and elevations along the trail are:

```
End of Bogachiel Trail(mi.32.7) . . . . . . . 0.0 Miles  5200 Feet
Spur to top of Bogachiel Peak . . . . . . . . 0.2 Miles  5474 Feet
Good campsite . . . . . . . . . . . . . . . . . . . 0.9 Miles  5000 Feet
Soleduck Trail (Left) . . . . . . . . . . . . . . . 2.1 Miles  5050 Feet
     (8.4 miles long, 3100 feet elevation gain)

Cat Ck. Ridge (Leave High Divide)  . . . . 3.0 Miles  5100 Feet
Ocarina Lake (Good campsite)  . . . . . . . 3.4 Miles  4900 Feet
Cat Creek Way Trail . . . . . . . . . . . . . . . 4.0 Miles  4500 Feet
     (4.5 miles long, 1250 feet elevation gain)

Bear Grass Hill . . . . . . . . . . . . . . . . . . . 5.1 Miles  4800 Feet
     (End of maintained trail)

Stream (50 feet below trail) . . . . . . . . . . 5.5 Miles  4800 Feet
End of Trail . . . . . . . . . . . . . . . . . . . . . 6.2 Miles  5000 Feet
```

High Divide - Bailey Range Trail was originally planned to continue across the Bailey Range to Long Ridge Trail, near Ludden Peak, but it ends here at a steep cliff. One can cross the range using the popular Bailey Range Traverse which begins here, but it should only be attempted by experienced cross country hikers with appropriate equipment.

244

We now return to mile 219.3 of Highway 101.

	HIGHWAY 101 MILES from I-5	MILE NUMBER	
SOLEDUCK RIVER ROAD Sol Duc Hot Springs Resort	148.0	219.3	TURNOUT
	149.6	217.7	SLOW VEHICLE TURNOUT
	150.2	217.1	SLOW VEHICLE TURNOUT
	150.6	216.7	SLOW VEHICLE TURNOUT
2918	151.0	216.3	
TURNOUT	151.2	216.1	
TURNOUT	152.0	215.3	
	152.1	215.2	HECKLE STREET
	153.6	213.7	TURNOUT
	154.3	213.0	EAST SNIDER ROAD To: 3040 (E. TWIN RIVER RD)
	154.9	212.4 SOL DUC RIVER	
COOPER RANCH ROAD 29	155.4	211.9	KLAHOWYA CAMPGROUND (ONF) PIONEERS PATH NATURE TRAIL

FSR 29 twists and turns its way south through Olympic National Forest to Sitkum River. There, it turns west and follows the river to FSR 2900-070, the access road for Rugged Ridge Tr. It continues, past unmaintained Klahanie Campground (ONF), and returns to Highway 101 at mile 193.2 just north of Forks. This trail is usually reached from the other end of FSR

Klahowya Campground is nestled in among the tall trees on the Soleduck River. It is set back far enough from the highway to provide a feeling of seclusion. There are 55 sites (no hook-ups), with a maximum trailer size of 21 feet. There are fire places, tables, potable water, flush toilets, a boat ramp and a nature trail.

29. The route to Rugged Ridge Trail, the trail itself and Klahanie Campground, are described on page 249.

Pioneers Path Nature Trail (0.3 Miles Long) makes a loop south of the campground. It starts from near the end of the camping loop, beyond the day use parking area. The trailhead is on the right, opposite sites 49-55. Overflow and large RV parking are on the left.

	155.7 211.6 SOL DUC RIVER	
RIVERSIDE ROAD	156.0 211.3	SNIDER ROAD TO: 3040 (E. TWIN RIVER RD)
RIVERSIDE ROAD	156.1 211.2	
TURNOUT	156.4 210.9	
	157.3 210.0 MILEPOST	
	157.8 209.5	MILLER ROAD
	158.1 209.2 LEAVING OLYMPIC NAT'L FOREST	
	159.1 208.2	(WEST TWIN RIVER ROAD) 30
HILLSTROM ROAD	161.0 206.3 TAVERN	Tavern
	161.2 206.1 BEAR CREEK	
	161.3 206.0	BEAR CREEK ROAD
Bear Creek Motel and RV Park Hungry Bear Cafe	161.4 205.9 MOTEL RV PARK RESTAURANT	

The RV park has 11 sites with hook-ups.

HIGHWAY 101

MILES   MILE
from NUMBER
I-5   ____

BEAR CREEK REC. AREA (DNR)
ALBEN WAHLGREN CAMPGROUND
(DNR)

161.5   205.8
CAMPGROUND

Wahlgren Memorial Campground (Maximum trailer length 21 ft.) has ten sites (no hook-ups). There are tables, fire rings, potable water and pit toilets. There are three short nature trails that start on the right side of the camping loop road near its junction with the spur to the day use parking area. The trailhead overlooks the river and has a map of the trails.

163.0   204.3
ENTERING SAPPHO

163.4   203.9
GAS RESTAURANT

BURNT MOUNTAIN ROAD
COASTAL SCENIC ROUTE

TO: STATE HIGHWAY 112
     OZETTE AREA OF ONP
     NEAH BAY

163.5   203.8

RIXON ROAD

163.6   203.7
SOL DUC RIVER

CLARK ROAD
PAVEL ROAD
STATE SALMON HATCHERY
INTERPRETIVE CENTER

163.7   203.6
CAMPGROUND

RAYONIER TUMBLING RAPIDS
REST AREA AND CAMPGROUND

There are 9 sites (No hook-ups) and a cooking shelter at this rest area. It has flush toilets and potable water.

164.1   203.2
SOL DUC RIVER

164.7   202.6

SOL DUC AVENUE

165.3   202.0

E. LAKE PLEASANT ROAD
(ROSE ROAD)

	MILES from I-5	MILE NUMBER	
	165.4	201.9	BEAVER ROAD
CONLEY ROAD	165.8	201.5	
	166.4	200.9	LAKE PLEASANT COUNTY PARK

This one acre day use area has a boat launch, a swimming beach and a playground.

	MILES from I-5	MILE NUMBER	
Beaver Mini-Market Mobil	166.8 C-STORE	200.5 GAS	LAKE PLEASANT ROAD Lake Pleasant Grocery
BEAVER POST OFFICE	166.9 POST OFFICE	200.4	
PRICE ROAD LAOTIAN ROAD	167.1	200.2	
Old Chief's RV Park The Galley Cafe Coin Laundry	167.3 MILEPOST RV PARK LAUNDRY RESTAURANT	200.0	
	167.4 TAVERN	199.9	Loop Tavern LAKE CREEK ROAD
	168.4	198.9	SLOW VEHICLE TURNOUT
GRAVEL PIT ROAD	168.6	198.7	
	169.2	198.1	TURNOUT
SALMON DRIVE	169.9	197.4	
MAXFIELD ROAD	170.1	197.2	
IVERSON ROAD	170.3	197.0	
SHUWAH ROAD	170.8	196.5	
GAYDESKI ROAD	171.2 RANGER STATION	196.1	RANGER STATION (ONP/ONF) LUCKEN ROAD
KLAHN ROAD	172.5	194.8	
FRENCHY'S TAVERN	172.6 TAVERN	194.7	

	173.0	194.3
	SOL DUC RIVER	

WHITCOMB-DIMMEL ROAD	173.3	194.0
PUBLIC FISHING		

29	174.1	193.2	**PRIVATE ROAD**

TO: KLAHANIE CAMPGROUND
    RUGGED RIDGE TRAIL

We will turn left here to make an excursion to the Rugged Ridge trailhead. To continue on Highway 101, please turn to mile 193.2 on page 251.

FOREST SERVICE ROAD 29

FSR 29 follows the South Fork Calawah to FSR 2900-070, the access road to Rugged Ridge Trail. After we leave it to explore Rugged Ridge Trail, FSR 29 continues east, paralleling the Sitkum River, for about 10 miles, There it turns north. It twists and turns another ten miles or so, and finally emerges at mile 211.9 of Highway 101, opposite the entrance to Klahowya Campground. The road is paved to the junction with FSR 2900-070. See Map 10.1 on page 235.

	FS ROAD 29		
	MILES	MILES	
	from	to	
	HWY. 101	FSR 2900-070	
	0.0	11.2	
	HIGHWAY 101		
2902	3.6	7.6	
UNMARKED ROAD	5.0	6.2	
	MILEPOST		
	5.3	5.9	**LARGE FLAT TURNOUT**
	5.4	5.8	**KLAHANIE CAMPGROUND 2900-011**
	CAMPGROUND		

This unmaintained campground (no tables or water) is not marked on maps or at the road. Some areas have fallen into disrepair. The road is rough.

These privations keep people away in droves, so your solitude is unlikely to be encroached upon. The campground does have a vault toilet that is still serviced.

2900-015

5.7	5.5
6.0	5.2
7.9	3.3
8.7	2.5
10.0	1.2

2932

UNMARKED ROAD

2923

MILEPOST

11.2   0.0

PAVEMENT ENDS

2900-070

RUGGED RIDGE TRAIL - 2.2 Miles

Just after you turn right, past the Sitkum River bridge, there is a closed road to an Elk Management area on your right, and a flat turnout on the left.

The trailhead for Rugged Ridge Trail is on your right 2.2 mi. from FSR 29. Just beyond the trailhead is a parking area on your left that looks out over a bluff. From the parking area you see a patchwork of clearcuts of differing ages. The old clearcuts have had time enough to heal, and contrast sharply with the devastation of the more recent ones.

RUGGED RIDGE TRAIL
(3.0 Miles Long)
Trail 883

Rugged Ridge Trail gains 350 feet of elevation in its first half, then loses 600 feet as you complete the journey to South Fork Calawah River. There is a profusion of ferns and mosses along the way. The trail crosses several streams with picturesque cascades that you can see from the trail. Near the end is Seven Step Falls. At the end of Rugged Ridge Trail, you must cross the South Fork Calawah River to reach Indian Pass Trail (See page 260.). There is no bridge, and the crossing can be dangerous in winter and spring.

Distances and elevations along the trail are:

FS Road 2900-070, mile 2.2	0.0 Miles	1000 Feet
Enter Olympic National Park	0.2 Miles	1200 Feet
High Point of Trail	1.6 Miles	1350 Feet
South Fork Calawah River	3.0 Miles	745 Feet

We now return to mile 193.2 of Highway 101.

HIGHWAY 101

MILES	MILE
from	NUMBER
I-5	
174.1	193.2

PRIVATE ROAD

29

TO: RUGGED RIDGE TRAIL

174.2 193.1   Smokehouse Restaurant
RESTAURANT   LA PUSH ROAD

TO: MORA CAMPGROUND (ONP)
RIALTO BEACH   BEACH HIKES

BEACH HIKES LA PUSH & MORA ROADS

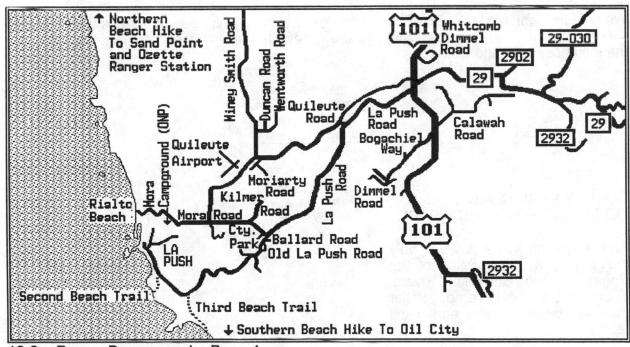

10-3   RIALTO BEACH AND LA PUSH AREA

Here we turn right into La Push Road. We will divert from La Push road for a visit to Rialto Beach in the coastal area of Olympic National Park, then press on to the beach trails southeast of La Push. La Push is a quiet fishing village in the Quileute Indian Reservation. There are two tourist resorts in La Push, and boats can be chartered for salmon fishing.

The description of Highway 101 resumes on page 256 at mile 193.1.

LA PUSH ROAD

MILES from HWY. 101	MILES to LA PUSH	
0.0	13.5	
HIGHWAY 101		
3.0	10.5	QUILEUTE AIRPORT ROAD
5.0	8.5	
CROSSROADS		
5.2	8.3	TURNOUT
5.4	8.1	WILSON ROAD PUBLIC FISHING
7.6	5.9	Three Rivers Resort MORA ROAD
RESORT RV PARK C-STORE GAS RESTAURANT LAUNDRY		This Resort has 9 RV sites with hook-ups, cabins, showers, gas, a store, a laundry and a cafe.

We will turn right into Mora Road here for an excursion to Rialto Beach. Please note that until we return to La Push Road the mileages shown refer to the distances from Highway 101, and the distances to Rialto Beach.

MORA ROAD

MILES from HWY. 101	MILES to RIALTO BCH.	
7.8	4.8	LEYENDECKER ROAD
7.9	4.7	COUNTY PARK ROAD LEYENDECKER COUNTY PARK
COUNTY PARK		

COUNTY PARK ROAD
LEYENDECKER COUNTY PARK

This 3-acre park is a day-use only picnic area at the junction of the Bogachiel and Soleduck Rivers. There is a boat ramp, trailer parking, picnic tables and vault toilets.

	8.0 4.6	
	SOLEDUCK RIVER	
	8.4 4.2	KILMER ROAD
GREEN ROAD	8.8 3.8	
RICHWINE ROAD	9.8 2.8	QUILEUTE AIRPORT ROAD
	10.3 2.3	
	ENTER OLYMPIC NATIONAL PARK	
SLOUGH TRAIL	10.8 1.8	MORA CAMPGROUND NATURE TRAIL
	NATIONAL PARK ENTRANCE BOOTH	

MORA CAMPGROUND NATURE TRAIL

This 0.3 mile long trail goes to James Pond then ends near the amphitheater.

SLOUGH TRAIL
(0.9 Miles Long)

This 0.9 mile nature trail loops back to Mora Road near the Olympic National Park boundary. There is a spur at about the 0.6 mile mark that leads down to Quileute River.

MORA RANGER STATION (ONP)	10.9 1.7
	RANGER STATION

MORA CAMPGROUND (ONP)	11.0 1.6
	CAMPGROUND

Mora Campground (max. trailer size 21 feet) has 95 sites (no hook-ups), but the trees and lush vegetation make it seem secluded and private.

Facilities include tables, fire places, potable water, amphitheater, flush toilets and a dump station. There is a short nature trail starting near the amphitheater.

BOAT LAUNCH PARKING	11.7 0.9

VIEWPOINT	12.4 0.2

RIALTO BEACH
N. WILDERNESS BEACH HIKE

| | 12.6 | 0.0 |

The road ends in a large parking loop, with the beach to the left. The trails start near the amenities block at the end of the loop. There are picnic tables, and fire grates among the trees on both sides of the path to the beach. The beach hikes start at the end of the paved path. Good objectives for short hikes are Hole In The Wall (1.0 mi.), a tunnel carved by the sea; the Chilean Memorial (2.5 mi.); and Norwegian Memorial (7.0 mi.)

NORTH WILDERNESS BEACH HIKE
(17.3 Miles Long)

Rialto Beach is the starting point for the North Wilderness Beach hike to Sand Point (17.3 miles), Cape Alava (20.6 miles). It is 3.0 miles and 3.3 miles respectively from Sand Point and Cape Alava to the Ozette Ranger Station at the end of Ozette Lake Road. It is also 3.3 miles to the Makah Indian Reservation Boundary on Shi Shi Beach. See page 203 for details of these trails.

The Quileute River cannot be crossed at the beach, so you must go by road to Third Beach Trail (See page 255.) to hike the South Wilderness Beach Hike to Oil City. Be sure to obtain a tide table from the Mora Ranger Station before setting out on a beach hike, and use the overland trails that are provided in the more dangerous spots.

We now return to La Push Road.

LA PUSH ROAD

MILES	MILES
from	to
HWY. 101	LA PUSH

	7.6	5.9	MORA ROAD
			MORA CAMPGROUND
			RIALTO BEACH

BALLARD ROAD
OLD LA PUSH ROAD

| | 7.7 | 5.8 |

OLD LA PUSH ROAD

| | 8.1 | 5.4 |

THIRD BEACH TRAIL
(1.5 Miles Long)

Third beach trail takes you through dense forest to the coastal bluff. In contrast to Second Beach, Third Beach is quiet and serene, and one can get his feet wet without being washed out to sea. A waterfall cascades from the rim of the bluff at the south end of the beach, and there are numerous tidepools. The trailhead and a toilet are located at the east end of the parking area.

SOUTH WILDERNESS BEACH HIKE
(15.8 Miles Long)

Third Beach is the starting point for the South Wilderness Beach Hike. The Quileute River cannot be crossed at the beach, so you must drive to Rialto Beach to hike the North Wilderness Beach Hike to Sand Point and Cape Alava.

The South Wilderness Beach hike is 15.8 miles long, and takes you to the Hoh River about half a mile from Oil City. The Hoh River cannot be crossed at the beach. Oil City has neither oil nor a city. There is, however, a parking area at the end of the road coming from Highway 101 about 12 miles distant.

Be sure to take tide tables on your beach hikes and use the overland trails that have been provided in the more dangerous places.

We now return to La Push Road.

SECOND BEACH TRAIL
(0.6 Miles Long)

Like Third Beach Trail, Second Beach Trail takes you through the dense forest to the coastal bluff. Unlike Third Beach though, Second Beach is the scene of a dramatic contest between the land and the sea. At high tide, huge breakers crash into the beach, trying to wrest it away from the land. An enormous seastack holds vigil over this pitched battle for real estate, having fought, and so far, won, its own battles with the sea over countless eons. The trailhead is at the western end of the parking area.

	LA PUSH ROAD		
	MILES from HWY. 101	MILES to LA PUSH	
FIRST BEACH La Push Ocean Park Resort	13.4 RESORT RV PARK ENTER LA PUSH	0.1	

La Push Ocean Park Resort has rooms, cabins and RV sites with hook-ups. It is on your left, fronting First Beach just as you enter La Push.

Shoreline Resort	13.5 RESORT STORE	0.0	La Push Grocery

We now return to mile 193.1 of Highway 101.

	HIGHWAY 101		
	MILES from I-5	MILE NUMBER	
	174.2 RESTAURANT	193.1	Smokehouse Restaurant **LA PUSH ROAD**
	174.9 CALAWAH RIVER	192.4	

FORKS

Forks is the last large town until you reach Hoquiam and Aberdeen, more than 100 miles to the south. (Aberdeen is where Washington Highway 12 leaves Highway 101 to take you back east to Olympia.) Forks is a good jumping-off place for exploring just about every different terrain that Olympic National Park has to offer. To the west are the Pacific Beaches. As you move eastward you have the forested Calawah and Bogachiel Valleys, A short drive south takes you to the mosses and ferns of the Hoh Valley's temperate rain forest. It is one of only three such rain forests in the world. (The others are in Chile and New Zealand's South Island.)

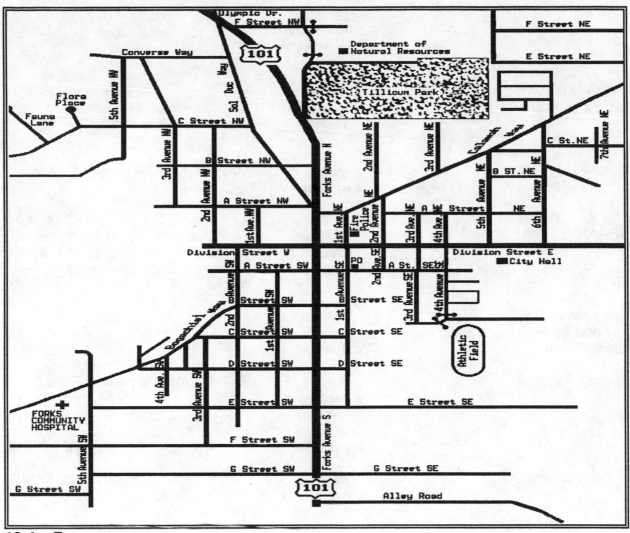

10-4 FORKS

Left	MILES from I-5	MILE NUMBER	Right
CALAWAH WAY Clark's Vagabond Restaurant	175.6 DIVISION STREET RESTAURANT GAS TAVERN	191.7	NW Garden Chinese Restaurant Mobil Service Station Texaco Service Station Hang Up Tavern
Hungry Harry's Cafe	175.7 A STREET SE, SW FAST FOOD	191.6	Main St. U Bake Pizzas & Subs
LIBRARY	175.8 B STREET SE, SW HOSPITAL	191.5	Forks community Hospital is six blocks to the right. B Street becomes Bogachiel Way in two blocks.
Forks Motel Pay and Save Supermarket Pacific Pizza	175.9 SUPERMARKET C STREET SE, SW	191.4	
Seafirst Bank	176.0 E STREET SE, SW GIFT SHOP	191.3	Rain Country Apparel & Gifts
	176.1	191.2	F STREET SW
	176.2 G STREET SE, SW	191.1	FERN HILL ROAD
Forks 101 RV Park Forks 101 RV Park has 18 sites, hook-ups, showers and laundry.	176.3 RV PARK SUPERMARKET	191.0	Thriftway Supermarket Northwestern National Bank
	176.4	190.9	Town Motel
VISITORS INFORMATION CABIN PICNIC AREA FITNESS TRAIL (0.3 Miles Long)	176.9	190.4	FORKS MUNICIPAL AIRPORT
	177.2 LEAVING FORKS HOSPITAL	190.1	HOSPITAL RUSSELL ROAD
	177.3 MILEPOST	190.0	
	177.7	189.6	TURNOUT
	180.8	186.5	FUHRMAN ROAD

181.3	186.0
CAMPGROUND	

BOGACHIEL STATE PARK

The Bogachiel State Park has 42 camp sites (no hook-ups) on the forested banks of the Bogachiel River. It can accommodate RV's up to 35 feet long, and it has tables, fireplaces, a cooking shelter, showers, flush toilets and a dump station.

FOREST SERVICE ROAD 2932

We will take a short side trip here to the Bogachiel Trail trailhead. The description of Highway 101 resumes at mile 186.0 on page 264.

FS ROAD 2932

MILES	MILES
from	to
HWY. 101	BOGACHIEL TR.

0.0	5.5	
HIGHWAY 101		
0.4	5.1	
PAVEMENT ENDS		
0.6	4.9	TURNOUT
0.9	4.6	TURNOUT
2.1	3.4	SIGN: "WARNING - PRIMITIVE ROAD FOR NEXT 1.5 MILES"
TURNOUT	3.5	2.0
TURNOUT	4.2	1.3
4.5	1.0	TURNOUT
4.8	0.7	TURNOUT
STEEP ROAD		
5.5	0.0	BOGACHIEL TRAIL
END OF ROAD		

BOGACHIEL TRAIL

The trail starts from about the middle of the parking area on your right.

BOGACHIEL TRAIL
(32.7 Miles Long)

The Bogachiel Trail (4850 feet elevation gain) follows the Bogachiel River to the North Fork Bogachiel River where it begins a gradual ascent. The ascent becomes steeper near the source of the North Fork Bogachiel, where you climb to Slide Pass and Little Divide. The trail continues along the ridge between the Bogachiel and the Soleduck to Bogachiel Peak. Bogachiel Peak provides one of the most spectacular panoramic vistas in the peninsula. The Bogachiel and Calawah Valleys were undeveloped at the time of the creation of Olympic National Park, and today they remain the best examples of primitive wilderness in the park.

Distances and elevations along the trail are:

FSR 2932, Mile 5.5 . . . . 0.0 Miles   400 Feet
Enter Olympic National Park . . . . 2.0 Miles   350 Feet
Indian Pass Trail, Shelter . . . . 6.1 Miles   450 Feet
    (3.4 miles long, 590 feet elevation gain)

Tumwata Creek Trail . . . . 8.2 Miles   500 Feet
    (11.5 miles long, 2764 feet elevation gain)

Flapjack Camp . . . . 10.3 Miles   650 Feet
Fifteen Mile Shelter . . . . 14.4 Miles   1000 Feet
Hyak Shelter . . . . 17.4 Miles   1400 Feet
Twenty-one Mile Shelter . . . . 20.6 Miles   2214 Feet
Slide Pass . . . . 22.1 Miles   3600 Feet
Mink Lake Trail . . . . 24.8 Miles   4130 Feet
    (4.3 miles long, 2450 feet elevation gain)

Canyon Creek Trail . . . . 28.4 Miles   3550 Feet
    (3.1 miles long, 1620 feet elevation gain)

Seven Lakes Basin Trail . . . . 31.8 Miles   4900 Feet
    (0.9 miles long, 500 feet elevation loss)

Hoh Lake Trail . . . . 32.7 Miles   5200 Feet
    (6.5 miles long, 4900 feet elevation gain)

High Divide-Bailey Range Trail . . . . . . 32.7 Miles   5200 Feet
    (6.2 miles long, 1084 feet elevation loss)

There is a path leaving from the High Divide - Bailey Range Trail to the summit of Bogachiel Peak that should not be missed. The path is 0.2 miles from the end of Bogachiel Trail, and it takes you 0.1 miles to the summit for a superlative panoramic view of what looks like the whole of northwestern Washington.

INDIAN PASS TRAIL
(3.4 Miles Long)

Indian Pass Trail takes you north from Bogachiel Trail to South Fork Calawah River. Rugged Ridge Trail is on the other side of the river. It comes down from the ridge between the South

Fork Calawah and the Sitkum Rivers. There is no bridge at the river, and crossing can be quite dangerous when the water is high in winter and spring. Indian Pass Trail and Rugged Ridge Trail are the only ways into the Calawah Valley, so the primitive wilderness has been preserved here better than anywhere else in the peninsula.

Distances and elevations along the trail are:

        Bogachiel Trail, mile 6.1 . . . . 0.0 Miles 450 Feet
        Indian Pass . . . . 1.8 Miles 1041 Feet
        Rugged Ridge Tr.-S. Fork Calawah . . . . 3.4 Miles 745 Feet
            (3.0 miles long, 605 feet elevation gain)

We will now return to Bogachiel State Park at mile 186.0 of Highway 101 to rest up for Chapter 11. It begins with the rain forest of the Hoh River Valley and the trail to Mount Olympus.

Yahoo Lake from Yahoo Lake Campground on Washington Department of Natural Resources Road C-3100.

CHAPTER 11

HOH   HOH-CLEARWATER ROAD   S. COAST

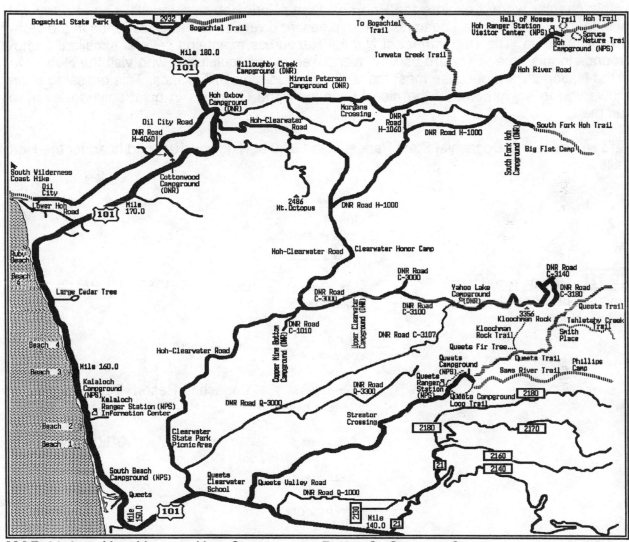

MAP 11-1   HOH VALLEY, HOH-CLEARWATER ROAD, S. OLYMPIC COAST

Temperate rain forests are found only in New Zealand, southern Chile, and here in the Pacific Northwest. The Hoh, Queets and Quinault Valleys have outstanding examples of all the features of rain forests. All three face the ocean on the west, and are saturated with rain. The average precipitation on the coast is over 145 inches (12 feet) per year. This figure

263

climbs to more than 200 inches (nearly 17 feet) per year at Mount Olympus. Even in summer, when there is relatively little rainfall, dense fogs compensate for the lack of rain.

The moisture supports a profusion of mosses and ferns which drape the trees. In the denser growths where the light is dim, the shapes produced by the vegetation on the trees stir the imagination. More than a few hikers have returned from these rain forests with absolute certainty that they have seen Sasquatch. Colonnades of trees often form straight lines that make them seem to be contrivances of a landscape architect. Others look like circus clowns on stilts. Colonnades come about when a fallen tree becomes a "nurse log" that provides a protected platform for the new generation of seedlings high above the fierce competition of the vegetation on the forest floor. The trees on stilts start out as seedlings on old stumps. They grow long roots from their high perches, and when the stumps disintegrate they are left with stilts.

In this chapter we will explore the Hoh and South Fork Hoh rain forests. Our journey will include more of the ocean beaches, and a pleasant diversion to the State lands in the Hoh-Clearwater area. The Department of Natural Resources maintains several excellent campgrounds in this area. They are usually overlooked by the multitudes who visit the Hoh Area of the National Park because most maps don't include the DNR roads. This omission often allows you to enjoy some of the nicest scenery in the Olympics in quiet solitude, even in summer.

Let's return now to Bogachiel State Park at mile 186.0 of Highway 101, and head for the Hoh Valley.

	HIGHWAY 101		
	MILES from I-5	MILE NUMBER	
2932 UNDIE ROAD BOGACHIEL TRAIL	181.3 CAMPGROUND	186.0	BOGACHIEL STATE PARK
	181.6 BOGACHIEL RIVER	185.7	
	181.8 RESORT GAS	185.5	Bogachiel Resort, Texaco Gas SMITH ROAD
	182.3	185.0	KALLMAN ROAD
	182.6 ENTER JEFFERSON CTY.	184.7	
TURNOUT	183.0	184.3	
TURNOUT	186.3	181.0	

To: HOH RAIN FOREST
OLYMPIC NATIONAL PARK
HOH CAMPGROUND (ONP)
HOH TRAIL
MOUNT OLYMPUS

HOH RIVER ROAD

Hoh River Road runs parallel to the north shore of the Hoh River to Hoh Campground. Hoh Ranger Station and Information Center, the trailheads for two nature trails and the trailhead for Hoh Trail are also located at the end of the road.

The road starts out by passing through several stump farms and stands of second growth trees. There is an occasional stretch of virgin forest even before you reach the park entrance. Beyond the park entrance is dense, virgin rain forest. Some of the Sitka Spruce are 300 feet tall. One of the larger ones is on display a few yards from a turnout right beside the road.

The Hoh trail is also 18.0 miles long. The first 12 miles are fairly flat, but then it climbs sharply to Blue Glacier on the slopes of Mount Olympus. Just before you reach Blue Glacier, you come to Glacier Meadows Camp which is still protected by trees. It makes a good base camp for climbing Mount Olympus.

Description of Highway 101 continues at mile 178.5 on page 272.

	HOH RIVER ROAD		
	MILES	MILES	
	from	to	
	HWY. 101	ROAD END	
TURNOUT	0.0	18.0	
	HIGHWAY 101		
	0.2	17.8	
	BRIDGE		
TURNOUT	0.3	17.7	
	0.6	17.4	TURNOUT

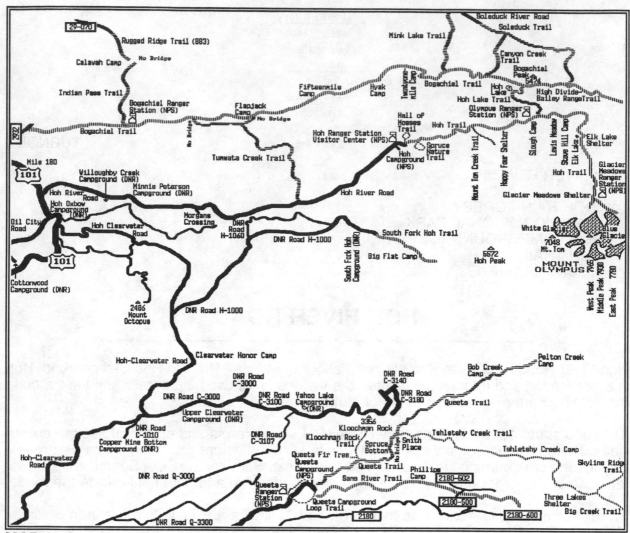

MAP 11-2   HOH VALLEY AND MOUNT OLYMPUS

HOH RIVER ROAD		
MILES	MILES	
from	to	
HWY. 101	ROAD END	
2.1	15.9	TURNOUT
ALDER CREEK		
3.5	14.5	TURNOUT
WILLOUGHBY CRK.		
3.6	14.4	WILLOUGHBY CK. CAMPGROUND (DNR)

There are five sites (maximum trailer size 21 feet) at Willoughby Creek Campground. There are pit toilets, but no hook-ups or potable water.

266

MILES from HWY. 101	MILES to ROAD END	
3.7	14.3	VIEWPOINT
3.8	14.2	VIEWPOINT
4.4	13.6	TURNOUT
4.6	13.4	VIEWPOINT
4.7	13.3	

MINNIE PETERSON CAMP (DNR)

There are six RV sites (maximum trailer length 21 feet) and one picnic site at Minnie Peterson Camp. It has well water, and pit toilets, but no hook-ups.

5.0	13.0	MILEPOST

5.6	12.4	Westward Hoh Store
GROCERIES GAS		(Sign: "Last Chance for
CABINS		Groceries, Gas")

BURGER SHACK

Burger Shack has a small store, several RV sites with hook-ups and fast food.

5.7	12.3	
FAST FOOD		
STORE		
RV PARK		

6.3	11.7	TURNOUT
6.4	11.6	TURNOUT
ROCK CREEK		
6.9	11.1	TURNOUT

7.2	10.8	MORGANS CROSSING CAMP (ONF)
BOAT RAMP		
CAMPGROUND		

Morgans Crossing has six sites that are suitable for self-contained RV's. There are no hook-ups, and no potable water. There is a boat ramp.

TURNOUT

7.4	10.6	
TOWER CREEK		

	MILES from HWY. 101	MILES to ROAD END	
	7.8	10.2	TURNOUT
	8.3	9.7	TURNOUT
TURNOUT	9.7	8.3	TURNOUT
	10.0 MILEPOST	8.0	
	10.2 CANYON CREEK	7.8	
	10.3	7.7	TURNOUT
	11.6	6.4	LEWIS RANCH
	12.0 ENTER NAT'L PARK	6.0	
TURNOUT	12.1	5.9	TURNOUT
TUMWATA CREEK TRAIL (Bogachiel-Hoh Trail)	12.6 ENTRANCE BOOTH OLYMPIC NATIONAL PARK	5.4	TRAIL PARKING AREA

TUMWATA CREEK TRAIL
(11.5 Miles Long)

Tumwata Creek Trail (2764 feet elevation gain) makes most of its elevation gain in its first three miles as it ascends a north-south ridge. Then it continues along a spur that runs more or less parallel to Tumwata Creek until it descends to the Bogachiel River. There is no water along the trail until you approach the Bogachiel. The trail forks into two branches when it reaches the river. The right branch goes to Flapjack Camp at mile 10.3 of Bogachiel Trail, and the left branch takes you to mile 8.2 of Bogachiel Trail. The Bogachiel River must be forded to reach the Bogachiel Trail at the end of both branches, so be sure to check on its status before you set out. Fording the Bogachiel can be dangerous at times.

Distances and elevations along the trail are:

Hoh River Road, Mile 12.6	0.0 Miles	436 Feet
South end of ridge	3.0 Miles	2900 Feet
North end of ridge	5.0 Miles	3200 Feet
Bogachiel River - Trail Forks	10.0 Miles	1000 Feet
Opp. Flapjack Camp (Right)	10.9 Miles	580 Feet
Opp. Mile 8.2 Bogachiel Tr.	11.5 Miles	550 Feet

12.8	5.2	TURNOUT

BOAT RAMP

13.3	4.7	TURNOUT

14.0	4.0	TURNOUT

15.5	2.5	BIG SPRUCE TREE

This huge Sitka Spruce is 270 feet tall, and thirteen feet in diameter. It is estimated to be 700 years old.

16.9	1.1	TURNOUT

17.6	0.4	TURNOUT

17.9	0.1
ROAD FORKS	

18.0	0.0

HOH RANGER STATION
HOH VISITOR CENTER
HALL OF MOSSES NATURE TRAIL
SPRUCE NATURE TRAIL
HOH TRAIL

All three of these trails can be reached from the rear entrance of the Visitor Center.

The Hall of Mosses Nature Trail is a 0.75 mile loop (to the left) through the trees to a colonnade of big leaf maples that is shrouded in ferns and mosses.

Spruce Nature Trail is a 1.25 mile loop branching right from the Hoh Trail near its start. It passes through a stand of large conifers, then descends to the river bank before returning to the Hoh Trail.

HOH CAMPGROUND (ONP)
HIKER PARKING AREA

Hoh Campground has 95 campsites (maximum trailer size 21 feet) nestled among the trees on the banks of the Hoh River. There are no hook-ups.

It has grates, tables, potable water, flush toilets, a dump station and a public telephone. There are naturalist walks and campfire programs in summer.

269

HOH TRAIL
(18.0 Miles Long)

The Hoh Trail (4422 feet elevation gain) is mostly flat for the first 12 miles as it ambles along beside the Hoh River through the dense jungle of the rain forest. The trees are often reshaped into bizarre forms by the ubiquitous ferns and mosses. As the sun sinks in the west, there are frequent sightings of elephants and giraffes. Scientists would like to study these nocturnal species that are so far from their normal habitat, but they secrete themselves so well that, so far, no trace of them has been uncovered after the sunrise has blossomed into broad daylight.

Look to your left as you approach Olympus Ranger Station, and you will see a ghost forest of silver trees that were killed by the 1978 Hoh Lake fire. The contrast is startling as you emerge from the teeming life of the rain forest. Past the Ranger Station, you return to the dense forest. Many of the conifers are 250 to 300 feet high and up to 12 feet thick. At Stove Creek Camp the trail starts to climb. The ascent is fairly gentle at first, but beyond the Hoh bridge you are on the slopes of Mount Olympus. After you stop on the bridge to take a few photos of the 150 foot gorge that the Hoh has carved here, you face a relentless climb for the remainder of the hike.

The trail forks just beyond Glacier Meadows. Both branches lead to Blue Glacier, the start of the climb to the summit of Mount Olympus. The view from the lateral moraine, across the glacier to Snow Dome and the peaks of Mount Olympus is superb. Everyone who reaches the moraine is tempted to go on to the summit. It is a fantastic climb, but it should only by attempted by parties of experienced, well equipped mountaineers. The distances are deceptive, the glacier is riddled with crevasses, and the weather can turn from sunny to dreadful in a matter of minutes. Most of the fatalities on Mount Olympus have been caused by the absence of essential equipment and inadequate mountaineering experience.

Distances and elevations along the trail are:

Hoh Ranger Station Visitor Center	0.0 Miles	578 Feet
Viewpoint	1.5 Miles	600 Feet
Mount Tom Creek Trail (Camp)	2.8 Miles	660 Feet
(1.2 miles long, 150 feet elevation gain)		
Happy Four Shelter	5.6 Miles	800 Feet
Slough Camp	7.9 Miles	900 Feet
Olympus Ranger Station	9.0 Miles	948 Feet
Hoh Lake Trail	9.5 Miles	1000 Feet
(6.5 miles long, 4900 feet elevation gain)		
Lewis Meadow	10.3 Miles	1000 Feet
Stove Hill Camp	12.0 Miles	1080 Feet
Hoh Bridge	13.0 Miles	1357 Feet
Elk Lake Camp	14.6 Miles	2558 Feet
Glacier Meadows	17.0 Miles	4200 Feet
Trail Forks near Ranger Station	17.1 Miles	4200 Feet
Lateral Moraine (Left)	18.0 Miles	5000 Feet
Indian Rock (Right)	17.5 Miles	4700 Feet

MOUNT TOM CREEK TRAIL
(1.2 Miles Long)

Mount Tom Creek Trail (140 feet elevation gain) is unmaintained, and has virtually disappeared on the south side of the Hoh River. The reason for its neglect is the fact that it is not safe to ford the Hoh here until late in the summer. The trail branches to the right from mile 2.8 of the Hoh Trail. There is a campsite immediately after you join the trail, on the north side of the river. On the south side of the river, the trail totally disappears from time to time as it follows the east bank of Mount Tom Creek for 1.1 miles. Mount Tom Shelter has been removed from the west bank of the creek at the end of the trail.

HOH LAKE TRAIL
(6.5 Miles Long)

Hoh Lake Trail (4900 feet elevation gain) starts at mile 9.5 of the Hoh Trail, half a mile east of Olympus Ranger Station. It is a beautiful high country trail with lots of open country and magnificent vistas. You pay for these vistas with steep ascents and lots of switchbacks as you climb to Bogachiel Peak. A spur trail leading to the summit of Bogachiel Peak leaves the High Divide - Bailey Range Trail 0.2 miles beyond the end of Hoh Lake Trail. Bogachiel Peak should not be missed. There are 360° panoramic vistas of the whole northwest corner of Washington from the summit.

This trail also takes you through the devastation of the 1978 Hoh Lake fire. If you observe closely, you will see small trees beginning to reclaim the open areas and the silvery ghost forest created by the fire.

The Hoh Lake Trail ends at a three-way junction with the Bogachiel Trail (32.7 miles long, see page 260), and the High Divide - Bailey Range Trail (6.2 miles long, see page 244). The Bogachiel Trail connects to trails leading to the Soleduck area of the National Park

Distances and elevations along the trail are:

Hoh Trail, mile 9.5	0.0 Miles	1000 Feet
Enter 1978 Hoh Lake Fire area	1.0 Miles	1500 Feet
Crest of ridge	3.5 Miles	3500 Feet
C.B. Flats	4.8 Miles	4050 Feet
Hoh Lake	5.3 Miles	4500 Feet
Bogachiel Trail (Left)	6.5 Miles	5200 Feet
(32.7 miles long, 4850 feet elevation gain)		
High Divide-Bailey Range Tr.(Rt.)	6.5 Miles	5200 Feet
(6.2 Miles Long, 1084 feet elevation loss)		

We will now return to mile 178.5 of Highway 101. After a brief diversion on Oil City Road we will explore the Bert Cole State Forest, and the South Fork Hoh Trail, a very nice trail in the neglected area south of Hoh River.

	HIGHWAY 101	
	MILES	MILE
	from	NUMBER
	I-5	
HOH RIVER ROAD	188.8	178.5
OIL CITY ROAD	189.9	177.4
To: COTTONWOOD CAMPGROUND (DNR)		
OCEAN BEACH TRAIL		

OIL CITY ROAD

Oil City Road takes you through private and state-owned land to a small parking area half a mile west of Oil City. Another half mile walk along the north bank of the Hoh River brings you to the beach. Oil City Road is the objective of the South Wilderness Beach Hike (See page 255.) which starts from Third Beach near La Push. There is neither oil nor city at Oil City. In fact, there is nothing at Oil City except houses — three of them, by my count.

This beach is an excellent place for beachcombing, especially in winter when the sea becomes quite violent. It spits out flotsam that ranges from gigantic driftwood logs to fragile glass fishing floats.

Description of Highway 101 continues at mile 177.4 on page 273.

	OIL CITY ROAD		
	MILES	MILES	
	from	to	
	HWY. 101	ROAD END	
TURNOUT	0.0	10.1	
TURNOUT	1.3	8.8	TURNOUT
DNR ROAD H-4060	2.3	7.9	
COTTONWOOD CAMPGROUND (DNR)			

Cottonwood Campground (maximum trailer size 21 feet) is 0.9 miles from Oil City Road on DNR Road H-4060. It has six sites and a picnic shelter on the Hoh River. None of the sites have hook-ups. There are toilets, potable water and a short nature trail.

TURNOUT	2.8	7.3	
TURNOUT	3.8	6.3	

MILES from HWY. 101	MILES to ROAD END	
4.3	5.8	
ANDERSON CREEK		
4.5	5.6	TURNOUT
4.9	5.2	
PAVEMENT ENDS		
5.1	5.0	TURNOUT
5.4	4.7	DNR ROAD H-3000
6.9	3.2	DNR ROAD H-4500
TURNOUT	7.6	2.5
8.5	1.6	
WOODEN BRIDGE		
9.5	0.6	
FOSSIL CREEK		
OIL CITY		
Road to Hoh River bottom.	9.6	0.5
9.9	0.2	TRAIL PARKING AREA
ENTER OLYMPIC NAT'L PARK		There is a toilet on the right near the parking area. Parking is not permitted in the turnaround at the end of the road.
10.1	0.0	
TURNAROUND		
BEACH TRAIL		

We now return to mile 177.4 of Highway 101 and continue our journey to the south.

HIGHWAY 101

MILES from I-5	MILE NUMBER
OIL CITY ROAD To: COTTONWOOD CAMPGROUND (DNR)	189.9	177.4
OCEAN BEACH TRAIL		

HOH OXBOW CAMPGROUND

190.5   176.8

Hoh Oxbow Campground (maximum trailer size 21 feet) has no hook-ups or potable water. It has twelve sites, tables and toilets. It also has an interpretive river trail.

190.7   176.6   TURNOUT

HOH RIVER

TURNOUT

191.0   176.3

HOH - CLEARWATER ROAD
(CLEARWATER HONOR CAMP ROAD)
(HOH MAINLINE ROAD)

191.3   176.0

BERT COLE STATE FOREST

To: SOUTH FORK HOH TRAIL
     YAHOO LAKE
     KLOOCHMAN ROCK

HOH-CLEARWATER ROAD

The area south of the Hoh River is largely ignored by the throngs of people who visit the national park, only a few miles away. I think this is so because cartographers fill this space with legends in old gothic typefaces that warn: "TERRA INCOGNITA" and "THERE BE DRAGONS HERE". Or, to be even more intimidating, they leave the space blank. Since the area is not developed as a tourist area, and the maps are quite skimpy, I will try especially hard to include enough landmarks for you to keep your bearings as you proceed.

The Hoh - Clearwater Road is paved for its entire length, and most of the gravel roads are well maintained. There are several excellent DNR campgrounds, most of which have short nature trails. For those who are unable to hike the 3.4 mile Kloochman Rock Trail which starts from mile 2.3 of Queets Trail, Kloochman Rock (3356 feet) is accessible by road from here. Although logging in the State Forest has marred the vista in recent years, the view is still spectacular.

Another attraction of this area is Yahoo Lake. Since it is a few hundred yards from the road, and the road has very little traffic anyway, you feel as though you are in a remote wilderness only minutes after you leave your car.

Description of Highway 101 continues at mile 176.0 on page 283.

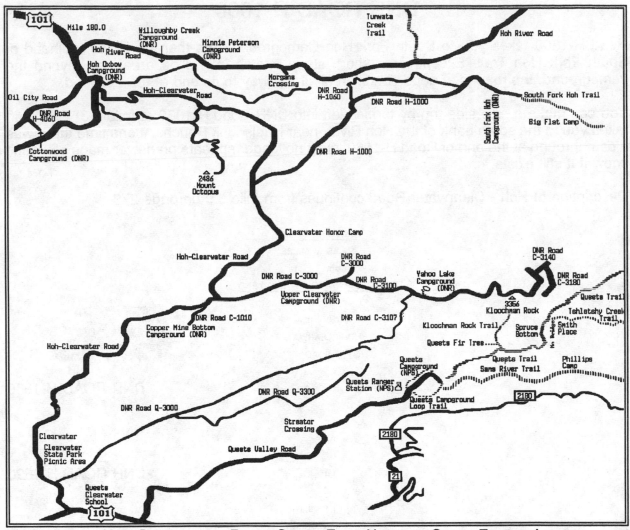

MAP 11-3 HOH-CLEARWATER ROAD, SOUTH FORK HOH AND STATE FOREST LANDS

HOH-CLEARWATER ROAD

	MILES	MILES
	from	to
	HWY.101 N.	HWY.101 S.
	0.0	29.8
	HIGHWAY 101,	
	MILE 176.0	
	1.3	28.5
	WINFIELD CREEK	
DNR ROAD H-1200	4.5	25.3
DNR ROAD H-1000	6.9	22.9
To: S. FORK HOH CAMPGROUND SOUTH FORK HOH TRAIL		

DNR ROAD H-1000

Road H-1000 takes you to South Fork Hoh Campground, and then on to the trailhead of South Fork Hoh Trail. Except for a short, steep stretch in a slide area just beyond the campground, the road is in good condition all of the way to its end at the trailhead.

You can make a nice side trip by turning left into DNR Road H-1060 at mile 2.3. This road takes you to the south bank of the Hoh River, near Huelsdonk Ranch. At one time there was a campground at the end of Road H-1060, but it no longer appears on newer maps so I don't know if it still exists.

Description of Hoh - Clearwater Road continues from mile 6.9 on page 278.

	DNR Road H-1000		
	MILES	**MILES**	
	from	to	
	HOH-CLEARWATER RD	ROAD END	
	0.0	10.4	
	HOH-CLEARWATER		
	ROAD		
	0.2	10.2	DNR ROAD H-1500
	0.9	9.5	
	BRIDGE		
	1.0	9.4	DNR ROAD H-1520
	1.1	9.3	
	MAPLE CREEK		
	1.2	9.2	DNR ROAD H-1600
			DNR ROAD H-1700
DNR ROAD H-1060 HUELSDONK RANCH	2.3	8.1	
	2.5	7.9	
	BRIDGE		
	2.6	7.8	DNR ROAD H-1800
	PAVEMENT ENDS		
	5.0	5.4	
	MILEPOST		
	5.4	5.0	DNR ROAD H-1064
	6.0	4.4	
	WASHOUT CREEK		

	MILES from HOH-CLEARWATER RD	MILES to ROAD END	
DNR ROAD H-1009	6.3	4.1	
	6.4	4.0	DNR ROAD H-1068
	6.7	3.7	DNR ROAD H-1070
TURNOUT	6.9	3.5	
	VIRGINIA FALLS CREEK		
	7.4	3.0	DNR ROAD H-1080
TURNOUT	7.6	2.8	TURNOUT
	MARSH CREEK		
	7.7	2.7	S. FORK HOH CAMPGROUND (DNR)
	S. FORK HOH R.		

South Fork Hoh Campground (maximum trailer size 21 feet) has no hook-ups or potable water. There are three sites, tables and toilets.

DNR ROAD H-1088	8.2	2.2	
	SLIDE AREA		
DNR ROAD H-1090	8.6	1.8	
DNR ROAD H-1094	9.9	0.5	
DNR ROAD H-1095	10.3	0.1	
	10.4	0.0	SOUTH FORK HOH TRAIL
	END ROAD H-1000		

SOUTH FORK HOH TRAIL
(3.3 Miles Long)

South Fork Hoh Trail (70 feet elevation gain) begins from the far right corner of the flat parking area at the end of Road H-1000. Since this trail no longer takes you to the high country, and it takes a bit of effort to reach the trailhead, it seldom has very much traffic. The infrequent traffic has emboldened the Roosevelt Elk. Fishermen, who constitute most of the traffic here, often report sightings of a small herd of these shy creatures.

Even if you don't see any elk, the sparse traffic has preserved the rain forest in a more pristine state than that found in more accessible tourist attractions. There are several examples of huge fir and spruce trees along this trail. In contrast to the high traffic areas, one also notices that the epiphytes dangling from the trees have learned how to grow closer to the ground than the reach of a human arm.

Although the trail ends after 3.3 miles, experienced hikers often go cross country from the end of the trail to Hoh Peak (5572 feet), and Mount Tom (7048 feet). This is also the easiest way for climbers to reach the Valhallas, the western peaks of Mount Olympus.

Distances and elevations along the trail are:

```
End of DNR Road 1000  . . . . . . . . . . . . . 0.0 Miles  800 Feet
Olympic National Park Boundary . . . . . . . 0.4 Miles  750 Feet
Big Flat Camp  . . . . . . . . . . . . . . . . . . 1.3 Miles  732 Feet
Camp beside River (Right)  . . . . . . . . . . 2.5 Miles  750 Feet
End of Trail . . . . . . . . . . . . . . . . . . . . 3.3 Miles  800 Feet
```

We now return to mile 6.9 of Hoh - Clearwater Road.

	HOH-CLEARWATER ROAD		
	MILES from HWY.101 N.	MILES to HWY.101 S.	
DNR ROAD H-1000	6.9	22.9	
To: S. FORK HOH CAMPGROUND SOUTH FORK HOH TRAIL			
	7.2	22.6	TURNOUT
	9.2	20.6	TURNOUT
	10.0	19.8	
	UPPER SNAHAPISH RIVER		
CLEARWATER CORRECTION CENTER	11.5	18.3	
DNR ROAD C-2000	12.0	17.8	
	13.2	16.6	DNR ROAD C-2700
	14.5	15.3	TURNOUT
	14.6	15.2	TURNOUT
DNR ROAD C-3000	16.1	13.7	

To: UPPER CLEARWATER CAMPGROUND
    YAHOO LAKE CAMPGROUND
    KLOOCHMAN ROCK VISTA

DNR ROADS C-3000 AND C-3100

Although there has been extensive logging in this area, even the clearcuts have their own special beauty. As the roads climb higher, you gain enough perspective to appreciate the patterns that the loggers have created. You can look down on the sunbursts where the logs have been skidded up hill; and the serpentine network patterns of the roads emerge in the absence off trees. Very often the morning fog on summer mornings isolates small clumps of trees into surrealistic islands that seem to float on clouds. Apart from the attraction of idyllic Yahoo Lake and the Kloochman Rock Vista the scenic drive itself makes this diversion worth while.

Description of Hoh - Clearwater Road continues from mile 16.1 on page 281.

	DNR C-3000/C-3100	
	MILES from HOH-CLEARWATER RD.	MILES to KLOOCHMAN ROCK

	MILES from HOH-CLEARWATER RD.	MILES to KLOOCHMAN ROCK	
	0.0	14.0	HOH-CLEARWATER ROAD, MILE 16.1
	0.6	13.4	BULL CREEK
DNR ROAD C-2800	1.4	12.6	
	2.3	11.7	TURNOUT
UNMARKED ROAD	2.8	11.2	
	3.3	10.7	UPPER CLEARWATER CAMPGR. (DNR)

Upper Clearwater Campground (maximum trailer size 21 feet) has 6 RV sites and 3 picnic only sites. None have hook-ups. It has potable water, toilets and a boat launch. There is an interpretive river trail which starts from near the beginning of the campsite loop.

	3.4	10.6	CLEARWATER R.

DNR ROAD C-3000

	4.0	10.0	ROAD FORKS

DNR ROAD C-3100

Road C-3000 goes to Grand Epling and Upper Road C-2000 via Road C-3700.

We turn to the right here, into Road C-3100 (the gravel one) to continue our journey to Yahoo Lake and Kloochman Rock.

	MILES from HOH-CLEARWATER RD.	MILES to KLOOCHMAN ROCK	
TURNOUT	4.9	9.1	
	5.0	9.0	
MILEPOST 1.0			
TURNOUT	6.2	7.8	
	6.8	7.2	
SLIDE AREA			
DNR ROAD Q-3000	7.2	6.8	DNR ROAD C-3100 DNR ROAD C-3140
ROAD FORKS			

Keep right here for Yahoo Lake and Kloochman Rock.

	7.5	6.5	TURNOUT
	8.3	5.7	TURNOUT
	9.0	5.0	
MILEPOST 5.0			
DNR ROAD C-3100	9.5	4.5	DNR ROAD C-3107 to Q-3000
DNR ROAD C-3150	9.8	4.2	
	9.9	4.1	TURNOUT
	10.0	4.0	TURNOUT
MILEPOST 6.0			
YAHOO LAKE CAMPGROUND (DNR) PARKING AREA	10.1	3.9	

To reach the campground (walk-in only) you walk a short distance, over a rise that isolates it from the road. After crossing two small bridges, the campground is to the left, and a nature trail to the right. It has six campsites and a shelter with a wood stove. There is no potable water. Behind the shelter, to the right, there are pit toilets.

	MILES from HOH-CLEARWATER RD.	MILES to KLOOCHMAN ROCK	
The campsites at Yahoo Lake are dispersed among the trees along the first third of a loop trail around the lake.	10.1	3.9	
	11.7	2.3	TURNOUT
	12.4	1.6	TURNOUT
TURNOUT	12.7	1.3	
	14.0 KLOOCHMAN ROCK	0.0	

The campsites at Yahoo Lake are dispersed among the trees along the first third of a loop trail around the lake.

Although it is not readily apparent from the campground, the lake and a fringe of trees are all that was left when the area was logged. It is a pleasant place to spend a summer afternoon listening to bird calls, watching water striders skitter across the water and contemplating the delicate blue of dragon flies.

We now return to mile 16.1 of Hoh-Clearwater Road.

	HOH-CLEARWATER ROAD		
	MILES from HWY.101 N.	MILES to HWY.101 S.	
DNR ROAD C-3000	16.1 SNAHAPISH RIVER	13.7	
To: UPPER CLEARWATER CAMPGROUND YAHOO LAKE CAMPGROUND KLOOCHMAN ROCK VISTA			
DNR ROAD C-1010 COPPER MINE BOTTOM CAMPG. (DNR)	16.5	13.3	

Copper Mine Bottom Campground (max. trailer size 21 feet) has no hook-ups, or potable water. It is located at the end of DNR Road C-1010 (gravel), 1.4 miles from Hoh-Clearwater Road.

	MILES from HWY.101 N.	MILES to HWY.101 S.	
There are 9 campsites, a kitchen shelter with a wood stove, toilets and a hand boat launch. The campground floods when it is wet, but the sites are on raised platforms for tents.	16.5	13.3	
There is a 500 year old, 250 foot tall Sitka spruce growing right in the campground, near site 8. There are two trails: Sampson's Trail which starts near the kitchen shelter; and an interpretive trail which begins from near site 9.			
CHRISTMAS CREEK	18.7	11.1	
CLEARWATER R.	20.2	9.6	TURNOUT
SHALE CREEK	21.3	8.5	
DNR ROAD C-1100	21.7	8.1	
MILEPOST	25.0	4.8	
JEFFERSON COUNTY COURTHOUSE ANNEX	26.8	3.0	
HURST CREEK PARK PICNIC AREA (CLEARWATER STATE PARK)	27.1	2.7	
DNR ROAD Q-3000	27.8	2.0	
	28.1	1.7	TURNOUT
QUEETS RIVER	29.0	0.8	
HIGHWAY 101 MILE 146.9	29.8	0.0	

We now return to mile 176.0 of Highway 101.

HIGHWAY 101

MILES   MILE
from NUMBER
I-5   ____

HOH-CLEARWATER ROAD
(CLEARWATER HONOR CAMP ROAD)
(HOH MAINLINE ROAD)

	191.3 176.0	

	191.6 175.7	**Hoh River Resort**
	C-STORE GAS	
	RESORT RV PARK	Hoh River Resort has 20 full hook-up RV sites, 10 tent sites and four cabins. It has showers, flush toilets, a dump station, a laundry and a small C-store.

	192.3 175.0	TURNOUT
	192.7 174.6	TURNOUT
TURNOUT	194.8 172.5	TURNOUT
TURNOUT	196.8 170.5	TURNOUT
	NOLAN CREEK	

	197.3 170.0	
	MILEPOST	

UNMARKED ROAD	197.0 170.3	

AYH Rain Forest Hostel   198.0   169.3

Rain Forest Hostel has indoor sleeping, showers and a communal kitchen. It also takes tent campers.

TURNOUT	198.7 168.6	
	198.9 168.4	FULLERTON ROAD
	199.6 167.7	LOWER HOH ROAD

To: HOH TRIBAL CENTER
LOWER HOH RIVER

200.5 166.8	
OLYMPIC NAT'L	
PARK BOUNDARY	

SOUTH OLYMPIC COAST

The beaches from the Hoh Indian Reservation boundary in the north, to the Quinault Indian Reservation boundary in the south are included in the Olympic National Park. Although there is no marked trail, the beach can be hiked the entire 13.5 miles from the Hoh River to South Beach Campground. Access to the beaches is provided by 10 short trails that start from turnouts or parking areas along Highway 101 between Ruby Beach and South Beach Campground. The longest of these trails is about 500 yards long, but most are only about 100 yards long.

Be sure to obtain tide tables before you set out on a beach hike. There is a ranger station just south of Kalaloch Lodge, on the left, at mile 157 of Highway 101. The hiking distance to the Hoh River, along the beach north from Ruby Beach, is 2.8 miles. The hike ends near the end of Lower Hoh River Road in the Hoh Indian Reservation.

Distances between landmarks along the beach to the south are as follows:

Ruby Beach	to	Beach 6	0.9 Miles
Beach 6	to	small stream	0.9 Miles
Small stream	to	Steamboat Creek	0.4 Miles
Steamboat Creek	to	Beach 4	2.4 Miles
Beach 4	to	Beach 3	0.6 Miles
Beach 3	to	Kalaloch Creek	2.5 Miles
Kalaloch Creek	to	Beach 2	1.3 Miles
Beach 2	to	Beach 1	0.9 Miles
Beach 1	to	South Beach Campground	0.8 Miles

Although the easy access makes this stretch of beach very popular, it is large enough that one never feels particularly crowded. There are great sunsets everywhere, and each beach has its own special attractions, such as the seastacks at Ruby Beach, and the tidepools, at Beach 4. In winter you can marvel at the ability of the surf to toss huge driftwood trees up on the same beach where it creates the fragile spindrift. Winter is also great for beachcombing.

Don't be intimidated by the size of the campgrounds here. Even though there are large numbers of sites, they are so well laid out in small loops that one never feels crowded. You should, however, remember that the campgrounds are all filled early in the day in summer. It is very unlikely that you will get any of the ocean side sites unless you stake your claim well before lunchtime.

There is a small store, gas, a restaurant and a gift shop at Kalaloch Lodge. This will be your last chance to stock up on necessities until you get to Amanda Park. There are also several shops and restaurants at Quinault along Quinault South Shore Road.

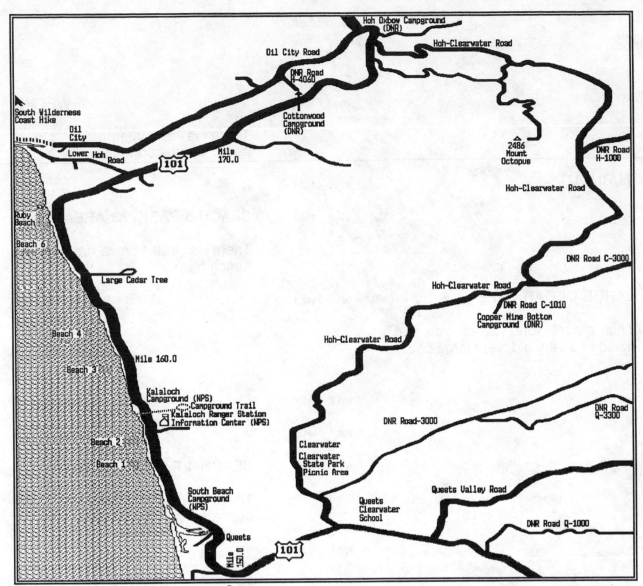

MAP 11-4 SOUTH OLYMPIC COAST

We will return to Highway 101 now. It runs parallel to the beach until it turns inland again just beyond South Beach Campground.

HIGHWAY 101	
MILES	MILE
from	NUMBER
I-5	
202.7	164.6

RUBY BEACH PARKING AREA
RUBY BEACH TRAIL

A short road leads to the 0.2 mi. long trail at the north end of the parking lot. Toilets and trash bins are at the south end.

	MILES from I-5	MILE NUMBER	
	203.8	163.5	VIEWPOINT

There is an interpretive plaque about Destruction Island here.

TURNOUT	204.2	163.1	
	204.6	162.7	BEACH 6 PARKING AREA

There is a 0.1 mile trail to the beach here.

LARGE CEDAR TREE	205.0	162.3	

This gravel road takes you 0.4 miles to a very old, very large cedar tree.

	205.2	162.1	TURNOUT
	205.7	161.6	TURNOUT
	206.8	160.5	BEACH 4 PARKING AREA

There is a 0.1 mile long trail to the beach here.

	207.1	160.2	TURNOUT
	207.2	160.1	TURNOUT
	207.3	160.0 MILEPOST	
	207.4	159.9	BEACH 3 PARKING AREA

There is a 0.1 mile trail to the beach here.

	208.1	159.2	TURNOUT
	208.3	159.0	TURNOUT
TURNOUT	208.7	158.6	
TURNOUT	209.0	158.3	TURNOUT

286

	HIGHWAY 101		
	MILES from I-5	MILE NUMBER	
TURNOUT	209.3	158.0	TURNOUT
KALALOCH CAMPGROUND (ONP)	209.6	157.7	DNR ROAD K-1000

Kalaloch Campground (maximum trailer length 21 feet) has 179 sites, none with hook-ups. It has grates, tables, piped water flush toilets and a dump station. In summer there are campfire programs and nature walks.

Some of the sites are located right on the edge of the bluff that overlooks the beach, but you have to get there early to get one of them.

There are two short trails that start from the southeast corner of the campground. The trail to the left (1.0 miles round trip) goes across the highway to the forest. The one to the right goes 0.2 miles to the beach.

	209.8	157.5	TURNOUT
	210.0 KALALOCH CREEK	157.3	
	210.2 C-STORE GAS RESTAURANT RESORT PHONE GIFT SHOP	157.1	Kalaloch Beach Ocean Village Kalaloch Lodge

Kalaloch Lodge is situated on the high bluff that overlooking the sea. There is a staircase to the beach in the northwest corner of the resort. The gift shop is in the restaurant.

RANGER STATION (ONP) INFORMATION CENTER	210.3 RANGER STATION PHONE	157.0	
UNMARKED ROAD	211.0	156.3	
TURNOUT	211.1	156.2	BEACH 2 PARKING AREA

HIGHWAY 101

MILES   MILE
from NUMBER
I-5   ___

TURNOUT	212.0	155.3		**BEACH 1 PARKING AREA**

Spruce Burl Loop Trail (0.1 mi. long, and a 0.1 trail to the beach start here. There is a toilet near the parking area.

	212.9	154.4	**SOUTH BEACH CAMPING AREA**

South Beach Camping Area (maximum trailer size 36 feet) has sites for self-contained RV's only. It has no hook-ups, toilets, potable water nor other amenities.

213.2 154.1
OLYMPIC NAT'L
PARK BOUNDARY

TURNOUT	213.8	153.5	TURNOUT
TURNOUT	214.3	153.0	
	214.4	152.9	TURNOUT

215.1 152.2
QUEETS RIVER

QUEETS MINI MART	215.3	152.0	
		C-STORE	

UNMARKED ROAD	215.6	151.7	TURNOUT
TURNOUT	215.7	151.6	TURNOUT

215.8 151.5
ENTERING
JEFFERSON CTY.

217.3 150.0
MILEPOST

TURNOUT	218.2	149.1

219.3 148.0
ENTERING GRAYS
HARBOR COUNTY

	HIGHWAY 101	
	MILES MILE	
	from NUMBER	
	I-5 ___	

HOH-CLEARWATER ROAD   220.04   146.9   TURNOUT
(CLEARWATER MAINLINE ROAD)

Description of Hoh-Clearwater Road
starts on page 274.

QUEETS CLEARWATER SCHOOL   221.3   146.0

QUEETS VALLEY ROAD   222.7   144.6

To: QUEETS CAMPGROUND
     QUEETS TRAIL
     KLOOCHMAN ROCK TRAIL

Description of Queets Valley Road will begin at this point in Chapter 12.

Bridge over Graves Creek at the end of South Shore Quinault Road.

CHAPTER 12

QUEETS   QUINAULT

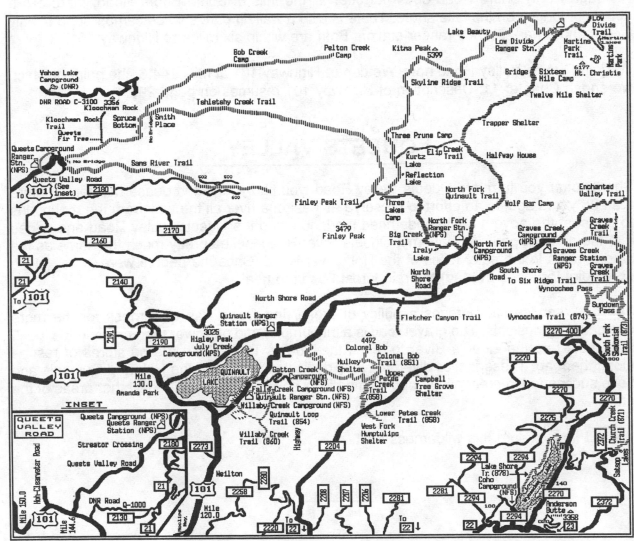

MAP 12-1   QUEETS RIVER VALLEY AND QUINAULT AREA

In Chapter 12 we will visit the Queets and Quinault rain forests. These two areas, although only a few miles apart, are quite different. Part of the difference can be accounted for by the park service policy of maintaining the Queets Valley as a wilderness area.

The park service gained control of the only access road into the Queets Valley some years ago, and most of the land in a corridor which follows the river has returned to its natural state. In many areas it is becoming difficult to distinguish the second growth trees from virgin forest. In contrast to the Hoh and the Quinault areas, there are no tourist services in the Queets Valley. Also, the road and Queets Campground are more primitive than those in the more popular areas. These features discourage people with large RV's and those with time constraints from visiting the Queets Valley.

The Quinault area teems with tourist services. On Highway 101 and on South Shore Road there are lodges, restaurants, RV parks, stores, a coin laundry, and a post office. There are three forest service campgrounds and a forest service ranger station on South Shore Road. All are within four miles of Highway 101.

Although North Shore Road does not offer all the frills of South Shore Road, there are a couple of lodges on the lake shore. There is also a walk-in park service campground at July Creek and a park service ranger station. Both are within six miles of Highway 101.

We join Queets Valley Road now. We depart Highway 101 at mile 144.6, the point at which we ended Chapter 11. Description of Highway 101 resumes on page 296.

QUEETS VALLEY

Shortly after you turn into Queets Valley Road, you find yourself in dense rain forest. More than 35 years ago, in an effort to preserve at least one river all the way from the mountains to the sea, the government condemned the land along the Queets Valley Road and added it to the national park. At that time, Queets River Road looked pretty much the same as the stump farms in the early miles of the Hoh River Road. Once the people were gone, (still a sore point for those evicted) the rain forest began to heal.

The park service still pursues a policy of preserving Queets as wilderness for the more dedicated enthusiasts. The gravel road is a bit bumpier and narrower than one might expect. One must ford the Queets River to reach the Queets Trail. There are no stores or resorts along the road. These tactics divert the less dedicated tourists to the Hoh and Quinault, and have succeeded in preserving opportunities for a solitude available in few other areas of the park.

We will now explore this wilderness a bit.

QUEETS RIVER ROAD	
MILES	MILES
from	to
HWY. 101	ROAD END
0.0	13.9
HIGHWAY 101	
MILE 144.6	

The ranger station is set back from the road. The 3 mile loop trail that starts at the campground crosses the road here.

QUEETS CAMPGROUND LOOP TRAIL
(3.0 Miles Long)

Queets Campground Loop Trail is an easy walk, mostly through virgin forest and old second growth on both sides of the road. It starts from the left side of the road, 0.1 mile west of the main entrance to the campground. Just beyond the ranger station, it crosses the Queets River Road and returns to the end of the road on the other side. The last 0.3 miles of it coincides with Sams River Trail.

Distances and elevations along the trail are:

293

```
Queets River Road, Mile 13.6 . . . . . . . . .0 Miles  290 Feet
Queets Ranger Station . . . . . . . . . . . . .1.2 Miles  270 Feet
Queets River Road, Mile 12.7 . . . . . . . .1.3 Miles  270 Feet
Junction Sams River Trail . . . . . . . . . . .2.7 Miles  300 Feet
    (12.0 miles long, 1100 feet elevation gain)

Queets River Road, Mi. 13.9 (End)  . . . . .3.0 Miles  290 Feet
```

	QUEETS RIVER ROAD	
	MILES	MILES
	from	to
	HWY. 101	ROAD END
QUEETS CAMPGROUND	13.7	0.2

Queets Campground is not recommended for RV's, but small ones might be able to squeeze in. It has 26 sites (no hook-ups) laid out haphazardly among the trees on the river bank. There are grates, tables and pit toilets.

ANOTHER CAMPGROUND ENTRANCE	13.8	0.1

SMALL TRAILHEAD PARKING AREA	13.9	0.0
	END OF ROAD	

SAMS RIVER TRAIL
QUEETS CAMPGROUND LOOP TRAIL

QUEETS TRAIL
QUEETS CAMPGROUND LOOP TRAIL

There is a notice board at the end of the road which usually provides advice as to the best place to ford the Queets River.

SAMS RIVER TRAIL
(12 Miles Long)

Sams River Trail (1100 feet elevation gain) switches back and forth across the boundary between the national forest and the national park. As a result, it has become an orphan, and has not been maintained in many years. The trail disappears frequently, and is often covered by windfalls, especially where logging in the national forest has taken its toll. If one is willing to exert the effort of a little pathfinding, he will be rewarded with a trek through the rain forest wilderness, usually in complete solitude. There are good views of Kloochman Rock, and excellent examples of enormous trees in the virgin forest parts of the hike. There is no sign marking the trail, which starts from the end of Queets Valley Road and coincides with the Queets Campground Trail for the first 0.3 miles. The trail has become quite faint so watch carefully for its beginning on the left at the fork.

Distances and elevations along the trail are:

```
End of Queets River Road (Right) . . . . .   0.0 Miles   290 Feet
Trail forks, keep left . . . . . . . . . . . . . .   0.3 Miles   300 Feet
First Canyon . . . . . . . . . . . . . . . . . . .   3.0 Miles   500 Feet
Nat'l Park/Nat'l Forest Boundary . . . . . .   4.5 Miles   650 Feet
Camp Phillips (N. Bank of River) . . . . . .   5.0 Miles   600 Feet
FS Road 2180-500 (Bridge) . . . . . . . . .   8.0 Miles   900 Feet
Camp . . . . . . . . . . . . . . . . . . . . . . . . 10.0 Miles  1000 Feet
Waterfall, End of Trail . . . . . . . . . . . . 12.0 Miles  1400 Feet
```

QUEETS TRAIL
(15.4 Miles Long)

Queets Trail (520 feet elevation gain) starts from the other side of Queets River, which must be forded. Since the best place to ford the river varies depending on the water level, you may have to ford Sams River as well. There is a notice board at the end of Queets River Road which provides information about the safest places to ford the rivers. There is a path at the end of the road that takes you down a steep bluff to river level. Fording the Queets is dangerous when the water is high. The current is swift, and the stones on the bottom are slippery. Use a brace, and wear rough soled shoes when you cross.

The trail itself is an easy walk along the river bottom. There are signs of the early settlers in the first couple of miles. The trail wanders among the huge trees and glades of this marvelous rain forest. Elk, which are usually quite shy, are often sighted from the trail. Beyond the end of the maintained trail, one can strike out to Queets Basin and Mount Olympus. The cross country traverse should only be attempted by experienced hikers with appropriate equipment.

Distances and elevations along the trail are:

```
N. Bank Queets River (No Bridge) . . . . . .  0.0 Miles   280 Feet
Barn . . . . . . . . . . . . . . . . . . . . . . . . .  1.6 Miles   375 Feet
Kloochman Rock Trail (Left) . . . . . . . . . .  2.3 Miles   350 Feet
     (3.4 miles long, 3000 feet elevation gain)

Lower Tshletshy Ford . . . . . . . . . . . . . .  3.9 Miles   400 Feet
Spruce Bottom Camp . . . . . . . . . . . . . .  4.9 Miles   426 Feet
Path to Smith Place Camp-0.2 mi. . . . . . .  5.6 Miles   480 Feet
Tshletshy Creek Trail . . . . . . . . . . . . . .  5.6 Miles   480 Feet
     (16.2 miles long, 3140 feet elevation gain)

Harlow Bottom . . . . . . . . . . . . . . . . . . .  7.5 Miles   500 Feet
Bob Creek Camp . . . . . . . . . . . . . . . . . 11.0 Miles   800 Feet
Pelton Crk. Shelter- End of Trail . . . . . . 15.4 Miles   800 Feet
```

KLOOCHMAN ROCK TRAIL
(3.4 Miles Long)

Kloochman Rock Trail (3000 feet elevation gain) starts at mile 2.3 of Queets Trail. To your left, 0.2 miles from Queets Trail, it takes you to Queets Fir, the world's largest Douglas fir tree. The tree is on a side path to your left. It is estimated to be at least 1000 years old. Its trunk is over 14 feet thick, and it is over 200 feet tall. It may have been taller at one time, because the 200 feet is measured to the point where the top was broken off long ago.

Although the vista from Kloochman rock has been impaired in recent years by logging operations, it is still well worth the effort expended in the 3.4 mile hike. Kloochman Rock can also be reached by DNR Road C-3100 via Hoh - Clearwater Road. (See page 279.)

TSHLETSHY CREEK TRAIL
(16.2 Miles Long)

Tshletshy Creek Trail (3140 feet elevation gain) is unmaintained, and shown on most maps as abandoned. It starts at mile 5.6 of Queets Trail. You must ford the Queets River again shortly after the beginning of the trail. The trail is in such poor condition that it should be regarded as a cross country hike. Only experienced, well equipped cross country hikers should attempt it. For much of the route you force your way through a marvelous conifer jungle, with frequent crossings of Tshletshy Creek. Allow plenty of time for direction finding and scouting, especially for the last one-third of the journey. At the end, the trail climbs the divide and joins Big Creek Trail near Three Lakes Camp. Big Creek Trail will take you to Irely Lake and North Fork Quinault Road.

Distances and elevations along the trail are:

Queets Trail, mile 5.6	0.0 Miles	480 Feet
Smith Place Camp, Cabin	0.2 Miles	460 Feet
First crossing Tshletshy Creek	0.8 Miles	480 Feet
Tshletshy Creek Camp	9.2 Miles	1360 Feet
Last crossing Tshletshy Creek	14.4 Miles	2275 Feet
Three Lakes Shelter-End of Trail	16.2 Miles	3600 Feet
Big Creek Trail, mile 6.9	16.2 Miles	3600 Feet

(7.1 miles long, 3100 feet elevation gain)

We will now return to mile 144.6 of Highway 101, and press on to the Quinault Valley.

HIGHWAY 101	
MILES from I-5	MILE NUMBER

QUEETS VALLEY ROAD	222.7	144.6

	222.9 144.4	SLOW VEHICLE TURNOUT
	ENTER GRAYS	
	HARBOR COUNTY	
TURNOUT	223.5 143.8	
DNR ROAD Q-1000 To: 21 VIA FSR 2130	224.0 143.3	
SLOW VEHICLE TURNOUT	224.3 143.0	
SLOW VEHICLE TURNOUT	225.8 141.5	
	226.2 141.1	SLOW VEHICLE TURNOUT
	227.3 140.0	
	MILEPOST	
TURNOUT	227.5 139.8	
	NORTH FORK	
	RAFT RIVER	
SLOW VEHICLE TURNOUT	227.7 139.6	
TURNOUT	229.1 138.2	
21	229.7 137.6	

21

(WEST BOUNDARY ROAD)
To: 2180-500

FSR 2180-500 meets mile 8.0 of
Sams River Trail. See page 294.

	230.3 137.0	SLOW VEHICLE TURNOUT
TURNOUT	232.7 134.6	
	233.6 133.7	TURNOUT
	BOULDER CREEK	
	234.8 132.5	
	TEN O'CLOCK CRK	
	234.9 132.4	TURNOUT
	235.3 132.0	Abandoned shake mill

TURNOUT   236.0   131.3   TURNOUT

2190

(CLEARY CREEK ROAD)   236.6   130.7
                                           DRY CREEK

To: HIGLEY PEAK LOOKOUT
TRAIL

Higley Creek Lookout Trail is 0.6
miles long with an elevation gain of
225 feet. It begins from mile 9.6 of
FSR 2190. There is parking for two
cars at the trailhead, but no sign
marking the trail.

Higley Peak is 3025 feet high,
enabling you to see the entire
Quinault Valley.

                                           237.3   130.0
                                           MILEPOST

Eudies Luncheon   237.5   129.8
Chevron Station   FAST FOOD GAS
                                              PHONE

Brannon's Automotive & Chevron   238.0   129.3
                                           PRAIRIE CREEK

HAAS ROAD   238.1   129.2

QUINAULT NORTH SHORE ROAD   238.6   128.7

QUINAULT VALLEY

The Quinault Valley is fairly densely settled on both shores of Lake Quinault, but it never seems crowded. There are several resorts and other tourist facilities near the lake, but by the time you get only a few miles from Highway 101, on either of the main roads you feel like you are in the wilderness again. Both roads entering the Quinault Valley penetrate deeply into the rain forest of the national park. At the end of both roads, there are long trails that take you to the passes in the high country. From North Shore Road, North Fork Quinault Trail takes you to Low Divide, where you can descend to the Elwha, retracing the steps of the Press Party expedition of 1890. Alternatively, you can return to North Shore Road via Skyline Trail and Big Creek Trail.

From South Shore Road, Enchanted Valley Trail takes you to the glaciers of Anderson Pass. At Anderson pass you must choose between West Fork Dosewallips, Duckabush and North Fork Skokomish Trails to take you out of the national park to the east. All three have special attractions that will make your selection difficult. Or, you might return to South Shore Road via North Fork Skokomish, Six Ridge and Graves Creek Trails.

Description of Highway 101 continues at mile 128.7 on page 304.

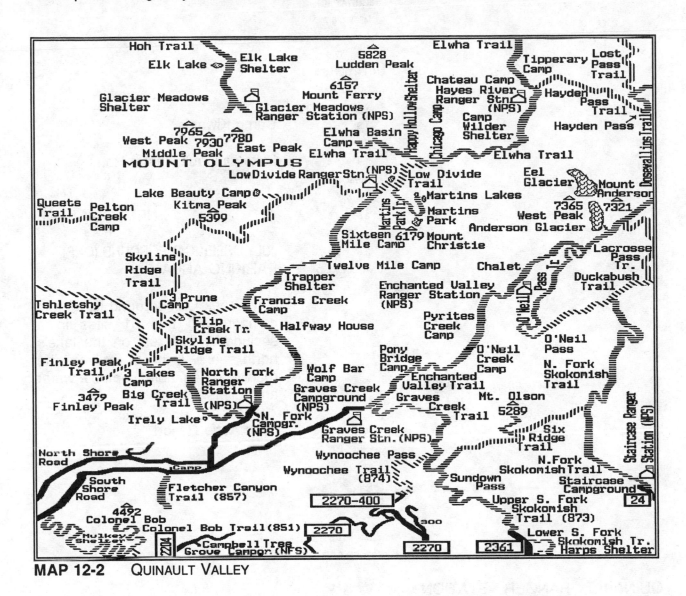

MAP 12-2   QUINAULT VALLEY

QUINAULT NORTH SHORE ROAD

North Shore Road takes you along the shore of Lake Quinault, then through the rain forest, more or less parallel to Quinault River. Just before the river forks you are offered a bridge to South Shore Road. North Shore road will take you to the trails that go north and west from the Quinault Valley. Near the end of the road there is a primitive campground and a ranger station.

MILES	MILES
from	to
HIGHWAY 101	ROAD END

0.0   17.3

HIGHWAY 101

MILE 128.7

0.3   17.0

ENTER OLYMPIC

NATIONAL PARK

1.3   16.0   Camp Kiwanis

1.9   15.4   Lake Quinault Resort Hotel

RESORT

2.8   14.5   HEMLOCK LANE

3.5   13.8   JULY CREEK CAMPGROUND (ONP)

CAMPGROUND   PARKING AREA

July Creek Campground (a walk-in campground) has 31 sites in a secluded rain forest on the lake's north shore. It is not far from the road, and has tables, potable water and toilets.

3.9   13.4   Loch Aerie Resort

RESORT

5.0   12.3

CANOE CREEK

5.5   11.8

KESTNER CREEK

QUINAULT   RANGER   STATION   5.6   11.7
(ONP)
                                   RANGER STATION

Joan's Ceramics   6.1   11.2

                                   GIFT SHOP

                                   6.8   10.5

                                   FINLEY CREEK

                                   7.9   9.4

                                   PAVEMENT ENDS

	MILES from HIGHWAY 101	MILES to ROAD END	
	10.0	7.3	
	BIG CREEK		
TURNOUT	12.6	4.7	
SERVICE ROAD	12.8	4.5	
	JOE CREEK		
NORTH SHORE ROAD	14.0	3.3	BRIDGE TO SOUTH SHORE ROAD To: GRAVES CREEK CAMPGROUND
	14.6	2.7	SERVICE ROAD
	15.1	2.2	TURNOUT
	16.1	1.2	TURNOUT
BIG CREEK TRAIL (IRELY LAKE TRAIL)	16.6	0.7	TRAILHEAD PARKING AREA

To: SKYLINE RIDGE TRAIL

BIG CREEK TRAIL
(7.1 Miles Long)

Big Creek Trail (3100 feet elevation gain) passes through terrain that ranges from rain forest in the river bottom, to sub-alpine when it gains the top of the ridge between the Queets and Quinault Rivers. At Three Lakes one can continue on the abandoned Tshletshy Creek Trail to the Queets area, or take the Skyline Ridge Trail, a glorious high country trail. Skyline Ridge Trail follows the ridge north to Kitma Peak, then turns east to join the North Fork Quinault Trail near Low Divide.

Distances and elevations along the trail are:

North Shore Road, Mile 16.6 . . . . 0.0 Miles   500 Feet
Path to Irely Lake (Left 0.1 mi.) . . . . 1.1 Miles   600 Feet
Bridge . . . . 4.0 Miles 1330 Feet
Worlds largest yellow cedar tree . . . . . . 5.9 Miles 2700 Feet
Skyline Ridge Trail (Left) . . . . 6.6 Miles 3200 Feet
   (20.5 Miles Long, 2100 feet elevation gain)

Three Lakes Camp . . . . 7.0 Miles 3400 Feet
Tshletshy Creek Trail (Abandoned) . . . . 7.0 Miles 3400 Feet
   (16.2 Miles Long, 3140 feet elevation gain)

SKYLINE RIDGE TRAIL
(20.5 Miles Long)

Skyline Ridge Trail (2100 feet elevation gain) is a superb high country trail. It starts at mile 6.6 of Big Creek Trail near Three Lakes Camp. It follows the ridge between Queets and Quinault Rivers north to Kitma Peak (5399 feet). There it turns east to join the North Fork Quinault Trail near Low Divide. Having climbed to the ridge top on the Big Creek Trail, one tends to think that the hard part is finished. It isn't. The trail continually switches from one side of the ridge to the other, and all the little ascents add up to a lot of effort.

The scenery gets even better at Kitma Peak and beyond, where one of the park's most isolated wildernesses is visible in wide vistas from above the tree line. The best view is from the summit of Kitma Peak. The peaks and glaciers of Mount Olympus are only seven miles away. The panorama of virgin rain forest in the U-shaped Queets Valley far below will set a new standard of what a wilderness should look like. Beyond Kitma Peak, the trail descends to the trees from time to time so you can rest your eyes after looking at the incredible scenery.

Distances and elevations along the trail are:

Big Creek Trail, mile 6.6	0.0 Miles	3200 Feet
Oval Lake	2.0 Miles	3850 Feet
Elip Creek Trail	2.9 Miles	3800 Feet
(4.6 miles long,feet elevation gain))		
Three Prune Camp	4.3 Miles	3600 Feet
Kitma Peak	9.3 Miles	5150 Feet
Promise Creek Pass	11.0 Miles	4980 Feet
High Camp	11.5 Miles	5300 Feet
Hee Haw Pass	12.5 Miles	4500 Feet
Lake Beauty Camp,(left 0.3 mile)	13.5 Miles	4700 Feet
Beauty Pass	14.0 Miles	5000 Feet
Seattle Creek	16.5 Miles	4200 Feet
N. Fork Quinault Tr.- mi. 15.9	20.5 Miles	3550 Feet
(16.4 miles long, 3082 feet elevation gain)		

FINLEY PEAK TRAIL
(0.5 Miles Long)

All that remains of Finley Peak Trail (300 feet elevation gain) is a 0.5 mile segment that starts from the junction of Big Creek Trail and Tshletshy Creek Trail at Three Lakes Camp, and goes south for about half a mile. The views from the ridge are good, and there are abundant huckleberries in late summer.

Past the end of the trail, one can force his way through the dense undergrowth to Finley Peak, the site of the Olympic National Forest's first fire lookout. The cabin was pulled down a few years after the National Park was created.

We now return to Quinault North Shore Road.

	MILES	MILES	
	from	to	
	HIGHWAY 101	ROAD END	

BIG CREEK TRAIL (IRELY LAKE TRAIL)	16.6	0.7	TRAILHEAD PARKING AREA

	16.9	0.4	NORTH FORK CAMPGROUND
	CAMPGROUND		

North Fork Campground has eight sites set back from the road near the North Fork Quinault River. It is not recommended for RV's. There is a toilet.

NORTH FORK RANGER STATION	17.2	0.1	
	RANGER STATION		

NORTH FORK QUINAULT TRAIL (NPS) PARKING AREA	17.3	0.0	TOILET
	END OF ROAD		

NORTH FORK QUINAULT TRAIL
(16.4 Miles Long)

North Fork Quinault Trail (3082 feet elevation gain) climbs gradually for the first ten miles or so, then steepens somewhat for the remainder of the journey to Low Divide. Beyond Low Divide Ranger Station the trail is known as Low Divide Trail until it reaches the other side of the pass and joins Elwha Trial. The route follows pretty much the same path as that followed by the Press Party Expedition who were the first to cross Low Divide in 1890.

The trail does not rise above the trees until near its end. There is a meadow at Low Divide, which is the only bit of high country on the whole traverse from Quinault North Shore Road to the beginning of Elwha Trail at Whiskey Bend Road nearly 45 miles to the north.

By combining parts of North Fork Quinault Trail, Elip Creek Trail, Skyline Trail and Big Creek Trail, you can get a 21.1 mile loop that gives you a look at several entirely different environments.

Distances and elevations along the trail are:

End of N. Shore Road, mile 17.3	0.0 Miles	520 Feet
Wolf Bar Camp	2.5 Miles	630 Feet
Rustler Creek Trail (Left)	3.6 Miles	750 Feet
(2.5 miles long, 750 feet elevation gain)		

```
Halfway House Camp . . . . . . . . . . . . . 5.2 Miles    800 Feet
Camp, North bank of Elip Creek  . . . . . . 6.4 Miles    900 Feet
Elip Creek Trail (Left) . . . . . . . . . . . . . 6.5 Miles  1060 Feet
     (4.6 miles long, 750 feet elevation gain)

Francis Creek Camp . . . . . . . . . . . . . . 7.0 Miles  1100 Feet
Trapper Shelter  . . . . . . . . . . . . . . . . 8.5 Miles  1200 Feet
Twelvemile Shelter . . . . . . . . . . . . . . 11.5 Miles  1800 Feet
Sixteenmile Camp  . . . . . . . . . . . . . . 12.3 Miles  2000 Feet
Glacier Creek . . . . . . . . . . . . . . . . . 14.4 Miles  2800 Feet
Skyline Trail . . . . . . . . . . . . . . . . . . 15.9 Miles  3550 Feet
     (20.5 miles long, 2100 feet elevation gain)

Low Divide Shelter . . . . . . . . . . . . . . 16.1 Miles  3560 Feet
Low Divide Ranger Station . . . . . . . . . 16.4 Miles  3602 Feet
Low Divide Trail . . . . . . . . . . . . . . . . 16.4 Miles  3602 Feet
     (3.1 miles long, 1400 feet elevation gain)
```

RUSTLER CREEK TRAIL
(2.5 Miles Long)

Rustler Creek Trail (750 feet elevation gain) is not marked. It begins just past a bridge on the North Fork Quinault Trail at mile 3.6. The trail is not maintained, and it disappears so often that most would consider it a cross country hike. The rewards are an excellent example of rain forest, and the remains of an old cabin and a forge at an abandoned mine.

ELIP CREEK TRAIL
(4.6 Miles Long)

Elip Creek Trail (2740 feet elevation gain) connects North Fork Quinault Trail to Skyline Ridge Trail, making a 21.1 mile loop possible, using Skyline Ridge Trail and Big Creek Trail to return to Quinault North Shore Road.

Elip Creek Trail starts from mile 6.5 of North Fork Quinault Trail. Near the beginning of the trail, there are a lot of trees which have been blown over by the wind. Then, dense, gloomy forest resumes. The forest gradually thins out, until, near the end of the trail, you are in the sub-alpine zone. Just before you reach Skyline Ridge Trail, you come to One Tent Camp at mile 4.5.

We now return to mile 128.7 of Highway 101, and follow it to Quinault South Shore Road at mile 124.0.

HIGHWAY 101	
MILES from I-5	MILE NUMBER
QUINAULT NORTH SHORE ROAD 238.6	128.7

JJ's Restaurant	238.7	128.6	
Adams RV Park	RESTAURANT		
	RV PARK		
Lake Quinault Elks Club	240.4	126.9	
	240.6	126.7	Amanda Park Mercantile Store
	C-STORE	GAS	Amanda Park Restaurant
	RESTAURANT		Amanda Park Texaco Station
CLOSED ROAD	240.8	126.5	
	QUINAULT RIVER		
TURNOUT	241.1	126.2	TURNOUT
QUINAULT SOUTH SHORE ROAD	241.8	125.5	

QUINAULT SOUTH SHORE ROAD

South Shore Road takes you around the south and east shores of Lake Quinault to the community of Lake Quinault. Here you will find three forest service campgrounds, a forest service ranger station, two resorts, restaurants, stores, an RV Park, a laundromat, gas stations and a post office. There are also three short trails.

A few miles beyond the community of Lake Quinault you penetrate the rain forest again. You will get glimpses of the river and the mountains beyond as the road proceeds to Graves Creek in the national park. There is another campground and a ranger station at Graves Creek. It is also the starting point for Enchanted Valley Trail, an arterial trail that gives you access to West Fork Dosewallips Trail, Duckabush Trail and North Fork Skokomish Trails via Anderson Pass. These trails lead to the eastern reaches of the national park, and expose an excellent variety of features of the national park. The features will range from rain forests to glaciers, and from isolated wilderness to the early attempts to settle the area now abandoned to the national park.

Description of Highway 101 resumes at mile 125.5 on page 316 in Chapter 13.

SOUTH SHORE ROAD

MILES	MILES
from	to
HIGHWAY 101	ROAD END
0.0	19.1
HIGHWAY 101	
MILE 125.5	

1.3 17.8 **QUINAULT RAIN FOREST TRAIL**
(BIG TREE GROVE NATURE TRAIL)
QUINAULT LOOP TRAIL
PARKING AREA

There is a small picnic area near the entrance to the parking area. Quinault Rain Forest Trail is a short loop trail that takes you through a grove of 500 year old Douglas firs. The trail ends at a junction with Quinault Loop Trail which will take you back to the parking area.

QUINAULT LOOP TRAIL
(4.0 Miles Long)

Quinault Loop Trail is a flat nature trail that meanders through the forest on both sides of the road. It has several convenient entrance points, and can be easily walked in either direction. This description of the trail starts from the parking area near Willaby Creek, and goes counter clockwise.

Parking area near Willaby Creek . . . . 0.0 Miles
Quinault Rain Forest Nature Trail . . . . 0.1 Miles
Lodge Trail . . . . 1.8 Miles
S. Shore Rd. parking near Falls Crk. Campgr. . . . . 2.7 Miles
Willaby Creek Campground . . . . 3.9 Miles
Parking Area Near Willaby Creek . . . . 4.0 Miles

WILLABY CAMPGROUND (NFS)

1.5 17.6
CAMPGROUND

Willaby Campground (max. trailer size 16 feet) has 19 sites near the lake. It has tables, potable water, flush toilets and a boatramp.

Lake Quinault Lodge
Quinault Lodge Restaurant
Chevron Gas Station

2.0 17.1
LODGE GAS
RESTAURANT

LODGE TRAIL

Lodge Trail is a short trail. It starts across the road from the lodge, and goes 0.7 miles to Quinault Loop Trail.

	2.1	17.0	Lake Quinault Mercantile
	C-STORE		Snack Bar
	FAST FOOD		

RANGER STATION (NFS)　　　　　2.2　16.9

PARKING AREA　　　　　　　　　2.3　16.8　　ACCESS TO QUINAULT LOOP TRAIL
ACCESS TO QUINAULT LOOP TRAIL　　BRIDGE

The Quinault Loop Trail goes between the ranger station and the creek to the lake shore.

Just beyond the bridge there is a road to the right. Quinault Loop Trail re-enters the forest at a bend in this road, about 50 yards from South Shore Road.

FALLS CREEK CAMPGROUND (NFS)　　2.4　16.7

Falls Creek Campground (maximum trailer size 16 feet) has 19 campsites in the trees near the lake. There are no hook-ups. It has a cooking shelter, tables, potable water, flush toilets and a boat launch.

GATTON CREEK CAMPGROUND (NFS)　　2.7　16.4
　　　　　　　　　　　　　　　CAMPGROUND

Gatton Creek takes the other two campgrounds' overflow. It has tables, potable water and flush toilets.

Rain Forest Resort Village　　　　　3.2　155.9　　POST OFFICE
Rain Forest Restaurant　　　　RESORT RV PARK　Laundromat
Rain Forest RV Park (31 sites　　RESTAURANT GAS　General Store
with hook-ups)　　　　　　C-STORE PROPANE　Chevron Gas
　　　　　　　　　　　　　　LAUNDROMAT
　　　　　　　　　　　　　　POST OFFICE

　　　　　　　　　　　　　5.9　13.2　　　　　　　　　TURNOUT

　　　　　　　　　　　　　6.0　13.1　　COLONEL BOB TRAIL

COLONEL BOB TRAIL
(7.2 Miles Long)

Colonel Bob Trail (4260 feet elevation gain) takes you to the summit of Colonel Bob (4492 feet). It is the tallest of four peaks in the Colonel Bob Wilderness area of the national forest.

The trail starts across the road from three houses. It seems strange to have the trailhead for a wilderness trail that is almost in town. The trail starts climbing immediately, and continues to climb most of the way to Colonel Bob. Portions of the trail twist and turn, sometimes descending, to get around obstacles in the terrain. The descents are a mixed blessing, as you know you will have to make back the elevation loss later in the trail.

From the top, you have 360° views. There is an unobstructed view of the Quinault area, with Mount Olympus as a backdrop. Looking south you see numerous forested ridges with little pockmarks of clearcuts.

Distances and elevations along the trail are:

Quinault S. Shore Road, mile 6.0	0.0 Miles	230 Feet
Mulkey Shelter	4.0 Miles	2160 Feet
Upper Petes Creek Trail (Right)	5.5 Miles	3300 Feet
(2.4 miles long, 2260 feet elevation gain)		
Moonshine Flats	6.3 Miles	3500 Feet
Summit of Colonel Bob	7.2 Miles	4492 Feet

	SOUTH SHORE ROAD		
	MILES from HIGHWAY 101	MILES to ROAD END	
UNMARKED ROAD	6.3	12.8	
	6.7	12.4	TURNOUT
TURNOUT UNMARKED ROAD	7.5	11.6	
	7.8 PAVEMENT ENDS	11.3	
UNMARKED ROAD	7.8	11.2	
UNMARKED ROAD	8.1	11.0	
TURNOUT	8.4	10.7	
TURNOUT	8.6	10.5	
UNMARKED ROAD	8.8	10.3	
	9.1 MILEPOST	10.0	UNMARKED ROAD
	9.7	9.4	UNMARKED ROAD

	10.4	8.7	TURNOUT
TURNOUT	10.9	8.2	
	BRIDGE		
TURNOUT	11.3	7.8	
COTTONWOOD CAMPGROUND	11.4	7.7	FLETCHER CANYON TRAIL
(ABANDONED)	CAMPGROUND		

Cottonwood Campground has been abandoned, and it is not maintained. The grates, tables and toilets etc. have all been removed. It is located 0.2 miles from South Shore Road, at the end of a rough, dusty road. Remain alert, as the road is unmarked and is easy to miss. It comes just beyond the road to Fletcher Canyon Trail.

FLETCHER CANYON TRAIL
(2.3 Miles Long)
Trail 857

Fletcher Canyon Trail (1100 feet elevation gain) starts from a small clearing at the end of a 0.1 mile road that leaves South Shore Road to the right at mile 11.4. It is not marked, and somewhat overgrown with vegetation. You will need to watch carefully, as it is very easy to miss. The trail is only maintained for the first mile, but a determined hiker can continue for another 1.3 miles.

Distances and elevations along the trail are:

Quinault S. Shore Road, Mi.11.4	0.0 Miles	400 Feet
End of maintained trail	1.0 Miles	1200 Feet
Fletcher Bowl Camp	1.9 Miles	1450 Feet
End of trail	2.3 Miles	1500 Feet

	11.8	7.3
	OLYMPIC NAT'L	
	PARK BOUNDARY	
	LUNCH CREEK	
TURNOUT	12.5	6.6

309

	MILES from HIGHWAY 101	MILES to ROAD END	
TURNOUT BRIDGE TO NORTH SHORE ROAD	12.8	6.3	
		CANNINGS CREEK	
	13.5	5.6	
		HOWE CREEK	
TURNOUT	13.9	5.2	
	14.4	4.7	TURNOUT
TURNOUT	15.6	3.5	
TURNOUT	16.6	2.5	
	16.9	2.2	TURNOUT
	18.5	0.6	GRAVES CRK RANGER STATION (ONP)
GRAVES CREEK CAMPGROUND (ONP)	18.7	0.4	

Graves Creek Campground (maximum trailer size 21 feet) has 45 sites among the trees near the bank of East Fork Quinault River. There are no hook-ups. it has grates, tables, potable water and flush toilets.

There is a one mile loop trail starting from near the western-most toilet block.

GROUP USE AREA	18.8	0.3	
ENCHANTED VALLEY TRAIL GRAVES CREEK TRAIL PARKING AREA	19.1	0.0	
	ROAD END		

There is a toilet, a stock unloading area and a parking area at the end of the road.

ENCHANTED VALLEY TRAIL
(18.9 Miles Long)

Enchanted Valley Trail (3860 feet elevation gain) is an arterial trail that gives access to the eastern portions of the national park. It connects with O'Neil Pass Trail, giving you access to Duckabush Trail and North Fork Skokomish Trail. Then, at Anderson Pass, the trail continues as West Fork Dosewallips Trail.

The trail starts out in the rain forest at the end of Quinault South Shore Road using the route of an abandoned road. It climbs gently and displays its scenery as it follows the East Fork Quinault River for 13 miles to Enchanted Valley Chalet. From there the trail gets steeper as you ascend to the glaciers of Anderson Pass.

Distances and elevations along the trail are:

End of S. Shore Road at mi.19.1	0.0 Miles	600 Feet
Graves Creek Trail (right)	0.1 Miles	646 Feet
End of abandoned road	2.4 Miles	1178 Feet
Pony Bridge Camp	3.0 Miles	903 Feet
O'Neil Crk Shelter (0.1 Mi.right)	7.0 Miles	1179 Feet
Noname Creek Camp	8.5 Miles	1320 Feet
Pyrites Creek Camp	10.0 Miles	1450 Feet
Pyrites Creek Trail	10.0 Miles	1450 Feet

(3.0 miles long, 2350 feet elevation gain)

Suspension footbridge	12.6 Miles	1920 Feet
Enchanted Valley Chalet	13.3 Miles	2000 Feet
World's Largest Western Hemlock	15.2 Miles	2100 Feet
O'Neil Pass Trail (right)	16.9 Miles	3200 Feet

(7.4 Miles Long, 1750 feet elevation gain)

Anderson Pass	18.9 Miles	4464 Feet
W. Fork Dosewallips Trail	18.9 Miles	4464 Feet

(9.1 miles long, 2560 feet elevation gain)

PYRITES CREEK TRAIL
(3.0 Miles Long)

Pyrites Creek Trail (2350 feet elevation gain) has not been maintained in years, but there are some very good vistas that make the trip worth while. It starts from mile 10.0 of Enchanted Valley Trail and goes to The Crows Foot (the confluence of three branches of Pyrites Creek). The trail is so faint,that your best bet is to pretend that you are on a cross country hike.

O'NEIL PASS TRAIL
(7.4 Miles Long)

O'Neil Pass Trail (1750 feet elevation gain) connects Enchanted Valley Trail to Duckabush Trail. North Fork Skokomish Trail joins Duckabush Trail 3.4 miles from O'Neil Pass. If you turn right into North Fork Skokomish Trail, you have the choice of going to Staircase, or turning right again at Six Ridge Trail and returning to the Quinault area via Graves Creek Trail. The sweeping views of the valleys offer dramatic contrast to the glacier encrusted mountains from the high vantage of O'Neil Pass Trail.

Distances and elevations along the trail are:

```
Enchanted Valley Trail Mi. 16.9 . . . . . . . 0.0 Miles  3200 Feet
White Creek crossing . . . . . . . . . . . . . 0.7 Miles  3760 Feet
Heart Lake Way Trail . . . . . . . . . . . . . 3.8 Miles  4300 Feet
      (0.5 miles long, 870 feet elevation gain)

Basin on Overlook Peak . . . . . . . . . . . 5.7 Miles  4700 Feet
O'Neil Pass . . . . . . . . . . . . . . . . . . . 7.4 Miles  4950 Feet
Duckabush Trail . . . . . . . . . . . . . . . . 7.4 Miles  4950 Feet
      (22.2 miles long, 4550 feet elevation gain)
```

GRAVES CREEK TRAIL
(8.6 Miles Long)

Graves Creek Trail (4000 feet elevation gain) strikes out uphill at mile 0.1 of Enchanted Valley Trail. Though only 8.6 miles long, this trail connects with Wynoochee Trail, South Fork Skokomish Trail and Six Ridge Trail to give you access to the southeast corner of the national park, and the adjacent national forest lands. The trail follows the course of Graves Creek east to Success Creek, then south to the junction with Wynoochee Trail. It then bends back to the north to Six Ridge Pass. As you travel through the high country you see splendid views of the interior mountains and Mount Olympus. From Six Ridge Pass you can see Mount Cruiser and Mount Lincoln in the Sawtooth Range. In the distance to the southeast Mount Rainier seems to be suspended from the sky by its snowy summit.

Distances and elevations along the trail are:

```
Enchanted Valley Trail, mile 0.1 . . . . . . 0.0 Miles   646 Feet
Success Creek Camp, No Bridge . . . . . 3.5 Miles  1880 Feet
Camp on Graves Creek . . . . . . . . . . . . 5.3 Miles  2520 Feet
Wynoochee Trail (Right) . . . . . . . . . . . 6.1 Miles  2700 Feet
      (3.7 miles long, 1100, feet elevation gain)

Sundown Lake Way Trail (Right) . . . . . . 6.6 Miles  3400 Feet
      (1.0 miles long, no elevation gain)

Upper S. Fork Skokomish Trail . . . . . . . 7.2 Miles  3820 Feet
      (7.0 miles long, 2800 feet elevation gain)

Lake Sundown Shelter . . . . . . . . . . . . . 7.5 Miles  3900 Feet
Six Ridge Pass . . . . . . . . . . . . . . . . . . 8.6 Miles  4650 Feet
Six Ridge Trail . . . . . . . . . . . . . . . . . . 8.6 Miles  4650 Feet
      (9.6 Miles Long, 3080 feet elevation gain)
```

We leave the rainforest now. In Chapter 13 we will return to mile 125.5 of Highway 101 and make our way to Forest Service Road 22 to explore the southwestern corner of Olympic National Forest.

Vista from the Trailhead of Wynoochee Trail at the end of Forest Service Road 2270-400.

CHAPTER 13

HUMPTULIPS WYNOOCHEE HOQUIAM-ABERDEEN

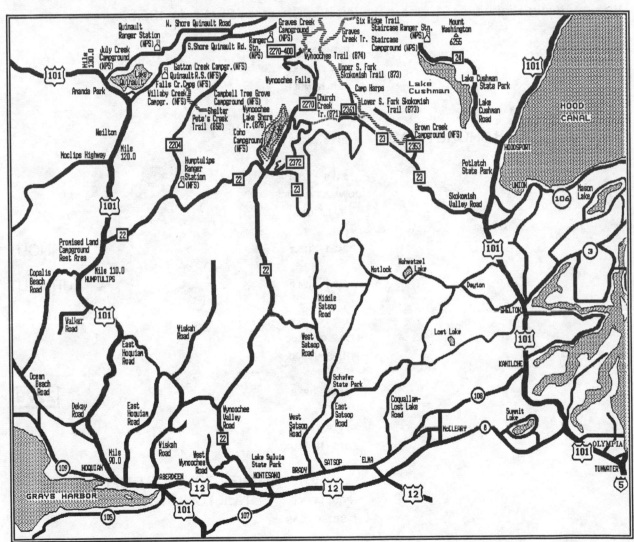

MAP 13-1 SOUTHERN OLYMPIC PENINSULA

In this chapter we will explore those parts of the national forest that are reached from Forest Service Road 22. First, we visit Campbell Tree Grove, a drive-through stand of large fir trees that have been granted a reprieve by the Forest Service. We then head for Wynoochee Dam. Wynoochee Dam was constructed by the US Corps of Engineers, primarily for flood control.

There is a picnic area and an information center near the dam, and the forest service has built a trail that encircles the lake. Next we go to Wynoochee Trail. It connects this area to Enchanted Valley, South Fork Skokomish and North Fork Skokomish Trails.

We will leave our old friend, Highway 101, at mile 83.5 in Aberdeen, where we join US Highway 12. Highway 101 continues south to Washington State Highway 105, the south coast ocean beaches, and, eventually, to Oregon's north coast.

US Highway 12 will take us past the south end of Forest Service Road 22 and to Montesano and Elma. Just beyond the Elma exit, US Highway 12 goes to the right. The main road continues as Washington State Highway 8, which rejoins Highway 101 at mile 361.6 on the western edge of Olympia. This last junction completes the 325 mile loop through the Olympic Peninsula.

We now rejoin Highway 101 where we left it in Chapter 12, at mile 125.5.

	HIGHWAY 101		
	MILES from I-5	MILE NUMBER	
QUINAULT SOUTH SHORE ROAD	241.8	125.5	
	241.9 QUINAULT NATURE AREA, ONF	125.4	
	242.1	125.2	TURNOUT
	243.1	124.2	TURNOUT
	243.4 LEAVE QUINAULT NATURE AREA ONF	123.9	
	243.5	123.8	2273
	243.9 ENTER NEILTON	123.4	
	244.3 POST OFFICE C-STORE GAS	123.0	NEILTON POST OFFICE NEILTON STORE
MEADOWLAND FLAT	244.9	122.4	
	247.1	120.2	MOCLIPS HIGHWAY HATCHERY OCEAN BEACHES

To: (109)

	MILES from I-5	MILE NUMBER	
	247.3	120.0	
		MILEPOST	
	247.8	119.5	TURNOUT
2258 QUINAULT RIDGE ROAD NEILTON POINT	249.1	118.2	
	249.2	118.1	
		LEAVE ONF	
2220 NEWBURY CREEK ROAD BURNT HILL LOOKOUT	250.2	117.1	
TURNOUT	251.1	116.2	
TURNOUT	253.8	113.5	
22 WYNOOCHEE-DONKEY CREEK ROAD CAMPBELL TREE GROVE WYNOOCHEE LAKE	254.7	112.6	

Here we turn left to explore the West Fork Humptulips and Wynoochee areas. Check your gas and supplies. The nearest food store and gas station is 57 mi. from here via FSR 22 or 70 mi. via FSR 23.

If you need supplies, Humptulips Store is three miles south on Highway 101. At Axford Prairie, three miles beyond Humptulips, there are two restaurants, two stores, diesel fuel and gas.

Highway 101 continues at mile 112.6 on page 328.

WEST FORK HUMPTULIPS VALLEY

This area lies wholly within the national forest. Like all national forest lands south of the national park between Lake Cushman and Lake Quinault, it has been heavily logged with very little consideration for its recreational users. The forest service is saddled with a 99 year concession to a large timber company, and appears to have given up the struggle to salvage

317

any of the vistas which were once virgin forest. Even Colonel Bob Wilderness is affected. West Fork Humptulips Road has been constructed along its southern boundary, so views to the south and east from the wilderness area usually include a patchwork of clear-cuts, second growth and virgin forest.

I should point out that it is my opinion that even clear-cuts have a unique beauty when they are seen from far enough away. Removing the trees can open up broad expanses that give you an entirely different perspective than one might get from fleeting glimpses snatched from within the deep forest.

Unfortunately, there is another casualty of the logging activities. What was once an extensive network of trails has largely disappeared as the logging roads penetrate ever deeper.

The junction of Forest Service Road 22 and Highway 101 is not signed, and it is not included on the NFS/NPS map. It is a good, paved road that goes to your left (east) three tenths of a mile north of Promised Land Rest Area and Campground. Shortly after you turn you will see a sign noting the distances to Campbell Tree Grove, and Lake Wynoochee. Then at mile 0.2 you will see the familiar brown forest service shield confirming that you are in fact on the right road.

	FS ROAD 22		
	MILES from HIGHWAY 101	MILES to US HWY.12	
	0.0	54.9	
	HIGHWAY 101		
	MILE 112.6		
TURNOUT	0.5	54.4	
ROAD 7930	3.8	51.1	
	4.1	50.8	UNMARKED ROAD
	4.7	50.2	TURNOUT
	5.0	49.9	
	MILEPOST		
TURNOUT	5.8	49.1	
2203	7.7	47.2	
	BRIDGE		
2204 W. FORK HUMPTULIPS ROAD HUMPTULIPS RANGER STATION (NFS) PETE'S CREEK TRAIL CAMPBELL TREE GROVE CAMPGROUND	8.2	46.7	TURNOUT

318

FS ROAD 2204 - W. FORK HUMPTULIPS ROAD

Here we make an excursion to Campbell Tree Grove. The road runs parallel to the river to its beginnings, between Moonlight Dome (4122 feet) and the national park boundary. Along the way, we pass through both deep forest and the devastation of recent clear-cuts. At the junction with FSR 2220 and FSR 2280 there is a high bridge over the West Fork Humptulips that merits a stop for photos.

The forest service has built a road through Campbell Tree Grove, allowing those of us who lack the mobility to negotiate a hiking trail to sample this small stand of large fir trees.

Description of Forest Service Road 22 continues at mile 46.7 on page 322.

FS ROAD 2204

MILES	MILES
from	to
FSR 22	TREE GROVE

0.0	13.9	
FSR 22, MI.8.2		
0.2	13.7	HUMPTULIPS RANGER STATION (NFS)
RANGER STATION		
0.9	13.0	2207
2.6	11.3	UNMARKED ROAD
2.9	11.0	2208
3.0	10.9	
PAVEMENT ENDS		
3.6	10.3	2204-031
4.1	9.8	
ONE LANE BRIDGE		
WEST FORK		
HUMPTULIPS RIV.		

2204-040

2220
2280
TURNOUT

4.2	9.7	
4.9	9.0	
5.9	8.0	RECENT CLEAR CUT

UNMARKED ROAD

6.1 7.8

2204-070

6.9 7.0   UNMARKED ROAD
TURNOUT

FS ROAD 2204		
MILES	MILES	
from	to	
FSR 22	TREE GROVE	
7.0	6.9	UNMARKED ROAD
8.1	5.8	UNMARKED ROAD
9.0	4.9	UNMARKED ROAD
9.8	4.1	2204-090
10.0	3.9	
	MILEPOST	

| UPPER PETES CREEK TRAIL | 10.8 | 3.1 | LOWER PETES CREEK TRAIL PARKING AREA |

UPPER PETES CREEK TRAIL
(2.4 Miles Long)
Trail 858

Upper Petes Creek Trail (2360 feet elevation gain) starts out from the trailhead with and easy grade, but as it switchbacks its way up the side of Quinault Ridge, it grows steeper with every step. The trail is within the Colonel Bob Wilderness, so you will find interesting vegetation all the way to its junction with Colonel Bob Trail. Near the end of the trail one should be alert for rock slides.

Distances and elevations along the trail are:

                Trailhead, FSR 2204 Mile 10.8 . . . . 0.0 Miles 1000 Feet
                Petes Creek Crossing . . . . 1.0 Miles 1600 Feet
                Small Campsite . . . . 2.0 Miles 2480 Feet
                Colonel Bob Trail . . . . 2.4 Miles 3360 Feet
                    (7.2 miles long, 4460 feet elevation gain)

LOWER PETES CREEK TRAIL
(1.0 Miles Long)
Trail 858

Lower Petes Creek Trail (300 feet elevation loss) is an easy hike. In places, the trail is flat. It takes you down to the confluence of Petes Creek and West Fork Humptulips River. There is a shelter on the other side of the river, but extreme caution should be exercised in fording it in spring and early summer. The peak you see to the southeast is Stovepipe Mountain (3610 feet).

Distances and elevations along the trail are:

Trailhead, FSR 2204 Mile 10.8 . . . . 0.0 Miles 1000 Feet
West Fork Humptulips River . . . . 0.9 Miles 700 Feet
West Fork Shelter (across river) . . . . . . 1.0 Miles 700 Feet

We now return to Forest Service Road 2204.

| | FS ROAD 2204 | | |
	MILES from FSR 22	MILES to TREE GROVE	
UPPER PETES CREEK TRAIL	10.8	3.1	LOWER PETES CREEK TRAIL PARKING AREA
	10.9 PETES CREEK	3.0	
	12.4	1.5	TURNOUT UNMARKED ROAD
	13.0	0.9	TURNOUT
	13.9	0.0	2204-110 CAMPBELL TREE GROVE CAMPGROUND (NFS)

Campbell Tree Grove Campground (maximum trailer size 21 feet) has six tent sites, and three trailer sites (no hook-ups). There are picnic tables, potable water and toilets.

FSR 2204 continues beyond the campground, following the river for another three miles.

CAMPBELL TREE GROVE

Campbell Tree Grove is at the foot of Moonlight Dome (4122 feet). Although logging is quite extensive in the entire area surrounding the grove, this remnant of tall trees has been spared. The Douglas Firs here are much larger than the species usually seen in this area. This grove is similar to the one near Willaby Creek, through which Quinault Rainforest Nature Trail passes. The campground road continues on to form a 0.4 mile loop through the grove.

We now return to mile 8.2 of Forest Service Road 22.

	MILES from HIGHWAY 101	MILES to US HWY.12	
2204 W. FORK HUMPTULIPS ROAD	8.2	46.7	TURNOUT
	1-LANE ROAD		
2205	8.8	46.1	
	9.4	45.5	UNMARKED ROAD
	9.7	45.2	UNMARKED ROAD
	9.8	45.1	UNMARKED ROAD
	10.0	44.9	
	MILEPOST		
	10.3	44.6	UNMARKED ROAD
	12.2	42.7	UNMARKED ROAD
LARGE FLAT AREA	12.3	42.6	
2206	12.9	42.0	
	13.0	41.9	2270
	PAVEMENT ENDS		
2281	14.8	40.1	
	15.0	39.9	
	MILEPOST		
	15.6	39.3	UNMARKED ROAD
2200-460	16.7	38.2	
	17.0	37.9	UNMARKED ROAD
2200-340	17.2	37.7	
LARGE FLAT TURNOUT	17.9	37.0	
	18.1	36.8	UNMARKED ROAD
	18.5	36.4	LARGE FLAT TURNOUT
	18.8	36.1	TURNOUT
2200-260	19.0	35.9	

19.3 35.6	TURNOUT
BIG CREEK	

2294

19.6 35.3

This not the road to Wynoochee Dam and Coho Campground. FSR 2194 makes a large loop, returning to FSR 22 about one mile south of Coho Campground. You will save many miles of rough roads by continuing on FSR 22 for another 1.8 miles to the other end of the FSR 2294 loop.

2200-100

19.8 35.1   **WYNOOCHEE LAKE FISH**
WYNOOCHEE RIVER   **COLLECTION STATION**

2200-240

20.2 34.7

20.3 34.6   **2200-220**

2294

21.4 33.5

WYNOOCHEE DAM
COHO CAMPGROUND (NFS)
WYNOOCHEE LAKE SHORE TRAIL

WYNOOCHEE DAM AREA

Eight tenths of a mile after leaving FSR 22, there is a large parking area on the right at the foot of the dam. The path on the east side of the parking area is Wynoochee Lake Shore Trail. It leads to a picnic area at the top of the dam. Just beyond the parking area on FSR 2294 is a bridge over the Wynoochee River. Across the bridge is a gravel road to the left. On the right is the parking area for the Corps of Engineers Information Center, viewpoint and picnic area. There are toilets in the main building.

Four tenths of a mile beyond the Wynoochee bridge is FSR 2200-100. The Corps of Engineers Project Office, picnic area and a dump station are to the right. Coho Campground is straight ahead on FSR 2294.

Coho Campground (max. trailer size 36 feet) is two tenths of a mile beyond FSR 2200-100 (1.4 miles from FSR 22). It has 71 sites, none with hook-ups. There are picnic tables, potable water, flush toilets, a dump station, a boat launch and a dock. In addition to Wynoochee Lake Shore Trail, which passes the campground near the shore of the lake, Chetwood Trail — a

323

short nature trail — starts from B loop, near site 42. There is a large parking area for day use, and another one near the boat launch for boat trailers. There is a toilet block with flush toilets in the boat trailer parking area.

WYNOOCHEE LAKE SHORE TRAIL
(12.0 Miles Long)
Trail 878

Wynoochee Lake Shore Trail has a lot of steep ups and downs as it circles the lake, but there is no really dramatic elevation gain. It starts at Coho Campground, and I have described it as going clockwise. You can however join it from several other places along FSR 2294 and FSR 2270, and hike it in either direction with about the same effort. You should note before you start out that there is no bridge over the Wynoochee River at the north end of the lake. Additionally, this trail is not maintained on a regular basis, so you are sometimes confronted with large windfalls and pathfinding difficulties. The hike includes both virgin forest and second growth.

The trail is difficult to find from Coho Campground. The steep, paved road down to the boat launch is probably as good a place as any to start. About 50 or 60 feet from the parking area at the top, you will see the trail going off to the right toward the dam and the Wynoochee River bridge. Turn right here if you want to hike the trail in a counter-clockwise direction. If you continue down to the boat launch and follow the loop in the road to the left at the bottom, you will see a concrete slab at the north end of the loop. The trail starts out rather steeply up a forested hillside from just behind the slab. The path that goes to the right to the water's edge is a beach access trail. It does not join the Wynoochee Lake Shore Trail. Most of the time the trail overlooks the lake from a hundred feet or so above it. Half a mile from the start, there is a path to Chetwood Campground, a small walk-in, boat-in campground on the lake shore. Tenas Campground, which has been abandoned by the Forest Service, is on the upper east shore of the lake at mile 6.6 of the trail. This primitive campground can also be reached by turning left from FSR 2270 at mile 4.6 into FSR 2270-180.

Distances along the trail are:

Coho Campground	0.0 Miles
Path to Chetwood Campground (right)	0.4 Miles
Wynoochee River (No Bridge)	6.0 Miles
Tenas Campground (Abandoned)	6.6 Miles
Wynoochee Dam	12.0 Miles
Coho Campground	12.2 Miles

We now return to mile 21.4 of Forest Service Road 22.

FS ROAD 22

MILES from HIGHWAY 101	MILES to US HWY.12
21.4	33.5

2294

	FS ROAD 22	
	MILES	MILES
	from	to
	HIGHWAY 101	US HWY.12

UNMARKED ROAD   21.6   33.3

2270

To: **23**   21.7   33.2   **GRISDALE**

WYNOOCHEE FALLS   **MONTESANO**

WYNOOCHEE TRAIL

FSR 23 (mile 33.1) joins FSR 2270 from the right about 200 yards north of this intersection. FSR 23 begins from Skokomish Valley Road, 5.6 miles west of mile 339.7 of Highway 101. (See page 41.)

FSR 22 goes south (right) here. It leaves the national forest in about three miles. The scenery consists mostly of stump farms and small stands of second growth. The road ends at US Highway 12, west of Montesano.

                             37.9   17.0

                       PAVEMENT BEGINS

12 EAST   OLYMPIA   54.9   0.0   **ABERDEEN**   **WEST** **12**

We now return to the beginning of FSR 2270 at its junction with FSR 22 and make our way to Wynoochee Trail.

WYNOOCHEE VALLEY

At the point where FSR 22 makes a right angle turn to the south (mile 21.7), FSR 2270 makes a right angle turn to the north. It follows the eastern shore of Wynoochee Lake for the first few miles, passing several small access roads to the lake shore. Near the north end of the lake, FSR 2270-180 goes to the left, taking you to Tenas Campground which has been abandoned by the forest service.

FSR 2270 forks 1.3 miles beyond the turnoff to Tenas Campground. Both branches are FSR 2270. They are the ends of a loop. I recommend that you take the right branch as I have described below. It will shorten your trip to the Wynoochee Trail trailhead considerably, and the road is in better condition. Wynoochee Falls Campground, which has also been abandoned by the forest service is two miles north of the fork on the right branch.

	FS ROAD 2270	
	MILES	MILES
	from	to
	FSR 22	FSR 2270-400
	0.0	11.7
	FSR 22 Mi. 21.7	

MILES	MILES
from	to
FSR 22	FSR 2270-400

0.1 11.6

23

To: SKOKOMISH RIVER VALLEY
HIGHWAY 101, MILE 339.7

To: **2372**

ANDERSON BUTTE TRAIL
SATSOP RANGER STATION
CHURCH CREEK TRAIL

Anderson Butte Trail (0.3 miles long, 560 feet elevation gain) starts at the end of FSR 2372-020. (See page 46.)

Church Creek Trail (3.5 miles long, 1650 feet elevation gain) starts from FSR 2361-600. It is described on page 45.

1.9 9.8
SUTTER CREEK

2270-140

2.4 9.3

3.1 8.6
SIXTEEN CREEK

2270-180

4.6 7.1

TENAS CAMPGROUND (ABANDONED)

2372

SATSOP LAKES
CHURCH CREEK TRAIL
SATSOP RANGER STATION
ANDERSON BUTTE TRAIL
To: **23**

This road looks like a short, easy way to Satsop Lakes. It is not. This end of the road is very steep, narrow and twisty. Unless you have a suitable vehicle you should start from the other end of FSR 2372 at mile 32.3 of FSR 23.

UNMARKED ROAD

4.8 6.9

2270-200

5.0 6.7

UNMARKED ROAD

5.4 6.3

	MILES from FSR 22	MILES to FSR 2270-400	
2270 (WESTERN SECTION OF LOOP)	5.9	5.8	**2270** (EASTERN SECTION OF LOOP)
	7.8	3.9	**2270-240**
2270-260 WYNOOCHEE FALLS CAMPGROUND (ABANDONED)	8.0	3.7	
WATERFALL	9.6	2.1	**2270-300**
	9.8	1.9	SHORT ROAD TO CREEK
	10.5	1.2	TURNOUT
	11.7	0.0	**2270-400**

WYNOOCHEE FALLS CAMPGROUND (ABANDONED)

Although there are no amenities such as tables or toilets, and the road is rough, Wynoochee Falls Campground has spacious, sunny campsites.

To: WYNOOCHEE TRAIL

FSR 2270-400 turns sharply to the right from a curve in FSR 2270 that turns sharply to the left. It is narrow and twisty, and has a couple of places that are extremely narrow due to washouts. I recommend that you walk the remaining 1.7 miles to Wynoochee Trail if your vehicle is large or heavy. There is a campsite on each side of the road as you start FSR 2270-400.

The trail starts from the end of a hairpin turn, 1.7 miles from FSR 2270. Just past the trailhead, the road is closed.

WYNOOCHEE TRAIL
(3.7 Miles Long)
Trail 874

Wynoochee Trail (1100 feet elevation gain) takes you to Graves Creek Trail in the national park via Wynoochee Pass. There, you can either turn left to go to Quinault South Shore

Road, or turn right for South Fork Skokomish Trail and Six Ridge Trail. Six Ridge Trail takes you to Mount Olsen Trail and North Fork Skokomish Trail.

You leave the patchwork of clear-cuts in the national forest when you enter the national park 0.3 miles from the trailhead. As the trail steepens, you cross several streams with picturesque cascades. The forest here consists of unusually large trees. The western hemlocks are among the largest in the peninsula, even though the elevation of the trail is relatively high. Three tenths of a mile beyond Wynoochee Pass you are offered Sundown Lake Way Trail as a short-cut to Sundown Lake. This trail saves you about a mile in distance. It also saves you the effort of regaining about 700 feet of elevation lost in the descent to Graves Creek Trail via Wynoochee Trail. it does however have lots of ups and downs.

Distances and elevations along the trail are:

FSR 2270-400, Mile 1.7 . . . . 0.0 Miles 2500 Feet
Enter Olympic National Park . . . . 0.3 Miles 2700 Feet
Cross Wynoochee River . . . . 1.6 Miles 2800 Feet
Wynoochee Pass . . . . 2.2 Miles 3600 Feet
Sundown Lake Way Trail . . . . 2.5 Miles 3400 Feet
    (1.0 miles long, lots of ups and downs)

Graves Creek Trail . . . . 3.7 Miles 2700 Feet
    (8.6 miles long, 4000 feet elevation gain)

SUNDOWN LAKE WAY TRAIL
(1.0 Miles Long)

Sundown Lake Way Trail starts and ends at the same elevation as it goes from mile 2.5 of Wynoochee Trail to mile 6.6 of Graves Creek Trail. There are a lot of ups and downs along the way. The trail is not maintained, the tread is quite rough, and it is sometimes hard to find. These factors mitigate against its main purpose — avoiding the 700 foot descent to Graves Creek Trail via Wynoochee Trail, then immediately regaining the 700 feet to get to Sundown Lake.

Although the route via Wynoochee Trail is about one mile longer, it probably entails less effort, especially if you are burdened with a heavy pack.

Now we return to mile 112.6 of Highway 101 to continue our journey south to Hoquiam and Aberdeen.

HIGHWAY 101	
MILES	MILE
from	NUMBER
I-5	

22 WYNOOCHEE-DONKEY CREEK ROAD   254.7   112.6

	255.0 112.3	**PROMISED LAND REST AREA AND CAMPGROUND (ITT-RAYONIER)**

This pleasant campground has 15 sites, none with hook-ups. It has tables, a kitchen shelter, and flush toilets. several of the sites are beside Stevens Creek Pond, which is used for spawning and rearing salmon and steelhead trout.

Oxbow Tavern
McNUTT ROAD

257.3   110.0
MILEPOST
TAVERN
HUMPTULIPS

258.1   109.2
C-STORE GAS
POST OFFICE

COPALIS BEACH ROAD
Humptulips Store Unocal 76 Gas
HUMPTULIPS POST OFFICE
STATE FISH HATCHERY
OCEAN BEACHES

PARK N RIDE

258.2   109.1

258.3   109.0
HUMPTULIPS RIV.

EAST HUMPTULIPS ROAD

258.9   108.4

PUBLIC FISHING

259.0   108.3

BADGER ROAD

260.6   106.7

BOWES ROAD

260.7   106.6
RESTAURANT
C-STORE GAS
DIESEL TAVERN

Golden Eagle Cafe
Chevron Gas, Diesel
Red Rooster Tavern, Gas
Li'l Prairie Mart Store

260.8   106.5

WALKER ROAD

262.5   104.8
GIFT SHOP

Cleary Gift Shop

EAST HOQUIAM ROAD

265.3   102.0

	HIGHWAY 101	
	MILES MILE	
	from NUMBER	
	I-5	

LARSON BROS. ROAD   266.5 100.8
SCOUT CAMP

                                    267.3 100.0
                                   MILEPOST

UNMARKED ROAD   269.4 97.9

                                    269.9 97.4   **FAILOR LAKE ROAD**
                                           PUBLIC FISHING

UNMARKED ROAD   272.1 95.2

EDGE ROAD   273.3 94.0

                                   273.6 93.7   **DEKAY ROAD**

                                   274.0 93.3
                                   W. BR. HOQUIAM

                                   275.5 91.8   **OCEAN BEACH ROAD**
                                       GAS   Three Way Service

D & L Cafe   275.9 91.4
Y Motel   CAFE   MOTEL

Broken Arrow Mobil Court   277.2 90.1

                                   277.3 90.0
                                   MILEPOST

To: (109)   278.3 89.0
                                   LITTLE HOQUIAM

HOQUIAM AND ABERDEEN

Hoquiam, Aberdeen and Cosmopolis form a single urban area with a population of 30,000. Located on Grays Harbor, they are the gateway cities to both the Olympic Peninsula and to Washington's south coast. For those heading north, it is the last major commercial center until Forks, more than a hundred miles from here.

The highway divides in Hoquiam. Eastbound traffic follows the one-way streets Simpson Avenue, Park Street and Heron Street to the east side of Aberdeen where Heron Street joins Wiskah Street. There the road is reunited as Highway 12 to Olympia. Westbound traffic continues on Wiskah Street when it becomes one-way. This route follows one-way streets Alder Street, Sumner Avenue and Riverside before rejoining as Highway 101 near the Junction of Lincoln and Emerson Avenue.

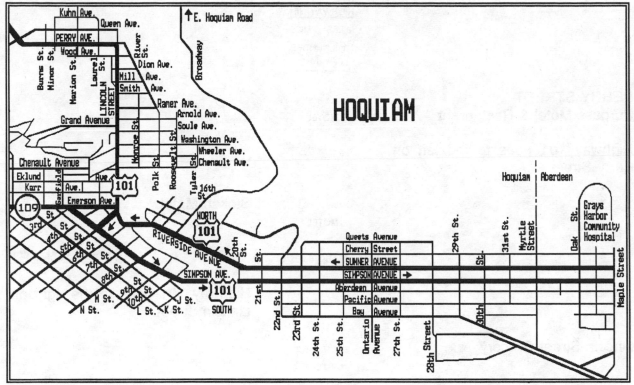

MAP 13-2   HOQUIAM

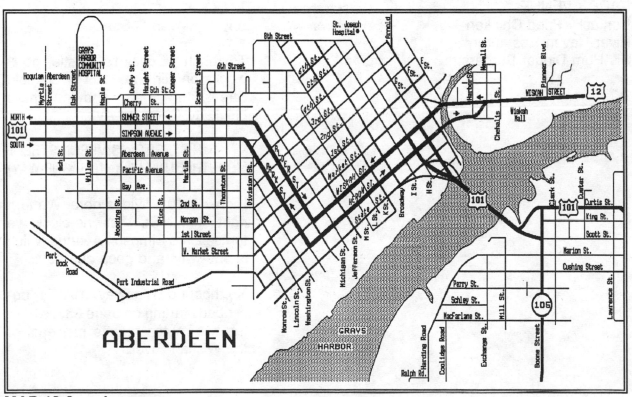

MAP 13-3   ABERDEEN

PERRY STREET

Burgess Motel & Restaurant

278.4 88.9

MOTEL

Highway 101 goes to the left on Perry Street

278.5 88.8

MOTEL

Stoken Motel

278.8 88.5

LINCOLN STREET

Highway 101 goes to the right on Lincoln Street.

Lincoln Street Grocery

279.1 88.2

C-STORE

RAMER AVENUE

Wesley's Gull Express Lane

Hole In One Donuts

KARR AVENUE

Kentucky Fried Chicken

River Haven Restaurant

Als Hum-Dinger Burgers

279.6 87.7

C-STORE GAS

FAST FOODS

RESTAURANT

HOQUIAM'S CASTLE (109)

OCEAN SHORES

TAHOLA

Seven-Eleven C-Store

To reach Hoquaim's Castle, go 3 blocks on Highway 109 to Garfield Street, turn right and go three blocks to Chenault Ave.

279.8 87.5

5TH STREET to SIMPSON STREET (SOUTHBOUND HWY. 101 - ONE-WAY)

Highway 101 divides here. We turn right into 5th St. After one block, we turn left into Simpson Avenue which is one-way, and goes due east.

Northbound Highway 101 is described starting on page 337, where the two routes reunite just east of the Wiskah River.

	HIGHWAY 101		
	MILES from I-5	MILE NUMBER	
Smitty's In & Out	279.9	87.4	Ralph's Chevron
Safeway Supermarket	6TH STREET		Gambur's Cafe
	FAST FOOD GAS		Golden Dragon #1
	SUPERMARKET		
	7TH STREET		
	RESTAURANT		
Ernie's Mobil	280.0	87.3	
Duffy's Family Restaurant	8TH STREET		
	GAS		
	RESTAURANT		
Ken Harrison's Texaco	280.1	87.2	
Swanson's Grocery	9TH STREET		
	GAS FOOD STORE		
	280.4	86.9	
	HOQUIAM RIVER		
Rosa's U-Bake Pizza	280.7	86.6	
	23RD STREET		
	FAST FOOD		
Hank's Service & Garage	280.8	86.5	
	24TH STREET		
	GAS		
	280.9	86.4	
	25TH STREET		
	281.0	86.3	Simpson Ave. Shell Food Mart
	ONTARIO STREET		
	C-STORE GAS		
	281.3	86.0	Casa Mia Mexican Restaurant
	29TH STREET		
	RESTAURANT		
	281.4	85.9	Anjo's Quick Stop
	30TH STREET		
	C-STORE		
	281.6	85.7	
	MYRTLE STREET		
	ENTER ABERDEEN		
	ASH STREET		
	281.7	85.6	
	OAK STREET		

Harbor ThrifTway Supermarket

281.8   85.5
WILLOW STREET
SUPERMARKET

281.9   85.4
MAPLE STREET
RESTAURANT
WOODING STREET

Chinese Village Restaurant

282.0   85.3
DUFFY STREET

282.1   85.2
HAIGHT STREET
RESTAURANT
C-STORE
RICE STREET

Lighthouse Drive-in
Seven-Eleven

282.2   85.1
CONGER STREET
RESTAURANT

Chico's Mexican Restaurant

Dairy Queen

282.3   85.0
MARTIN STREET
FAST FOOD

282.4   84.9
N. SCAMMEL ST.
JEFFRIES STREET
RESTAURANT

Duffy's Family Restaurant

282.5   84.8
THORNTON STREET
WILLIAMS STREET

282.6   84.7
DIVISION STREET
4TH STREET

PARK STREET
Highway 101 turns right here into Park Street.

Park St. Shell Food Mart

282.7   84.6
3RD STREET
C-STORE

282.8   84.5
2ND STREET

282.9   84.4
1ST STREET
MARKET STREET

334

WEST HERON STREET Highway 101 goes to the left into West Heron Street.	283.0 84.3 W. WISKAH ST. W. HERON STREET	
Pizza Hut Turn left into Alder Street, then left again into W. Wiskah Street for Pizza Hut.	283.1 84.2 ALDER STREET FAST FOOD	
Olympic Inn Motel **Sidney's Family Restaurant** **Denny's Restaurant**	283.2 84.1 MICHIGAN STREET JEFFERSON ST. RESTAURANT MOTEL	
	283.3 84.0 M STREET SUPERMARKET	**Safeway Supermarket**
	283.4 83.9 L STREET	
Misty's Restaurant	283.5 83.8 K STREET RESTAURANT GAS	**City Center Unocal Service**
	283.6 83.7 BROADWAY I STREET	**Smoke Shop Cafe**
[12] EAST	283.7 83.6 H STREET LEAVE HWY.101 BEGIN HWY. 12	SOUTH [101] To: (105) COSMOPOLIS OCEAN BEACHES

LEAVE HIGHWAY 101 JOIN US HIGHWAY 12

Here we say goodbye to our old friend, Highway 101. We have come nearly 284 miles as we followed its loop through the Olympic Peninsula. From here it goes south to Raymond and South Bend, then follows the coast to the Columbia River. There it turns inland to cross the river, entering Oregon near Astoria.

To return to Olympia, we continue straight ahead on Heron Street which has now become US Highway 12. Highway 12 takes us 21.2 miles, or about half the distance to Olympia before it too abandons us just east of Elma. Highway 12 goes to the southeast, to Oakville, then joins Interstate Highway 5 north of Centralia.

Again, we continue on straight ahead on Washington State Highway 8 when US Highway 12 exits to the right. Highway 8 takes us 20 miles to the east where we close the loop with Highway 101. Interstate Highway 5 in Olympia is 5.7 miles east of the junction. To continue on to Olympia, stay on the main highway as it veers to the right to merge with Highway 101. Shelton and the Olympic Peninsula are to the North. To return to the Olympic Peninsula, take the Highway 101 North - Shelton Exit to the right, cross over the expressway and turn left to re-enter headed in the opposite direction.

We now proceed on Heron Street (US Highway 12 East) to its reunion with Wiskah Street. There we will describe westbound US Highway 12 and northbound Highway 101 before continuing our journey to Olympia.

Westbound US Highway 12 becomes one-way at Newell Street. If you are coming from Olympia, just continue straight ahead on Wiskah Street. The two one-way sections of Highway 101 are reunited at the junction with Washington State Highway 109 in Hoquiam.

Description of Highway 12 east of Newell Street begins on page 341.

US HIGHWAY 12

	MILES from	MILES to
	MILE 83.6	-HWY 101- MILE 361.6

Louise's Mexican Restaurant	0.0	41.2
Billy's Restaurant	H STREET	
	RESTAURANT	
	0.1	41.1
	G STREET	
	0.2	41.0
	F STREET	
	WISKAH RIVER	
Burger King	0.3	40.9
	FAST FOOD	
	0.4	40.8
	HARBOR STREET	

[12] WEST
    WISKAH STREET

0.5 40.7
NEWELL STREET
HWY. REUNITED

ONE-WAY ends

Heron Street (Highway 12 East) merges into Wiskah Street.

HIGHWAY 12 WEST & HIGHWAY 101 NORTH

The highway divides here into two one-way streets here. US Highway 12 westbound and US Highway 101 northbound follow Wiskah Street which is one-way to the west.

We will divert here for a description of the westbound and northbound route. Description of the eastbound route back to Olympia continues on page 341.

Description of the eastbound route back to Olympia continues on page 341.

US HIGHWAY 12

MILES MILES

from to

MILE 83.6 -HWY 101- MILE 361.6

	0.5 40.7	Towne Motel
	NEWELL STREET	
	HIGHWAY DIVIDES	
	MOTEL	
	0.4 40.8	
	HARBOR STREET	
Burger King	0.3 40.9	KANSAS STREET
	FAST FOOD	
	0.2 41.0	Pourhouse Tavern
	WISKAH RIVER	
	F STREET	
	TAVERN	

[101] SOUTH

To: (105)

**COSMOPOLIS
OCEAN BEACHES**

0.1 41.1	Dan's Chevron
G STREET	
GAS	
HWY 101 NORTH	

Turn left here for the ocean beaches. Continue on straight ahead for Olympia and the eastern leg of Highway 101 North to the Olympic Peninsula.

Time Out Tavern
New China Restaurant

0.0 41.2
H STREET
END OF HWY 12
TAVERN
RESTAURANT

US HIGHWAY 12 ENDS   JOIN HIGHWAY 101

The mileage figures shown from this point to the reunion of northbound and southbound Highway 101 are in the same format as Highway 101 southbound. The figure on the left is the distance to Interstate Highway 5 in Olympia via the loop through the peninsula. The figure on the left is the Highway 101 mile number. The mile number is also the distance to the Washington-Oregon boundary.

	HIGHWAY 101	
	MILES MILE	
	from NUMBER	
	I-5 ——	
101 SOUTH	283.7 83.6 H STREET	
	283.6 83.7 I STREET BROADWAY RESTAURANT	**Golden Dragon Restaurant #2** **Ships Galley Restaurant** **Home Plate Cafe**
	283.5 83.8 K STREET FAST FOOD	**Godfather's Pizza**
Rocky's U-Bake Pizza	283.4 83.9 L STREET FAST FOOD GAS	**Texaco Service Station**
	283.3 84.0 M STREET	
Denny's Restaurant Red Barrel Restaurant Red Lion Motel	283.2 84.1 JEFFERSON ST. RESTAURANT MOTEL MICHIGAN STREET	**Thunderbird Motel** **Wiskah Cookhouse**
ALDER STREET	283.0 84.3 ALDER STREET	

Highway 101 goes to the right into Alder Street. There is a Pizza Hut in the next block of Wiskah Street

	282.9 84.4 MARKET STREET 1ST STREET
	282.8 84.5 2ND STREET

SUMNER STREET

Here Highway 101 turns left into Sumner Street.

282.7 84.8
3RD STREET

282.6 84.7
4TH STREET
DIVISION STREET
BEGIN
SUMNER ST.
FAST FOOD

282.5 84.8
WILLIAMS STREET
THORNTON STREET

282.4 84.9
JEFFRIES STREET
SCAMMEL STREET

282.3 85.0
MARTIN STREET

282.2 85.1
CONGER STREET

282.1 85.2
RICE STREET
HAIGHT STREET

282.0 85.3
DUFFY STREET

281.9 85.4
WOODING STREET
MAPLE STREET

281.8 85.5
WILLOW STREET

281.7 85.6
OAK STREET

281.6 85.7
ASH STREET
MYRTLE STREET
ENTER HOQUIAM

281.5 85.8
31ST STREET

Shakey's Pizza Parlor

Western Buffet

339

MILES   MILE
from NUMBER
I-5   ___

281.4   85.9
30TH STREET

281.3   86.0
29TH STREET

281.2   86.1
28TH STREET

281.1   86.2
27TH STREET

281.0   86.3
ONTARIO STREET

Fairway Food Mart

280.9   86.4
25TH STREET

280.8   86.5
24TH STREET

280.7   86.6
23RD STREET

280.6   86.7
22ND STREET

280.5   86.8
21ST STREET

280.4   86.9
BEGIN RIVERSIDE
2OTH STREET

Highway 101 bends to the right here and the street changes its name from Sumner to Riverside.

280.2   87.1
19TH STREET

280.1   87.2
MUSEUM

Polson Museum

280.0   87.3
16TH STREET
15TH STREET

279.9   87.4
14TH STREET
HOQUIAM RIVER
LINCOLN STREET

After crossing the river, Highway 101 turns sharply to the right (north) and becomes Lincoln Street.

	MILES from I-5	MILE NUMBER
[101] SOUTH 5TH STREET	279.7	87.6
(109) OCEAN SHORES TAHOLA	279.6	87.7

Northbound Highway 101 and southbound Highway 101 are reunited here. Description of Highway 101 for those people who are headed north continues at mile 87.5 on page 332.

We now return to the point at which the highway divided, mile 0.5 of US Highway 12 at Newell Street. Highway 12 is named Wiskah Street, and we will be headed east for Olympia.

US HIGHWAY 12

MILES   MILES
from   to
MILE 83.6 -HWY 101- MILE 361.6

	MILES from	MILES to	
[12] WEST WISKAH STREET	0.5	40.7	WISKAH STREET EAST [12] (End ONE-WAY)
	NEWELL STREET HWY. REUNITED		Eastbound Hwy. 12 merges into Wiskah Street from Heron St.
	0.6	40.6	Aberdeen Mobil Station
	CHEHALIS STREET C-STORE GAS		Sunshine Food
Pietro's Pizza	0.7	40.5	
	FAST FOOD		
Wiskah Mall Baskin Robbins Ice Cream	0.8	40.4	King Arthur's Restaurant
	RESTAURANT		
Flamingo Motel Kentucky Fried Chicken	0.9	40.3	McDonalds Skippers Seafood & Chowder
	MOTEL FAST FOOD		
Duffy's Family Restaurant	1.0	40.2	Price Plus Warehouse Foods
	RESTAURANT SUPERMARKET		
	1.7	39.5	JUNCTION CITY ROAD
	LEAVE ABERDEEN		

COPELAND ROAD	1.9 GAS	39.3	Hilltop Gull
LAKE ABERDEEN ROAD Skookum Mobil & RV Park	2.9 RV PARK	38.3	
LAKE ABERDEEN STATE STEELHEAD HATCHERY	3.5 C-STORE	37.7 GAS	Central Park Shell Food Mart
STRADER LANE YORK DRIVE	4.5	36.7	
	4.9 RESTAURANT	36.3	Park Place Restaurant
	5.0	36.2	Lincshire Center Market
	5.1 C-STORE	36.1 GAS	Central Park Chevron SOLKI DRIVE Seven-Eleven C-Store
	5.6	35.6	PIONEER ROAD
RAIN VAAN ROAD	5.7	35.5	
HIRSHBECK HEIGHTS ROAD Park Motel	5.8	35.4	
	6.1 HILL ROAD	35.1	
	6.3	34.9	DEER PARK ROAD
	6.6	34.6	BRYERWOOD
WEST WYNOOCHEE ROAD	8.2	33.0	ALDERGROVE DRIVE

Although this is not FSR 22 to Wynoochee Lake, you can follow it for about three miles to Geissler Road which connects with FSR 22 after crossing the Wynoochee River in about 1.5 miles.

	8.4 WYNOOCHEE RIVER	32.8	

22 **WYNOOCHEE VALLEY ROAD**

9.4   31.8

DEVONSHIRE ROAD

Wynoochee Valley Road takes you about 35 miles to Wynoochee Dam in Olympic National Forest. It is paved for about half the distance. It provides access to FSR 23, and several trails in the national forest. Beyond Wynoochee Dam it continues west some 20 miles to mile 112.6 of Highway 101, 3 miles north of Humptulips. It is described beginning on page 317.

9.8   31.4

SYLVIA CREEK

10.0   31.2

MILEPOST

**MONTESANO
SYLVIA LAKE STATE PARK**

10.5   30.7

RESTAURANT

C-STORE GAS

107

To: 101 SOUTH

**RAYMOND
SOUTH BEND**

**WEST SATSOP ROAD
BRADY
SCHAFER STATE PARK**

14.7   26.5

15.8   25.4

SATSOP RIVER

16.4   24.8

SATSOP

GAS FOOD PHONE

**OAKRIDGE RECREATION
OAKRIDGE GOLF COURSE**

18.2   23.0

SCHOUWEILER RD.

8 **EAST**

21.2   20.0

ELMA

FOOD PHONE

GAS DIESEL

RV PARK LODGING

**OAKVILLE
CENTRALIA**

SOUTH 12

LEAVE US HIGHWAY 12 JOIN STATE HIGHWAY 8

US Highway 12 goes to the right here. We continue straight ahead on State Highway 8 to go to the eastern segment of the Highway 101 Loop and Olympia. The mileage figures shown below are the Highway 8 mile numbers and the remaining distance to Highway 101's eastern leg.

	WA HIGHWAY 8		
	MILES from HWY 12	MILES to HWY 101	
	0.0	20.0	
	BEGIN WA HWY 8		
GRAYS HARBOR FAIRGROUNDS GRAYS HARBOR PAVILION & PARK	1.0	19.0	SOUTHERN UNION ROAD
	1.1	18.9	
	CLOQUALLAM CRK.		
	1.8	18.2	REST AREA
	2.4	17.6	
	HEISE ROAD		
	4.1	15.9	
	WILDCAT CREEK		
	6.0	14.0	
(108) McCLEARY SHELTON			
McCLEARY McCLEARY MUSEUM HOSPITAL	7.5 HOSPITAL GAS PHONE	12.5	MALONE
	9.0	11.0	
	MOX-CHEHALIS RD		
	10.0	10.0	
	MILEPOST		
	10.5	9.5	
	ENTER THURSTON COUNTY		
	10.8 COOPER ROAD	9.2	THURSTON COUNTY ORV SPORTS PARK
	12.7	7.3	REST AREA

WA HIGHWAY 8		
MILES	MILES	
from	to	
HWY 12	HWY 101	

SUMMIT LAKE ROAD
SUMMIT LAKE SHORE ROAD — 13.4 6.6

15.4 4.6 — KENNEDY CREEK ROAD
RESTAURANT — Ranch Kitchen
TAVERN

16.2 3.8 — ROCK CANDY MOUNTAIN ROAD

SUMMIT LAKE ROAD

Summit Lake Antiques — 17.0 3.0

WILSON ROAD — 17.5 2.5 — WINSLOW DRIVE

Summit Lake Grocery — 17.8 2.2
Mobil Service Station — C-STORE GAS

PERRY CREEK ROAD — 19.9 0.1 — OLD OLYMPIC HIGHWAY

SHAKER CHURCH ROAD — 20.0 0.0
END OF WA HWY 8
JCT. HWY. 101

The merger of Highway 8 and Highway 101 completes our loop through the Olympic Peninsula. It is 5.7 miles to the end of Highway 101 at its junction with Interstate Highway 5 in Olympla.

To head north on Highway 101 toward Shelton, take the Mud Bay Road, Highway 101 North exit 0.6 miles beyond the point where east bound Highway 101 merges with Highway 8 from the right. At the end of the exit you turn left, cross over the expressway, and turn left again at the entrance ramp for Highway 101 North.

The remaining 5.7 miles of Highway 101 to the Interstate are described on pages 18 - 22. I wish you a pleasant journey. (See pages 1 through 345 to do the whole trip again.)

APPENDIX 1
LIST OF TRAILS

ANDERSON RANCH TRAIL 216
ANDERSON GLACIER TRAIL 99
APPLETON PASS TRAIL 223
AURORA RIDGE TRAIL 238
AURORA DIVIDE TRAIL 229
AURORA CREEK TRAIL 230
BADGER VALLEY TRAIL 183
BALDY TRAIL 155
BARNES CREEK TRAIL 228
BIG CREEK NATURE TRAIL 63
BIG CREEK TRAIL 301
BLACK & WHITE LAKES WAY TRAIL 69
BOGACHIEL TRAIL 260
BOULDER LAKE TRAIL 223
BUCKHORN LAKE WAY TRAIL 144
CAMERON CREEK TRAIL 157
CANYON CREEK TRAIL 243
CAPE ALAVA TRAIL 203
CASCADE ROCK TRAIL 209
CAT CREEK WAY TRAIL 224
CEDAR CREEK TRAIL 43
CEDAR LAKE WAY TRAIL 156
CHURCH CREEK TRAIL 45
CHURCH CREEK SHELTER TRAIL 43
COLONEL BOB TRAIL 307
CONSTANCE PASS TRAIL 100
COX VALLEY TRAIL 182
CRYSTAL RIDGE TRAIL 222
DEER RIDGE TRAIL 153
DODGER POINT TRAIL 217
DOSEWALLIPS TRAIL 97
DRY CREEK TRAIL 66
DRY CREEK TRAIL 43
DUCKABUSH TRAIL 88
ELIP CREEK TRAIL 304
ELK LAKE TRAIL 78
ELK MOUNTAIN WAY TRAIL 166
ELWHA TRAIL 213
ENCHANTED VALLEY TRAIL 310
FAIRHOLM CAMPGROUND NATURE TRAIL 232
FALLSVIEW LOOP NATURE TRAIL 107
FALLSVIEW CANYON TRAIL 108
FINLEY PEAK TRAIL 302
FLAPJACK LAKES TRAIL 68
FLETCHER CANYON TRAIL 309
GEYSER VALLEY TRAIL 215
GOLD CREEK TRAIL 137
GRAND RIDGE TRAIL 165
GRAND PASS TRAIL 183

GRAVES CREEK TRAIL 312
GRIFF CREEK TRAIL 211
HAPPY LAKE RIDGE TRAIL 220
HAYDEN PASS TRAIL 217
HEART LAKE WAY TRAIL 90
HEATHER CREEK TRAIL 143
HEATHER PARK TRAIL 174
HIGH DIVIDE - BAILEY RANGE TRAIL 244
HOH LAKE TRAIL 271
HOH TRAIL 270
HURRICANE HILL TRAIL 211
HURRICANE HILL LOOKOUT TRAIL 180
INDIAN PASS TRAIL 260
INTERROREM NATURE TRAIL 87
JEFFERSON RIDGE TRAIL 77
KLOOCHMAN ROCK TRAIL 295
KRAUSE BOTTOM TRAIL 215
LACROSSE BASIN TRAIL 90
LACROSSE PASS TRAIL 89
LAKE CREEK TRAIL 176
LAKE ANGELES TRAIL 175
LAKE CONSTANCE TRAIL 96
LENA LAKE TRAIL 79
LILLIAN RIVER TRAIL 217
LITTLE QUILCENE TRAIL 120
LITTLE RIVER TRAIL 208
LONG RIDGE TRAIL 215
LOST PASS TRAIL 100
LOVERS LANE 241
LOW DIVIDE TRAIL 218
LOWER PETES CREEK TRAIL 320
LOWER SOUTH FORK SKOKOMISH TRAIL 42
LOWER DUNGENESS TRAIL 138
LOWER GRAY WOLF TRAIL 154
LOWER MAYNARD BURN WAY TRAIL 140
LOWER BIG QUILCENE TRAIL 111
MARTINS PARK TRAIL 218
MARYMERE FALLS TRAIL 229
MEADOW LOOP TRAILS 179
MILDRED LAKES WAY TRAIL 83
MINK LAKE TRAIL 240
MOUNT WALKER TRAIL 106
MOUNT TOWNSEND TRAIL 114
MOUNT JUPITER TRAIL 90
MOUNT ZION TRAIL 120
MOUNT STORM KING TRAIL 228
MOUNT HOPPER TRAIL 70
MOUNT LINCOLN WAY TRAIL 68
MOUNT ELLINOR TRAIL 62
MOUNT ROSE TRAIL 64

APPENDIX 2
LIST OF ROADS AND HIGHWAYS

INDEX

ORDER FORM

TELEPHONE ORDERS: Call 1 (206) 754-0152. Have your VISA or Mastercard Ready.

POSTAL ORDERS: **NOSADO PRESS**
318 Security Building (OP)
203 East Fourth Avenue
Olympia, WA 98501 U.S.A.

Please send me _____ copies of "Barney's Book on the Olympic Peninsula" at $17.95 per copy plus Shipping Charges. (Please add an additional 7.8% for Sales Tax on books shipped to Washington addresses.) I understand that I can return the book(s) for a full refund — <u>for any reason</u> — no questions asked.

SHIPPING CHARGES:

BOOK RATE: $1.75 for the first book, plus 75 cents for each additional book sent to the same address. (Surface shipping may take three to four weeks for delivery.)

AIR MAIL: $3.00 per book.

METHOD OF PAYMENT:

☐ Check or Money Order
☐ Credit Card (VISA or Mastercard)

Card Number: _ _ _ _   _ _ _ _   _ _ _ _   _ _ _ _

Name as shown on card: _____

Expiration Date: _____ / _____

Name:_____

Address: _____

City:_____ **State:**_____ **Zip:**_____

GIFT ORDER ADDRESS:

Send Gift to: _____

Address: _____

City:_____ **State:**_____ **Zip:**_____

GIFT ORDER ADDRESS:

Send Gift to: _____

Address: _____

City: _____ **State:** _____ **Zip:**_____